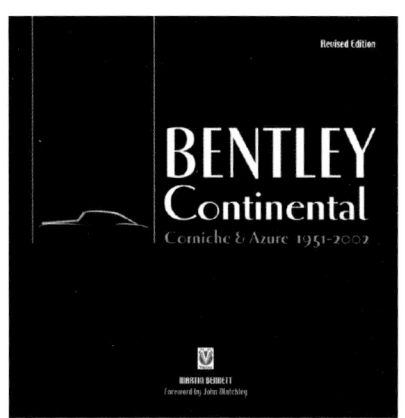

Other great books from Veloce –

Speedpro Series

4-cylinder Engine – How to Blueprint & Build a Short Block For High Performance (Hammill)
Alfa Romeo DOHC High-performance Manual (Kartalamakis)
Alfa Romeo V6 Engine High-performance Manual (Kartalamakis)
BMC 998cc A-series Engine – How to Power Tune (Hammill)
1275cc A-series High-performance Manual (Hammill)
Camshafts – How to Choose & Time Them For Maximum Power (Hammill)
Competition Car Datalogging Manual, The (Templeman)
Cylinder Heads – How to Build, Modify & Power Tune Updated & Revised Edition (Burgess & Gollan)
Distributor-type Ignition Systems – How to Build & Power Tune New 3rd Edition (Hammill)
Fast Road Car – How to Plan and Build Revised & Updated Colour New Edition (Stapleton)
Ford SOHC 'Pinto' & Sierra Cosworth DOHC Engines – How to Power Tune Updated & Enlarged Edition (Hammill)
Ford V8 – How to Power Tune Small Block Engines (Hammill)
Harley-Davidson Evolution Engines – How to Build & Power Tune (Hammill)
Holley Carburetors – How to Build & Power Tune Revised & Updated Edition (Hammill)
Honda Civic Type R, The – High-Performance Manual (Cowland & Clifford)
Jaguar XK Engines – How to Power Tune Revised & Updated Colour Edition (Hammill)
MG Midget & Austin-Healey Sprite – How to Power Tune New 3rd Edition (Stapleton)
MGB 4-cylinder Engine – How to Power Tune (Burgess)
MGB V8 Power – How to Give Your, Third Colour Edition (Williams)
MGB, MGC & MGB V8 – How to Improve New 2nd Edition (Williams)
Mini Engines – How to Power Tune On a Small Budget Colour Edition (Hammill)
Motorcycle-engined Racing Car – How to Build (Pashley)
Motorsport – Getting Started in (Collins)
Nissan GT-R High-performance Manual, The (Gorodji)
Nitrous Oxide High-performance Manual, The (Langfield)
Rover V8 Engines – How to Power Tune (Hammill)
Speed secrets – Today's techniques for 4-stroke engine blueprinting & tuning (Swager)
Sportscar & Kitcar Suspension & Brakes – How to Build & Modify Revised 3rd Edition (Hammill)
SU Carburettor High-performance Manual (Hammill)
Successful Low-Cost Rally Car, How to Build a (Young)
Suzuki 4x4 – How to Modify For Serious Off-road Action (Richardson)
Tiger Avon Sportscar – How to Build Your Own Updated & Revised 2nd Edition (Dudley)
TR2, 3 & TR4 – How to Improve (Williams)
TR5, 250 & TR6 – How to Improve (Williams)
TR7 & TR8 – How to Improve (Williams)
V8 Engine – How to Build a Short Block For High Performance (Hammill)
Volkswagen Beetle Suspension, Brakes & Chassis – How to Modify For High Performance (Hale)
Volkswagen Bus Suspension, Brakes & Chassis – How to Modify For High Performance (Hale)
Weber DCOE, & Dellorto DHLA Carburetors – How to Build & Power Tune 3rd Edition (Hammill)

Those Were The Days ... Series

Alpine Trials & Rallies 1910-1973 (Pfundner)
American 'Independent' Automakers – AMC to Willys 1945 to 1960 (Mort)
American Station Wagons – The Golden Era 1950-1975 (Mort)
American Trucks of the 1950s (Mort)
American Trucks of the 1960s (Mort)
American Woodies 1928-1953 (Mort)
Anglo-American Cars from the 1930s to the 1970s (Mort)
Austerity Motoring (Bobbitt)
Austins, The last real (Peck)
Brighton National Speed Trials (Gardiner)
British Lorries of the 1950s (Bobbitt)
British Lorries of the 1960s (Bobbitt)
British Touring Car Championship, The (Collins)
British Police Cars (Walker)
British Woodies (Peck)
Café Racer Phenomenon, The (Walker)
Dune Buggy Phenomenon (Hale)
Dune Buggy Phenomenon Volume 2 (Hale)
Endurance Racing at Silverstone in the 1970s & 1980s (Parker)
Hot Rod & Stock Car Racing in Britain in the 1980s (Neil)
Last Real Austins, The, 1946-1959 (Peck)
MG's Abingdon Factory (Moylan)
Motor Racing at Brands Hatch in the Seventies (Parker)
Motor Racing at Brands Hatch in the Eighties (Parker)
Motor Racing at Crystal Palace (Collins)
Motor Racing at Goodwood in the Sixties (Gardiner)
Motor Racing at Nassau in the 1950s & 1960s (O'Neil)
Motor Racing at Oulton Park in the 1960s (McFadyen)
Motor Racing at Oulton Park in the 1970s (McFadyen)
Superprix (Page & Collins)
Three Wheelers (Bobbitt)

Truckmakers

DAF Trucks since 1949 (Peck)

Enthusiast's Restoration Manual Series

Citroën 2CV, How to Restore (Porter)
Classic Car Bodywork, How to Restore (Thaddeus)
Classic British Car Electrical Systems (Astley)
Classic Car Electrics (Thaddeus)
Classic Cars, How to Paint (Thaddeus)
Reliant Regal, How to Restore (Payne)
Triumph TR2, 3, 3A, 4 & 4A, How to Restore (Williams)
Triumph TR5/250 & 6, How to Restore (Williams)
Triumph TR7/8, How to Restore (Williams)
Volkswagen Beetle, How to Restore (Tyler)
VW Bay Window Bus (Paxton)
Yamaha FS1-E, How to Restore (Watts)

Essential Buyer's Guide Series

Alfa GT (Booker)
Alfa Romeo Spider Giulia (Booker & Talbott)
BMW GS (Henshaw)
BSA Bantam (Henshaw)
BSA Twins (Henshaw)
Citroën 2CV (Paxton)
Citroën ID & DS (Heilig)
Fiat 500 & 600 (Bobbitt)
Ford Capri (Paxton)
Hinckley Triumph triples & fours 750, 900, 955, 1000, 1050, 1200 – 1991-2009 (Henshaw)
Honda SOHC Fours (Henshaw)
Jaguar E-type 3.8 & 4.2-litre (Crespin)
Jaguar E-type V12 5.3-litre (Crespin)
Jaguar XJ 1995-2003 (Crespin)
Jaguar/Daimler XJ6, XJ12 & Sovereign (Crespin)
Jaguar/Daimler XJ40 (Crespin)
Jaguar XJ-S (Crespin)
MGB & MGB GT (Williams)
Mercedes-Benz 280SL-560DSL Roadsters (Bass)
Mercedes-Benz 'Pagoda' 230SL, 250SL & 280SL Roadsters & Coupés (Bass)
Mini (Paxton)
Morris Minor & 1000 (Newell)
Norton Commando (Henshaw)
Porsche 928 (Hemmings)
Rolls-Royce Silver Shadow & Bentley T-Series (Bobbitt)
Subaru Impreza (Hobbs)
Triumph Bonneville (Henshaw)
Triumph Stag (Mort & Fox)
Triumph TR6 (Williams)
VW Beetle (Cservenka & Copping)
VW Bus (Cservenka & Copping)
VW Golf GTI (Cservenka & Copping)

Auto-Graphics Series

Fiat-based Abarths (Sparrow)
Jaguar MKI & II Saloons (Sparrow)
Lambretta Li Series Scooters (Sparrow)

Rally Giants Series

Audi Quattro (Robson)
Austin Healey 100-6 & 3000 (Robson)
Fiat 131 Abarth (Robson)
Ford Escort MkI (Robson)
Ford Escort RS Cosworth & World Rally Car (Robson)
Ford Escort RS1800 (Robson)
Lancia Delta 4x4/Integrale (Robson)
Lancia Stratos (Robson)
Mini Cooper/Mini Cooper S (Robson)
Peugeot 205 T16 (Robson)
Saab 96 & V4 (Robson)
Subaru Impreza (Robson)
Toyota Celica GT4 (Robson)

WSC Giants

Ferrari 312P & 312PB (Collins & McDonough)
Matra Sports Cars – MS620, 630, 650, 660 & 670 – 1966 to 1974 (McDonough)

General

1½-litre GP Racing 1961-1965 (Whitelock)
AC Two-litre Saloons & Buckland Sportscars (Archibald)
Alfa Romeo Giulia Coupé GT & GTA (Tipler)
Alfa Romeo Montreal – The dream car that came true (Taylor)
Alfa Romeo Montreal – The Essential Companion (Taylor)
Alfa Tipo 33 (McDonough & Collins)
Alpine & Renault – The Development of the Revolutionary Turbo F1 Car 1968 to 1979 (Smith)
Alpine & Renault – The Sports Prototypes 1963 to 1969 (Smith)
Alpine & Renault – The Sports Prototypes 1973 to 1978 (Smith)
Anatomy of the Works Minis (Moylan)
André Lefebvre, and the cars he created at Voisin and Citroën (Beck)
Armstrong-Siddeley (Smith)
Art Deco and British Car Design (Down)
Autodrome (Collins & Ireland)
Autodrome 2 (Collins & Ireland)
Automotive A-Z, Lane's Dictionary of Automotive Terms (Lane)
Automotive Mascots (Kay & Springate)
Bahamas Speed Weeks, The (O'Neil)
Bentley Continental, Corniche and Azure (Bennett)
Bentley MkVI, Rolls-Royce Silver Wraith, Dawn & Cloud/Bentley R & S-Series (Nutland)
Bluebird CN7 (Stevens)
BMC Competitions Department Secrets (Turner, Chambers & Browning)
BMW 5-Series (Cranswick)
BMW Z-Cars (Taylor)
BMW Boxer Twins 1970-1995 Bible, The (Falloon)
Britains Farm Model Balers & Combines 1967-2007, Pocket Guide to (Pullen)
Britains Farm Model & Toy Tractors 1998-2008, Pocket Guide to (Pullen)
Britains Toy Models Catalogues 1970-1979 (Pullen)
British 250cc Racing Motorcycles (Pereira)
British at Indianapolis, The (Wagstaff)
British Cars, The Complete Catalogue of, 1895-1975 (Culshaw & Horrobin)
BRM – A Mechanic's Tale (Salmon)
BRM V16 (Ludvigsen)
BSA Bantam Bible, The (Henshaw)
Bugatti Type 40 (Price)
Bugatti 46/50 Updated Edition (Price & Arbey)
Bugatti T44 & T49 (Price & Arbey)
Bugatti 57 2nd Edition (Price)
Caravans, The Illustrated History 1919-1959 (Jenkinson)
Caravans, The Illustrated History From 1960 (Jenkinson)
Carrera Panamericana, La (Tipler)
Chrysler 300 – America's Most Powerful Car 2nd Edition (Ackerson)
Chrysler PT Cruiser (Ackerson)
Citroën DS (Bobbitt)
Classic British Car Electrical Systems (Astley)
Cliff Allison, The Official Biography of – From the Fells to Ferrari – (Gauld)
Cobra – The Real Thing! (Legate)
Concept Cars, How to illustrate and design (Dewey)
Cortina – Ford's Bestseller (Robson)
Coventry Climax Racing Engines (Hammill)
Daily Mirror World Cup Rally 40, The (Robson)
Daimler SP250 New Edition (Long)
Datsun Fairlady Roadster to 280ZX – The Z-Car Story (Long)
Diecast Toy Cars of the 1950s & 1960s (Ralston)
Dino – The V6 Ferrari (Long)
Dodge Challenger & Plymouth Barracuda (Grist)
Dodge Charger – Enduring Thunder (Ackerson)
Dodge Dynamite! (Grist)
Donington (Boddy)
Draw & Paint Cars – How to (Gardiner)
Drive on the Wild Side, A – 20 Extreme Driving Adventures From Around the World (Weaver)
Ducati 750 Bible, The (Falloon)
Ducati 750SS 'roundcase' 1974, The Book of the (Falloon)
Ducati 860, 900 and Mille Bible, The (Falloon)
Dune Buggy, Building A – The Essential Manual (Shakespeare)
Dune Buggy Files (Hale)
Dune Buggy Handbook (Hale)
Edward Turner: The Man Behind the Motorcycles (Clew)
Fast Ladies – Female Racing Drivers 1888 to 1970 (Bouzanquet)
Ferrari 288 GTO, The Book of the (Sackey)
Fiat & Abarth 124 Spider & Coupé (Tipler)
Fiat & Abarth 500 & 600 2nd Edition (Bobbitt)
Fiats, Great Small (Ward)
Fine Art of the Motorcycle Engine, The (Peirce)
Ford F100/F150 Pick-up 1948-1996 (Ackerson)
Ford F150 Pick-up 1997-2005 (Ackerson)
Ford GT – Then, and Now (Streather)
Ford GT40 (Legate)
Ford In Miniature (Olson)
Ford Model Y (Roberts)
Ford Thunderbird From 1954, The Book of the (Long)
Formula 5000 Motor Racing, Back then ... and back now (Lawson)
Forza Minardi! (Vigar)
Funky Mopeds (Skelton)
GM In Miniature (Olson)
GT – The World's Best GT Cars 1953-73 (Dawson)
Hillclimbing & Sprinting – The Essential Manual (Short & Wilkinson)
Honda NSX (Long)
Intermeccanica – The Story of the Prancing Bull (McCredie & Reisner)
Jack Sears, The Official Biography of – Gentleman Jack (Gauld)
Jaguar, The Rise of (Price)
Jaguar XJ 220 – The Inside Story (Moreton)
Jaguar XJ-S (Long)
Jeep CJ (Ackerson)
Jeep Wrangler (Ackerson)
John Chatham – 'Mr Big Healey' – The Official Biography (Burr)
Karmann-Ghia Coupé & Convertible (Bobbitt)
Lamborghini Miura Bible, The (Sackey)
Lamborghini Urraco (Landsem)
Lambretta Bible, The (Davies)
Lancia 037 (Collins)
Lancia Delta HF Integrale (Blaettel & Wagner)
Land Rover, The Half-ton Military (Cook)
Laverda Twins & Triples Bible 1968-1986 (Falloon)
Lea-Francis Story, The (Price)
Lexus Story, The (Long)
little book of smart, the New Edition (Jackson)
Lola – The Illustrated History (1957-1977) (Starkey)
Lola – All the Sports Racing & Single-seater Racing Cars 1978-1997 (Starkey)
Lola T70 – The Racing History & Individual Chassis Record 4th Edition (Starkey)
Lotus 49 (Oliver)
Marketingmobiles, The Wonderful Wacky World of (Hale)
Mazda MX-5/Miata 1.6 Enthusiast's Workshop Manual (Grainger & Shoemark)
Mazda MX-5/Miata 1.8 Enthusiast's Workshop Manual (Grainger & Shoemark)
Mazda MX-5 Miata: The Book of the World's Favourite Sportscar (Long)
Mazda MX-5 Miata Roadster (Long)
Maximum Mini (Booij)
Mercedes-Benz SL – 113-series 1963-1971 (Long)
Mercedes-Benz SL & SLC – 107-series 1971-1989 (Long)
MGA (Price Williams)
MGB & MGB GT– Expert Guide (Auto-doc Series) (Williams)
MGB Electrical Systems Updated & Revised Edition (Astley)
Micro Caravans (Jenkinson)
Micro Trucks (Mort)
Microcars at Large! (Quellin)
Mini Cooper – The Real Thing! (Tipler)
Mitsubishi Lancer Evo, The Road Car & WRC Story (Long)
Montlhéry, The Story of the Paris Autodrome (Boddy)
Morgan Maverick (Lawrence)
Morris Minor, 60 Years on the Road (Newell)
Moto Guzzi Sport & Le Mans Bible, The (Falloon)
Motor Movies – The Posters! (Veysey)
Motor Racing – Reflections of a Lost Era (Carter)
Motorcycle Apprentice (Cakebread)
Motorcycle Road & Racing Chassis Designs (Noakes)
Motorhomes, The Illustrated History (Jenkinson)
Motorsport In colour, 1950s (Wainwright)
Nissan 300ZX & 350Z – The Z-Car Story (Long)
Nissan GT-R Supercar: Born to race (Gorodji)
Northeast American Sports Car Races 1950-1959 (O'Neil)
Off-Road Giants! – Heroes of 1960s Motorcycle Sport (Westlake)
Pass the Theory and Practical Driving Tests (Gibson & Hoole)
Peking to Paris 2007 (Young)
Plastic Toy Cars of the 1950s & 1960s (Ralston)
Pontiac Firebird (Cranswick)
Porsche Boxster (Long)
Porsche 356 (2nd Edition) (Long)
Porsche 908 (Födisch, Neßhöver, Roßbach, Schwarz & Roßbach)
Porsche 911 Carrera – The Last of the Evolution (Corlett)
Porsche 911R, RS & RSR, 4th Edition (Starkey)
Porsche 911, The Book of the (Long)
Porsche 911 – The Definitive History 1963-1971 (Long)
Porsche 911 – The Definitive History 1971-1977 (Long)
Porsche 911 – The Definitive History 1977-1987 (Long)
Porsche 911 – The Definitive History 1987-1997 (Long)
Porsche 911 – The Definitive History 1997-2004 (Long)
Porsche 911SC 'Super Carrera' – The Essential Companion (Streather)
Porsche 914 & 914-6: The Definitive History of the Road & Competition Cars (Long)
Porsche 924 (Long)
Porsche 928 (Long)
Porsche 944 (Long)
Porsche 964, 993 & 996 Data Plate Code Breaker (Streather)
Porsche 993 'King Of Porsche' – The Essential Companion (Streather)
Porsche 996 'Supreme Porsche' – The Essential Companion (Streather)
Porsche Racing Cars – 1953 to 1975 (Long)
Porsche Racing Cars – 1976 to 2005 (Long)
Porsche – The Rally Story (Meredith)
Porsche: Three Generations of Genius (Meredith)
RAC Rally Action! (Gardiner)
Rallye Sport Fords: The Inside Story (Moreton)
Redman, Jim – 6 Times World Motorcycle Champion: The Autobiography (Redman)
Rolls-Royce Silver Shadow/Bentley T Series Corniche & Camargue Revised & Enlarged Edition (Bobbitt)
Rolls-Royce Silver Spirit, Silver Spur & Bentley Mulsanne 2nd Edition (Bobbitt)
Russian Motor Vehicles (Kelly)
RX-7 – Mazda's Rotary Engine Sportscar (Updated & Revised New Edition) (Long)
Scooters & Microcars, The A-Z of Popular (Dan)
Scooter Lifestyle (Grainger)
Singer Story: Cars, Commercial Vehicles, Bicycles & Motorcycle (Atkinson)
SM – Citroën's Maserati-engined Supercar (Long & Claverol)
Speedway – Motor Racing's Ghost Tracks (Collins & Ireland)
Subaru Impreza: The Road Car And WRC Story (Long)
Supercar, How to Build your own (Thompson)
Tales from the Toolbox (Oliver)
Taxi! The Story of the 'London' Taxicab (Bobbitt)
Tinplate Toy Cars of the 1950s & 1960s (Ralston)
Toleman Story, The (Hilton)
Toyota Celica & Supra, The Book of Toyota's Sports Coupés (Long)
Toyota MR2 Coupés & Spyders (Long)
Triumph Bonneville!, Save the – The inside story of the Meriden Workers' Co-op (Rosamond)
Triumph Motorcycles & the Meriden Factory (Hancox)
Triumph Speed Twin & Thunderbird Bible (Woolridge)
Triumph Tiger Cub Bible (Estall)
Triumph Trophy Bible (Woolridge)
Triumph TR6 (Kimberley)
TWR Story, The – Group A (Hughes & Scott)
Unraced (Collins)
Velocette Motorcycles – MSS to Thruxton Updated & Revised (Burris)
Virgil Exner – Visioneer: The Official Biography of Virgil M Exner Designer Extraordinaire (Grist)
Volkswagen Bus Book, The (Bobbitt)
Volkswagen Bus or Van to Camper, How to Convert (Porter)
Volkswagens of the World (Glen)
VW Beetle Cabriolet (Bobbitt)
VW Beetle – The Car of the 20th Century (Copping)
VW Bus – 40 Years of Splitties, Bays & Wedges (Copping)
VW Bus Book, The (Bobbitt)
VW Golf: Five Generations of Fun (Copping & Cservenka)
VW – The Air-cooled Era (Copping)
VW T5 Camper Conversion Manual (Porter)
VW Campers (Copping)
Works Minis, The Last (Purves & Brenchley)
Works Rally Mechanic (Moylan)

From Veloce Publishing's new imprints:

Battle Cry!
Soviet General & field rank officer uniforms: 1955 to 1991 (Streather)

Hubble & Hattie
My dog is blind – but lives life to the full! (Horsky)
Smellorama – nose games for your dog (Theby)
Waggy Tails & Wheelchairs (Epp)
Winston ... the dog who changed my life (Klute)

www.veloce.co.uk

First published in 1998. Reprinted 2002, 2003 & 2006. This new revised edition published September 2009 by Veloce Publishing Limited, 33 Trinity Street, Dorchester DT1 1TT, England. Fax 01305 268864/e-mail info@veloce.co.uk/web www.veloce.co.uk or www.velocebooks.com. ISBN: 978-1-84584-210-9 UPC: 6-36847-04210-3
© Martin Bennett and Veloce Publishing 2009. All rights reserved. With the exception of quoting brief passages for the purpose of review, no part of this publication may be recorded, reproduced or transmitted by any means, including photocopying, without the written permission of Veloce Publishing Ltd. Throughout this book logos, model names and designations, etc, have been used for the purposes of identification, illustration and decoration. Such names are the property of the trademark holder as this is not an official publication.
Readers with ideas for automotive books, or books on other transport or related hobby subjects, are invited to write to the editorial director of Veloce Publishing at the above address.
British Library Cataloguing in Publication Data – A catalogue record for this book is available from the British Library. Typesetting, design and page make-up all by Veloce Publishing Ltd on Apple Mac. Printed in India by Replika Press.

Revised Edition

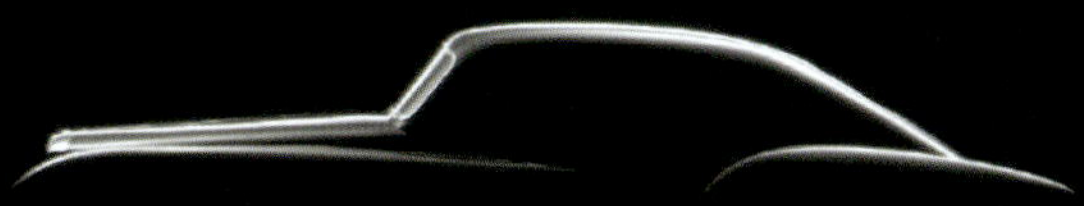

BENTLEY
Continental
Corniche & Azure 1951-2002

MARTIN BENNETT
Foreword by John Blatchley

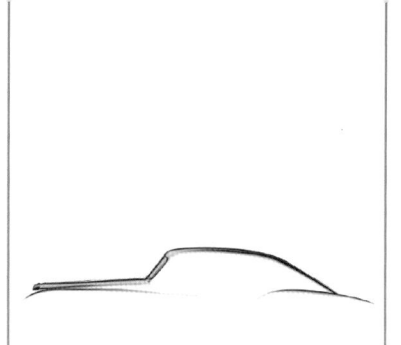

FOREWORD BY JOHN BLATCHLEY (1913-2008)

Although I have known Martin Bennett for only two years, I have already come to regard him as the leading guru on all matters Bentley and Rolls-Royce.

We met, quite by chance, on a visit to the Hunt House in Paulerspury, where, in the library, I was buying a copy of his much-acclaimed book *Rolls-Royce and Bentley: The Crewe Years*. In my retirement I had heard about this book, but had not seen it before. From subsequent perusal I learned more about the cars I had been styling for umpteen years than I had ever learned from any other source. This led to a long correspondence between Martin and myself, which continues to this day.

Through this correspondence I have come to know and appreciate the magnitude of Martin's knowledge about every area of design: engine, chassis and body, including styling, where he notably excels.

It is these attributes, allied to his wide acquaintance with Rolls-Royce personnel, from the board down, that gives Martin insights into Company policies and access to archive material not available to everyone. This privilege lends special authority to all his writings.

There could be no better qualified person than Martin Bennett to write the story of the Bentley Continentals. With his wealth of knowledge, his readable narrative style and great variety of illustrations, he has produced a book that will please everyone, from well-informed cognoscenti to less knowledgeable newcomers.

In the early chapters Martin has drawn together the various strands of information that exist relating to the background of the Continental marque; piecing together the whys and wherefores that led ultimately to the Company producing 'Olga,' that post-war miracle car around which all conversations about Bentley Continentals gyrate.

That Olga was, in fact, a 'Corniche' matters not. If anyone can sort it out, Martin can — and does so in this book.

John Blatchley
Chief Styling Engineer,
Rolls-Royce Ltd, Car Division,
1950-1969

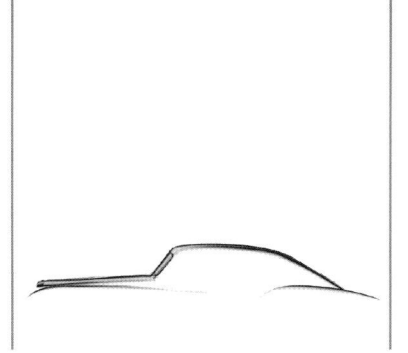

CONTENTS

INTRODUCTION 6
ACKNOWLEDGEMENTS 7

1. THE CONCEPT: CORNICHE II. 8
2. THE BENTLEY CONTINENTAL INTO PRODUCTION 27
    TECHNICAL SPECIFICATIONS – CONTINENTAL R TYPE 54
3. THE S TYPE CONTINENTAL 57
    TECHNICAL SPECIFICATIONS – CONTINENTAL S TYPE (S1) 91
4. A NEW ENGINE & MORE S TYPE CONTINENTALS 94
    TECHNICAL SPECIFICATIONS – BENTLEY CONTINENTAL S2 & S3 143
5. BENTLEY CONTINENTAL DESIGNERS & COACHBUILDERS 146
6. THE CORNICHE – & RETURN OF THE CONTINENTAL 167
    TECHNICAL SPECIFICATIONS – BENTLEY CORNICHE (1971-84) & CONTINENTAL (1984-95) . 186
7. A SUPERCAR FOR THE NINETIES & BEYOND 190
    TECHNICAL SPECIFICATIONS – CONTINENTAL R & DERIVATIVES 210

APPENDIX 1. CHASSIS & ENGINE NUMBERING SYSTEMS EXPLAINED 213
APPENDIX 2. BENTLEY CONTINENTAL MODIFICATION DATA, R TYPE TO S3, 1952-1966 . . 217
APPENDIX 3. GEARBOX & GEARCHANGE ANALYSIS, R TYPE CONTINENTAL 221
APPENDIX 4. CAR LISTINGS: R TYPE & S TYPE CONTINENTALS 222
INDEX 251

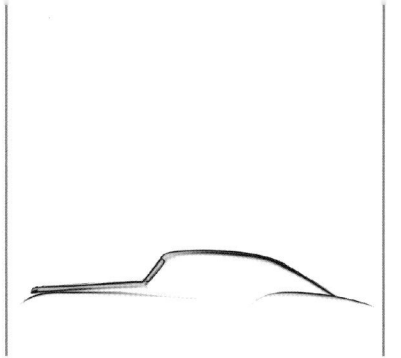

INTRODUCTION

The appellation 'Continental' is perhaps the most evocative in Bentley history, conjuring up as it does visions of fast motoring to the South of France, or through the Alps Maritimes, with silken power clothed in supremely elegant coachwork, and drivers and passengers enveloped in the heady aroma of Connolly hides and the rich glow of fine woodwork.

In order to determine the scope of this book, it was necessary to define exactly what a Bentley Continental is. Firstly, it is the models so described by their makers, all of which have characteristics not shared by their more ordinary brethren in the Bentley range: higher than standard performance and a special coachbuilt body, usually — though not always — with two rather than four doors.

If these are the defining features of a Bentley Continental, then it follows that at least one other model could qualify, even if it was not, at first, distinguished by the Continental model designation. I refer, of course, to the rare Bentley Corniche. The original Bentley Continental of 1951 was known within the Company as 'Corniche II' (the original Corniche was a pre-war experimental version of the Bentley Mark V). It therefore seems perfectly natural for the Corniche name to be revived for a latter-day, high performance Bentley coupé. This was a Bentley Continental just as surely as if it had been given that name; in fact, from 1984, it was belatedly renamed Bentley Continental in order to distinguish it from the Rolls-Royce Corniche, and this, as much as anything else, justifies its inclusion in this book.

Conversely, the Bentley Azure was to have been called the Bentley Continental R Convertible until literally weeks before introduction, and is a derivative of the fabulous Continental R. Thus, no argument is needed to categorise that superb motor car as a Bentley Continental; it more than qualifies on the counts of high performance and special coachwork.

An additional and vital feature of the earliest Bentley Continental (nowadays known as the R Type Continental) was its lighter than standard coachwork. However, this attribute was short-lived. Even before the R Type Continental was replaced by its larger and heavier successor, the demands of wealthy customers for more substantial seating, radios, electric windows, and the like, largely annulled the weight-saving that had been achieved as a key characteristic of the original Continental concept. Thereafter, light weight was no longer considered an essential Continental attribute. Improving tyre technology and progressively increasing engine power made weight-saving unnecessary. Indeed, the Azure weighed in at a hefty 2.6 tons and was certainly none the worse for it, performance-wise!

Today, the Bentley Continentals of old are highly desirable, sought-after motor cars — and for good reason. The engineering responsible for the smooth, silent performance and sure-footed handling is second-to-none, and the special coachwork was — and still is — a reminder of a time when unhurried craftsmanship was the order of the day. Even in times of recession Bentley Continentals, particularly the R Type Continental, hold their value and continue to be highly sought after. Those who are fortunate enough to own one value them very highly indeed. If the author were told that he had to choose one car to last the rest of his life, as his sole means of transport, he would have no hesitation in choosing a Bentley R Type Continental — preferably with lightweight seats and manual gearbox!

Although cars bearing the Bentley Continental appellation are still made at Crewe, cars which arguably continue to more than live up to their evocative and venerated model name, it has been decided to keep this revised edition within the original book's remit, leaving to other authors coverage of the new generation of models that have developed since the 1998 sale of Rolls-Royce Motor Cars Ltd to Volkswagen and the subsequent renaming of the Company to become Bentley Motors Ltd.

Right: R Type Continental H. J. Mulliner sports saloon BC11C at Windsor Castle. This was the Conduit Street showroom Trials car from February 1954.

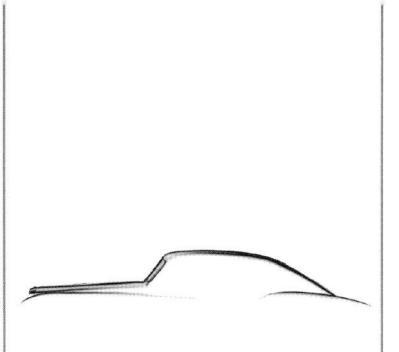

ACKNOWLEDGEMENTS

This book would not have been possible, or at the very least would have been very much the poorer, without the magnificent contributions of a number of people in several countries. The vast majority of the illustrations have been sourced, over a period of several decades, from the former Rolls-Royce Ltd Car Division, and its successors (now Bentley Motors Ltd), either directly or through other sources. The Company's photographer, Chris Ladley, was particularly helpful in the closing stages of assembling the illustrations. Many others were kindly provided by Klaus-Josef Roßfeldt, Peter Fischer, and Andrew Wood of P. & A. Wood.

Enormous assistance was forthcoming from the staff of the Rolls-Royce Enthusiasts' Club and Sir Henry Royce Memorial Foundation at the Hunt House in supplying, by facsimile, details of large numbers of individual cars, and I particularly mention the magnificent efforts of two gracious ladies, Barbara Westlake and Emma Newman.

My good friend Richard Mann, former Senior Quality Engineer at Mulliner Park Ward, gave freely of his time and knowledge, as well as locating some rare photographs and assisting in many valuable ways as the book progressed. Fellow authors Tom Clarke, Malcolm Bobbitt, Klaus-Josef Roßfeldt and Martyn Nutland are thanked for their encouragement and responses to calls for help. Peter Graham checked my car listings, suggesting amendments where they were needed.

I am especially grateful to John Blatchley, Chief Styling Engineer at Belper and Crewe in the early post-war period until his retirement in 1969, for his recollections, kind words of encouragement and, in particular, for readily agreeing to write the Foreword. Sadly, 'JPB' passed away in 2008.

The Bentley 'B in wings' logo is reproduced with the kind permission of its owner, Bentley Motors Ltd.

Illustrations not from the archives of Bentley Motors Ltd and the Company's former coachbuilder subsidiaries were contributed by the following:

John Donner – page 13; Tom Clarke – 23; Peter Fischer – 36 (upper), 39, 40 (upper), 61 (lower), 62 (upper left), 66 (upper), 75, 78 (top right), 81, 85 (lower), 87, 99 (upper), 111 (lower), 140 (lower), 141 (lower); Dr M. Nowka via Klaus-Josef Roßfeldt – 120 (top), 121; Klaus-Josef Roßfeldt – 38 (lower), 41 (lower), 50, 51 (lower), 108 (upper), 182 (upper right & lower), 208, 209; Keith Wherry – 63; Tom Solley – 78 (middle right), 90, 68; Brian Lewis – 79 (top); Bill Coburn – 84 (lower two); Alpine Eagle via Ashley James – 52, 53 (lower). P. & A. Wood – 100, 24 (top), 99 (lower), 111 upper), 122 (middle), 197; Jack Barclay Ltd – 113, 114 (lower), 141 (upper right), 154, 201, 202, 137; Davide Bassoli – 83 (upper); Brian McMillan – 168; Chris Ladley – 207.

A small number of photographs were taken by the author and a very small number are of unknown origin. I trust the photographers concerned will forgive the absence of acknowledgement.

Martin Bennett
Goulburn, New South Wales
Australia

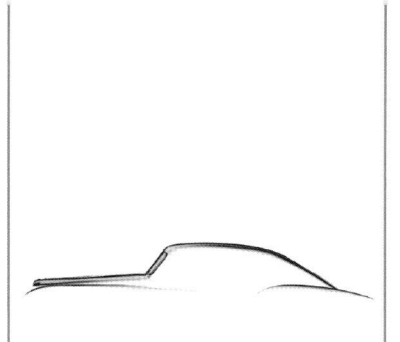

1. THE CONCEPT: CORNICHE II

In the late 1930s motorways in Britain were still twenty years away, but fast, limited access roads were already being built on the Continent, notably in Germany, enabling drivers to cruise at higher speeds for longer periods than was possible on even the best British 'A' roads.

The provision of Hall's Metal bearings on the Bentley 4¼-litre helped equip the Bentley for this new development, and the advent of the 1939 'M' series 4¼, with overdrive gearbox and improved engine lubrication system, meant that more effortless, prolonged high speed cruising was possible with reduced risk to the engine. Third gear became the direct drive, though the final drive ratio was lowered slightly.

At this time, some coachbuilders offering coachwork for Bentley chassis applied the appellation 'Continental' to certain body styles. It needs to be stressed that in every case this was a description of the coachwork and not a name sanctioned by the chassis maker, nor were the chassis in any way non-standard. That is not to say, though, that these cars did not influence the choice of model name for the post-war Bentley Continental. It should also be remembered that there were Continental variants of the Rolls-Royce Silver Ghost and Phantom II, and — in these instances — the Continental appellation was used by the chassis maker rather than the coachbuilder to identify a particular specification.

In 1938, a special Bentley 4¼-litre, chassis B27LE, the 'Embiricos' Bentley, was fitted with streamlined coachwork styled by Frenchman Georges Paulin and built by a small French coachbuilder, Pourtout, for André Embiricos of the Greek shipping dynasty. Its higher than standard performance was achieved by a combination of mechanical modifications, including a higher final drive ratio giving a top gear overall ratio of 2.87:1, and streamlined, low cross-section, lightweight coachwork.

In 1939, the Embiricos Bentley covered 114 miles in the hour at Brooklands. It proved capable of exceeding 120mph on the then new autobahns, and returned 20 miles per gallon at 80mph, all of which brings to mind the post-war Bentley Continental. After the war, when it was eleven years old, B27LE finished sixth at the 1949 Le Mans 24-hour Race with new owner H. S. F. Hay at the wheel. Hay entered B27LE twice more, finishing 14th in 1950 and 22nd in '51 following an unfortunate generator failure which left the driver without lights at night.

By the close of the 1930s, both the 'large' and 'small' Rolls-Royce models had acquired independent front suspension, but the Bentley was conspicuous for its leaf-sprung front beam axle. It was vital that the Bentley, being the sporting model of the range, be brought up to date in this respect and not be seen to lag behind the contemporary Rolls-Royce models. Thus, the final pre-World War II Bentley was the Mk V — the first manifestation of the 'Rationalised Range' of models then under development, with a new design of independent front suspension in a completely new chassis. Only eleven Mk Vs were completed before war curtailed motor car production. A special, high performance version of the Mk V, called the 'Corniche', was also under development.

An experimental Corniche, chassis 14-B-V, which reached the French testing stage, had the 2.87:1 overall top gear ratio of the Embiricos car, and bolt-on pressed steel wheels. In specification, the Mk V formed the basis of the post-war models, both Bentley and Rolls-Royce. In concept, the Corniche version anticipated the post-war Bentley Continental.

14-B-V was fitted with special, streamlined sports saloon coachwork designed, like the Embiricos car, by Georges Paulin and built by Vanvooren of Paris. The traditional Bentley radiator shell was discarded in favour of a streamlined grille of the style then popular, and the Marchal headlamps were integral with the bodywork. A high-efficiency dual exhaust system maximised available engine power.

14-B-V was seriously damaged in a roll-over accident in France. There is anecdotal evidence that it was later destroyed by a bomb on the quay at Dieppe, where it had been left by Ivan Waller (IMW) for shipment back to England just as war broke out. William Arthur Robotham (1899-1980), who was Deputy Chief Engineer and Head of the Experimental Department at the time, confirmed this in his book *Silver Ghosts and Silver Dawn* (Constable, 1970), though other sources claim that the chassis was returned to Derby and

1938 Bentley 4¼-litre, chassis B27LE – the 'Embiricos' Bentley, which was styled by Georges Paulin and built by Pourtout, a small French coachbuilder, for André Embiricos. In terms of its higher than standard performance, achieved by mechanical modifications which included a higher final drive ratio and streamlined, low cross-section, lightweight coachwork, this car must be regarded as the direct forerunner of the post-war Bentley Continental. The actual styling, in silhouette and certain detail, also inspired that of the H. J. Mulliner Continental. In 1939, the Embiricos Bentley covered 114 miles in the hour at Brooklands. When it was eleven years old, in 1949, B27LE finished sixth at Le Mans.

that only the body was destroyed in the Dieppe bombing raid. Sadly, Paulin was shot by a German firing squad for his work in the Resistance.

Consideration had been given to an eight-cylinder version of the Corniche, which could have been introduced as early as the 1940 Motor Show, using the straight-eight Rationalised engine. This could have resulted in a production 120mph Bentley more than a decade before the post-war Continental appeared. Some careful weight-saving would have been essential, if only because the tyres of the period would have demanded it. The two pre-war Experimental straight-eight Bentleys, 11-B-V ('Comet', or 'Scalded Cat', which showed itself capable of climbing Porlock* in top gear with four up), and 4-B-50 ('Cresta'), were both capable of 100mph, but were really too heavy to run at such speeds without becoming dangerous, or at the very least ruinously uneconomic in terms of tyre wear. The Corniche, 14-B-V, is said to have destroyed a set of tyres in twelve miles when an attempt was made to drive 100 miles in an hour on a German autobahn, which would have been comfortably within its capabilities but for the tyre factor.

After the war when motor car production resumed at Rolls-Royce, the Chassis Division (by now renamed the Car Division to reflect the fact that

The Embiricos Bentley led to the Corniche, also styled by Paulin. It was based on the Mk V chassis, which had independent front suspension. The streamlined coachwork was built by Vanvooren of Paris. Though a four-door saloon, the Corniche is an important milestone on the way to the Bentley Continental.

* Porlock Hill, in coastal west Somerset, was the yardstick of hill-climbing performance in pre-war and early post-war periods.

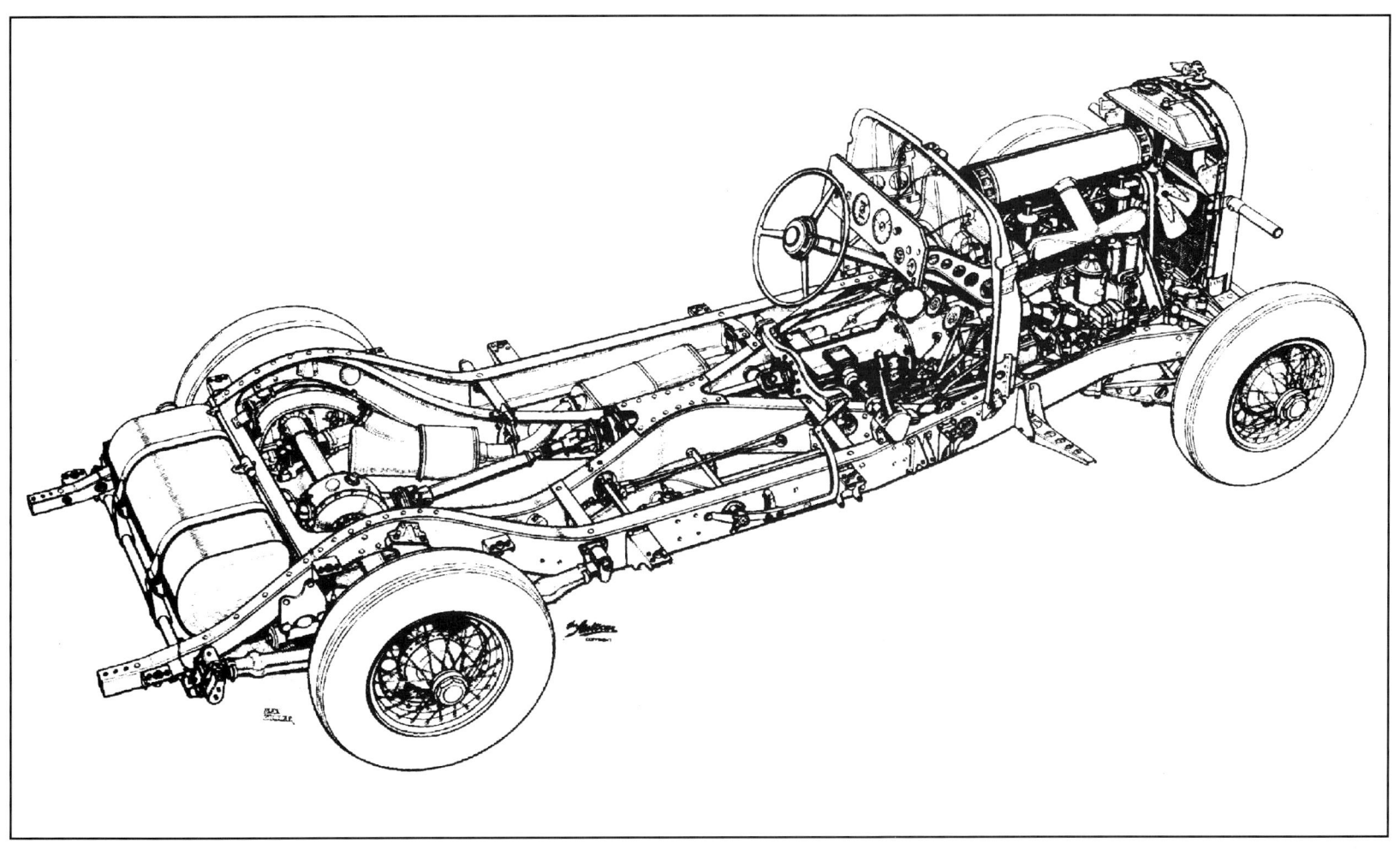

The Bentley Corniche used the Mk V chassis. The Mk V was developed barely in time for fewer than twenty chassis to be built before the outbreak of World War II, and only eleven are known to have been completed and fitted with coachwork. This model was a design leader in that its frame and other details of the chassis, including a new design of independent front suspension, were to have formed the basis of the 'Rationalised Range', using a common chassis design (though in various lengths) for all Rolls-Royce and Bentley models. The similarity between this chassis and that of the Mk VI and other early post-war models is very much in evidence. As such, this chassis was an important milestone in the development of the Bentley Continental.

complete cars were being made), was transferred from Derby to the war-time Merlin engine factory at Crewe, Cheshire. Though the first complete car built by the Company under one roof — the Bentley Mk VI standard steel saloon — offered performance levels and road manners that none of its peers could fully emulate, its appearance was anything but sporting and dated quickly. The Paris Rolls-Royce & Bentley distributor, Franco-Britannic Autos, with the redoubtable Walter Sleator (Sr) in charge, conceived a small series of special coachbuilt Mk VIs which it called 'Cresta', reviving the name of the pre-war Experimental Bentley. The styling was by Pininfarina and the first two-door saloon body was built by that Company at its Torino coachworks. Construction of the 'production' coachwork was entrusted to Facel Metallon ('Forge et Ateliers de Construction d'Eure-et-Loire' — FACEL) after Farina had built a second body.

Some of the Cresta's special chassis features, such as the lowered steering column and higher final drive ratio, subsequently became essential features of the Bentley Continental, and availability of this modified chassis no doubt gave impetus to the Continental project.

In the meantime, at home, the surviving British coachbuilders were gradually discarding the traditional coachbuilding methods and changing to, at first, 'composite', then all-metal construction methods. H. J. Mulliner & Co. was at the forefront of these developments with its all-metal 'lightweight' mode of construction, using light alloy extrusions instead of wood for body frames, and it was this expertise that stood Mulliner in good stead when the time came to develop the lightweight coachwork for the Bentley Continental.

The economic circumstances of early post-war Britain mitigated against very high-priced luxury motor cars and, paradoxically, in this instance, favoured cars which would appeal to export markets. In particular, the 'dollar gap' meant that there was an urgent need for more goods suitable for the American market.

Since 1947, the Chancellor of the Exchequer and Minister of Economic affairs in Clement Attlee's post-war Labour Government had been the grimly austere, Winchester and Oxford educated Sir Stafford Cripps, whose religious beliefs are said to have been the basis for his extreme left-wing views. Cripps's personal wealth allowed him the luxury of being able to choose austerity for himself, while imposing 'Austerity' on the nation as a whole with equal enthusiasm and, arguably, well beyond the point at which it could reasonably have been justified. Cripps's main tools for minimising inflation were the imposition of high taxation and a 'voluntary' wage-freeze. While the latter obviously had little bearing on the home market suitability of cars such as the Bentley Continental, a purchase tax at the staggering rate of 66.66 per cent had a definite inhibiting effect (even without taking into account the very high rates of income tax on large incomes) increasing the UK price to £7608 at the time of the car's introduction in 1952. Although the purchase tax rate was reduced to 50 per cent the following year, it was still

The Experimental Department based at Belper, near Derby, installed the 5.3-litre, in-line, eight-cylinder version of the range of engines then under development for the Rationalised Range of cars, into two Bentley Mk V chassis. This is the first of these Experimental chassis, 11-B-V. It was fitted with Park Ward saloon coachwork and called 'Comet' – though its performance gave rise to the colourfully descriptive but unofficial name of 'Scalded Cat.' Though capable of climbing Porlock in top gear with four up, it was a genuine 100mph car. Pressed steel wheels of the type envisaged for production were fitted.

The Bentley 'Cresta' – a concept initiated before the war for presentation at the 1939 Paris Salon. Events obliged postponement of the project until 1948 when it was revived at the instigation of Walter Sleator (Sr) of Franco-Britannic Autos, French special retailers for Rolls-Royce and Bentley cars (owned by Sleator), using the Mk VI chassis. The styling was by Pininfarina and the first car was built by them on chassis B323CD. After this prototype, a further example was built by Pininfarina and ten more were constructed, with styling variations, by Facel Metallon ('Forge et Ateliers de Construction d'Eure-et-Loire' – FACEL) of Paris. Approval was forthcoming from Rolls-Royce Ltd, who supplied special Mk VI chassis with shortened and lowered steering columns, 3.42:1 final drive ratios and kph speedometers. Availability of this special chassis gave impetus to the Bentley Continental project, which is also believed to have been instigated by Sr or, at the very least, strongly encouraged by him. This is B447CD, the first 'Cresta' to be built by Facel.

high enough to render the Continental effectively — if not actually — an 'export-only' model. Devaluation of the pound in 1949 had made life a little easier for those struggling to create appealing consumer goods for export against a continuing backdrop of difficult conditions at home.

It was under these conditions that the Bentley Continental, known as 'Corniche II' within the Company, was conceived in 1950. Under the direction of Chief Project Engineer Ivan Evernden (Ev), the Experimental Department, then based at Clan Foundry in Belper, a short distance north of Derby, took a Bentley Mk VI chassis fitted with 'Cresta' steering column and final drive, and the then still experimental 4566cc ('big bore') engine, and made a number of further changes intended to enhance the Mk VI's already creditable performance without detracting from its traditional attributes of silence and smoothness. Ev recalled that with the project halfway to fruition, Company management, perhaps concerned about development costs or whether there was a market for such a car, "got cold feet". However, Motor Car Division head, Dr Llewellyn Smith (LS), and head of the London Sales Department, Jack Scott (JS), were both sufficiently astute to support the project.

At that time, the Rolls-Royce Ltd Styling Department had not yet been created and styling work was still one of the rôles of Experimental. After spending the war on aero engine cowling design at the Company's Hucknall aero establishment, John P. Blatchley was now employed on styling work at Belper. Before the war Blatchley had been Chief Designer at Gurney Nutting, the famous London coachbuilding firm. He had arrived at Belper just in time to rescue the proposed standard steel saloon design for the Bentley Mk VI chassis, proposing a number of styling changes that added a little Gurney Nutting flair and transforming the rather bland prototype into a much more stylish design which proved more than acceptable to the Company's post-war clientele. In September 1951, Blatchley was appointed chief of the newly-created Styling Department which had been established at Crewe, thus becoming separate from the Experimental Department, which had been moved from Belper to Crewe in April of that year.

Conventional wisdom, as well as countless books and magazine articles, has taught us that the superb styling of the H. J. Mulliner coachwork of the prototype Bentley Continental (and most of the production Bentley R Type

This car, a 1949 Mk VI, chassis B9EW, with coupé coachwork by H. J. Mulliner & Co., was exhibited at the 1949 Earls Court Motor Show. It was the first to use that firm's newly developed, all-metal 'Lightweight' mode of construction, developed by Technical Director, Stanley Watts. This method used 'Reynolds Metal' extrusions for the body framing, and stood Mulliners in good stead for the Corniche II, or Bentley Continental project. Note the shallower (front to rear) Bentley radiator shell and alligator-type bonnet.

Continentals) was the work of Blatchley and Evernden. In his retirement, however, JPB disclaimed any credit for this project and recalled that his contribution was confined to some very early drawings of the basic styling concept required by Ev, from which Miss Cecily Jenner produced a water colour perspective (page 15) showing headlamps in the front wing extremities and other features which differed markedly from the final styling. Nevertheless, it was certainly Ev, as Chief Project Engineer, who proposed a body style based on the silhouette of the pre-war Embiricos Bentley. Paulin's design was brought up to date by raising the front wings to sweep across the doors, which were hung on the 'A' posts.

Rather than entrust building of the coachwork to their own coachbuilding subsidiary, Park Ward & Co., Rolls-Royce Ltd selected H. J. Mulliner & Co. for this task. This firm's recently developed, all-metal 'lighweight' mode of construction was precisely what the Continental project called for, and Mulliner's Technical Director, Stanley Watts, was known to be enthusiastic about the project. Watts had been responsible for the handsome and distinctive look of H. J. Mulliner coachwork in the late 1930s and the early post-war period, and final interpretation of the Bentley Continental's styling fell to him. It was Watts who produced the full-size drawing — the final stage of design work immediately preceding actual construction. As Technical

Dr F. Llewellyn Smith (LS), first post-war Managing Director of Rolls-Royce Ltd, Motor Car Division. LS encouraged the Bentley Continental; without his approval the project could not have gone ahead.

Director, Watts had been instrumental in developing the 'lightweight' mode of construction used to such effect on the Bentley Continental. George Moseley was taken on at H. J. Mulliner (from Harold Radford Ltd) especially to work with Watts on the Continental, and was put to work on the design of the all-metal lightweight structure.

Styling was also influenced by the results of aerodynamic tests carried out by Ev's assistant, Milford Read, using the wind tunnel at the Flight Test Establishment, Rolls-Royce Ltd's aero test facility in Hucknall, Nottinghamshire. A quarter-scale model was used for this testing: the first use of this type of model — much used in the United States — in shaping any Rolls-Royce or Bentley car. The form arrived at proved particularly aerodynamically efficient, with a comparatively small frontal area, steeply raked and sharply curved windscreen and 'fastback' roofline all contributing to this desirable attribute. Also, the finned rear wings were shown to contribute to lateral stability at speed, controlling high-speed 'yaw' and minimising any tendency for the car to be thrown off-line by side winds.

Although there is evidence that the stylists would have preferred a streamlined cowling, like that of the Embiricos car, to the traditional Bentley radiator shell, all development drawings show the Bentley radiator shell, and when the car appeared it was fitted with a 1½-inch lower version of the standard Mk VI grille. This was no bad thing as the Bentley radiator shell was notably streamlined in its own right and, on the Continental, was mounted with a pronounced rearward lean, largely flush with the coachwork. It is unlikely to have impaired aerodynamic efficiency. The prototype as

The Bentley Continental project was known as 'Corniche II' within the Company. Initial styling work was carried out by the Experimental Department at Belper under the direction of Chief Projects Engineer Ivan Evernden (Ev). This water-colour perspective was drawn by Cecily Jenner from the initial ideas of John Blatchley (JPB), who had found his niche as head of the Styling Department, then still part of the Experimental Department and located in a disused squash court at Belper. He was appointed Chief Styling Engineer when the Styling Department was officially created as a separate department in September 1951. At the time this perspective was drawn, probably late 1949 or early 1950, JPB was deeply involved in the abortive Bentley VIII project, which also featured headlamps in the wing noses, as seen here.

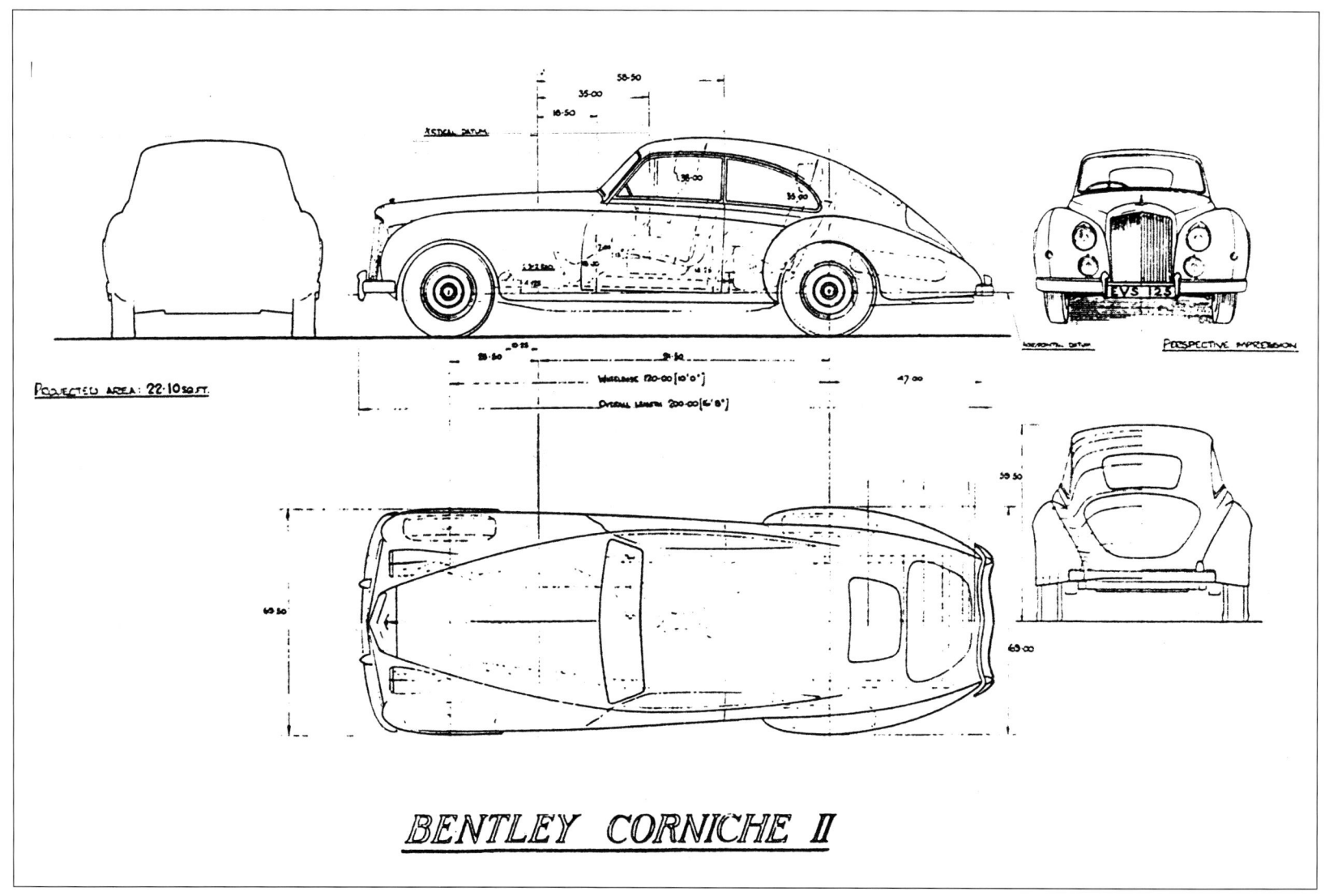

Above & opposite: These two Corniche II drawings show the progression of the design. The headlamps are now in their definitive position between bonnet and wings. Though modernised, with long front wings sweeping back over the doors to meet the rear wings, the outline in side elevation owes much to the 'Embiricos' Bentley. The second, 'revised' drawing, by Bill Allen, dated February 14th 1951, embodies a number of amendments. The 'fastback' roofline is flatter as it slopes toward the tail, with a larger backlight and boot-lid, the rear wings stand up higher at the rear to form 'fins', and the rear of the car tapers much less, seen in plan view.

originally built, and a few of the production cars, were fitted with radiator shells without the traditional dummy filler cap, or winged 'B' mascot, thus presenting an even smoother frontal appearance.

The Corniche II remit included a weight limit of 34cwt, and a top speed 20 per cent faster than that of the Mk VI standard steel saloon, which translated to within a whisker of 120mph. The weight limit was not so much in order to achieve the target top speed, though obviously it helped, but to keep within the limits imposed by the tyre manufacturers. The tyres then available would support sustained speeds of 115mph, provided the kerb weight on each tyre was limited to 8½cwt. The low weight also allowed a high rate of acceleration to be maintained against the high overall gearing.

The chassis was standard Mk VI, except for the improved efficiency exhaust system (which produces the distinctive 'note' for which the Continental is well known), higher compression ratio, higher final drive ratio, lowered steering column rake, a differently shaped petrol tank and lower radiator shell, which was mounted further forward. The exhaust system gave 25bhp more available power compared to the standard chassis. The impeccable steering mechanism and geometry of the Mk VI chassis were eminently suited to the projected high-speed motor car, and contributed in no small measure to its fine handling qualities. No attempt was made to lighten the chassis, all weight savings being achieved in the coachwork. The prototype Bentley Continental, experimental chassis 9-B-VI, was completed and on the road by August 1951.

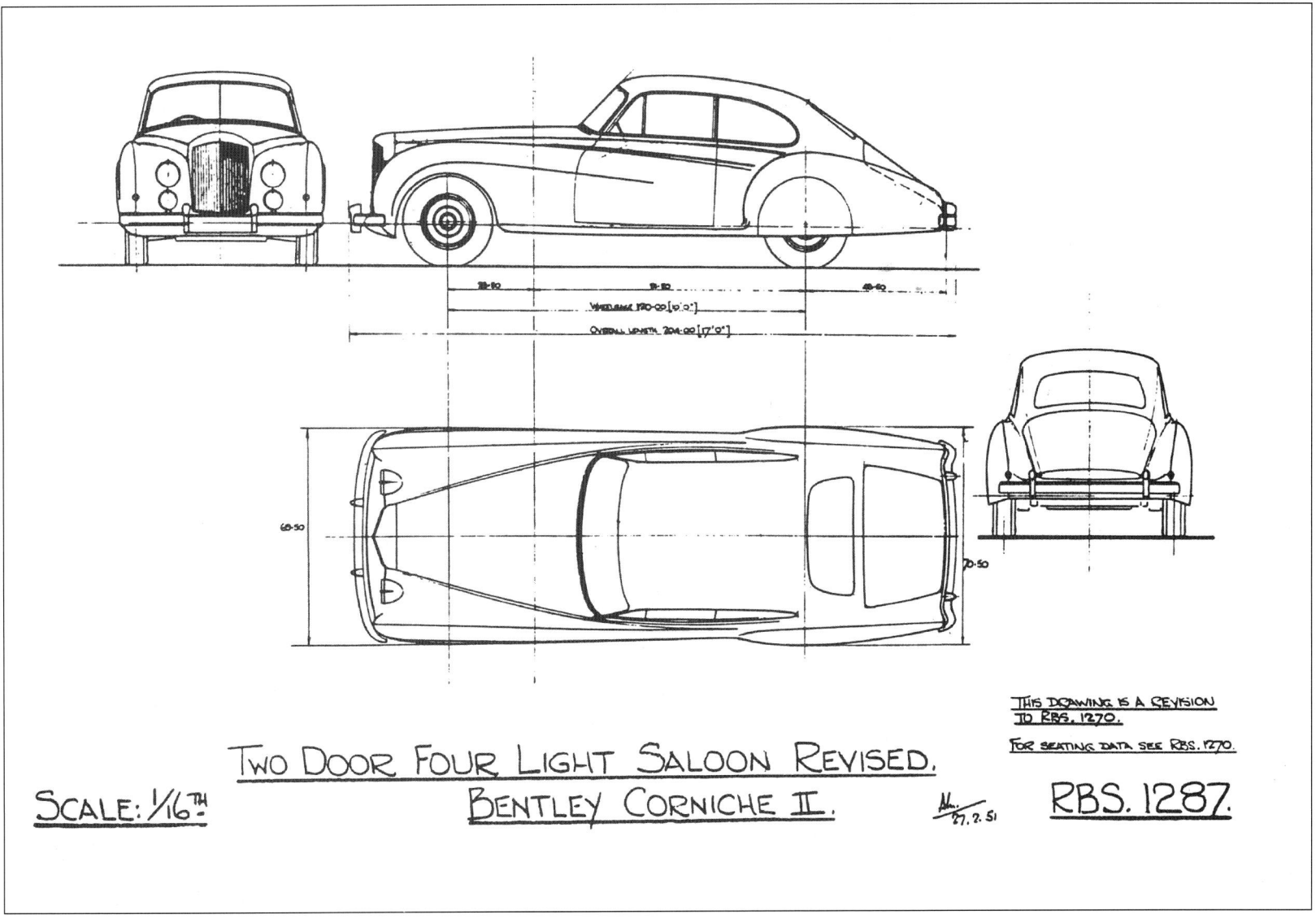

It received the Cheshire registration number OLG-490, which quickly gave rise to the name 'Olga' which has stuck ever since.

It might well be asked: why is this model called the R Type Continental if the chassis is Mk VI? The fact is that 9-B-VI pre-dated introduction of the standard Bentley R Type, with its longer chassis, revised rear spring arrangement and automatic choke. This, and the early ('A' series) production Continentals, used the Mk VI chassis and may be readily recognised, without looking under the bonnet or underneath the car, by their manual mixture control on the steering wheel boss. These cars could therefore, with complete accuracy, be described as Mk VI Continentals.

It was only well after production had gained momentum (at the introduction of the 'B' series) that the Continental was based on the R Type chassis. It is also relevant to consider that the Continental was never marketed as the R Type Continental, but was described by its makers simply as the Bentley Continental. As has so often happened with Rolls-Royce and Bentley model nomenclature, the term R Type Continental was applied retrospectively as a convenient means by which to distinguish the original Continental model from its successors, and this description has inevitably embraced the earliest cars which – strictly speaking – were Mk VIs rather than R Types.

The Mk VI chassis was a post-war development of the 'Rationalised Range' chassis designed before the war, the first manifestation of which was the 1939 Bentley Mk V, which had been built in small numbers just before the outbreak of war stopped all chassis production at Derby. The Bentley Corniche had been based on the Mk V chassis. The 4257cc, 6-cylinder, overhead inlet, side exhaust valve ('F-head') engine of the Mk VI had grown to 4566cc by the time the prototype Bentley Continental appeared. The fact that the Continental chassis was able to deliver such phenomenal performance with only minimal departures from the standard specification is testimony to how well Rolls-Royce development engineers had carried out their task of designing the early post-war cars, as well as how fundamentally right the pre-war 'Rationalised Range' concept really was.

Construction of the Bentley Continental coachwork followed

Corniche II used the then latest form of the Bentley Mk VI chassis with 4566cc engine and 'Cresta' modifications – lower steering column rake and higher final drive ratio. Also, the radiator shell was 1½in lower and mounted further forward than that of the standard chassis seen here. A special, low-loss exhaust system completed the specification. No attempt was made to lighten the chassis. The prototype and the earliest production Bentley Continentals used the BVI chassis and, strictly speaking, should therefore be characterised as Mk VI Continentals. However, the majority were built on the later R Type chassis and the whole model series, for want of a more appropriate tag, subsequently became known as the R Type Continental.

Previous page, bottom, this page & following two pages: Corniche II as built in 1951 as Experimental chassis 9-B-VI. The final form of the coachwork, by H. J. Mulliner & Co., was extremely successful, both aesthetically and practically. The bumpers were made of aluminium and the rear one was shaped to follow the contours of the car's tail. In the three-quarter front view, note the Marchal (French) head- and fog-lamps that were fitted at first. These were later replaced with standard Lucas units as seen in the front-on view, which also shows the modified horn grilles with every second bar removed. The three-quarter rear view offers a glimpse of the facia, with its 'nacelle' housing the speedometer and rev counter directly in front of the driver. Note the split, heavily curved windscreen and the absence of dummy filler cap and winged 'B' mascot on the radiator shell. The Cheshire registration number OLG-490 gave rise to the name 'Olga'.

H. J. Mulliner's newly-developed 'lightweight' system, using aluminium panels over a frame of extruded light alloy ('Reynold's metal'). Further weight savings were achieved by way of using aluminium tubular construction for the seat frames, light alloy bumpers and window frames, and a minimum of chrome decoration. The windscreen glass was supplied by Triplex which, at first, was reticent about its ability to supply such a sharply-curved screen in one piece — hence the central dividing bar on the prototype car.

Testing of 'Olga' in England revealed that the maximum attainable speed was 'only' 114mph on Dunlop MDT (Medium Distance Track) tyres. This speed corresponded to an engine speed of 3750rpm, which was 500rpm below the permissible maximum. It became clear that the chosen overall gearing ratio of 2.79:1 (with overdrive top gear) was too high.

'Olga' was taken to France for tests under the control of Walter Sleator (Sr), the Company's representative in Paris and one of the driving forces behind the Continental project. There, a speed of 119mph was achieved (with the help of a slightly favourable gradient) in the hands of an Experimental Department test driver. This corresponded to an engine speed of 3850rpm, which means that, theoretically at least, a speed of 140mph should have been

Chief Projects Engineer, Ivan F. Evernden MBE BSc (Ev), with his brainchild 9-B-VI 'Olga.' When this picture was taken, in the early 1960s, 'Olga' had again been fitted with Marchal lamps and had also received a new radiator shell with dummy filler cap and winged 'B' mascot. Ev was born in 1896 and died in 1980. He joined Rolls-Royce Ltd in 1916.

possible, given a more favourable stretch of road, and confirmed that the car was too highly geared. In France, a gearbox with direct top gear and a 3.07:1 rear axle was fitted, with complete success. On the Montlhéry track maximum speed increased slightly with the new gearing, while acceleration improved significantly. The average lap speed, as timed by the Automobile Club de France, was 118.75mph, and the best lap speed was within 0.25mph of 120mph, again using Dunlop MDT tyres at a pressure of 50lb/in^3.

Other test runs on India Shallow Tread road tyres produced a maximum

'Olga' undergoing a comprehensive, body-off restoration at the workshops of P. & A. Wood in the 1980s and after completion of the work. The chassis, which is the Mk VI pattern rather than R Type, was dismantled down to the bare frame. The car was returned to its then owner, Victor Gauntlett, in as-new condition. The Experimental chassis number 9-B-VI had given way to the additional 'A' series production number BC26A in 1954. In 1960/61 the car was overhauled at Hythe Road to make it ready for sale to its first private owner, Stanley Sedgwick.

of 115.5mph. Normal 6-ply tyres, as used on the standard Mk VI, lasted for as little as 20 miles in these high speed test conditions! Acceleration to 100mph took 36 seconds — considerably faster than any other saloon of the period. Though the Continental was only 0.2 of a second faster reaching 50mph than the standard Mk VI with the 4566cc engine, it gathered speed much more quickly from that point on and was nearly 4 seconds quicker to 70mph and more than 6 seconds quicker to 80mph.

The specification was settled and the stage set for production.

The prototype Bentley Continental, 'Olga,' following a magnificent body-off restoration for Mr Victor Gauntlett by P. & A. Wood. Originally Experimental chassis 9-B-VI, 'Olga' received the production chassis number BC26A before being sold by Rolls-Royce to Mr Stanley Sedgwick in 1961.

The first Bentley Continental. A delightful study of 'Olga,' chassis BC26A, at the Surrey home of the late Stanley Sedgwick, who owned this celebrated car for a quarter of a century from 1960, covering 100,000 miles in the first twelve years alone, which included some remarkable long-distance, high-speed motoring.

THE AUTOCAR, SEPTEMBER 12, 1952

The Autocar ROAD TESTS

Long graceful lines and a special low radiator shell, without the traditional filler cap and emblem, identify the Continental Bentley saloon. There are twin Marchal head lamps with amber bulbs, and auxiliary lamps, while the side lamps in the wings act also as direction indicators.

No. 1475: BENTLEY CONTINENTAL SPORTS SALOON

THE Continental sports saloon is a new stage in the evolution of the post-war Bentley. The first major change since the introduction of the post-war chassis was made last year, when an increase in the bore brought the engine swept volume up to 4½ litres. *The Autocar* Road Test of December 7, 1951, recorded that it enabled the standard four-door steel panelled saloon to reach a maximum speed of 100 m.p.h., accompanied by impressive acceleration, without the slightest sacrifice of the smoothness or silence for which the *marque* is renowned. The next step was to raise the compression to profit by the better fuel now available in overseas markets, and to fit lighter bodywork with lower drag characteristics, which would allow the great potentialities of this chassis to be more fully exploited. The reduction in drag permitted a higher axle ratio to be employed, and a close ratio gear box was installed to give the best acceleration. The resulting car, known as the Bentley Continental sports saloon, has been subjected to rigorous testing on the Continent for about a year, and *The Autocar* has recently been able to give it an extensive trial in Britain and on the Continent. It brings Bentley back to the forefront of the world's fastest cars, and its tremendous performance makes this one of the outstanding in the long series of Road Tests.

The car is being produced in limited numbers and is reserved for export only. Its price is high, the sterling figure being £4,890 without purchase tax, which means that by the time the foreign buyer has paid delivery charges and local taxes it will probably cost him between six and seven thousand pounds. The Continental Bentley may, therefore, be the most expensive production car in the world, but it also makes a strong claim to be the fastest four-five-seater

—DATA—

PRICE (basic), with two-door saloon body, £4,890. Not available in Great Britain.
Extras: Radio standard if requested.
Heater standard.
ENGINE: Capacity: 4,566 c.c. (278.633 cu in).
Number of cylinders: 6.
Bore and stroke: 92 × 114.3 mm (3.625 × 4.5 in).
Valve gear: Overhead inlet with push rods, side exhaust.
Compression ratio: 7 to 1.
B.H.P.: Not quoted.
Torque: Not quoted.
M.P.H. per 1,000 r.p.m. on top gear, 27.
WEIGHT (with 5 gals fuel), 33¼ cwt (3,739 lb).
Weight distribution (per cent) 50.1 F; 49.9 R.
Laden as tested: 36.8 cwt (4,120 lb).
Lb per c.c. (laden): 0.9
BRAKES: Type: F, leading and trailing shoe; R, leading and trailing shoe.
Method of operation: F Hydraulic. R Mechanical. Mechanical servo.
Drum dimensions: F, 12½in diameter, 2¼in wide. R, 12½in diameter, 2¼in wide.
Lining area: F, 186 sq in. R, 186 sq in (202 sq in per ton laden).
TYRES: 6.50—16in.
Pressures (lb per sq in): 30 F; 35 R (normal). 35 F; 40 R (for fast driving).
TANK CAPACITY: 18 Imperial gallons.
Oil sump, 16 pints.
Cooling system, 32 pints.
TURNING CIRCLE: 43ft 0in (L and R).
Steering wheel turns (lock to lock): 3¼.
DIMENSIONS: Wheelbase 10ft 0in.
Track: 4ft 8½in (F); 4ft 10¼in (R).
Length (overall): 17ft 2½in.
Height: 5ft 3in.
Width: 5ft 11½in.
Ground clearance: 7in.
Frontal area: 23.5 sq ft (approx).
ELECTRICAL SYSTEM: 12-volt. 54 ampère-hour battery.
Head lights: Single or double dip, as required; wattage as required.
SUSPENSION: Front, Coil springs and wishbones with anti-roll bar.
Rear, Half-elliptics.

PERFORMANCE

BENTLEY CONTINENTAL SPORTS SALOON

ACCELERATION: from constant speeds.
Speed, gear ratios and time in sec.

M.P.H.	3.077 to 1	3.740 to 1	4.750 to 1	8.230 to 1
10—30	8.2	6.9	5.3	3.4
20—40	7.4	6.0	4.8	3.5
30—50	7.4	6.1	5.1	—
40—60	7.4	6.8	5.7	—
50—70	8.4	7.1	6.1	—
60—80	9.6	8.4	—	—
70—90	12.1	10.8	—	—
80—100	14.6	14.4	—	—

From rest through gears to:

M.P.H.	sec
30	4.4
50	10.5
60	13.5
70	16.3
80	22.2
90	28.1
100	36.0

Standing quarter mile, 19.5 sec.

SPEED ON GEARS:

	M.P.H. (normal and max.)*	K.P.H. (normal and max.)
Top (mean)	115.4	185.7
(best)	116.9	188.1
3rd	80—100	129—161
2nd	60—77	97—124
1st	30—44	48—71

* At 4,300 r.p.m. limit on intermediate gears.

SPEEDOMETER CORRECTION: M.P.H.

Car speedometer	10	20	30	40	50	60	70	80	90	100
True speed	11.6	21.2	30.6	40.7	51.3	61.5	71.3	81.5	92.0	101.5

TRACTIVE RESISTANCE: 34 lb per ton at 10 M.P.H.

TRACTIVE EFFORT:

	Pull (lb per ton)	Equivalent Gradient
Top	287	1 in 7.8
Third	352	1 in 6.2
Second	442	1 in 5.0

BRAKES:

Efficiency	Pedal Pressure (lb)
97.0 per cent	116
91.5 per cent	100
58.7 per cent	50

FUEL CONSUMPTION:
19.4 m.p.g. overall for 438 miles. (14.6 litres per 100 km).
Approximate normal range 16-21 m.p.g. (17.7-13.5 litres per 100 km).
Fuel: Belgian Super for performance tests; 50-50 Pool and 80 octane for road running.

WEATHER: Dry, warm, sunny.
Air temperature 95-85 degrees F.
Acceleration figures are the means of several runs in opposite directions.
Tractive effort and resistance obtained by Tapley meter.
Model described in *The Autocar* of February 29, 1952.

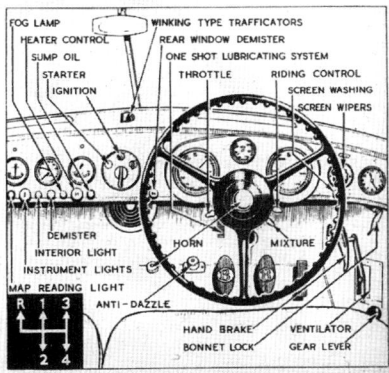

25

THE AUTOCAR, SEPTEMBER 12, 1952

The special radiator shell is smoothly faired into the bonnet and the concave curves of the wings, to give a new and modern appearance to the Continental Bentley. There is a curved windscreen supported in very slim pillars.

The graceful tail sweeps down between rear wings which terminate in twin stop and tail lamps, the stop lamps being also used as flashing direction indicators. The bumpers are in heavy-gauge light alloy and the exhaust pipe is chromium plated. Twin reversing lamps are grouped alongside the central number plate.

ROAD TEST . . . . continued

saloon in the world. Circumstances made it necessary to carry out the maximum speed tests on brand new tyres, which increase rolling resistance, and in the middle of a hot day, with an air temperature of 95 deg F, which reduces volumetric efficiency. Even so, a mean maximum speed of over 115 m.p.h. was recorded. One run, with driver only, was timed at 120 m.p.h., and it seems probable that in more favourable circumstances this speed might be more regularly reached. The acceleration from rest to 100 m.p.h. (36.0 sec) has not been approached by any other saloon car in *The Autocar's* experience and has been equalled by very few open sports cars. Acceleration in the gears is so well maintained that the usual tabulations have had to be extended to 100 m.p.h. for both top and third gears.

However, the figures, impressive though they are, do not tell the whole story. Whatever memorable motoring experiences one may have had, this was something different. It showed what can be achieved by the single-minded pursuit of perfection, not in seeking always to incorporate the latest technical innovation, but by ceaseless, resourceful and painstaking improvement of every minute detail on well-tried basic principles. Such a car is bound to be costly, and the British, who make it, cannot own it; but it goes abroad as proof that a nation where the creators are constantly subjected to the debasement of their own living standards can still keep alive the ideal of perfection for others to enjoy.

One might think that such tremendous performance could be used only on rare occasions, but the controls are so superbly responsive that the experienced driver quickly finds himself making full use of its potentialities, to over 100 m.p.h., then effacing the speed smoothly and quickly with a touch on the mechanical servo brakes. It is an experience that lulls the critical faculty and defies one to analyse the car step by step, but the effort must be made.

For the driver, the forward view through the wide, curved windscreen, with its very slim pillars, is excellent, the seating position is good for high-speed driving and the controls are well arranged. When the engine starts, there is a rasping noise, discreet and distant, but sufficient to indicate that this is something new in Bentleys, and there is a momentary snarl from the exhaust at the beginning of acceleration in each gear. These are absolutely the only aural concessions to high performance. Engine and gear-box are slightly audible in first gear, but otherwise, throughout the performance range, there is only that uncanny silence which indicates long and careful attention to every detail of design and construction.

With the high gearing employed, third is the natural ratio to employ for mountainous country or winding roads. It can be kept in use for miles on end, and for smoothness or silence is quite indistinguishable from top. The maximum available on this gear is 100 m.p.h. without trespassing by more than the thickness of the needle into the red zone on the rev counter, so that it caters for all normal needs. Anyone not familiar with the car has to feel the gear lever occasionally to remind himself which gear he is using. If there is any mechanical noise at speeds near the maximum, it is completely lost in the rush of the wind.

There is no need to specify a cruising speed; progress seems as smooth, easy and effortless at 100 m.p.h. as at 50. Nor is there any imperative need for frequent gear changing. It is possible to make a smooth, easy start on top gear and to accelerate relentlessly away to maximum speed without using the gear box at all. This is hardly to be recommended as normal practice, however, especially as gear changing is such

There is a folding central arm rest at the rear, and below the seat is a grille supplying fresh air from the ventilation system. The generous-sized rear quarter lights can be hinged outwards to act as air extractors.

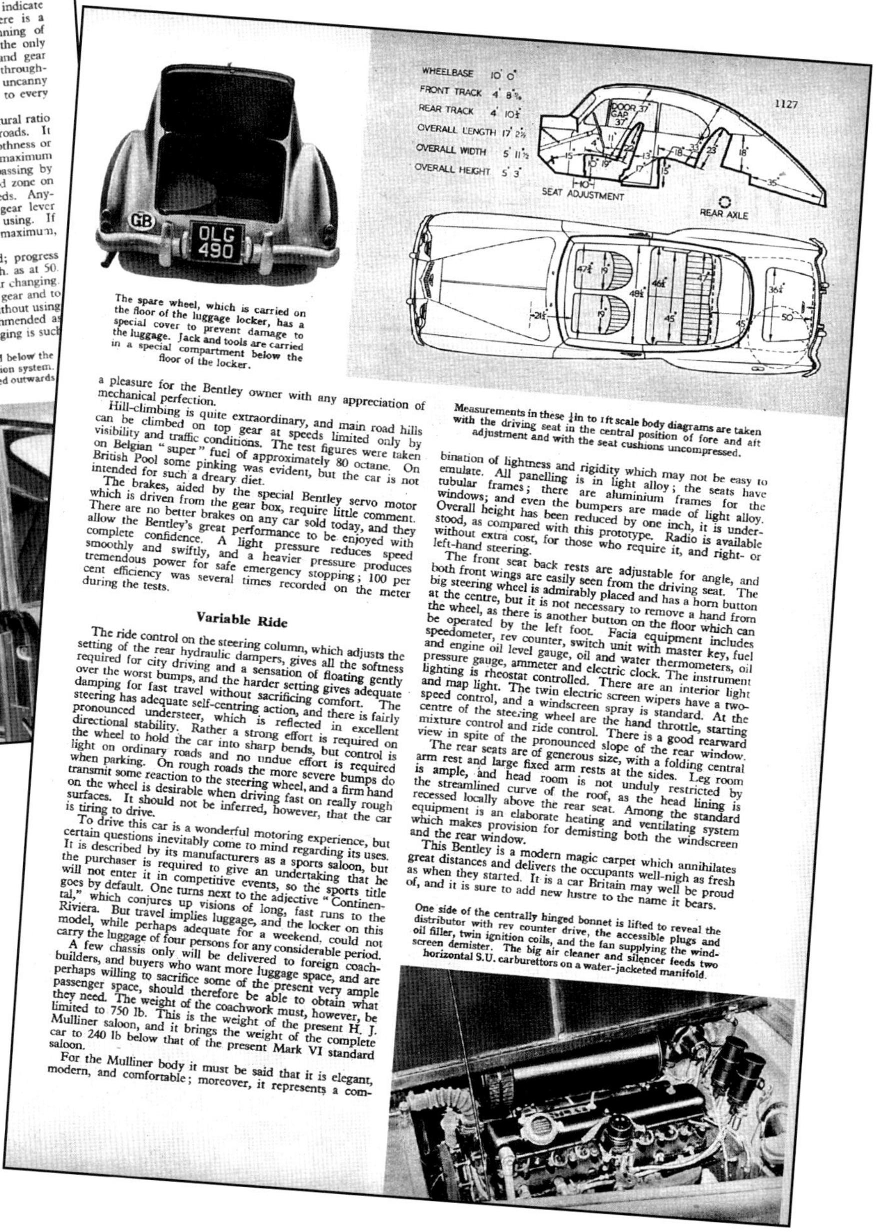

The massive facia in polished walnut is almost entirely occupied by instrument dials and switches. Below are seen one of the heater elements, the pendant pedal for the one-shot lubrication and a fresh-air duct by the throttle.

The spare wheel, which is carried on the floor of the luggage locker, has a special cover to prevent damage to the luggage. Jack and tools are carried in a special compartment below the floor of the locker.

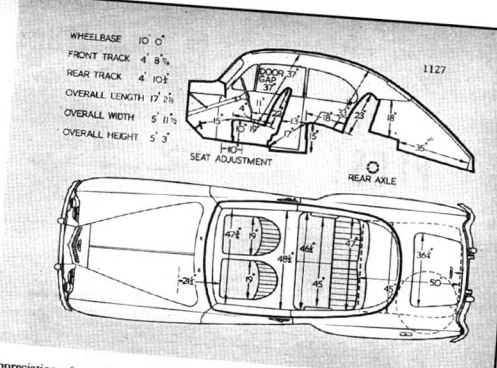

Measurements in these ⅛in to 1ft scale body diagrams are taken with the driving seat in the central position of fore and aft adjustment and with the seat cushions uncompressed.

a pleasure for the Bentley owner with any appreciation of mechanical perfection.

Hill-climbing is quite extraordinary, and main road hills can be climbed on top gear at speeds limited only by visibility and traffic conditions. The test figures were taken on Belgian "super" fuel of approximately 80 octane. On British Pool some pinking was evident, but the car is not intended for such a dreary diet.

The brakes, aided by the special Bentley servo motor which is driven from the gear box, require little comment. There are no better brakes on any car sold today, and they allow the Bentley's great performance to be enjoyed with complete confidence. A light pressure reduces speed smoothly and swiftly, and a heavier pressure produces tremendous power for safe emergency stopping; 100 per cent efficiency was several times recorded on the meter during the tests.

Variable Ride

The ride control on the steering column, which adjusts the setting of the rear hydraulic dampers, gives all the softness required for city driving and a sensation of floating gently over the worst bumps, and the harder setting gives adequate damping for fast travel without sacrificing comfort. The steering has adequate self-centring action, and there is fairly pronounced understeer, which is reflected in excellent directional stability. Rather a strong effort is required on the wheel to hold the car into sharp bends, but control is light on ordinary roads and no undue effort is required when parking. On rough roads the more severe bumps do transmit some reaction to the steering wheel, and a firm hand on the wheel is desirable when driving fast on really rough surfaces. It should not be inferred, however, that the car is tiring to drive.

To drive this car is a wonderful motoring experience, but certain questions inevitably come to mind regarding its uses. It is described by its manufacturers as a sports saloon, but the purchaser is required to give an undertaking that he will not enter it in competitive events, so the sports title goes by default. One turns next to the adjective "Continental," which conjures up visions of long, fast runs to the Riviera. But travel implies luggage, and the locker on this model, while perhaps adequate for a weekend, could not carry the luggage of four persons for any considerable period.

A few chassis only will be delivered to foreign coach-builders, and buyers who want more luggage space, and are perhaps willing to sacrifice some of the present very ample passenger space, should therefore be able to obtain what they need. The weight of the coachwork must, however, be limited to 750 lb. This is the weight of the present H. J. Mulliner saloon, and it brings the weight of the complete car to 240 lb below that of the present Mark VI standard saloon.

For the Mulliner body it must be said that it is elegant, modern, and comfortable; moreover, it represents a combination of lightness and rigidity which may not be easy to emulate. All panelling is in light alloy; the seats have tubular frames; there are aluminium frames for the windows; and even the bumpers are made of light alloy. Overall height has been reduced by one inch, it is understood, as compared with this prototype. Radio is available without extra cost, for those who require it, and right- or left-hand steering.

The front seat back rests are adjustable for angle, and both front wings are easily seen from the driving seat. The big steering wheel is admirably placed and has a horn button at the centre, but it is not necessary to remove a hand from the wheel, as there is another button on the floor which can be operated by the left foot. Facia equipment includes speedometer, rev counter, switch unit with master key, fuel and engine oil level gauge, oil and water thermometers, oil pressure gauge, ammeter and electric clock. The instrument lighting is rheostat controlled. There are an interior light and map light. The twin electric screen wipers have a two-speed control, and a windscreen spray is standard. At the centre of the steering wheel are the hand throttle, starting mixture control and ride control. There is a good rearward view in spite of the pronounced slope of the rear window.

The rear seats are of generous size, with a folding central arm rest and large fixed arm rests at the sides. Leg room is ample, and head room is not unduly restricted by the streamlined curve of the roof, as the head lining is recessed locally above the rear seat. Among the standard equipment is an elaborate heating and ventilating system which makes provision for demisting both the windscreen and the rear window.

This Bentley is a modern magic carpet which annihilates great distances and delivers the occupants well-nigh as fresh as when they started. It is a car Britain may well be proud of, and it is sure to add new lustre to the name it bears.

One side of the centrally hinged bonnet is lifted to reveal the distributor with rev counter drive, the accessible plugs and oil filler, twin ignition coils, and the fan supplying the windscreen demister. The big air cleaner and silencer feeds two horizontal S.U. carburettors on a water-jacketed manifold.

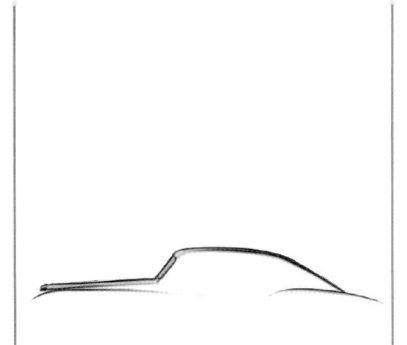

2. THE BENTLEY CONTINENTAL INTO PRODUCTION

It quickly became obvious that with the Bentley Continental Rolls-Royce had a winner. The production cars, or at least those that did not have to carry extra weight added by the demands of owners, were capable of 80 miles per hour in second gear, 100mph in third and a shade under 120mph in top — more than sufficient to claim the title of the world's fastest genuine four-seater car, as well as the most expensive production car. Moreover, it would easily return better than 20 miles per gallon of the low octane substance that passed for petrol in those days.

At first, the Continental was effectively an export-only car and, as such, earned for Britain a respectable amount of much needed export income.

Bentley Continental chassis were built alongside the standard chassis at Crewe, and dispatched in chassis form to H. J. Mulliner & Co., though the occasional chassis was shipped to a foreign coachbuilder and, later in the model's life, Park Ward received six chassis. Deliveries to owners and shippers of complete Bentley Continental cars commenced in June 1952. Deliveries of standard Bentley R Types started the same month, although, because chassis had been sent to coachbuilders some months earlier, initial ('A' series) Bentley Continental production was still based on the Mk VI chassis.

Most (192) of the 207 production cars had the H. J. Mulliner 'fastback' (for want of a better term) coachwork as fitted to 'Olga,' though with a number of minor changes for production. These included a new facia, one-piece windscreen, chrome-plated brass window frames and, for deliveries other than to France, standard Lucas fog- and headlamps in place of Olga's Marchal units. Also, the roofline was an inch lower than Olga's, and normal steel bumpers were fitted to nearly all of the production cars. Some of these changes, where ease of production won out over adherence to the original remit, voided hard-won weight-savings. Further weight gains were imposed by customer requests for bulkier front seats and other creature comforts, as well as the fitting of chrome strips and other decoration not required on the original concept. The Bentley Continental sales brochure gave the weight of the complete car as 33.5cwt and warned: "It will be appreciated that any variation from standard body specification involving increased weight will inevitably affect the performance of the car." A radio was included in the price but, in the interests of weight-saving, was only fitted at the customer's specific request.

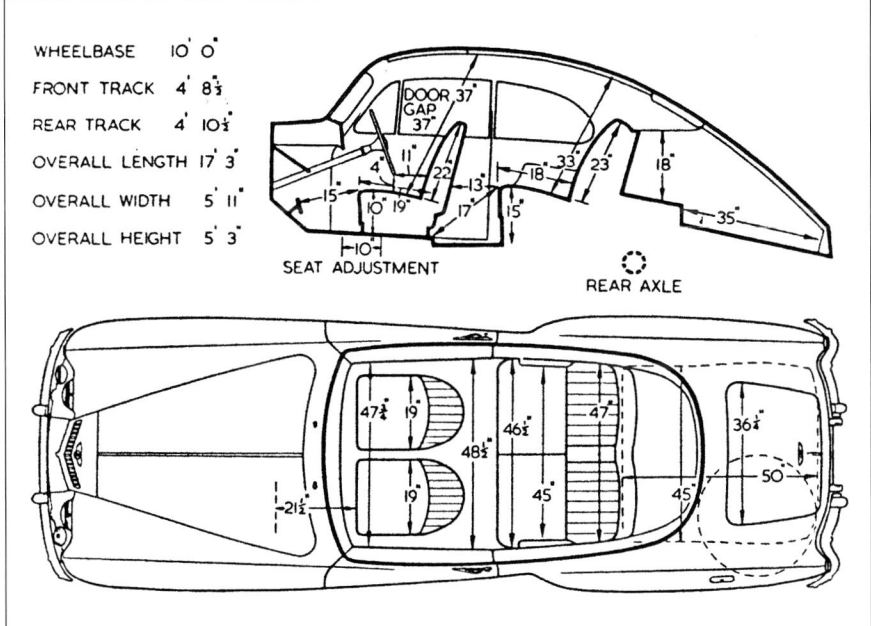

Plan and seating layout of the early Bentley Continental, actually based on the prototype's shape and dimensions, showing the small, lightweight bucket seats, the rear bumper shaped to follow the contours of the body, and the tail shape in plan view which was much less tapered than Evernden's original Corniche II design.

Only six Bentley R Type Continentals were fitted with coachwork by a British coachbuilder other than H. J. Mulliner. These were four drophead coupés and a brace of two-door saloons, all by Park Ward and all on late series chassis. It had been realised that with H. J. Mulliner supplying virtually all of the coachwork, the Bentley Continental was not yielding the maximum possible returns to Rolls-Royce Ltd, as Mulliner was then still an independent coachbuilder. An effective way of improving this situation was for Rolls-Royce to give its wholly-owned subsidiary Company, Park Ward, a role in supplying the coachwork. Chassis for the four Park Ward drophead coupés were specially strengthened by the Experimental Department.

In 1952, a series of high-level meetings in the Car Division resulted in the decision to hand responsibility for external styling of Park Ward coachwork to the Crewe Styling Office under John Blatchley (see Chapter Five). Park Ward's Chief Draughtsman, Peter Wharton (PJW), retained control over interior design, while structural design and detailing continued to be carried out by the Park Ward design and drawing office in High Road, Willesden. Peter Wharton was subsequently appointed Senior Stylist at Park Ward (and later H. J. Mulliner, Park Ward after the two firms merged) but, in practice, no coachwork was styled 'in-house' by Park Ward after 1952 — or at least none that was actually built.

The first Park Ward designs styled by John Blatchley under this policy were the drophead coupé and two-door saloon for the Bentley Continental, which nearly came too late for the R Type Continental, but were subsequently adapted very successfully for the larger S Type Continental chassis, on which they were built in much greater numbers. Although John Blatchley has frequently, but erroneously, been credited with styling the original (H. J. Mulliner) Bentley Continental, he did, in fact, style the later Park Ward version.

The remaining nine bodies on R Type Continental chassis were built by continental European coachbuilders: Franay (France) who built five bodies, Graber (Switzerland, three) and Pininfarina (Italy) who built a two-seater fixed head coupé.

Right-hand drive Continentals normally had the traditional Rolls-Royce right-hand, gate-type gear lever. Always a refined feature, this had been developed to perfection after the war and the expression, 'like a hot knife through butter,' was especially apt. The absence of synchromesh on first gear was of little consequence on the standard Mk VI and R Type, which would pull away in second gear at little more than idling revs. However, it was a little irksome in the case of the Continental which, due to its very high rear axle ratio, meant first gear was called upon much more frequently than

Above & left: Production Continentals employed the same lightweight method of construction as the prototype, with aluminium panels over a 'Reynolds Metal' light alloy framework. This is a very early production car, with lightweight bumpers and radiator shell fitted with the standard dummy filler cap and mascot. By the time production commenced, Triplex had been able to overcome the difficulties of producing such a sharply curved windscreen in one piece, and the centre dividing bar of the prototype was dispensed with. The roofline of the production cars was an inch lower than the prototype's, and the rear extremity of the rear wing was raised slightly. The grilles below the headlights are the standard pattern, designed by John Blatchley in 1946 to match the headlights and to finish off the front end appearance of the early post-war cars. These photographs were taken at Gunnersbury Park, West London, which was a favourite and convenient photographic location for coachbuilders' photographers, both before and after World War II.

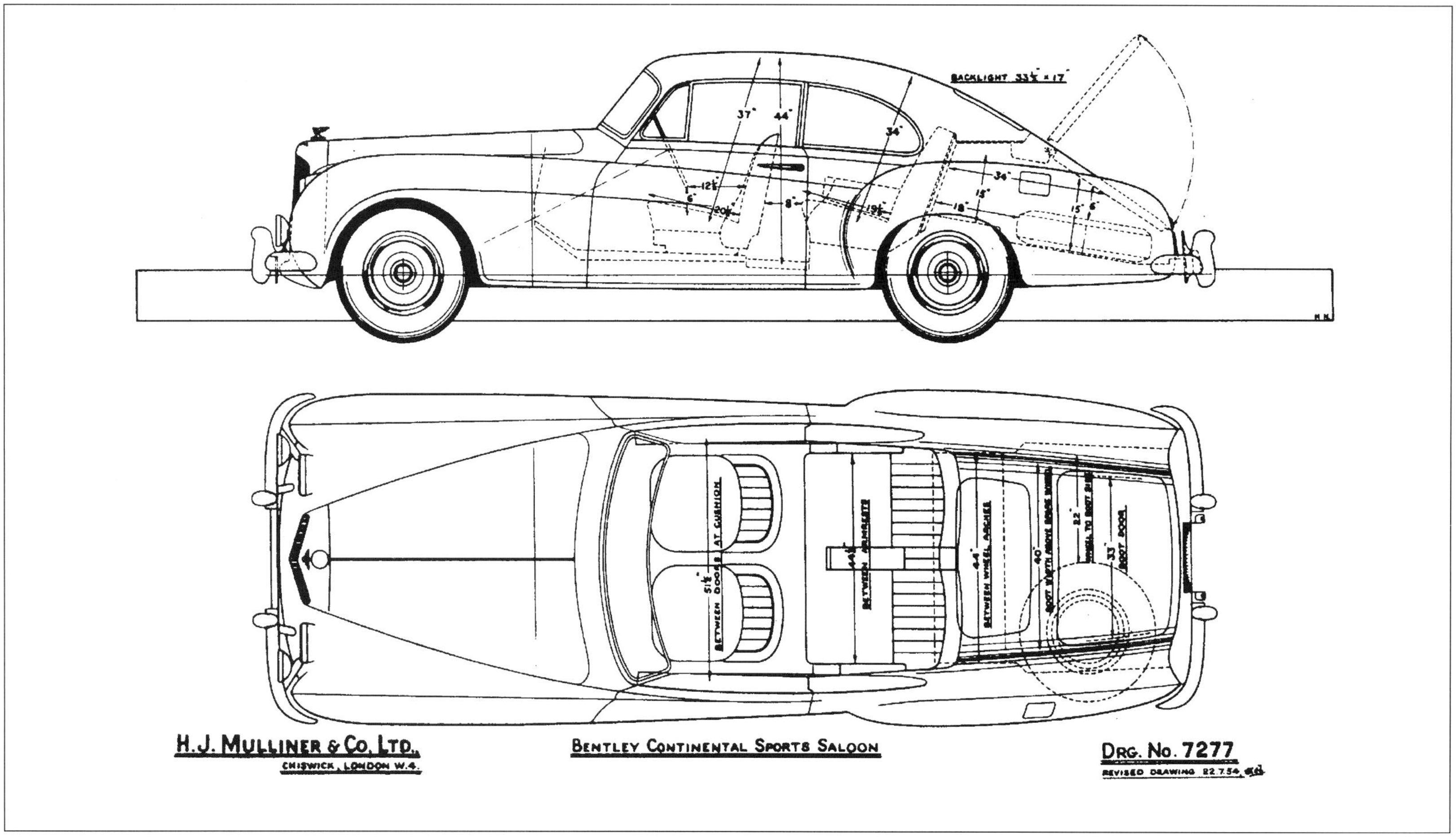

Line drawing of the production Continental, by H. J. Mulliner draughtsman Herbert Nye. Though the roofline was slightly flatter and an inch lower than that of the prototype, the rear headroom is shown to have increased by an inch! This drawing shows the heavy, export-type bumpers, with the straightened rear bumper that was fitted to the majority of production cars. An apron was provided here to fill what would otherwise have been an unsightly gap.

On production Continentals the prototype's separate nacelle for the speedometer and revolution counter gave way to this almost flat – but, in fact, slightly curved – one-piece facia. With variations, this became a feature of all Mulliner Continentals from the first production 'R Types' through to the S3, and was a fine setting for the comprehensive Bentley Continental instrumentation which took the form of individual gauges, rather than the four-in-one instrument of the standard chassis. There was even an oil temperature gauge (between the speedometer and the rev counter). To prevent reflections in the windscreen, the speedometer and rev counter were deeply recessed. Note the absence of a glove compartment on this very early car, and the oddments tray below the facia. The controls on the steering wheel indicate that this is an early synchromesh gearbox car without the automatic cold-start device: that is, a car based on the Mk VI chassis rather than that of the R Type.

The seating, in early Continentals at least, was built with weight minimisation in mind without sacrificing comfort. Later, customers seemed to rather miss the point and demanded heavier, thicker seats, which somewhat compromised the original concept. Headroom in the back seat was only slightly less than that of the standard steel saloon, which, given the Continental's sleek body shape, is rather remarkable.

The heart of the R Type Continental. The combination of higher performance engine, more efficient exhaust system, high gearing, light weight and wind-tunnel proven aerodynamic efficiency enabled the Continental to achieve a speed of 100mph in third gear and a top gear maximum of around 120mph, thereby easily qualifying it as the fastest genuine four-seater car in the world at the time.

on the standard cars, and experienced owners were accustomed to touching the synchromesh on second gear before engaging first. Complying with contemporary fashion, a steering column gearshift had been developed for left-hand drive cars, but this suited the Continental's sporting character less than ideally, and more than two-thirds of the left-hand drive manual geared cars had a centre, floor-mounted lever that worked through the gate on the right-hand side of the chassis. Whilst this was a little 'notchy' compared with the right-hand change, it was completely superior to the column change. In fact, the centre gear lever was sufficiently well-liked for half a dozen right-hand drive cars to have been so fitted.

For the 'D' series Continentals, with deliveries from July 1954 onwards, the engine bore was increased to 3.75 inches, giving a cubic capacity of 4887cc. The extra power provided would have been useful were it not for the fact that customers who insisted upon thicker, more luxurious seats (often with folding armrests), and other weight-adding items such as radio sets, electric windows and the like, had by now become the majority. The 4887cc engine was confined to the Continental chassis until the same capacity was adopted as standard for the S Type chassis the following year.

Just before introduction of the 4.9-litre ('D' series) Bentley Continental, an automatic gearbox became available as an option. The gearbox chosen was the Crewe-built version of the General Motors 'Hydramatic' (an epicyclic unit with four forward speeds and fluid coupling) that had already been available on the other models of the range for more than a year and a half. At first, before production commenced at Crewe, this option was restricted to

Following page: The overhead inlet, side exhaust ('F-head') layout was an essential feature of the Rationalised Range engines fitted to all the early post-war cars, including the Bentley Continental.

(continued on page 38)

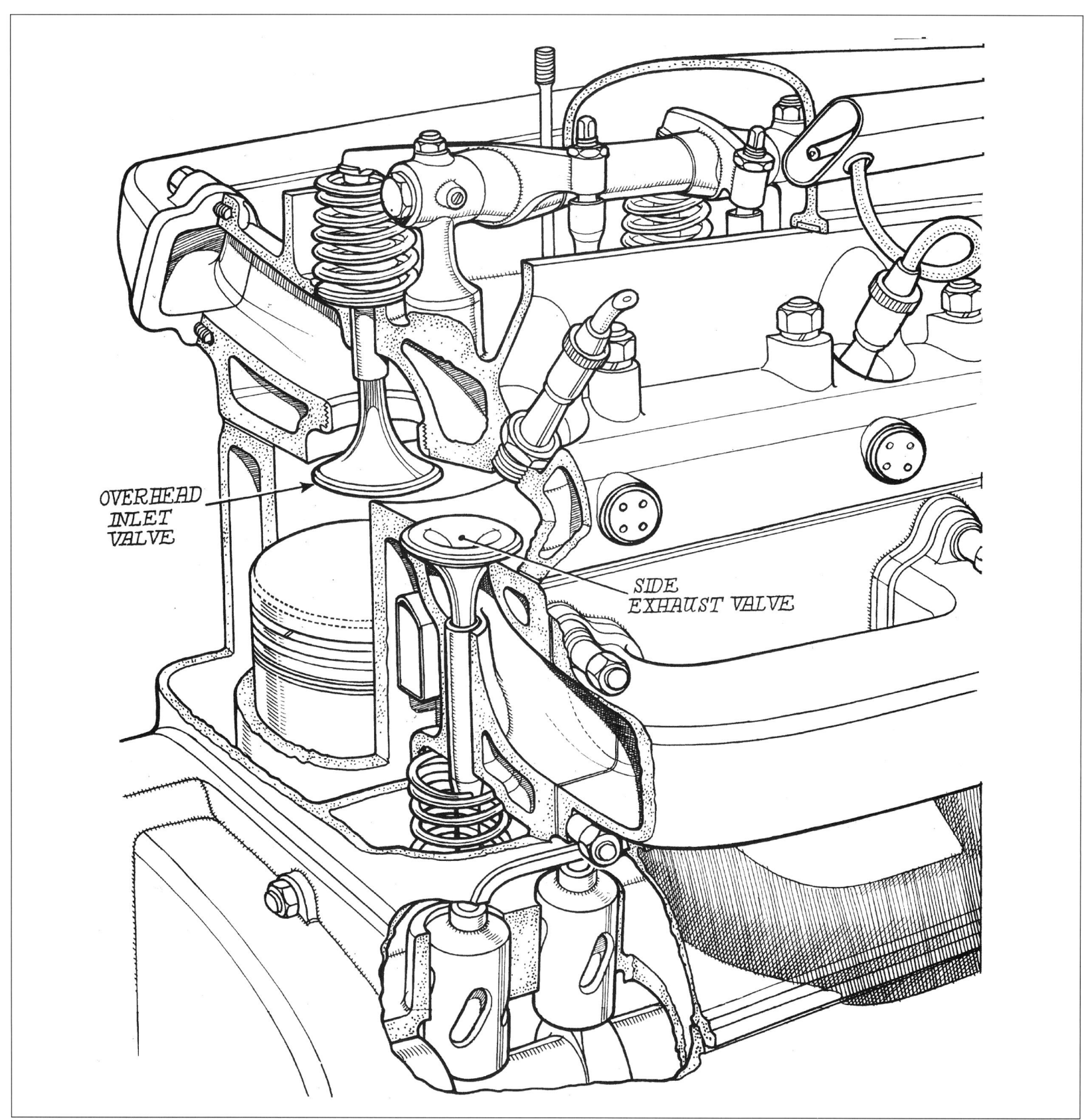

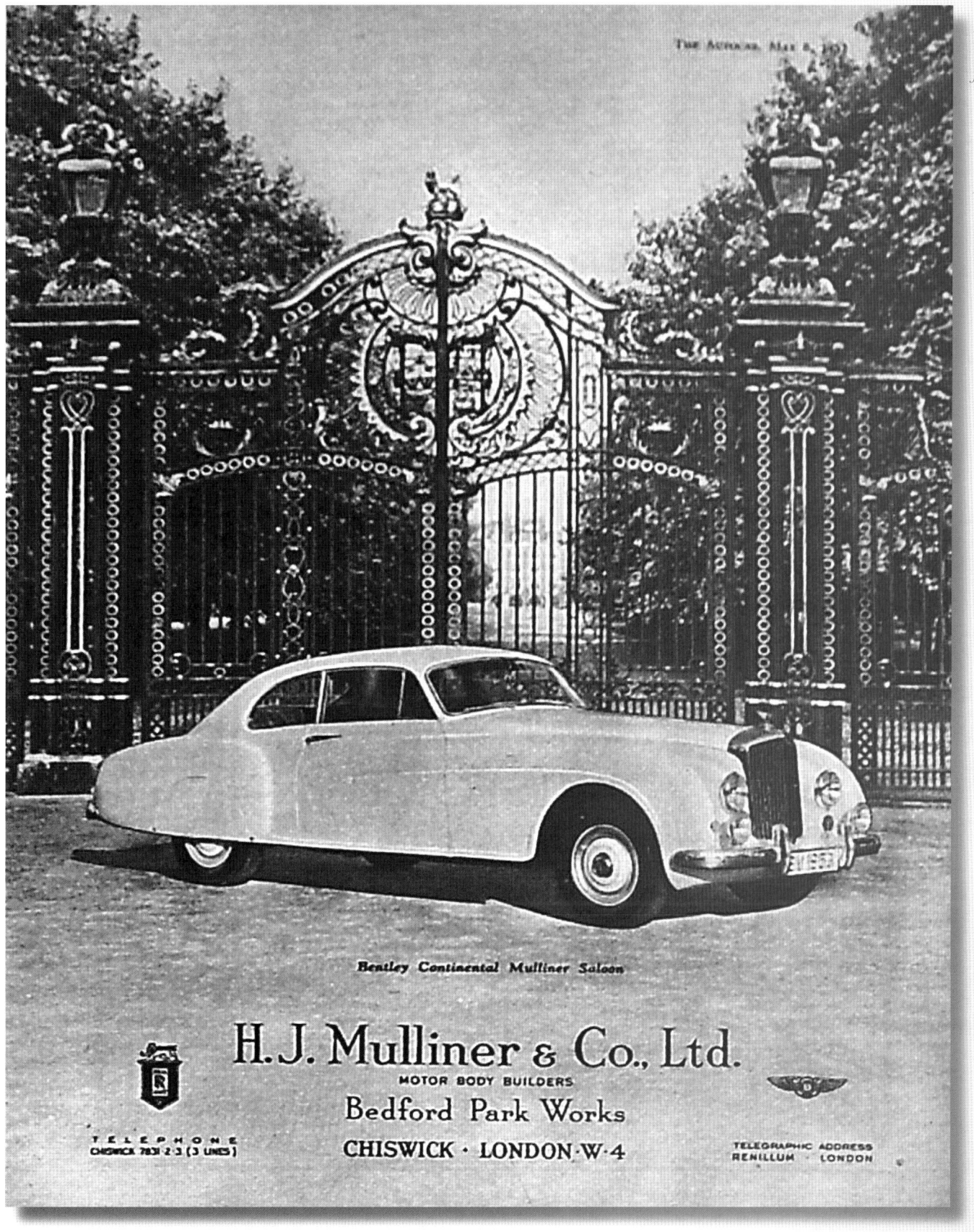

A period advertisement, from the May 8th 1953 edition of The Autocar, *placed by H.J. Mulliner & Co. to publicise the Bentley Continental.*

Though at first sight the tail shape of the H. J. Mulliner Bentley Continental appears less than ideal from the point of view of luggage carrying capacity, the picture, above left, shows the set of fitted luggage that could be accommodated. This is an early car with lightweight bumpers hugging the contours of the body and reversing lights flanking the numberplate. The pictures, above right show a later car, BC23B, with heavy Wilmot Breeden bumpers and overriders of a style which subsequently became standard for all Rolls-Royce and Bentley models. Note the dual lens rear lamps of this later car. The chrome embellisher mouldings on the waistline, sill and rear wing are non-standard for this body style, as is the shape of the rear wheel spat.

The fourth production Bentley Continental, BC4A, which was delivered in June 1952 to Briggs Cunningham, a US customer who nevertheless opted for right-hand drive. The lightweight bumpers and radiator shell with no cap or mascot show that this order uncompromisingly adhered to the original Continental remit. The body-hugging polished aluminium rear bumper is shown (left).

1952 Continental, chassis BC5A. Though this was only the fifth production car, weight-adding elements are already in evidence: the heavy steel, export-type bumpers and overriders, and even a short chrome moulding on the waistline. The radiator shell, however, is like that of the prototype, with no dummy filler cap or winged 'B' mascot. This serves to illustrate the freedom of choice available to the Bentley Continental purchaser.

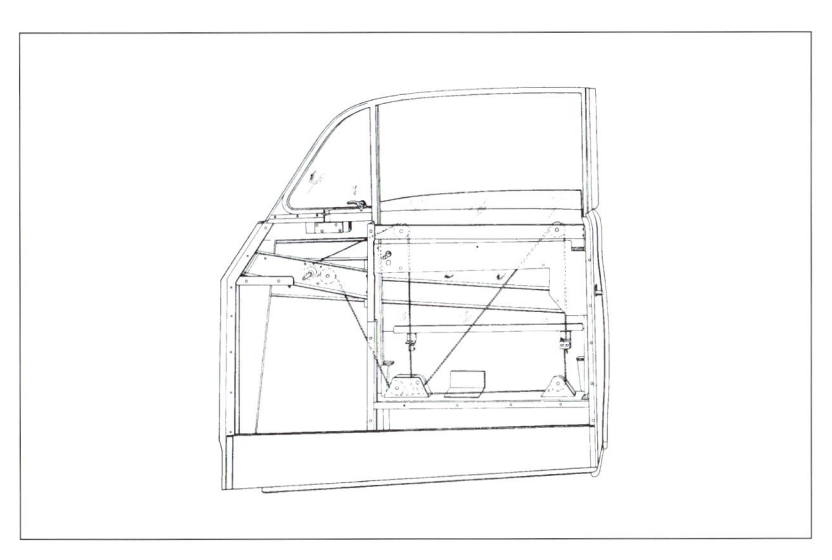

Above left: R Type Continental door construction detail, showing H. J. Mulliner's ingenious approach to weight-saving, with a Teleflex window-winding mechanism employing light steel cables. Some customers negated all this careful design work by specifying such weight-adding features as electric windows, as seen here on BC25B, above right. Note also the heavy seats with – unusually – pleated cushions.

BC10A, the tenth production Continental, following the original ideal in having no chrome waist moulding, but with the heavy steel bumpers that became standard very quickly and winged 'B' mascot on a dummy filler cap on the radiator shell.

BC25B, as well as having heavy bumpers, was fitted with heavy front seats and electric windows which, whilst adding to the feeling of luxury, somewhat compromised the original ideals.

Front interior of BC46D. The formerly open oddments compartment below the nearside of the facia now has a lid, while the steering column emerges from an additional wood panel which also incorporates the radio. The seats are heavier than provided for in the original Continental remit, but the windows are manually operated. The gear lever is shown in the first gear position – the only gear in which the lever goes this far forward.

export cars, the automatic gearboxes having been initially supplied by GM's Detroit Transmission Division and paid for with dollars. The deal with GM specified that the automatic gearbox would eventually be built in its entirety in a special area at the Crewe factory, and this was achieved fairly quickly; after which the export restriction was dropped. All automatic Continentals had the Crewe-built gearbox.

The selector for the automatic gearbox was mounted on the top of the steering column with the lever on the right-hand side on both left- and right-hand drive cars. The ability to make manual gear changes, and to hold the lower gears, suited the Continental's sporting character, though nowadays Continentals with the manual gearbox are much more sought after.

When Olga's career in the Experimental Department and as a press demonstrator came to an end, she was saved from scrapping — the usual fate of Rolls-Royce and Bentley prototypes — by the intervention of the late Stanley Sedgwick, who agreed to buy the by now rather tired car for a price arrived at by deducting her restoration cost from the then going rate of an R Type Continental in as-new condition. The Rolls-Royce Hythe Road Service and Repair depot overhauled the drive-train, suspension and brakes, and H. J. Mulliner & Co. restored the coachwork (actually sub-contracting the upholstery work to Wood & Pickett and the paintwork to Hooper Motor Services). Mr Sedgwick took delivery of an as-new 'Olga' in mid-1961.

The first 4.9-litre ('D' series) Continental, BC1LD, a left-hand drive chassis. This car is fitted with the chrome waist moulding and Wilmot Breeden heavy export bumpers and overriders, which, unlike the early lightweight type, did not follow the contours of the car's tail.

Before handing her over, Rolls-Royce changed the chassis number from 9-B-VI, her Experimental Department number, to a production number, BC26A — the last number in the 'A' series. Mr Sedgwick sold Olga in 1985, with 122,500 miles up since the 1961 rebuild, to Victor Gauntlett, who commissioned P. & A. Wood to carry out a superb body-off restoration, again returning her to as-new condition.

Production Bentley Continentals have achieved prodigious mileages in service, many exceeding 250,000 miles. Former Bentley Drivers' Club Chairman, Bill Medcalf's car, BC8C, had covered in excess of 360,000 miles when he sold it in 1997, still in virtually as-new condition. Bill found it to be a perfectly suitable car for everyday use, even in today's traffic conditions, and it was his car of choice for business trips from London to Glasgow, a round journey of 800 miles, as well as for long continental journeys, on which speeds of up to 110mph were reached with quiet ease. He once drove BC8C 6000 miles in one month! It should be added that Bill only sold this superb car to replace it with another R Type Continental, a 4.9-litre car which he took the precaution of acquiring before passing BC8C to its next fortunate owner!

The only slight disadvantages of using an R Type Continental as regular transport — and they are very slight indeed — are the steering, which is both low-geared by modern standards and rather heavy at parking speeds, and the brakes, which suffer from the old Rolls-Royce problem of 'servo-lag' — but, again, only at very low speeds. Both steering and brakes are a joy at all normal driving speeds, and the car's performance in no way handicaps the Bentley Continental driver in modern traffic.

BC47D. This later 'D' series car – though still with heavy bumpers – conforms more closely to the original ideal than does BC1LD on the previous page.

BC60D is a 4.9-litre Continental delivered in April 1955. Although like all of the later cars it has the heavy export bumpers, it is nevertheless equipped with the original lightweight seats, while a 'Webasto' sunshine roof enhances the pleasure of ownership.

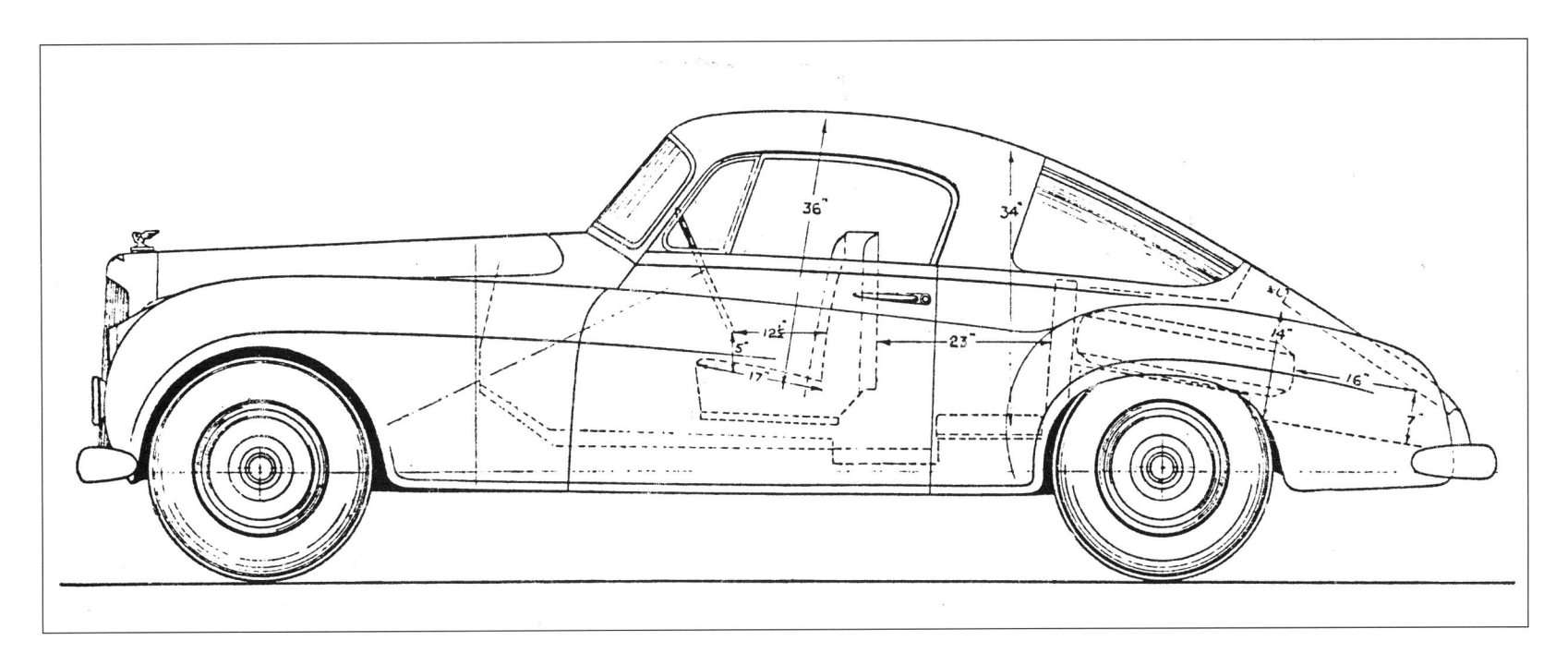

A very small number of Bentley Continental owners specified significant variations to the H. J. Mulliner design, of which this 2 + 2 fixed head coupé (above) was the most notable. A long-time Bentley customer, Australian-born R. G. McLeod had set a pattern of ordering shortened cars, with the normal wheelbase but a wheel more or less at each corner and coachwork with minimum overhang supplied to his design by H. J. Mulliner. This Continental on chassis BC50D was the fourth of these, having been preceded by plain, almost box-like coachwork on 1938 4¼-litre chassis B142MR (below), 1947 Mk VI B22AK and 1951 Mk VI B50MD. H. J. Mulliner & Co.'s drawing of BC50D shows the occasional rear seat. BC50D is one of only a handful of R Type Continentals known to have been destroyed – in this instance by fire in 1960.

PARK WARD COACHWORK
473, HIGH ROAD,
WILLESDEN
LONDON, NW10

BENTLEY CONTINENTAL SALOON

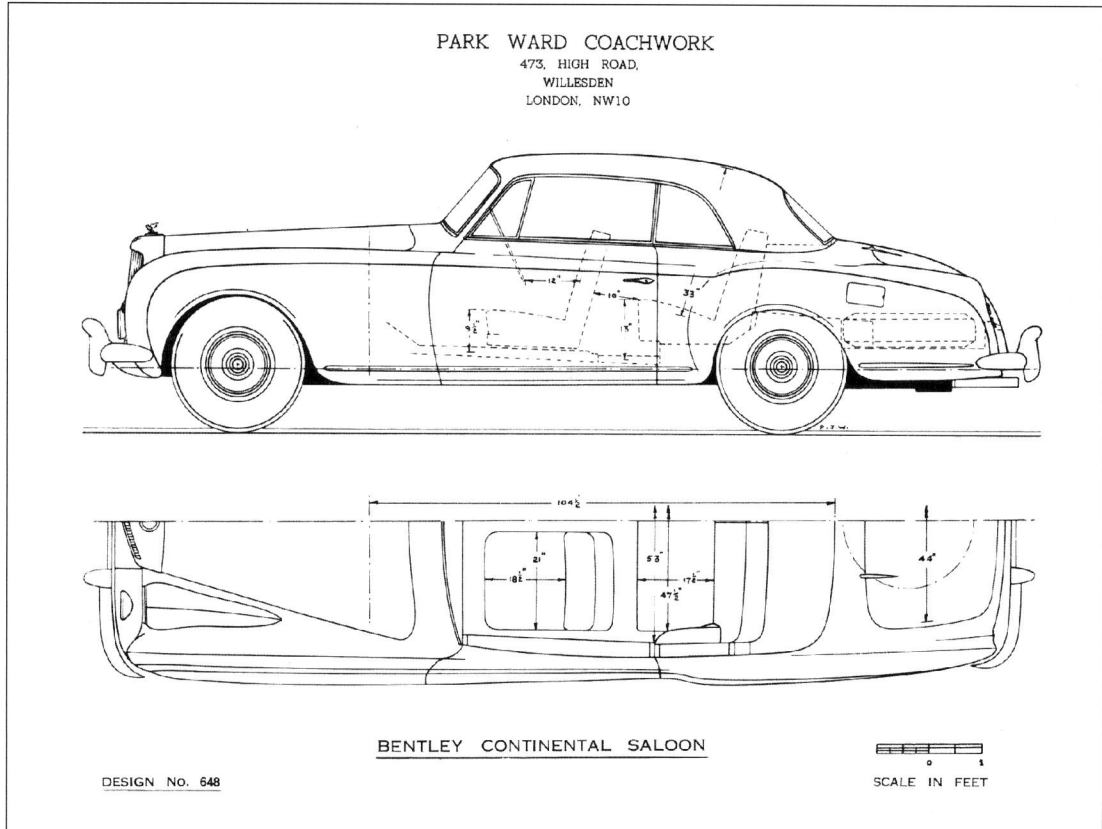

DESIGN No. 648

SCALE IN FEET

Above: Bentley Continental two-door saloon. Styling by John Blatchley, Crewe; structural design and construction by Park Ward, Willesden. Only two of these saloons were built on the R Type Continental chassis. Whilst it is difficult to positively identify which of the two this is, it is believed to be the first of them, BC24D. The aircraft behind is more easily identified as 'Aurora', one of BOAC's C-4 Argonauts, a Rolls-Royce Merlin-engined version of the DC-4 built by Canadair in 1949. Later owned by British Midland, this aircraft crashed at Ringway Airport, Stockport on June 4th 1967.

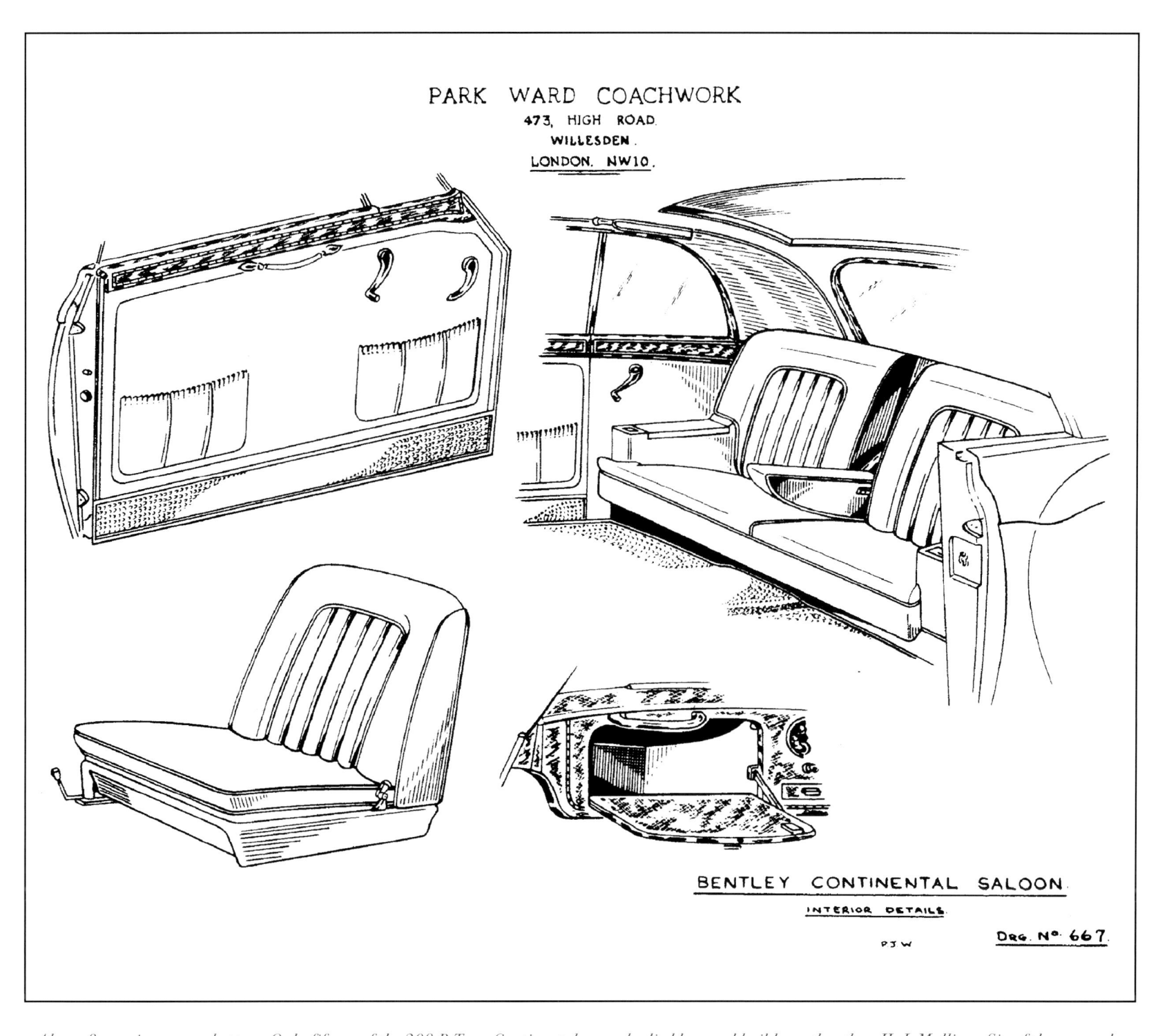

Above & previous page, bottom: Only fifteen of the 208 R Type Continentals were bodied by coachbuilders other than H. J. Mulliner. Six of these were by Park Ward, to two designs: a pair of two-door saloons, design number 648, and four drophead coupés, design number 647. These cars were the first Park Ward designs styled by Rolls-Royce Chief Styling Engineer, John Blatchley, who had taken over the external styling of Park Ward coachwork in 1952. The Park Ward designs for the S Type Continentals which followed were slight enlargements of these designs. Here, we see Park Ward Chief Draughtsman, Peter Wharton's, drawings of the two-door saloon and its interior design details. Though the external styling was the work of John Blatchley at Crewe, structural design and interior styling continued to be carried out by Park Ward's own drawing office at Willesden. Wharton (PJW) was later designated Chief Stylist at Park Ward (and later H. J. Mulliner, Park Ward), though, in practice, he never actually styled a complete car exterior.

This page & following: Period advertisements, from the October 6th 1954 edition of The Motor, *announcing the advent of Park Ward coachwork for the Bentley Continental.*

The Continental Bentley
with Coachwork by
PARK WARD

The Bentley Continental drophead coupe by Park Ward.

BENTLEY

announce

Two New Continental Models

The elegant Drophead Coupe and Sports Saloon by Park Ward provide exhilarating motoring for four passengers at speeds up to 120 m.p.h.

These new models, which are available with the automatic gearbox, are the only additions to the existing range of Rolls-Royce and Bentley cars which continue in their present form and will be exhibited at the Earls Court Motor Show.

Bentley Continental drophead coupé, chassis BC73C. This was the first Continental bodied by Park Ward. Again, styling by John Blatchley; structural design and construction by Park Ward. Although Park Ward had undoubtedly produced a remarkably fine motor car, the rear seat was somewhat dissapointing, being rather spartan and lacking both side and centre armrests.

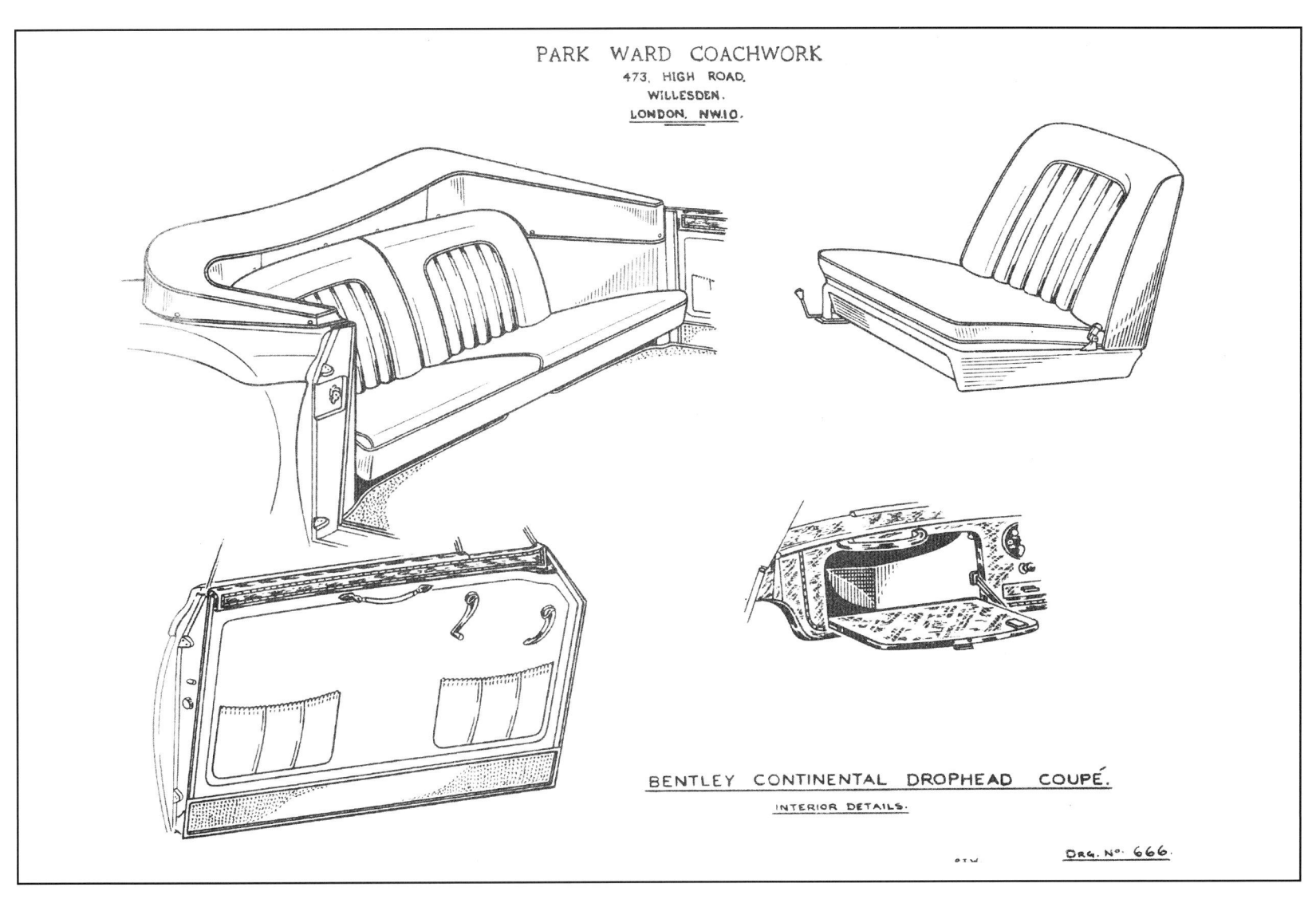

PJW's interior design drawing of the Park Ward drophead coupé.

BC73C from the rear showing the boot interior with the spare wheel not separated from the luggage, and the rather crude boot-lid prop.

The Park Ward drophead coupé coachwork for the R-type Continental chassis as announced, described and illustrated in the September 22nd 1954 edition of The Motor.

BC73C again. Note the very neat stowage of the convertible hood below its flush-fitting tonneau achieved by John Blatchley and Park Ward.

It is felt that, in this instance, Park Ward accomplished the task of designing and crafting the facia at least as successfully as had H. J. Mulliner, producing a strikingly beautiful piece of work.

The Swiss coachbuilding firm, Carrosserie Graber, built coachwork for three R Type Continentals, all drophead coupés. Two are shown here. The upper picture shows BC55C, which is still in original condition. The car in the two lower pictures is BC68D. Originally a drophead coupé similar to BC55C, in July 1957 it was converted to closed form by another Swiss firm, W. Köng, who incorporated the heavily wrapped-around rear window.

Nine R Type Continentals had continental European coachwork. Pininfarina built this remarkable two-seater fixed head coupé on chassis BC49C, its only body on a Bentley Continental chassis. This was one of six right-hand drive Continentals fitted with the centre gearchange. Note the Pininfarina badging on the front wing.

BC63LC started life with the familiar H. J. Mulliner 'fastback' coachwork, but was modified in 1960 to this rather less happy drophead coupé form by French coachbuilder Henri Chapron.

Above & opposite: Five R Type Continentals were bodied by French coachbuilder Franay. Three of these were based on the familiar H. J. Mulliner styling, as seen on chassis BC51LC (opposite page, top), but the example on 1954 4.9-litre chassis BC21D (opposite page, lower and above), presents a rather different line. In the three-quarter rear view (above), the three-piece wrap-around backlight is very much in evidence.

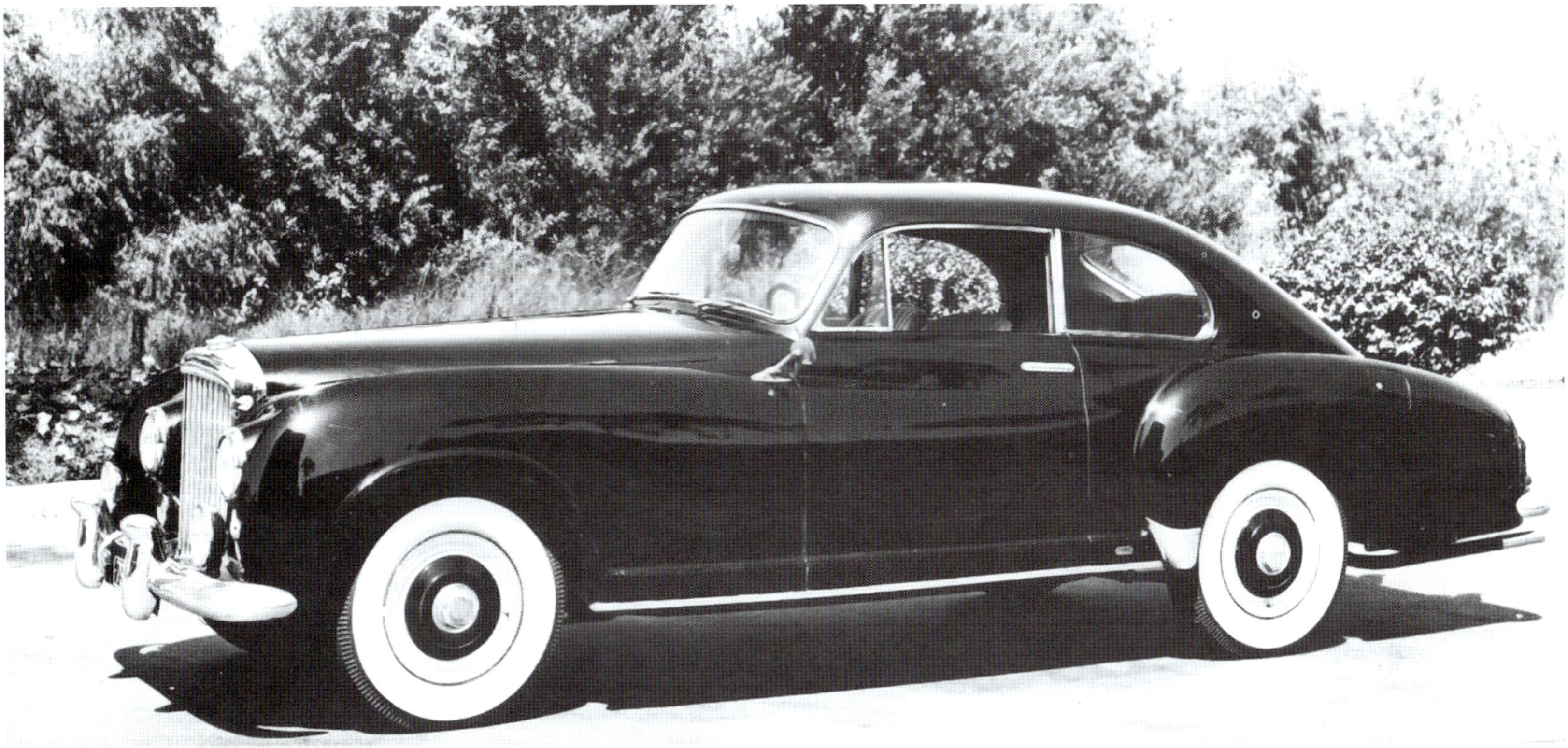

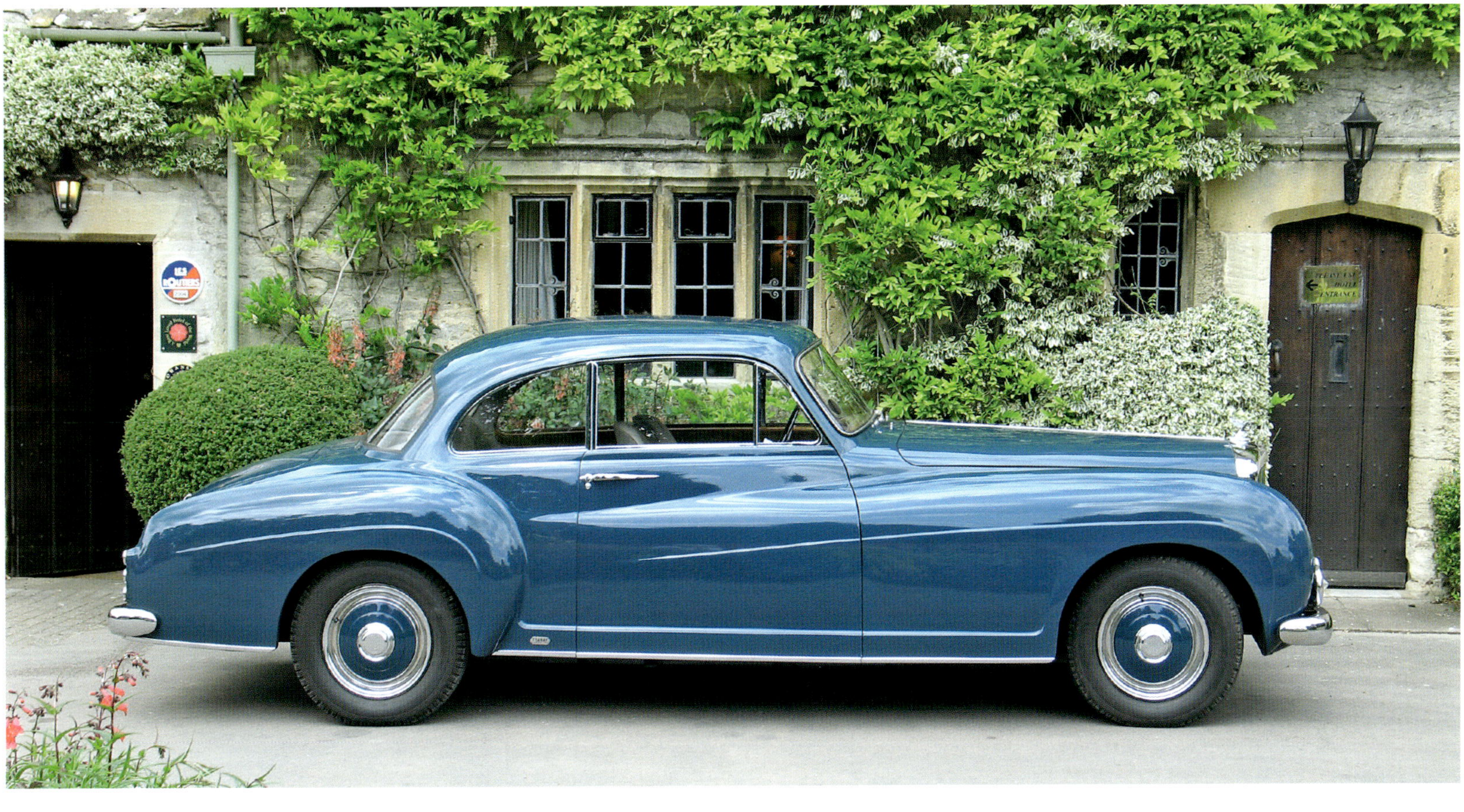

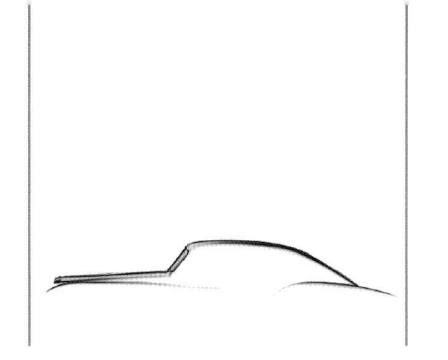

TECHNICAL SPECIFICATIONS – CONTINENTAL R TYPE

ENGINE

Dimensions
Six cylinders in-line. A to C series: Bore 3.625in (92mm), stroke 4.5in (114mm), cubic capacity 278.6in^3 (4566cc); D and E series onwards: bore 3.75in (95.25mm), stroke 4.5in (114mm), cubic capacity 298.2in^3 (4887cc). Compression ratio to chassis BC18A, 7.27:1; BC19A to BC3C, 7.1:1; BC4C onwards, 7.2:1.

Cylinder block/crankcase
Iron monobloc casting with 30 per cent chrome iron liners at tops of bores. D and E series (4887cc engine), full-length liners.

Crankshaft
1 per cent chrome molybdenum steel (EN.19) nitrided. Bolt-on balance weights. Seven main bearings of copper-lead-indium.

Pistons
Aluminium alloy (RR.53) tin plated. Granodised piston rings, one compression, one L-section and one slotted oil control ring.

Cylinder head
Aluminium alloy (RR.50) with inserted valve seats.

Valve gear
Overhead inlet, side exhaust valves. Exhaust valves in KE.965. Stellite coated seats and tips. Camshaft driven by helical gears.

Carburetters
'A' series: twin SU type H.6 (1¾in bore) with manual mixture control by lever on steering wheel boss. B to E series: twin SU type H.6 (1¾in bore) with automatic choke. Water-heated hot spot. Cars fitted with manual gearbox had a hand throttle control on steering wheel boss. Air intake silencer incorporating mesh air filter element (oil bath type air cleaner available for use in dusty conditions.)

Ignition system
Ignition by high tension coil and Delco-Remy distributor with twin contact breaker points. Firing order 1, 4, 2, 6, 3, 5.

Lubrication system
Helical gear oil pump in crankcase driven by skew gear from camshaft. Floating oil intake in sump incorporating gauze strainer. Full-flow filter on side of cylinder block. Pressure relief valve incorporating high and low pressure feeds. High pressure to the main and big-end bearings, camshaft bearings and

skew gear drive to oil pump and distributor, low pressure to valve gear and timing gears. Sump capacity 16 pints (2.4 US gallons, 9 litres).

Cooling system
Fixed radiator shutters. Thermostat on front of engine with radiator by-pass to give quickest possible warm-up from cold. Belt driven centrifugal coolant pump and fan.

CHASSIS

Dimensions
Overall length, early lightweight bumpers, 17ft 2½in (5245mm). Overall length, heavy export bumpers, 17ft 7½in (5372mm). Wheelbase 10ft 0in (3048mm). Front track 4ft 8½in (1435mm). Rear track 4ft 10½in (1486mm).

Frame
Channel section frame of riveted (welded from chassis BC21C) construction with cruciform centre bracing. Box section pan to support front suspension components.

Suspension
Front: independent by coil springs and rubber bushed wishbones, double-acting hydraulic dampers and anti-roll bar. Rear: semi-elliptic leaf springs protected by leather gaiters. Controllable hydraulic dampers by an oil pump mounted on the gearbox and an overriding control on the steering wheel boss.

Steering
Marles type cam and roller. Fore and aft side steering tube (drag link) to centre steering lever pivoted on front chassis crossmember and two-piece cross steering tube (track rod). Turns lock to lock 3½.

Transmission
Four forward speeds and reverse. Right-hand change (column change or more usually centre change on left-hand drive cars). Synchromesh on second, third and top gears. Ratios: Top 1:1, Third 1.34:1, Second 2.02:1, First 2.98:1, Reverse 3.15:1. Single dry-plate, centrifugally assisted clutch. Optional from chassis BC1D onwards, Rolls-Royce 4-speed automatic gearbox and fluid coupling, with selector mounted on the right of the steering column. Ratios: Top 1:1, Third 1.22:1, Second 1.54:1, First 2.67:1, Reverse 2.86:1. Two-piece propeller shaft with needle roller bearing universal joints and centre bearing. Rear axle: semi-floating type with hypoid gears. Ratio, 3.077:1.

Brakes
Hydraulic front, mechanical rear. Operation by means of friction disc servo on the offside of the gearbox, which applies the front brakes through a Lockheed master cylinder and assists application of the rear brakes. Handbrake on rear wheels by pull-out handle under right side of facia through a cable and mechanical linkage.

Exhaust system
Low loss single pipe system with two lagged expansion boxes.

Centralised lubrication system
All bearings in the steering and suspension systems, including the rear spring main leaf and shackles, fed with oil from a reservoir and pump mounted on the bulkhead in the engine compartment. Pump operated by a pedal under the facia, to be operated once every 100 miles (160km).

Fuel system
Rear mounted petrol tank, capacity 18 gallons (21.6 US gallons, 81.8 litres.) SU dual fuel pump mounted in the frame. Filter between tank and pump.

Electrical system
12 volt positive earth system with 55 amp/hour battery. Lucas special equipment dynamo and starter motor with reduction gearing and gentle-engagement pinion. Lucas built-in headlamps. Twin Lucas fog-lamps. Medium wave/Long wave Radiomobile radio with push-button tuning and two speakers available at no extra cost but in the interests of weight-saving not encouraged. Self-cancelling direction indicator switch on facia. Hot water type interior heater under front passenger seat with electric blower.

Other accessories
Trico vacuum operated windscreen washer.

Road wheels and tyres
16in steel disc well-base wheels, on five studs, carrying special high performance 6.50 x 16 India 'Speed Special' 6-ply tyres.

COACHWORK

Special coachwork built by the following coachbuilders:

H. J. Mulliner*	193
Park Ward	6
Graber	3
Franay	5
Pininfarina	1
Total*	208

*Including experimental car 9-B-VI, later renumbered BC26A.

PERFORMANCE DATA

The following results were obtained by The Autocar when road testing the prototype Bentley Continental (9-B-VI) in September 1952. For comparison purposes, figures obtained by the same journal for the 4½-litre Mk VI and R Type standard steel saloons are also given.

Acceleration through gears (seconds)	Mk VI	Continental	R Type (automatic)
0-30mph	4.5	4.4	4.4
0-60mph	15.2	13.5	13.8
0-100mph	-	36.0	-
Best maximum speed (mph):	100.0	116.9	106.5
Petrol consumption (mpg):	15.0-17.0	19.4	12.3

CHASSIS AND ENGINE NUMBERS

Chassis and engines are numbered consecutively, omitting 13.

Series	*Chassis numbers*	*Engine numbers*
A*	BC1A to BC25A	BCA1 to BCA24
B	BC1B to BC25B	BCB1 to BCB24
C	BC1C to BC78C	BCC1 to BCC77
D	BC1D to BC74D	BCD1 to BCD73
E	BC1E to BC9E	BCE1 to BCE9

Total: 208 cars
*Plus experimental car 9-B-VI, later renumbered BC26A.

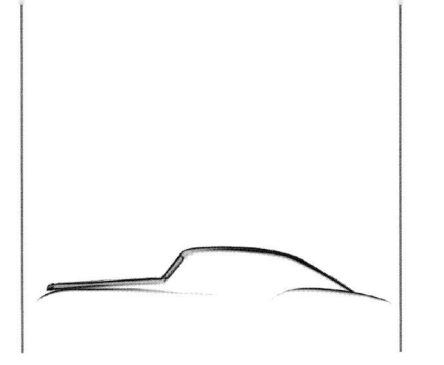

3. THE S TYPE CONTINENTAL

The Bentley Continental had become so established as a successful concept that its continuation into the S Series era was a foregone conclusion. The S Type was officially introduced in April 1955, though the the first S Type Continental chassis had been delivered to the coachbuilders the previous month.

Although, at a glance, the new chassis design appeared broadly similar to its predecessor, it was in fact entirely new, with a host of detail improvements. The welded box-section frame brought an improvement in torsional rigidity of no less than 50 per cent compared to its channel-section predecessor, at a weight penalty of a trifling 14lb.

Other changes to the chassis layout included a new semi-trailing wishbone front suspension layout, repositioning of the rear semi-elliptic springs inboard of the frame side members, and the addition of a substantial 'Z' type axle control rod, one end of which was attached to the right-hand frame side member and the other to the top of the axle casing. Each rear spring consisted of nine,

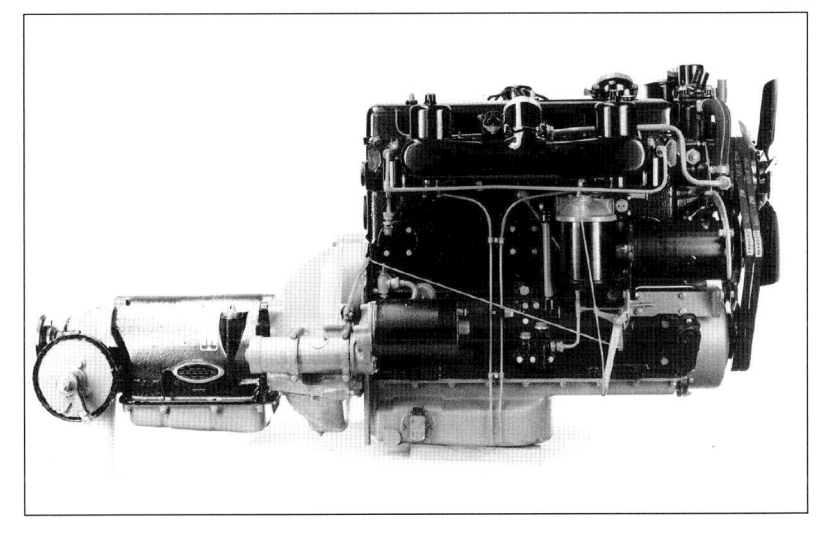

This is an early S1 engine with 1¾in SU type HD.6 carburetters and no pump for power-assisted steering. The rear extension of the automatic gearbox no longer incorporated a ride control pump as this feature was now electrically operated. The friction disc servo was speeded up on the S1 to address complaints of 'servo lag'. The type of air filter and silencer shown here was fitted to standard cars only. The Continental had a special type with paper filter.

Later S1 cars, Continentals included, were fitted with 2in SU type HD.8 carburetters as seen here. At the front of the rocker cover, just ahead of the oil filler cap, is the reservoir and pump for the power-assisted steering, which was offered as an option on all but the earliest cars. The starter motor on the right side of the engine indicates that this unit was destined for a left-hand drive car. Note the paired belts.

instead of seven leaves, with those on the right-hand side slightly thicker than their counterparts on the left, partly because the car was heavier on that side and partly to resist propeller shaft torque. Although they were still enclosed in leather gaiters, the rear springs were no longer fed with oil from the centralised chassis lubrication system, but were packed with grease instead.

The centralised lubrication system that had been a feature of the earlier model was retained on the S Type in a greatly abbreviated form, being confined to a few points on the front suspension and, on early cars, the steering ball-joints.

The braking system, while still based on the traditional friction-disc servo, was the subject of considerable improvement. Girling 'Autostatic' brakes were used, in which the shoes were in constant contact with the drums. The front brakes were of the two trailing shoe type, in order to avoid the 'self-servo' action of leading shoes often relied upon by other makers to provide a light pedal, but which were notorious for causing brake-fade under severe conditions. At the rear, leading and trailing shoes were used, actuated by a combined hydraulic and mechanical expander. For the first time, both front and rear brakes were hydraulically actuated, though the

Above & opposite: For the S1 Continental, H. J. Mulliner's famous 'fastback' styling, for want of a better term, acquired a higher, straight-through wingline with a new swageline on the rear wing. This was design number 7400, a noticeably bulkier car than its R Type predecessor. The Continental's radiator shell was an inch and a half lower than that of the standard cars.

direct mechanical linkage between the pedal and the rear brakes was retained and superimposed on the hydraulic actuation, mainly in order to provide the driver with 'feel' through the pedal.

Despite the reduced drum diameter dictated by the stylists' requirement for fifteen- instead of sixteen inch wheels, there was an increase in friction area amounting to almost 30 per cent. In response to criticisms of 'servo lag', servo speed was increased to 0.179 of the propeller shaft speed instead of 0.095. The set-up gave smooth, powerful, fade-free braking from the high speeds of which the Bentley Continental was so effortlessly capable, with pedal pressures so light that road testers were invariably taken by surprise.

In May 1956 (from chassis BC16BG), the master cylinder and fluid reservoir were duplicated, with an extra set of expanders for the front shoes. The system was split so that one circuit activated one shoe in each front drum, while the other worked the rear brakes and remaining shoes at the front. Thus, with the pedal still mechanically linked to the rear brakes, there were effectively three braking systems, each capable of stopping the car in the unlikely event of servo, hydraulic or mechanical failure. A twist-to-release handbrake, as fitted to left-hand drive R Types, was standard on the S Type.

The S Type saw the beginning of a move away from the Company's own distinctive — if archaic — terminology for the main steering linkage

Shadwell Harry Grylls (Gry) was Chief Engineer of the Car Division throughout the S Series era. He oversaw design and development of the V8 engine, introduced in 1959, and the monocoque cars announced in 1965. Gry joined Rolls-Royce Ltd in 1930 and died in 1983.

H. J. Mulliner draughtsman Herbert Nye's drawing of design number 7400 for the S1 Continental.

components. Thus, the 'cross steering tube' and 'side steering tube' became the more mundane track rod and drag link respectively: the former being a three-piece linkage, and the latter a transverse mounted affair connected to an extension on one of two idler levers pivoted between the chassis and the centre member of the track linkage. The steering was lower geared than that of the R Type, but this only partially accounted for the 4½ turns of the steering wheel lock-to-lock compared to the previous 3¾; and was mainly due to greater front wheel movement made possible by the new front suspension design. It gave the S Type a slightly smaller turning circle than its shorter predecessor.

The new front suspension layout comprised long lower, and short upper wishbones, with the upper pairs pivoted on the shafts of the horizontal piston-type shock dampers.

Early in 1956, power-assisted steering was offered as an option; at first, for export only. American motorists had, by that time, become accustomed to having power steering on large luxury cars, and a very expensive car without it would undoubtedly have met with some incredulity in that market. On cars fitted with power-assisted steering, the steering ratio was raised from 20.6:1 to 18.7:1, which meant a modest reduction in the turns of the wheel lock-to-lock to 4¼. No doubt, with the benefit of power assistance, the ratio could have been raised further, but Rolls-Royce was at that time committed

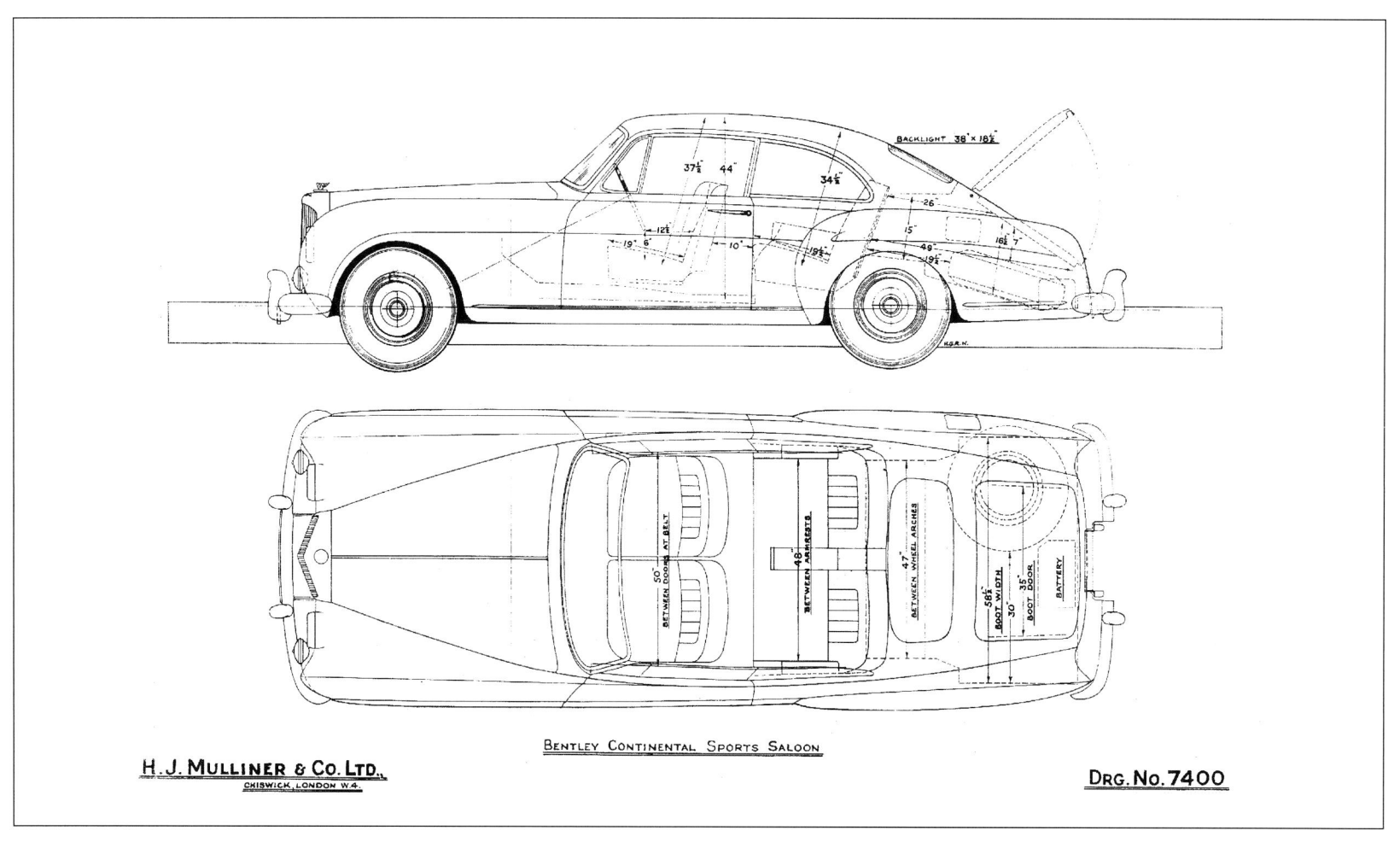

One fairly serious drawback of the fastback styling was the limitation it imposed on luggage capacity, particularly when one considers the continental touring nature of the car.

Inside, the facia was reminiscent of Mulliner's R Type Continental, but the seats, in pleated and bolstered style, were noticeably more substantial, adding further weight to what had already become a considerably heavier car than the original Continental concept had called for.

Above & following page, top: A very small number of S1 Continentals – around sixteen – were fitted with the manual gearbox. One of these, BC66BG, is the subject of these two photographs. The 'normal' and 'hard' ride control switch, which was normally mounted on the automatic gearbox selector quadrant bracket on the steering column, was relocated to just under the facia on these manual geared cars.

Above & opposite page: H. J. Mulliner design number 7400, chassis BC51BG, with additional air vents in the leading edges of the rear wings. This car also featured a considerable number of special interior features, some of which may be seen in the interior pictures. Note particularly the row of additional switches along the lower edge of the facia for a range of additional equipment, including an electric razor.

to tackling the now-scorned 'sneeze factor', which was the possibility of a car with very light but high-geared steering being thrown off-line by inadvertent slight movements of the steering wheel. It is on record that, at the time the PAS option was announced, a number of chassis being fitted with coachwork were retrospectively fitted — at considerable expense to the Company — in response to demands from customers that their cars be of the latest specification upon delivery.

The steering wheel hub was, for the first time, entirely free of control levers; the last of these (the 'ride control') gave way to a two-position switch on the side of the steering column. This switch, marked 'N' (normal) and 'H' (hard), operated solenoids in the rear dampers which altered the 'slow leak', doubling the degree of damping while the switch was in the 'H' position. Though this scheme did not allow the progressive ride control of the old system, it had the advantage of being much simpler, eliminating the need for the gearbox-driven oil pump and associated piping.

The engine of the new car was basically the 4887cc unit with full-length, high chromium content cylinder liners as fitted to the 'D' series R Type Continental, but with a new six-port cylinder head to improve breathing. The new head was attached by set bolts rather than studs as hitherto. The twin SU carburetters were of a new diaphragm type (HD.6) and were mounted

(continued on page 69)

This page: Continental, with only those minor changes necessary to lengthen it to suit the 123-inch wheelbase of the S1 chassis. A reliable recognition point is the door handle, which was relocated above the swageline on the S1. Both the two-door saloon and drophead coupé variants were exceedingly handsome cars. The saloon (top) is BC44AF. The detail (below right) shows the early round rear-lamps and direction indicators, with a rather bulbous protuberance on the rear wing top. Later, the standard S1 rear-lamp assembly was used and the top of the wing was restyled to present a, perhaps, neater appearance (main picture).

Advertising for the S1 Continental Park Ward two-door saloons. Left: the earliest version with the original rear-lamp arrangement, which can be glimpsed, and (right) the later variant with standard rear lamp assembly. Both adverts are from The Motor.

Two-tone colour schemes were popular on Park Ward coachwork, with the two shades divided along the wing swageline as seen (above) on chassis BC73BG. The different effect of a single colour is seen (below) in a Company photograph of an unidentified example.

A later variant of the Park Ward saloon had larger rear quarter-lights and a wrap-around rear window. (See also 'Coachwork evolution by airbrush,' page 89).

PARK WARD COACHWORK
473 HIGH ROAD
WILLESDEN
LONDON, N.W.10

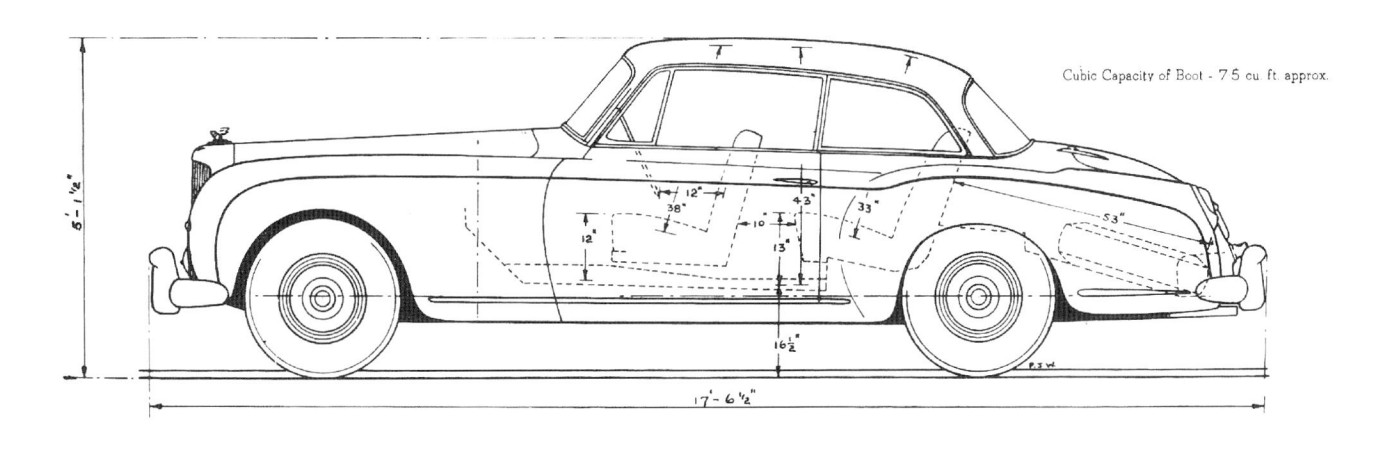

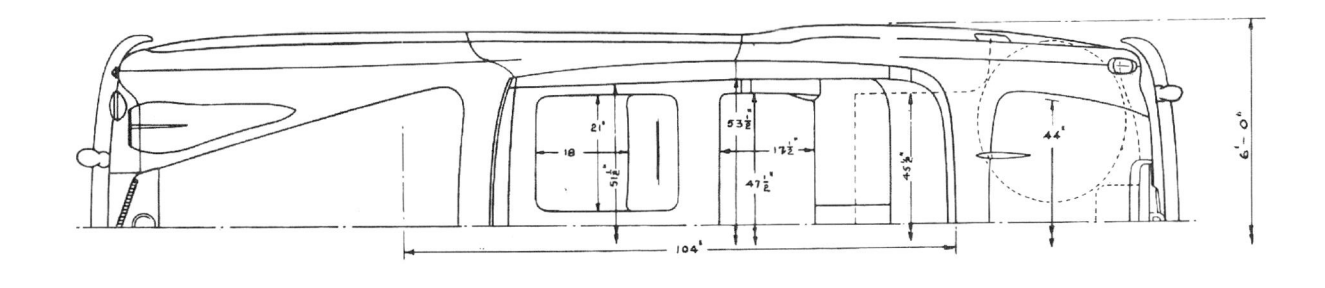

Cubic Capacity of Boot - 7.5 cu. ft. approx.

SCALE IN FEET

BENTLEY CONTINENTAL SALOON

DRG. No. 872

67

An advertisement placed by Park Ward & Co. in the October 18th, 1957 issue of Autosport. *The photograph used has been altered to show the later, larger rear quarter-light.*

THE BENTLEY CONTINENTAL

with coachwork by

PARK WARD

The styling of the Park Ward coachwork fitted to the Bentley Continental, includes certain modifications on the design of its predecessor. Enlarged quarter windows, hinged at the forward end, and a wrap-round backlight are two of the improvements which are incorporated in the elegant lines of the light-weight coachwork. The front seats have been " anatomically " designed to give better grip when cornering at speed. There is a Drophead Coupé version of the same car.

PARK WARD & CO. LTD · 473 HIGH ROAD · LONDON · N.W.10

on a revised induction manifold, one half of which was integral with the head, while the other half, carrying the carburetters, was bolted to it. This arrangement allowed the internal shape of the induction gallery to be more accurately controlled, while simplifying casting and facilitating future maintenance.

The Bentley Continental S Type differed from the early standard S Type chassis in having a higher (7.25:1) compression ratio, higher (2.92:1) final drive ratio, and 7.60 x 15 tyres instead of 8.20 x 15. These differences, together with the lower, more streamlined bodies fitted, gave the Continental a maximum speed of around 120mph, and faster acceleration than that of the standard cars in the upper speed range.

Between 1955 and 1959, the 4.9-litre, six-cylinder power unit underwent a continuous programme of modification and improvement, not least of which was the fitting of 2-inch (HD.8) carburetters, together with increased diameter (2-inch) inlet valves and raised compression ratio (from 7.25:1 to 8:1). The result was a silky smooth engine of great refinement and not inconsiderable power output; the latter was certainly more than 'adequate', as the Company was wont to somewhat modestly describe it!

Rather incongruously, perhaps, automatic transmission was standard on the Continental S Type, though a few cars (certainly fewer than 20) were fitted with synchromesh gearbox at customers' request. By mid-1957, this option had been withdrawn.

Although all but a handful of the previous R Type Continental chassis were fitted with H. J. Mulliner two-door sports saloon bodies, this was not the case with the Continental S Type, which saw a far greater variety of coachwork styles, eventually including four-door saloons.

H. J. Mulliner's famous 'fastback' design for the Continental R Type was developed for the S Type. It was lengthened to suit the larger chassis, the front wingline was raised to run parallel to the waistline, and stylish swaging was introduced into the rear wing. All pretence of lightweight

The Park Ward S1 Continentals included some intriguing interior features, like the folding rear seat that improved luggage capacity for two-person, long-distance touring. Note the luggage platform which folds out from under the seat cushion. The picnic set built into the door, consisting of 'Bandalasta' sandwich boxes and cups, fine Sheffield cutlery and 'Thermos' vacuum flasks (behind the right-hand sandwich box), was one of a range of luxury extras that could be fitted, at additional cost, to enhance even more the long-distance touring nature of these magnificent sporting cars. Note the buttons for the electric windows and the emergency winder handle in its clips on the inside of the scuttle, for operating the windows manually in the event of power failure.

This page & opposite: Park Ward & Co. specification for its two-door saloon coachwork on the S1 Continental chassis.

1587

Specification for Park Ward Coachwork

SALOON TO DESIGN No. 872
FOR BENTLEY CONTINENTAL CHASSIS

CONSTRUCTION Framework of special Park Ward Patent lightweight construction, covered with aluminium panels. Wide vision screen pillars and the scuttle reinforced.
Chromium plated superimposed moulding on lower edge of body and front wings.

SEATING Two persons in the front on sliding bucket type seats, the backs of which are adjustable for rake and tip forward to give access to the rear seat which accommodates two persons and incorporates a centre folding armrest. Combined glove box and hinged armrest fitted between front seats and adjustable armrest to each door, recessed to serve as door pull.
The rear seat cushion hinges upwards and the seat valance folds over and extends to provide for additional luggage carrying capacity.

DOORS Two, hung on front pillars, fitted with best quality locks, striking plates and concealed hinges, etc.
Push button release type exterior door handles.
Private lock fitted to both doors and interior safety catches incorporated in remote control interior handles.
Open pocket recess in each door.

WINDOWS Glasses to doors to drop flush and operated by mechanical lifts with winder handles.
Quarter windows arranged to hinge from forward end.
Wrap round backlight fixed and incorporating demister.
Swivelling ventilating windows incorporating drip channels fitted to front of doors.
Safety glass throughout.

ROOF Fixed and panelled.

WINDSCREEN Made in one panel, curved and permanently fixed, glazed with laminated safety glass.
Dual wipers fitted at base of screen.

DIRECTION INDICATORS Approved flashing type, wired to a time switch fitted on the instrument board capping.

VENTILATION Fresh air inlet to interior through frontal grilles.

WINGS Special Park Ward type wings integral with body with stone shields and mud lips.
Access to petrol filler by means of hinged door in offside rear wing, locked internally.

INSTRUMENT BOARD All instruments supplied with chassis fitted up thereon in approved manner.
Cubby hole on passenger's side having a hinged door and fitted with lock.
Cigar lighter fitted.
Grab handle to capping on passenger's side.
Pull-out picnic table under centre of board incorporating ashtray.

TRIMMING STYLE Of approved design.

continued

INTERIOR FITTINGS
One electric roof lamp, operated automatically with opening and closing of the doors. Switch provided also for independent operation.

Sun visors attached to screen rail with vanity mirror on passenger's visor.

Ashtrays in convenient position for rear seat passengers.

Interior driving mirror.

Spring-up type hand pulls fitted over quarters.

Slip pocket at each side of scuttle.

FLOOR COVERING
Floor to be covered with pile carpet, colour to tone with upholstery, suitably underlined.

Heel pads fitted to front carpet.

LUGGAGE AND TOOLS
Luggage boot at rear, access being gained by means of door hinged at the top and operated by push button release type handle incorporating lock.

Light in rear boot operated automatically by opening and closing of boot lid.

Road tools and small tools conveniently accommodated in rear boot.

SPARE WHEEL
One spare wheel and tyre supplied with chassis accommodated in the rear boot on the offside and fitted with carpet cover.

OTHER EQUIPMENT
Provision at front and rear for identification plates.

Combined stop-tail lamp, flasher lamp and reflector built into each rear wing.

Heating, demisting and defrosting equipment as provided with chassis.

Radio set as provided with chassis with controls recessed from behind instrument board.

Bumpers fitted to front and rear.

Concealed and internally operated locks to bonnet.

Connecting up lamp equipment supplied with chassis.

Windscreen spray equipment on scuttle, controlled by switch on instrument board.

EXTERIOR FINISH
Colour to standard range of shades and distribution to choice.

UPHOLSTERY
In best quality Vaumol leather to standard range of shades, with a cloth headlining to tone.

INTERIOR WOODWORK
Polished wood fillets, finishers, etc., of Walnut. Dadoes and Instrument board veneered on face.

NOTE:
For cars intended for use abroad, appropriate modifications would be made to such items as number plates, private door locks, etc., etc., to equip the car for the country concerned.

E. & O. E.
Park Ward & Company Limited reserve the right to alter this Specification at any time if the materials are not available or for any other reasons.

The Park Ward drophead coupé for the S1 Continental chassis shared the saloon's styling and, like the saloon, was adapted by John Blatchley from his earlier R Type design. This is the early version with round rear-lamps.

seats had by now been abandoned, as these were thickly padded, broad and … heavy! No attempt to describe the appearance of this coachwork could improve very much on the contemporary sales brochure, which described it as "flowing and purposeful and free from any needless excrescence"!

Park Ward's handsome two-door saloon and drophead coupé designs, styled by John Blatchley and built on a small number of late Continental R Type chassis, were enlarged for the new chassis. These cars, and particularly the closed version, had the advantage over the H. J. Mulliner car in substantially better luggage carrying capacity — obviously a boon on a car designed for continental touring.

For the first time, James Young Ltd had a modest share of the supply of coachwork for Bentley Continental chassis. In outward appearance James Young's two-door saloon was barely distinguishable from its Park Ward counterpart of earlier origins. This was, perhaps, a reflection of the fact that James Young's designer, A. F. McNeil, and John Blatchley, who styled Park Ward's coachwork from his Crewe styling office, had both been Gurney Nutting coachwork designers before the War and were good friends. John Blatchley, in his long retirement, told the author that he wished he had noticed this similarity at the time, "when I could perhaps have got some leg-pulling mileage out of it from old 'Mac'"!

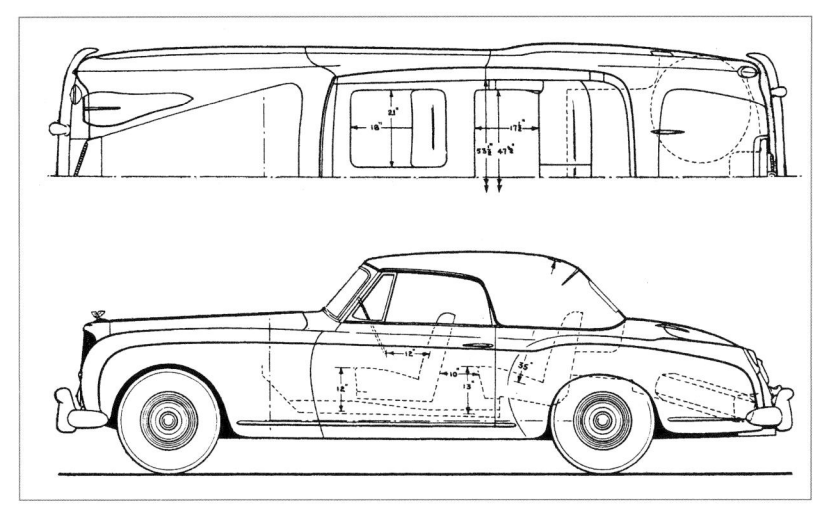

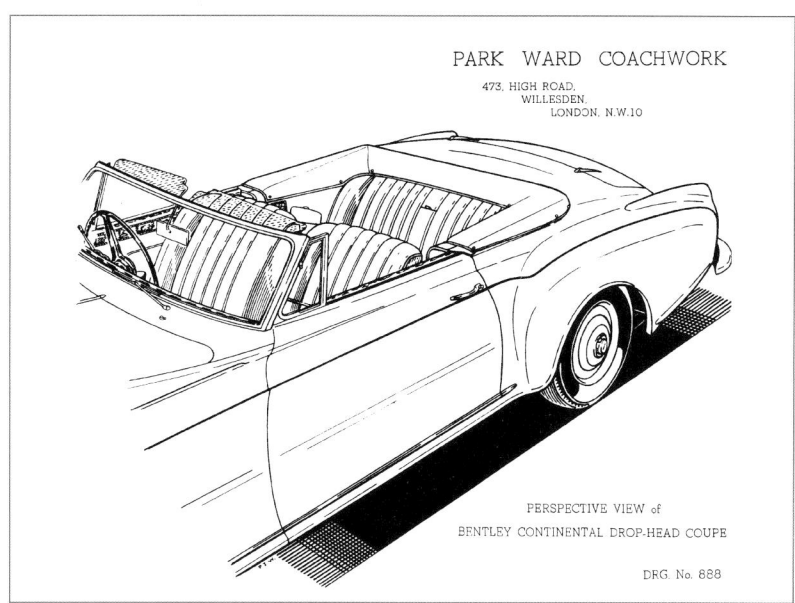

PARK WARD COACHWORK
473, HIGH ROAD,
WILLESDEN,
LONDON, N.W.10

PERSPECTIVE VIEW of
BENTLEY CONTINENTAL DROP-HEAD COUPE

DRG. No. 888

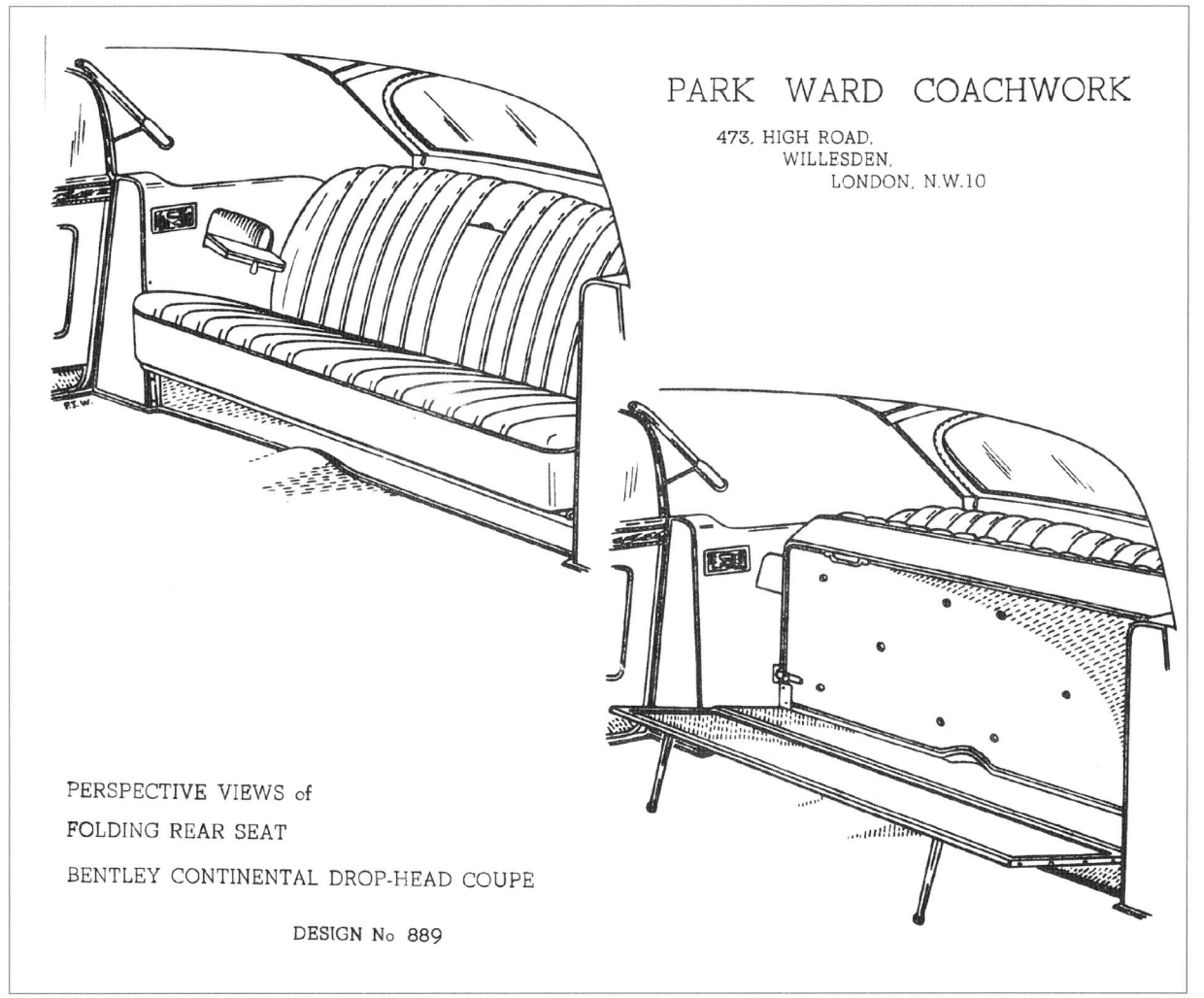

PARK WARD COACHWORK
473, HIGH ROAD,
WILLESDEN,
LONDON, N.W.10

PERSPECTIVE VIEWS of
FOLDING REAR SEAT
BENTLEY CONTINENTAL DROP-HEAD COUPE

DESIGN No 889

Line drawings of the Park Ward drophead coupé, and Peter Wharton's perspective and interior drawings showing the folding rear seat. Due to the drophead's limited rear seat width, which was reduced to make space for the hood mechanism, the side armrests were cleverly contrived to swing up into pockets to allow the seat cushion to fold up for extra luggage capacity. A zip fastener held the clear plastic rear window in place, allowing it to be opened whilst the fully-lined hood was raised.

The later Park Ward dropheads, like the saloons, had the standard S1 tail-light fittings, as seen on this example photographed outside the offices of the coachbuilder's works in High Road, Willesden.

The Park Ward S1 Continental facia was stylish and beautifully made, but instrument positioning would be better suited to one of the rare manual-geared cars, as the fuel and coolant temperature gauges are obscured by the gear selector quadrant on this automatic drophead coupé. The driver can see them only by leaning forward. The significance of the radiator mascot fitted to this example, apparently a leprechaun, is not known.

This page & overleaf: These four pictures, showing two Park Ward drophead coupés, again serve to illustrate the differing visual effects provided by single colours and two-tone schemes. On this page is S1 Continental Park Ward drophead coupé BC27EL, while on the opposite page is an unidentified car in delightfully English settings chosen by the Company's photographer. The picture showing the convertible hood raised reveals just how enormous were the blind spots interrupting rearward vision with this design. A trade-off was that the car was very cosy in this mode as the fully-lined hood and effective sealing made for a saloon-like interior.

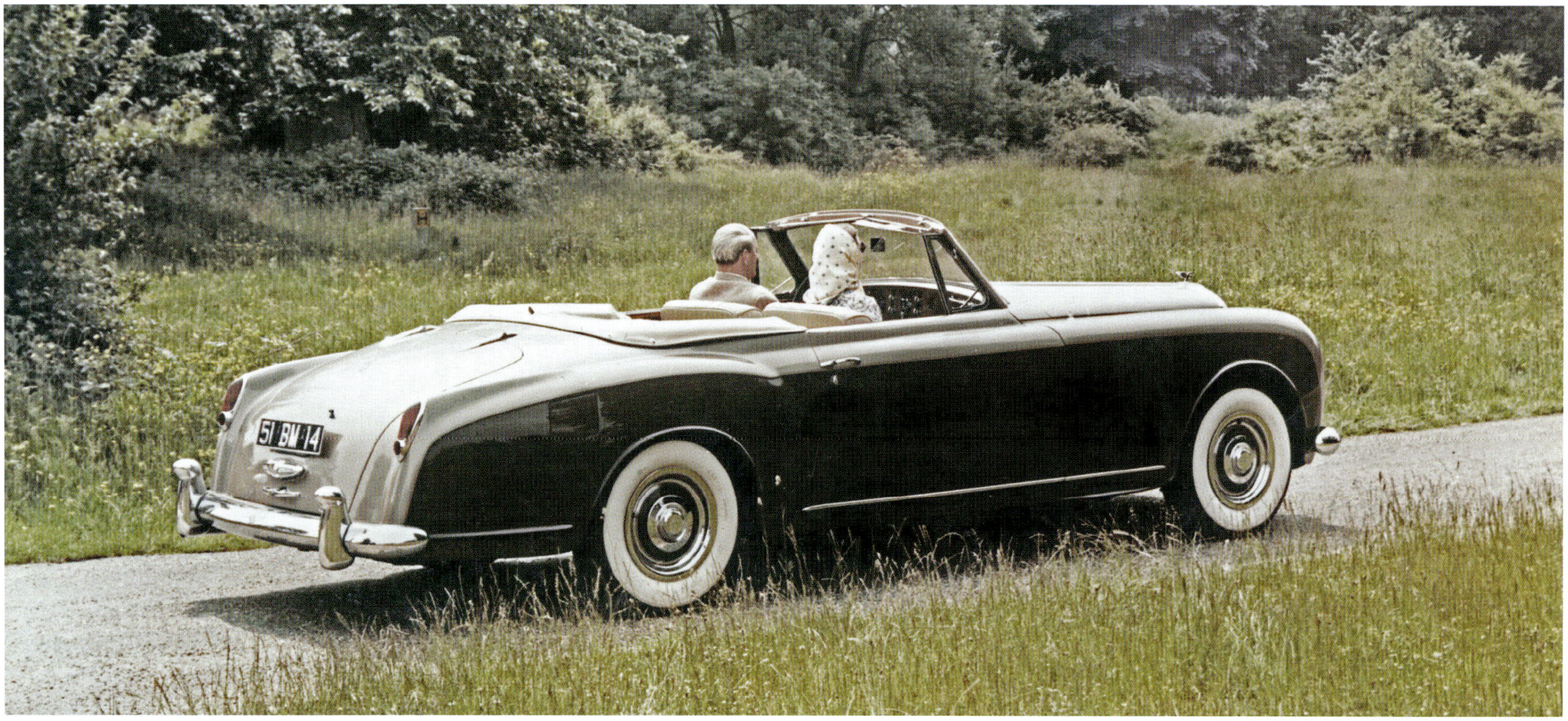
51 BM 14

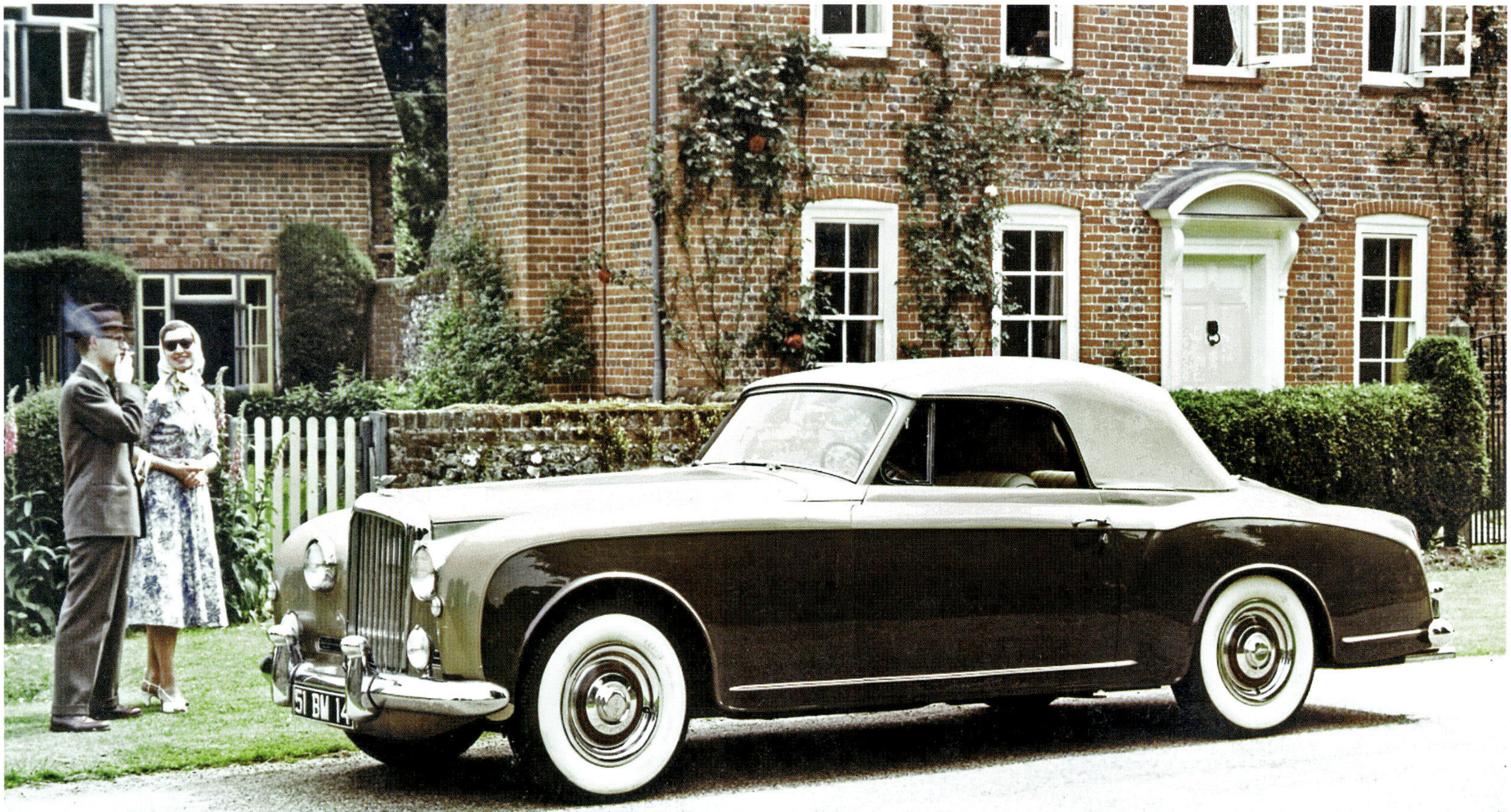
51 BM 14

The name 'Flying Spur' was taken from the family heraldic device of H. J. Mulliner Managing Director, Arthur Talbot Johnstone. A chrome winged spur radiator mascot was fitted to the first 'Flying Spur'.

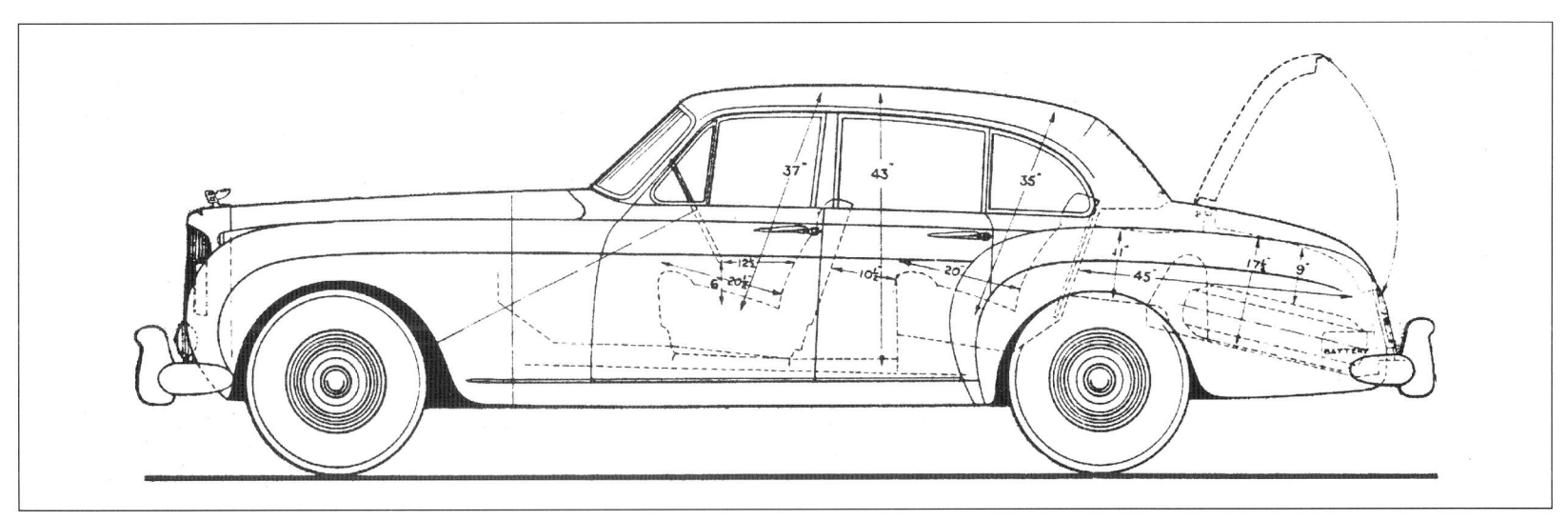

Although the Continental chassis was originally intended exclusively for two-door cars, H. J. Mulliner & Co. was eventually permitted, from 1957, to build a Continental four-door saloon. It was a beautifully styled and graceful six-light saloon, to which the coachbuilder gave the superb name 'Flying Spur'. The more practical and capacious boot, increased rear compartment headroom and legroom and ease of access to the rear compartment, all helped to make the 'Flying Spur' a more practical continental touring car than the same coachbuilder's two-door car. Top left is Herbert Nye's wash drawing of the 'Flying Spur', H. J. Mulliner design number 7443, together with a line drawing (bottom) showing the interior and boot dimensions, while centre left is the car 'in the metal'.

77

THE AUTOCAR, 27 SEPTEMBER 1957

— The Flying Spur —

H. J. MULLINER & CO.
have pleasure in introducing their new special light sports saloon "The Flying Spur". This is a comfortable 4 door body with ample room for 4/5 persons, giving good headroom and leg room for all occupants and permitting very easy entrance and exit to front and rear. Really good luggage accommodation is available.

This body is mounted on the same specification chassis as the well-known H. J. MULLINER 2 door Continental Saloon and thus makes available all the special and improved handling characteristics of that car with the added advantages and facilities of 4 doors.

With automatic gearbox and power assisted steering this remarkable car is now equally suitable for Town use and high speed Continental touring.

An example will be shown on our Stand No. 99 at the forthcoming Motor Show at Earls Court and a car is available for inspection and trial by appointment.

H. J. Mulliner & Co., Ltd.

Bedford Park Works.

CHISWICK · LONDON · W·4

By Appointment to Her Majesty The Queen Motor Carriage Builders

Telephone:
CHIswick 7831-2-3 (3 lines)
Telegraphic Addresses:
Renillum, London (Overseas)
Renillum, Chisk, London (Inland)

H. J. Mulliner & Co. advertisement in the 27th September, 1957 issue of The Autocar *for the firm's then-new 'Flying Spur' four-door saloon coachwork on the S1 Continental chassis.*

Above (both): For customers preferring more privacy for rear seat passengers, a four-light variant of the 'Flying Spur' was offered by H. J. Mulliner. Right is chassis BC2FM and, below, showing the boot shape, is BC9FM. Nowadays, this design is sometimes referred to as the 'blind rear quarter' Flying Spur.

In the 'blind' rear quarter of the four-light 'Flying Spur' there was a space for mirrored 'companions,' and these were provided at the customer's request. This car also has the optional, boot-mounted air conditioning, one of the outlets for which is seen here.

78

The final twenty H. J. Mulliner 'fastback' S1 Continentals were built to a modified design (number 7466), which differed in having higher swagelines on the wings, sidelights on the tops of the front wings, a slight flare to the wheelarches and detail interior differences, in order to give it a closer family resemblance to – and rationalise the front wings and certain other panels with – the 'Flying Spur' four-door saloon. Left is chassis BC5EL and below, the line drawing showing the revised details.

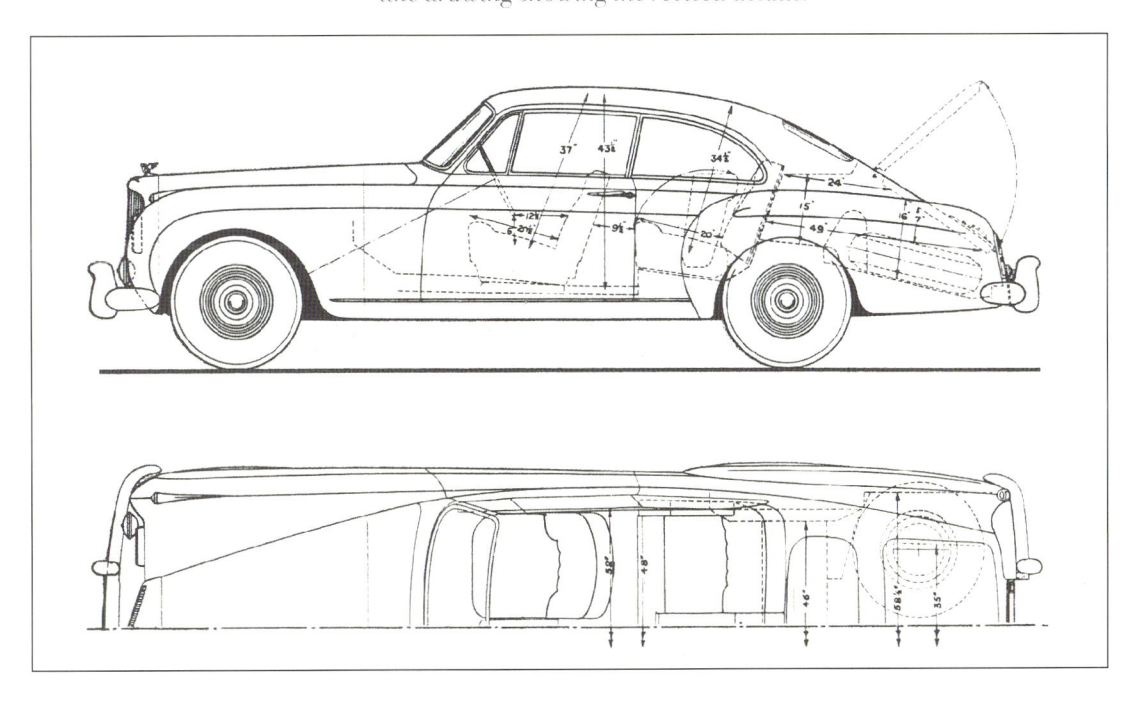

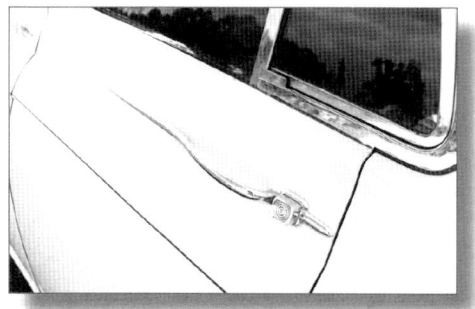

James Young Ltd, which built twenty bodies on S1 Continental chassis, initially offered only a two-door design which is easily mistaken for a Park Ward. The most reliable distinguishing features are the painted pillar forward of the rear quarter-light, and James Young's distinctive door handle with square push-button.

Right & following page: When permission was granted to Mulliner to build four-door Continentals, James Young followed suit with a particularly elegant four-light, four-door saloon. Right is the coachbuilder's publicity picture, taken at the photographer's favourite location in Barnfield Wood Road, near the Bromley works. On the opposite page are two known examples, showing the front and rear three-quarter views. The upper car is BC29EL, the lower one BC36FM. These cars are sometimes referred to as "James Young Flying Spurs," despite the name 'Flying Spur' belonging exclusively to H. J. Mulliner. The James Young coachwork is distinguishable from a four-light 'Flying Spur' by such features as sharp corners at the bottom of the windscreen, the continuous swageline across the front and rear wings, and the chrome rear window surround.

80

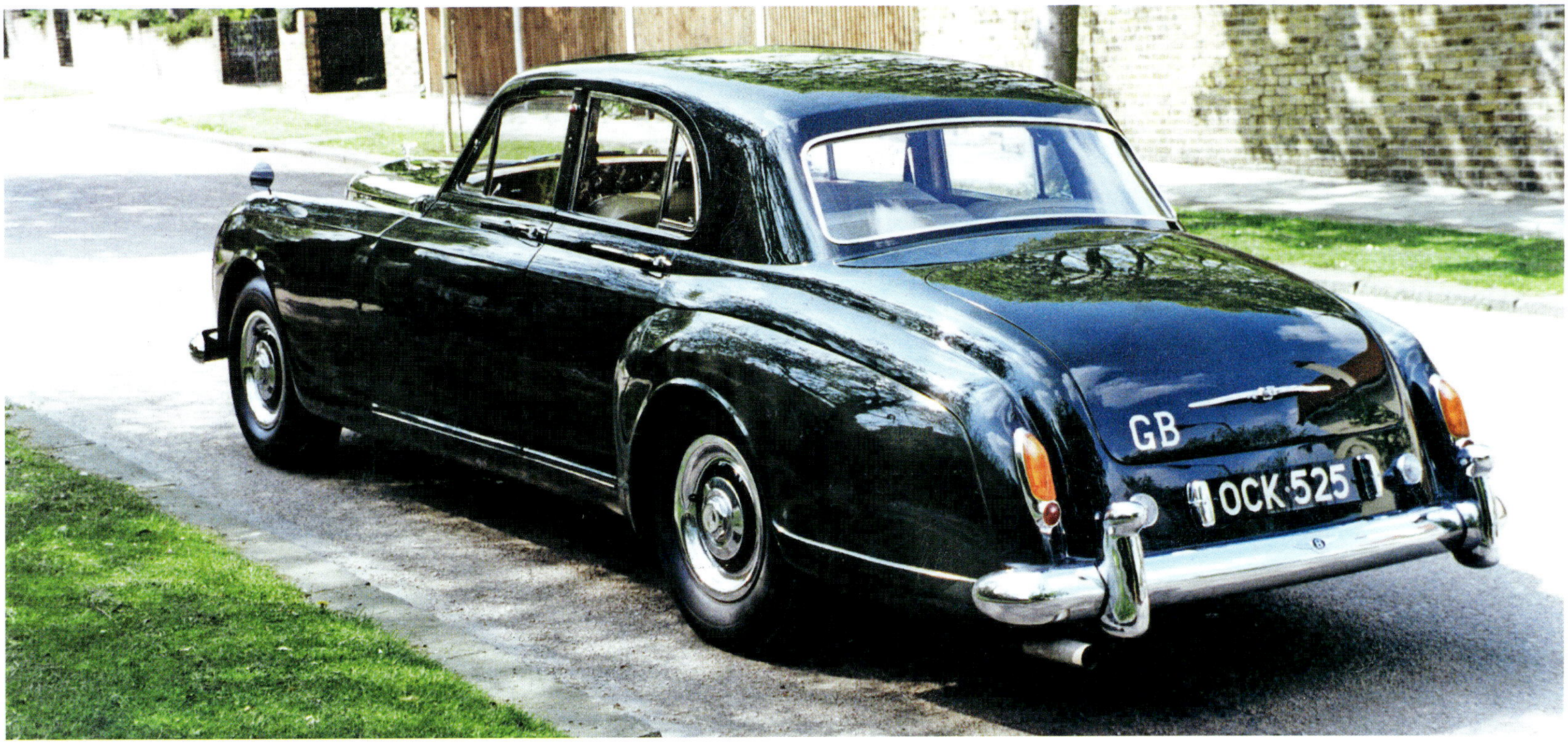
GB
OCK 525

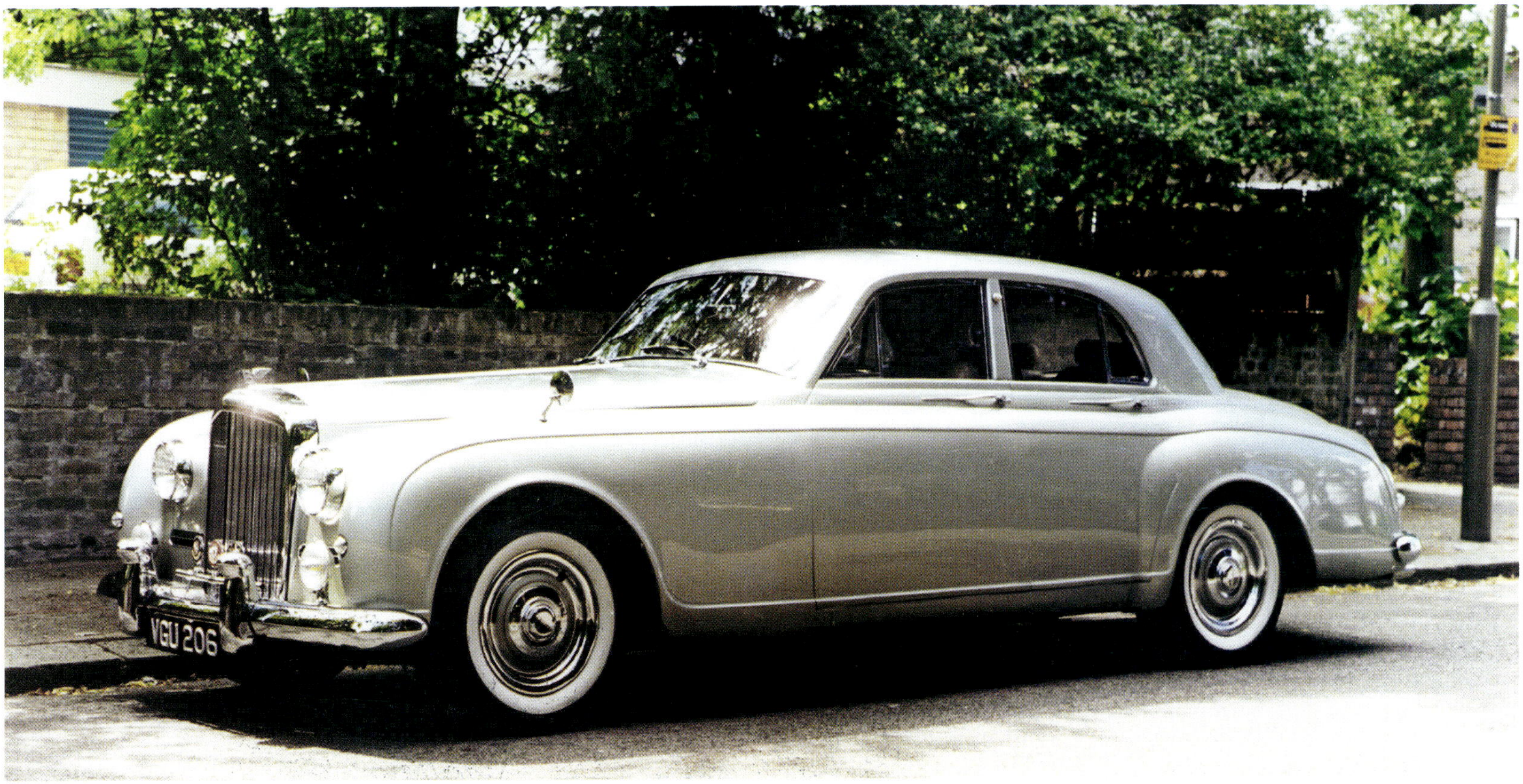
VGU 206

Hooper built only six bodies for the S1 Continental chassis, all four-door saloons to design number 8512, which was a most innovative and distinctive body style. On this page is BC18DJ, the prototype of the design which differs slightly from subsequent examples in having no front quarter-lights and a more pronounced curve at the end of the wing swageline.

Above is BC16GN, a 'production' Hooper design number 8512 saloon. Note the addition of front quarter-lights and slightly amended wing swageline. The interior photographs below, showing the leather-covered facia, are of the 1958 Earls Court Show car, chassis BC43EL.

Until 1957, the Bentley Continental had been a purely two-door car. H. J. Mulliner & Co., wishing to offer its customers a more practical car for fast continental touring, with more luggage capacity than its 'fastback' car, eventually succeeded in getting the nod from Rolls-Royce Ltd for a four-door Continental. The resultant saloon was called the 'Flying Spur,' after the family heraldic device of Mulliner director, Arthur Talbot Johnstone. In its standard guise it was a six-light car, with a large window aft of the rather narrow rear door but, in response to customer requests, it was also offered with a four-light configuration. The Flying Spur's superb styling was the work of George Moseley, who had by then become H. J. Mulliner's chief designer.

After introduction of the Flying Spur, H. J. Mulliner rationalised panel-making output by adapting the two-door 'fastback' saloon to use the Flying Spur front wings, and later a new two-door saloon was developed to overcome the 'fastback' car's luggage capacity shortcoming. The design of these later cars was a little unusual, at first, and the illustrations in 'Coachwork evolution by airbrush' (pages 86-87) show its evolution into an extraordinarily handsome car.

James Young also took advantage of being able to build four-door coachwork on the Continental chassis. These cars were all built to a four-light configuration, though later, a six-light design was developed for the following (S2 and S3) models.

Between them, British coachbuilders offered no fewer than seven distinct body styles on the S1* Continental chassis, all are illustrated in this chapter.

The designer's concept sketch of the Hooper S1 Continental saloon shows the 'grippy' front bucket seats with their heavily wrapped-around squabs – a highly desirable feature in a car with the Bentley Continental's performance and handling characteristics.

* After the introduction of the S2, the six-cylinder S Type cars became known as the S1.

H. J. Mulliner finally succumbed to the need for a more capacious boot for the two-door S1 Continental with the completely restyled car seen above. This is an interesting styling exercise, design number 7500, of which only a handful was built. Note the then fashionable wrap-around windscreen and backlight. Except for the prominent tail-fins and and rather unusual frontal treatment, both of which were aberrations for H. J. Mulliner, the result was aesthetically very successful. So much so that a subsequent 'cleaned up' version, the first of which is seen below on S1 Continental BC27GN, went on to become the standard Mulliner two-door design for the S2 Continental chassis. See also 'Coachwork Evolution by Airbrush,' pages 88 and 89.

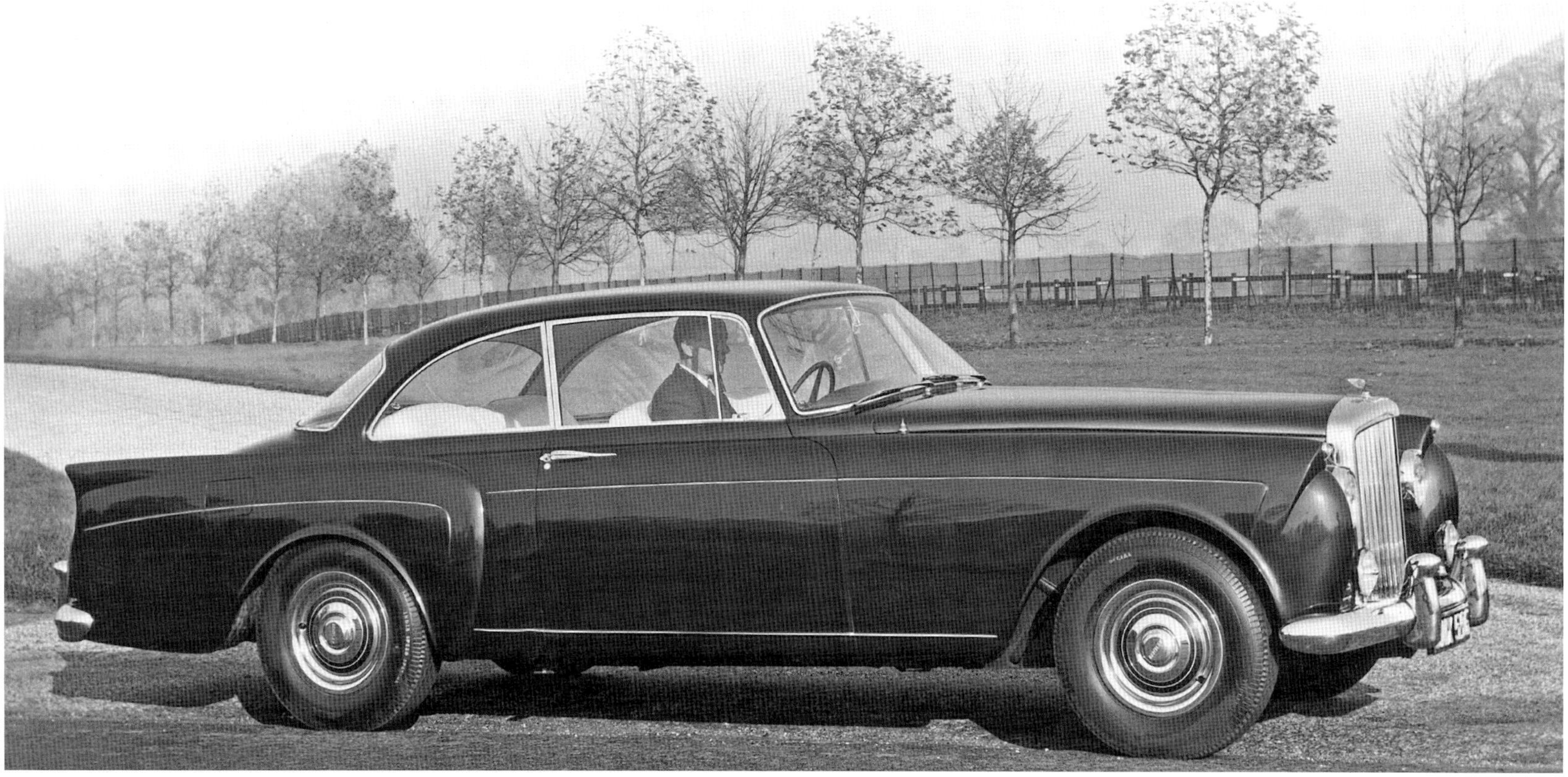

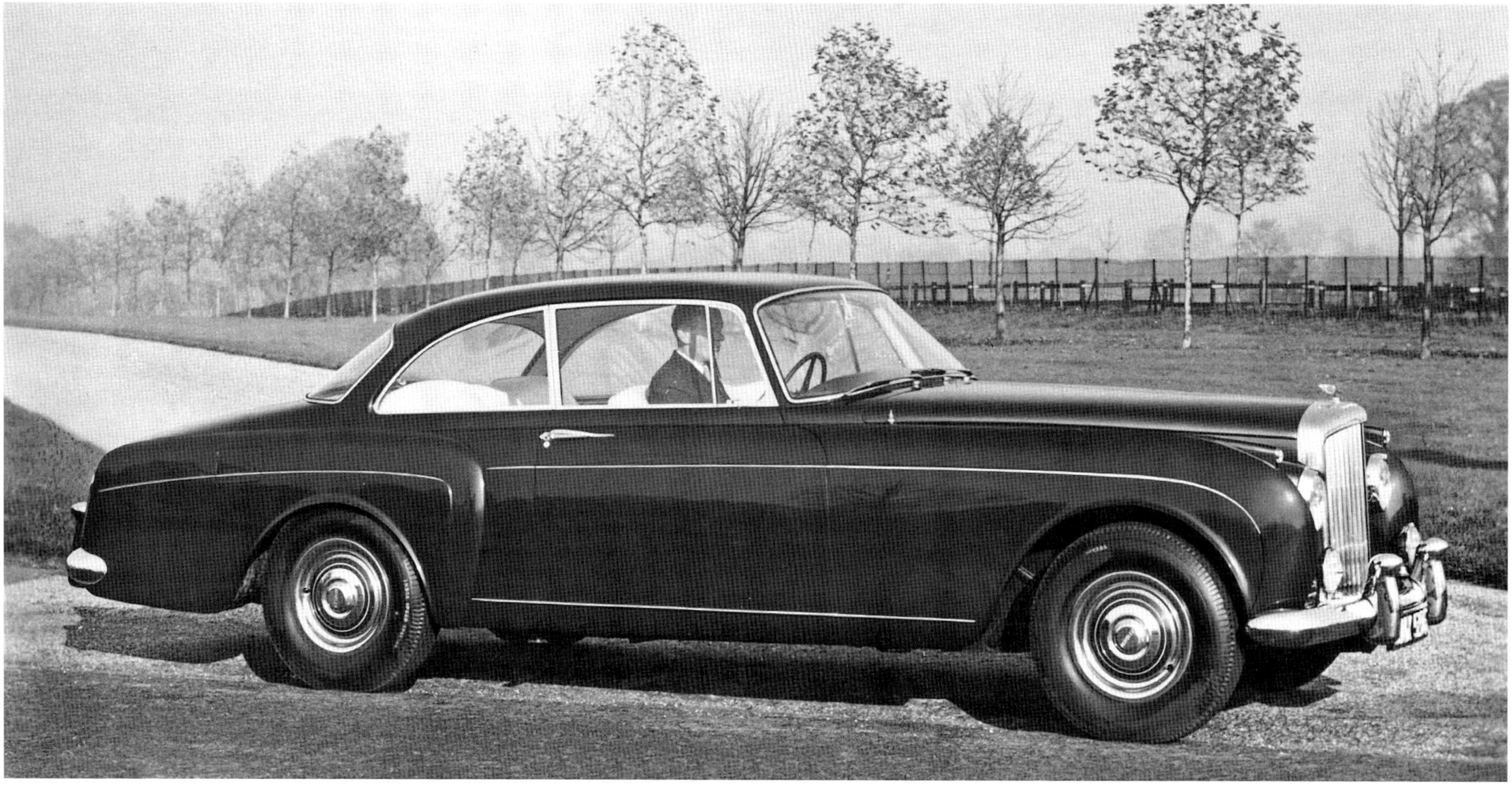

Coachwork evolution by airbrush – 1

Opposite & below: The airbrush is a miniature spraygun and was once an indispensable device for the coachwork designer. In photographic work it was used variously for repairing the image on old photographs and for retouching photographs when it is desired to alter the existing image. Coachwork stylists used them to make small changes to designs that were 'nearly there,' or which they wished to change for future production or to meet the requirements of an individual customer. In these three photographs we see how H. J. Mulliner's designer, probably George Moseley, used an airbrush to adapt a design that was not quite right. The upper picture shows design number 7500 for the Continental S1 chassis that was developed to address the inadequacy of the luggage capacity of the 'fastback' design. Small numbers had been built and sold but it was felt that the design would gain more acceptance without the tail-fins and unusual sculpturing of the front wings below the sidelamps. The photograph was airbrushed extremely skillfully (second picture) to achieve the superb design seen on chassis BC27GN (this). Unfortunately, this 'cleaned up' version of this styling came almost too late for the S1 chassis and BC27GN was the only one so fitted. However, it became the standard H. J. Mulliner two-door design for the Continental S2 and was later modified for the S3 Continental.

88

Coachwork evolution by airbrush – 2

Opposite & below: At Park Ward, an airbrush was similarly used, almost certainly by Peter Wharton, to amend the existing Continental S1 two-door saloon by 'installing' a longer rear quarter-light and a wrap-around rear window. The example shown (top) is chassis BC1CH. A mapping pen would have been used to deftly draw the chrome-plated quarter-light frame in the altered photo (second picture). Interestingly, more of the lawn behind the car, including the shadow of the tree, is visible through the larger glass area! Seen on its own, however, it is extremely unlikely that an untrained eye would be able to tell that the picture had been altered. The resultant design as built is seen below. Nowadays, computer technology has rendered unnecessary such highly-skilled handwork.

These two excellent photographs show the only S1 Continental not bodied by a British coachbuilder. The Swiss firm Graber built this stylish drophead coupé in 1956 on chassis BC25BG. Note the non-standard steering wheel.

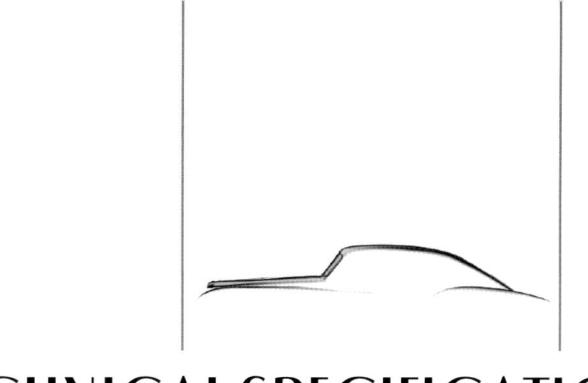

TECHNICAL SPECIFICATIONS – CONTINENTAL S TYPE (S1)

ENGINE

Dimensions
Six cylinders in-line. Bore 3.75in (95.25mm), stroke 4.5in (114mm), cubic capacity 298.2in^3 (4887cc). Compression ratio, 7.25:1. From chassis BC21BG, 8:1.

Cylinder block/crankcase
Iron monobloc casting with 30 per cent chrome iron liners at tops of bores.

Crankshaft
Nitrided molybdenum steel, fully machined and balanced. Integral balance weights. Seven main bearings of lead-indium lined steel.

Pistons
Light alloy split skirt.

Cylinder head
Aluminium alloy with inserted valve seats.

Valve gear
Overhead inlet, side exhaust valves. Case hardened nickel steel camshaft driven by helical gears.

Carburetters
Twin SU type HD.6 (1¾in bore). 8:1 compression engines, twin SU type HD.8 (2in bore). Automatic choke. Air intake silencer incorporating paper air filter element.

Ignition system
Ignition by high tension coil and Delco-Remy distributor with twin contact breaker points. Firing order 1, 4, 2, 6, 3, 5.

Lubrication system
Helical gear oil pump in crankcase driven by skew gear from camshaft. Floating oil intake in sump incorporating gauze strainer. Full-flow filter on side of cylinder block. Pressure relief valve incorporating high and low pressure feeds. High pressure to the main and big-end bearings, camshaft bearings and skew gear drive to oil pump and distributor, low pressure to valve gear and timing gears. Sump capacity 16 pints (2.4 US gallons, 9 litres).

Cooling system
Fixed radiator shutters. Thermostat on front of engine with radiator by-pass to give quickest possible warm-up from cold. Belt-driven centrifugal coolant pump and fan.

CHASSIS

Dimensions
Overall length, 17ft 8in (5385mm). Wheelbase, 10ft 3in (3124mm). Front track 4ft 10in (1473mm). Rear track 5ft 0in (1524mm.)

Frame
Welded box-section frame with cruciform centre bracing.

Suspension
Front: independent by coil springs, opposed piston hydraulic dampers and anti-roll bar. Rear: semi-elliptic leaf springs protected by leather gaiters. Electrically controllable hydraulic dampers by a switch on the left of the steering column to give 'normal' or 'hard' setting.

Steering
Marles type cam and roller connected by a transverse link to a three-piece track linkage. Power-assisted steering optional, at first for export only, from early B series. Turns lock to lock 4¼.

Transmission
Rolls-Royce 4-speed automatic gearbox and fluid coupling, with selector mounted on the right of the steering column. Ratios: Top 1:1, Third 1.45:1, Second 2.63:1, First 3.82:1, Reverse 4.3:1. Manual gearbox, with right-hand change lever, available on early cars. Two-piece propeller shaft with needle roller bearing universal joints and centre bearing.
Rear axle: hypoid bevel final drive with four-star differential and semi-floating halfshafts. Ratio 2.92:1.

Brakes
Rolls-Royce/Girling drum brakes. Hydraulic front, hydraulic/mechanical rear. Operation by means of friction disc servo on the offside of the gearbox, which applies the brakes hydraulically. Handbrake on rear wheels by pull-out, twist-to-release handle under facia through a cable and mechanical linkage. From chassis BC16BG, twin master cylinders and dupicated front hydraulic circuits.

Exhaust system
Single large bore system with three expansion boxes, each tuned to absorb a different range of frequencies.

Centralised lubrication system
Limited centralised system supplying the bearings in the steering and front suspension, with oil from a reservoir and pump mounted on the bulkhead in the engine compartment. Pump operated by a pedal under the facia, to be operated once every 100 miles (160km.) Rear springs packed with grease for life.

Fuel system
Rear mounted petrol tank, capacity 18 gallons (21.6 US gallons, 81.8 litres.) SU dual fuel pump mounted in the frame. Filter between tank and pump.

Electrical system
12 volt negative earth system with 55 amp/hour battery. Lucas special equipment dynamo and starter motor with planetary reduction gear and gentle-engagement pinion. Lucas built-in headlamps. Twin Lucas fog-lamps with twin filament bulbs for flashing direction indicators. Self-cancelling direction indicator switch on the facia. Medium wave/Long wave Radiomobile radio with push-button tuning and two speakers. Comprehensive interior heating/ventilation/demisting system. Refrigerated air conditioning available if required on later cars. Heated rear window. Trico electric windscreen washer system.

Road wheels and tyres
15in steel disc wheels, on five studs, carrying either 7.60 x 15 or 8.00 x 15 tyres depending on coachwork.

COACHWORK

Special coachwork fitted to all S1 Continentals as follows:

H. J. Mulliner	218
Park Ward	185
James Young	20
Hooper	6
Graber	1
Franay	1
Total	431

PERFORMANCE DATA

The following results were obtained by The Autocar when road testing Bentley S1 Continental (BC7AF) in December 1956. For comparison purposes figures obtained by the same journal for the S1 standard saloon are also given.

Acceleration through gears (seconds)	*S1*	*S1 Continental*
0-30mph	4.4	4.3
0-60mph	14.2	12.9
0-100mph	-	40.2
Best maximum speed (mph):	101.0	120.5
Petrol consumption (mpg):	14.0	15.2

CHASSIS AND ENGINE NUMBERS

Chassis and engines are numbered consecutively, omitting 13.

Series	*Chassis numbers*	*Engine numbers*
A	BC1AF to BC101AF*	BC1A to BC100A
B	BC1BG to BC101BG	BC1B to BC100B
C	BC1CH to BC51CH	BC1C to BC50C
D	BC1DJ to BC51DJ	BC1D to BC50D
E	BC1EL to BC51EL	BC1E to BC50E
F	C1FM to BC51FM	BC1F to BC50F
G	BC1GN to BC31GN	BC1G to BC30G

Total: 431 cars.

* Plus experimental car 27B, later renumbered BC102AF.

4. A NEW ENGINE & MORE S TYPE CONTINENTALS

The final version of the Continental S1 six-cylinder engine, with 8:1 compression ratio, 2-inch inlet valves and 2-inch SU carburetters, represented the practical limit of development of that engine. An experimental, petrol-injected version produced 210bhp, but not without some loss of refinement, when a smoother engine was being sought. Facing solid competition (particularly from the United States) in the areas of silence, refinement and weight-saving, as well as being clearly outclassed in power output, the in-line six had reached the end of the road by the close of the 1950s.

Further requirements called for an engine that was at least as light as the six, requiring no more bonnet space, but with the potential to develop much

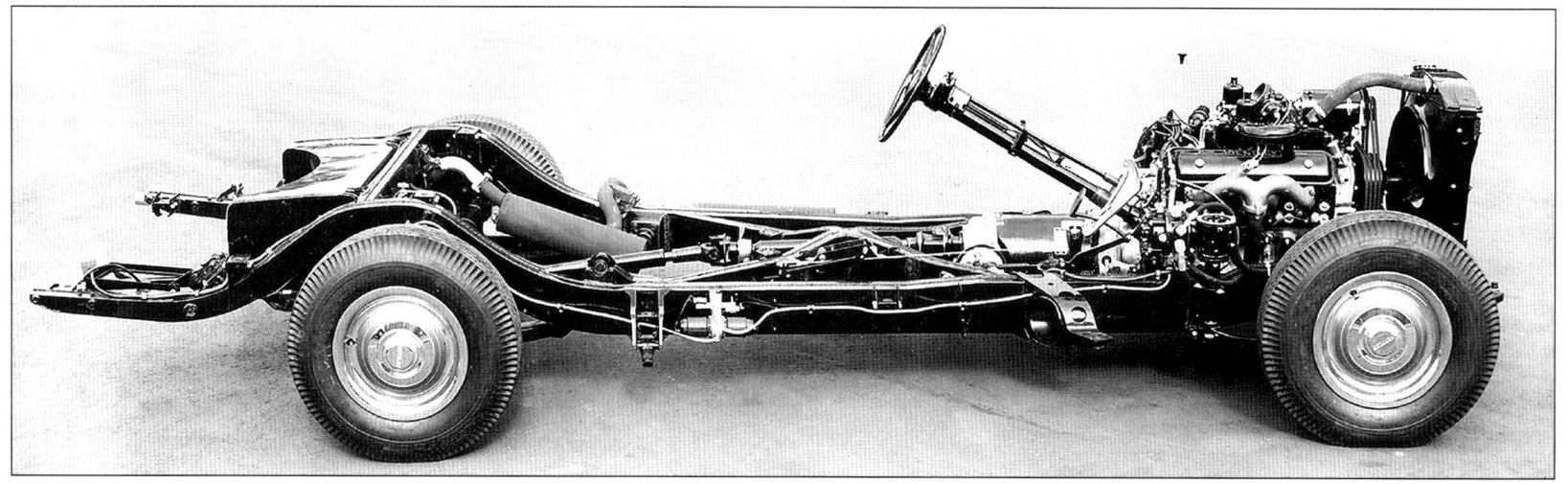

Two photographs of the S2 chassis. In the lower photograph it can be seen that, due to the extra width of the V8 engine, the steering box was located outside the frame. A transfer box with a pair of spiral pinions was provided to maintain the lateral position of the column. The projection below the radiator is the hydraulic actuating cylinder of the by now standard power-assisted steering. The Continental chassis was fitted with engine compartment rear bulkhead and side panels before it was delivered to the coachbuilder.

The gentleman on the left of this picture is Harry Grylls (Gry), Chief Engineer, with Ronald West (Wst), head of Engine Development at Crewe, admiring a prototype 'narrow' V8 engine, which was ultimately to power every Rolls-Royce and Bentley motor car from late 1959 until the late nineties – well over 80 per cent of all the cars ever built by Rolls-Royce.

The 6230cc V8 engine – painted in grey for photographic purposes – as fitted to the Bentley S2 Continental. The carburetters are 1¾-inch SU type HD.6, similar to those of the early six-cylinder S1 engine. The pump and reservoir for the standard power-assisted steering – as well as the compressor for the optional refrigerated air conditioning – are fitted. Note the take-off on the gearbox rear extension for the brake servo.

A feature of the S2 Continental chassis was four-shoe front brakes. More accurately, there were two pairs of half-shoes. This increased the total lining area by 25 per cent and provided smoother-acting, more evenly wearing brakes, and continued on early deliveries of the succeeding S3 Continental.

Above & opposite: The H. J. Mulliner two-door Continental lost its former familiar 'fastback' outline and adopted the lines of the much rarer car shown on pages 80 and 86. The result was this strikingly handsome sports saloon which, despite the now dated-looking, wrap-around glass front and rear, is arguably the best-looking of all Bentley Continentals. The H. J. Mulliner design number was 7514. The car above is chassis BC141AR.

more power. This is precisely what was achieved with the light alloy V8 announced in August 1959.

This new engine, the outcome of some six years of development work at Crewe, was a 90-degree 'oversquare' vee unit of 6230cc displacement, built largely of aluminium and weighing around the same as the old six, but capable of developing considerably more power. Since Rolls-Royce Ltd did not normally reveal the power output of its car engines at that time, preferring instead to describe the new unit, rather infuriatingly, as 'adequate' or 'sufficient', no published figures from the Company are available to illustrate precisely how much of an improvement the early V8 represented. However, 160bhp for the final version of the six as installed would be a reasonably accurate estimate, since the scraps of information that have escaped from the Company tell us that it produced 178bhp with open exhaust on the test bed. The last of the 6750cc, pre-fuel-injection V8s is known to have developed just under 200bhp at 4000rpm. Therefore, the early V8, with its shorter stroke, smaller carburetters and rather less efficient exhaust system, but unencumbered by emission control devices, could be estimated to have developed slightly less than 200bhp. It may be safely assumed, then, that the Bentley S2, announced in August 1959, enjoyed an increase in the power department of some 25 per cent, compared to the last of the six-cylinder cars.

In the interests of quiet running and ease of maintenance, tappet clearances on the new power unit were maintained hydraulically. Indeed, in an engine built almost entirely of aluminium, hydraulic tappets would have been all but indispensable. Like the automatic gearbox, the hydraulic tappets were, at first, 'bought out' from Detroit and later put into production at Crewe. It was not the first time Rolls-Royce had used hydraulic tappets in a motor car. They had been used as long ago as 1935 for the V12 Phantom III, which also had a light alloy block and crankcase. Unfortunately, the pre-war experience was not an unqualified success: in fact, the final ('D') series PIIIs appeared with solid tappets and most of the earlier cars were converted retrospectively. The cause of the trouble was sludge narrowing or blocking the passages leading to the hydraulic plungers, preventing the hydraulic tappet from functioning correctly and, consequently, leading to severe cam wear. This problem disappeared with the advent of modern engine oils and efficient filters and a similar system was employed on the V8 with complete confidence.

The cylinder liners were of cast iron, hand-fitted into the aluminium block and in direct contact with the inhibited glycol coolant ('wet' liners). For the first time in a Bentley, the bore dimension exceeded that of the stroke, the actual ratio being 0.876:1. As if to deliberately restrict the initial power

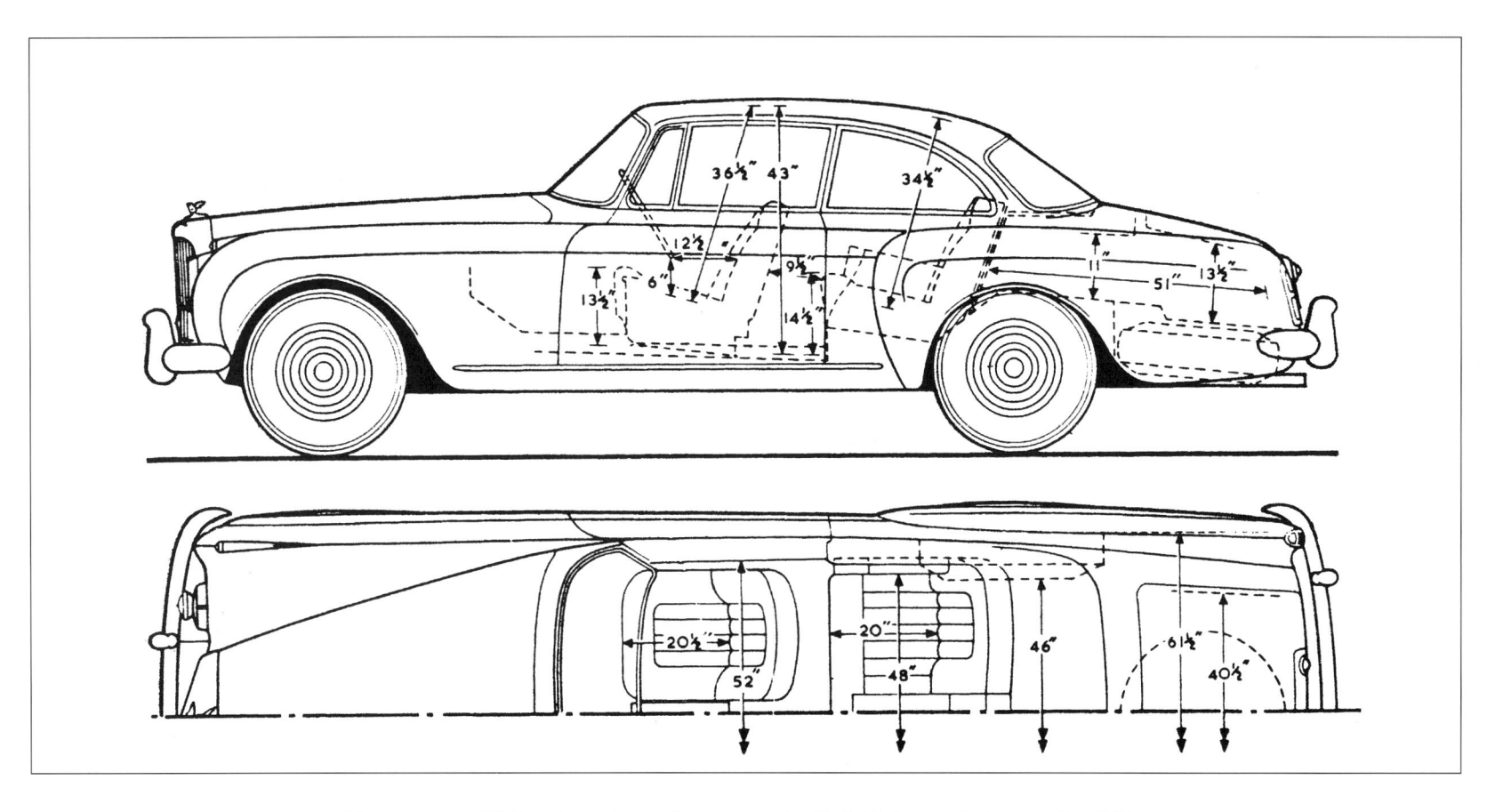

Line drawing, S2 Continental two-door saloon by H. J. Mulliner, design number 7514.

H. J. Mulliner design number 7514 'in the metal,' showing to particular effect the wrap-around windscreen and backlight.

Two more examples of H. J. Mulliner's superb two-door saloon for the S2 Continental, design number 7514, on chassis number BC55CZ (above) and BC48AR (below).

Although the 'fastback' coachwork style had been discontinued, one final example was built on an early left-hand drive S2 Continental chassis, BC41LAR, for a customer in France. As on the final twenty S1 'fastbacks', the front wings were the 'Flying Spur' pattern, and the lower S2 Continental radiator shell is believed to have been in painted finish from new.

output of the V8, the choice of carburetter — 1¾-inch SUs — represented a reversion to the carburetter fitted to the 1955-57 six-cylinder engine. The induction manifolding was arranged so that each carburetter served cylinders 1 and 4 of one bank and 2 and 3 of the other bank.

The Bentley S2, with the new engine, was introduced in August 1959, and the first batch of S2 Continental chassis had been in coachbuilders' hands the previous month. Few chassis modifications were necessary to accommodate the new engine. Some transmission components were strengthened and provision was made for new engine mountings. Additionally, because the steering box had to be moved outside the frame to make way for the wider engine, it was necessary to add a pair of pinions at the base of the column in order to maintain the same lateral position of the steering wheel, which was smaller, thinner rimmed and positioned slightly closer to the facia. At the rear of the chassis, the S2 Continental initially had the same final drive ratio (2.92:1) as its predecessor, but from chassis BC100BY the standard S2's ratio of 3.08:1 was adopted for the Continental, mainly due to concerns at Crewe that coachwork was becoming too heavy for a 'tall' axle ratio.

A significant break with tradition was abandonment of what remained of the 'one-shot' centralised chassis lubrication system in favour of long-life grease lubrication at twenty-one points.

With the more powerful engine and higher final drive ratio, the S2 Continental comfortably out-performed its predecessor, with a top speed in the region of 120mph and acceleration to 70mph around four seconds quicker. Enhanced performance naturally, meant an increase in fuel consumption, but, at the higher cruising speeds of which the S2 was more effortlessly capable, fuel economy was marginally better than for its six-cylinder equivalent.

The Bentley S2 Continental differed from the standard S2 chassis in its higher final drive ratio and new four-shoe front brakes. In order to blend with the sleek coachwork customarily built on the Continental chassis, and to present a reduced frontal area, the bonnet sloped down in an elegant curve

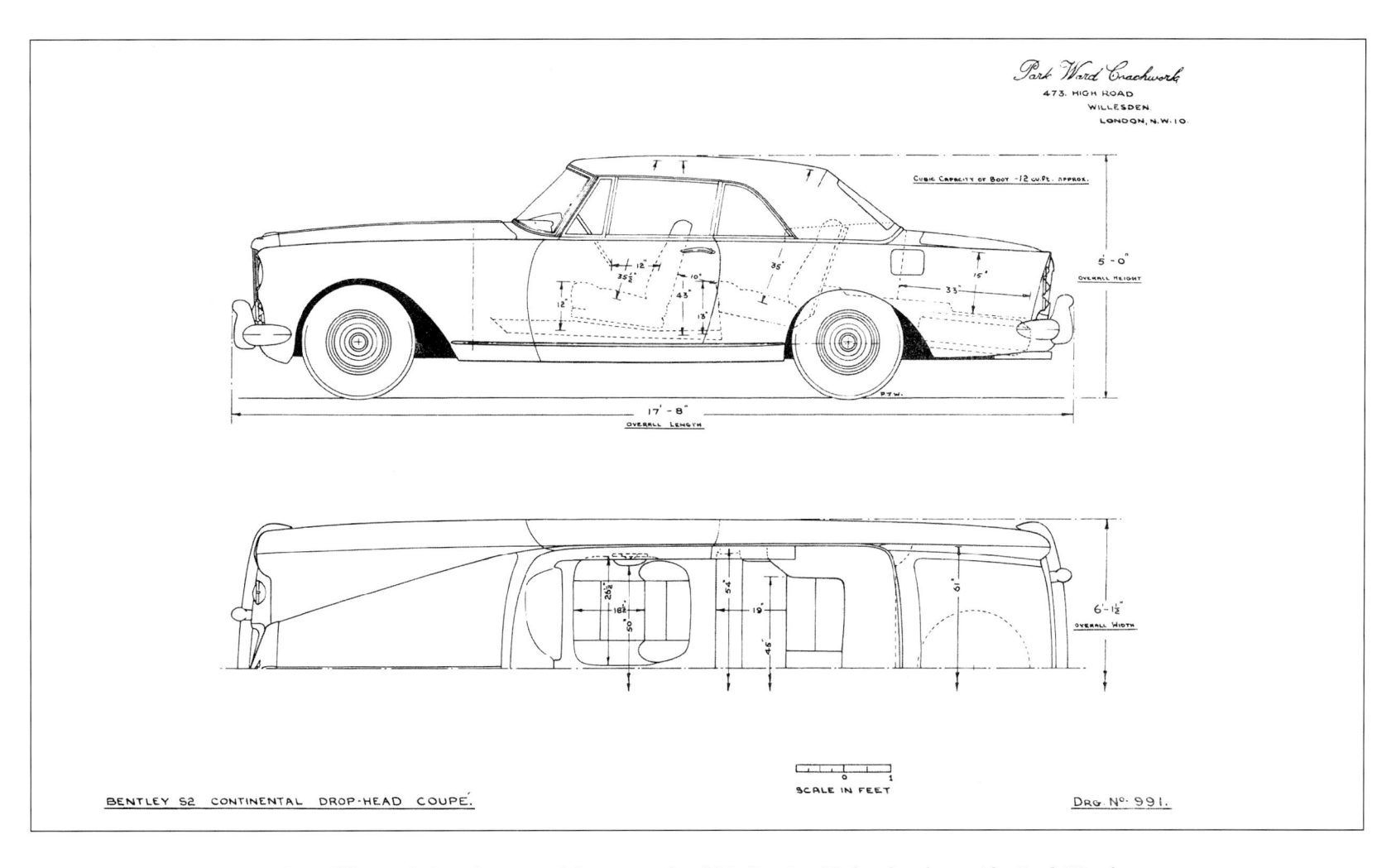

Peter Wharton's line drawing of design number 991, Bentley S2 drophead coupé by Park Ward.

Vilhelm Koren's bold and innovative design was only built in drophead coupé guise for the S2 Continental, though a two-door saloon version had been designed as well. Park Ward was the coachbuilder, and the drophead design number was 991. The styling is sometimes erroneously attributed to Graber. This is Peter Wharton's masterful drawing of the 'Korenental,' as it was called at Crewe and Willesden.

Particularly with the hood lowered, Koren's styling was superb, for all its simplicity. There had never been a Bentley like this before, and Crewe Styling Department Chief John Blatchley's faith in Koren had not been misplaced, despite some misgivings from the Motor Car Division management. This example is pictured in the courtyard at Park Ward's High Road, Willesden premises, with the offices behind and Vilhelm Koren at the wheel.

Unlike on the later monocoque Corniche convertible there were no coil springs to get in the way of the hood mechanism, which allowed the hood to fold deeply into the rear of the body. The stowed hood was covered by a tonneau. Note the recessed headlamp treatment.

to a new radiator shell. This was not just lower than its predecessor's but also departed from the traditional tall, rearward raked Bentley radiator in that it was mounted with a slight forward lean which gave it a jaunty, 'fast' appearance. By this time, most of the efforts of the coachbuilders were concentrated on the Bentley Continental chassis.

H. J. Mulliner's famous 'fastback' styling was not perpetuated for the Continental S2, though one final body was built on chassis BC41LAR. The standard two-door coachwork was now a particularly pleasing design based on a prototype that had been fitted to S1 chassis BC27GN, while the four-door 'Flying Spur' coachwork remained essentially unchanged. H. J. Mulliner & Co. had been acquired by Rolls-Royce Ltd in 1959, and the new owners had set about rationalising the available coachwork styles. H. J. Mulliner effectively became the coachbuilder for two- and four-door closed body styles, while Park Ward, which had been acquired before the war, concentrated its energies on a single drophead coupé design.

The Park Ward drophead coupé coachwork for the Continental S2 was styled in the Crewe Styling Department by Vilhelm Koren, a Norwegian freelance stylist who had been 'discovered' by 'Doc' Llewellyn Smith (LS)

The hood was electro-hydraulically power operated and was interlocked with the automatic gearbox selector so that it could only be operated in the neutral position.

With the hood erected, the interior was as comfortable and draught-free as a saloon.

The three-quarter rear view emphasises just how significant a break with styling tradition Koren's design represented. The rear seat could be folded flat to form a platform for additional luggage – a feature not new to Park Ward Bentleys. Like that of the S1 Continental drophead, the backlight was secured by means of a zip fastener so that it could be opened. Extensive use of welded steel for the frame and fixed panels, using aircraft construction methods, was a first for the British coachbuilding trade, and formed the basis of the construction principles employed for the later Silver Shadow/Bentley T Series two-door cars and subsequent Corniche and Camargue models.

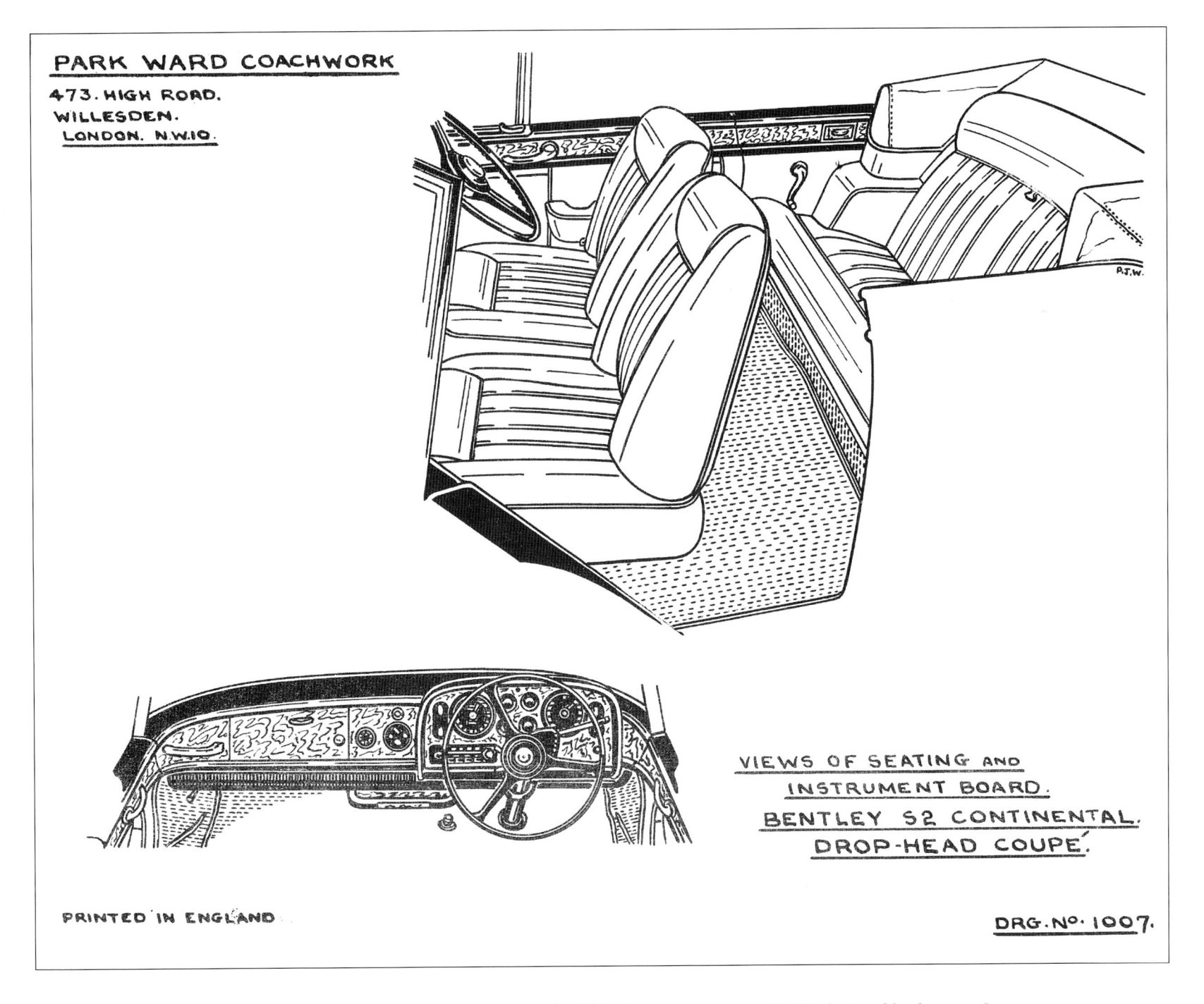

Peter Wharton's interior design drawings, design number 991, showing the 'anatomically' designed bucket-type front seats.

and John Blatchley (JPB) on a visit to the Turin Motor Show, where they had admired a Koren-styled Alfa-Romeo coupé. Koren had been prevailed upon to work with the Crewe styling team to design the new generation of Bentley Continentals.

Koren's drophead coupé styling for the Park Ward Continental S2 featured a straight-through wingline, headlamps in the outer extremities of the front wings and a finned treatment for the rear wings. The interior was equally radical, by Rolls-Royce standards, with the comprehensive Continental instrumentation stylishly grouped in a walnut veneered 'nacelle' directly in front of the driver. The upper and lower edges of the facia were padded and covered with leather, usually black, and this padding was extended along the door cappings. With a slightly 'wrapped-around' windscreen, the whole effect was thoroughly modern and very striking.

If this was somewhat out of character for a product of Rolls-Royce

(continued on page 110)

This page & opposite: Park Ward & Co. specification for the Koren-designed drophead coupé coachwork on the S2 Continental chassis.

7959

Specification for Park Ward Coachwork

DROPHEAD COUPE TO DESIGN No. 991
FOR BENTLEY S 2 CONTINENTAL CHASSIS

CONSTRUCTION — Framework of special Park Ward lightweight steel and alloy construction covered with steel and alloy panels. Wide vision screen pillars and the scuttle reinforced. Chromium plated superimposed moulding on lower edge of body and front wings.

SEATING — Two persons in the front on sliding bucket type seats, the backs of which are adjustable for rake and tip forward to give access to the rear seat which accommodates two persons and incorporates a centre folding armrest.
The rear seat backrest hinges forwards on to cushion to provide for additional luggage carrying capacity.

DOORS — Two, hung on front pillars, fitted with best quality locks, striking plates and concealed hinges, etc.
Push button release type exterior door handles.
Private lock with weathershield fitted to both doors and interior safety catches incorporated in remote control interior handles.
Recessed pockets in each door.
Adjustable armrest on each door recessed to serve as door pull.

WINDOWS — Glasses to doors and quarters to drop flush and operated by mechanical lifts with winder handles.
Swivelling ventilating windows with drip channels fitted to front of doors.
Safety glass throughout.

HEAD — Park Ward type power operated head fitting, covered with suitable available material to standard range of shades. Supplementary inner lining of cloth to tone with upholstery. Large rear curtain made to open and fold down by zip fastener when desired. Envelope cover of leather to match upholstery provided for hood when down and with bag for stowing when not in use.

WINDSCREEN — Wrap round wide vision type made in one panel and permanently fixed, glazed with laminated safety glass.
Dual wipers fitted at base of screen.

DIRECTION INDICATORS — Approved flashing type, wired to a time switch and operated by lever on steering column.

VENTILATION — Fresh air inlet to interior through frontal grilles.

continued

WINGS — Special Park Ward type rear wings of steel and front of aluminium integral with body, with stone shields and mud lips.
Access to petrol filler by means of hinged door in nearside rear wing, locked internally.

INSTRUMENT BOARD — All instruments and switches supplied with chassis fitted up thereon in approved manner.
Cubby hole on passenger's side having a hinged door and fitted with lock.
Cigar lighter fitted.
Grab handle on passenger's side.
Pull-out picnic table underneath board with combined ashtray.

TRIMMING STYLE — Of approved design.

INTERIOR FITTINGS — One electric light at rear operated automatically with opening and closing of the doors. Switch provided also for independent operation.
Ashtrays in convenient positions for rear seat passengers.
Interior driving mirror.
Sun visors attached to screen rail with vanity mirror on passenger's visor.
Slip pocket provided at each side of scuttle.

FLOOR COVERING — Floor to be covered with pile carpet, colour to tone with upholstery, suitably underlined.
Heel pads fitted to front carpet.

LUGGAGE AND TOOLS — Luggage boot at rear, access being gained by means of counter balanced door hinged at the top and operated by push button release type handle incorporating lock with weathershield.
Road tools and small tools conveniently accommodated in rear boot.
Light in rear boot operated automatically by opening and closing of boot lid.

SPARE WHEEL — One spare wheel and tyre supplied with chassis accommodated in compartment below luggage boot floor.

OTHER EQUIPMENT — Flasher lamp, stop-tail-reflector lamp and reverse lamp built into each rear wing.
Bumpers as supplied with chassis fitted to front and rear.
Heating, demisting and defrosting equipment as provided with chassis.
Radio Set with speaker as provided with chassis with controls recessed in instrument panel facia.
Windscreen spray equipment on scuttle controlled by switch on instrument board.
Concealed and internally operated locks to bonnet.
Connecting up lamp equipment supplied with chassis.
Provision at front and rear for identification plates.

EXTERIOR FINISH — In cellulose process, colour to standard range of shades.

UPHOLSTERY — In best quality Vaumol leather to standard range of shades.

INTERIOR WOODWORK — Door and quarter dadoes and instrument board walnut veneered on face, incorporating soft padded cappings covered in leather on top and bottom edges.

NOTE: For cars intended for use abroad, appropriate modifications would be made to such items as number plates, private door locks, etc., etc., to equip the car for the country concerned.

E. & O. E. — Park Ward & Co. Limited reserve the right to alter this Specification without notice if the materials are not available or for any other reasons.

PRINTED IN ENGLAND

This interior view shows how the customarily comprehensive Bentley Continental instrumentation is grouped within a leather surrounded, walnut veneered nacelle, forming a strikingly handsome display in front of the driver. The rigid Perspex sun visors could hardly be expected to satisfy present-day safety design standards!

A final look at Park Ward's design number 991 drophead coupé, showing the hood stowed and the windows fully open. Behind is a Rolls-Royce 'Continental'-powered light aircraft.

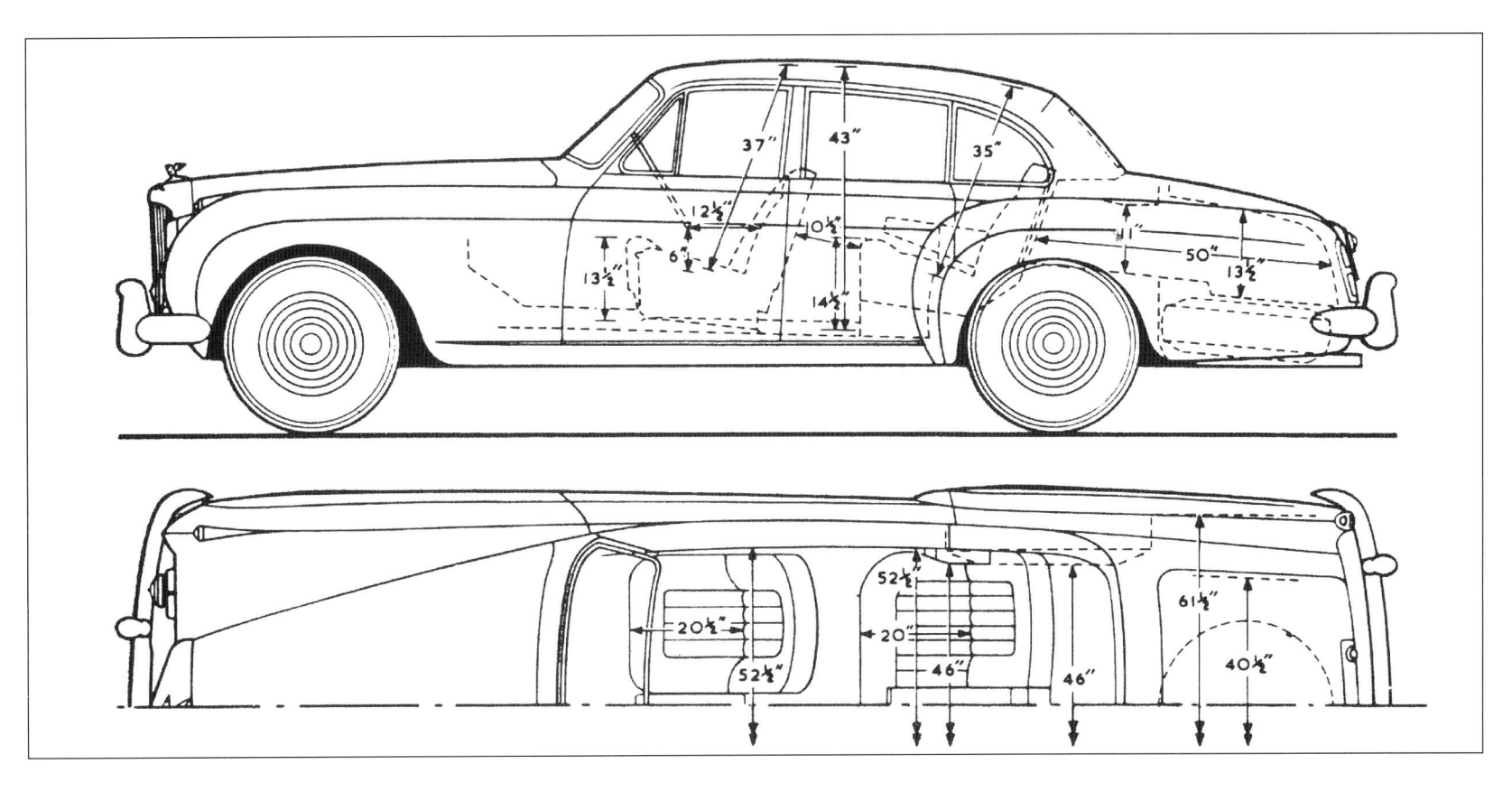

Line drawing, S2 Continental 'Flying Spur' saloon by H. J. Mulliner.

Above & following page: H. J. Mulliner's 'Flying Spur' saloon remained unchanged for the S2 Continental, except that the bonnet was lowered at the front to suit the squatter radiator shell and the boot-lid was extended downwards to eliminate the loading lip, with the numberplate and reverse lights moved from the body onto the boot-lid. The final series of these cars had the standard S3-pattern rear lights in lieu of the special H. J. Mulliner 'cathedral' type.

Ltd, it was refreshingly so, and undoubtedly won the Company some new business. LS is known to have been unconvinced by the wisdom of all this, as was Chief Engineer Harry Grylls (Gry), but the car sold well and vindicated the faith that JPB had shown in Koren. Within the Company, Koren's design was light-heartedly known as the 'Korenental.'

Park Ward & Co., with their not inconsiderable aeronautical experience, adopted aircraft techniques in the construction of Koren's drophead coupé. Also, steel was used much more extensively than hitherto. The floor, scuttle, rear seat pan, boot, rear wings and 'saddle' panel were all steel, welded into a single, immensely strong body structure. Indeed, it could be said that coachbuilding was undergoing a transformation at Park Ward and becoming more akin to body engineering. With unitary construction cars just around the corner, this was to prove an essential transition.

Before coachbuilding came to an end at their famous Western Avenue coachworks, Hooper & Co. built their final Bentley body — a four-door saloon — on the very first S2 Continental chassis, BC1AR. This design was essentially unchanged from that of Hooper's S1 cars.

S2 Continental H. J. Mulliner 'Flying Spur' saloon, chassis BC109CZ. Remarkably, this car completed 437,000 miles from new in the hands of its original owner, Mr H. C. Green, until he passed away. P. & A. Wood, who have maintained the car since 1967, overhauled the engine at 275,000 miles. Andrew Wood remarked that it drives as well as the best and that, given further careful use and maintenance, it will be capable of completing a million miles. The unusual colour was the choice of Mr Green and his wife.

A late (1962) S2 Continental H. J. Mulliner 'Flying Spur', chassis BC123CZ.

H. J. Mulliner & Co. continued to offer the four-light version of its 'Flying Spur' saloon as an alternative to the standard six-light design. Late S2s used the larger tail-light units of a type that subsequently became standard on the S3, and the Mulliner Continentals adopted this fitting in place of the former 'cathedral' type. The car in these two pictures is therefore identifiable as a late S2, while the absence of a winged 'B' radiator mascot suggests Swiss delivery, probably chassis BC76LCZ. The photograph was taken in Merrington Road, West Brompton, which was a convenient photographic stopping point on the route taken by company drivers delivering cars from the coachbuilders' works in west London to Lillie Hall, Fulham, where cars were held in bond and prepared for shipping.

A. F. McNeil's colour wash drawing (below) shows how James Young Ltd's four-door sports saloon coachwork for the S2 Continental had developed into a six-light car, design number CV.100, though retaining unchanged the wingline of the six-cylinder car. The upper photograph was taken at the photographer's favourite location in Parklangley,

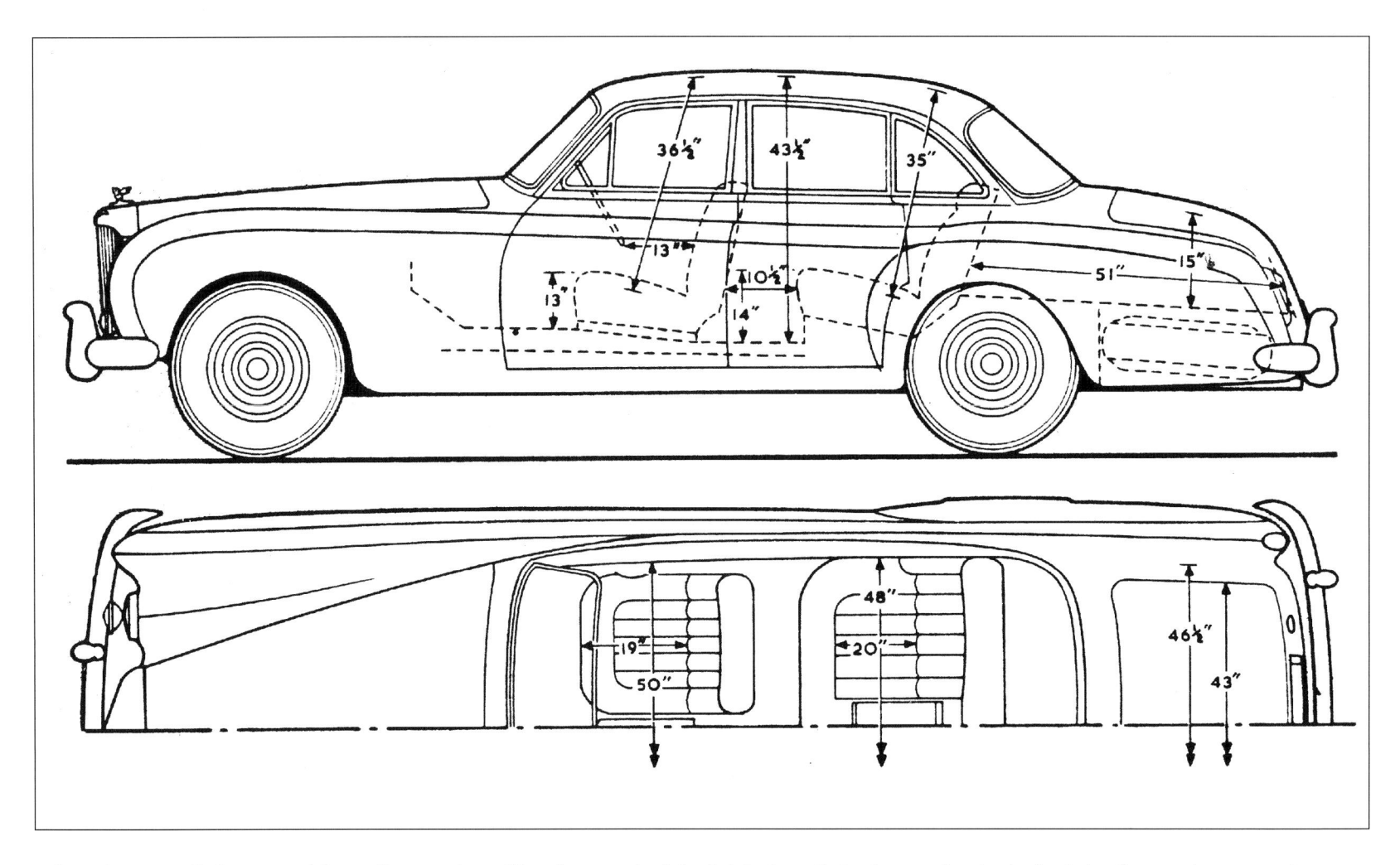

Line drawing, S2 Continental James Young saloon. The photograph of the finished car (below) was taken in the Berkeley Square showroom of parent Company Jack Barclay Ltd.

114

Autocar road test, 30th December 1960, of the Bentley S2 Continental James Young saloon.

Autocar road tests

1802

BENTLEY S2 Continental

The radiator shell of the Continental Bentley leans forward slightly, and is 2·35 in. lower and 3in. farther forward than that of the S2. Scuttle height is 2in. lower. Badges and number plate on this car are, of course, special for the owner

VERY seldom indeed has a privately owned car been offered and accepted by *The Autocar* for full road test, but since Bentley Continentals are built only to order in very small numbers, and the waiting list is long, an exception has been made in this case. The car is the property of Jack Barclay—hence the registration JB 1—and Bentley Motors have checked the car and given their approval to the test.

S2 Continental Bentleys are not available with other than specialist coachwork. The chassis is very similar to that of the short wheelbase S2 Bentley, but there are optional final drive ratios, a slightly higher geared one being offered to give 28·4 m.p.h. per thousand r.p.m. in top gear instead of 27·0 m.p.h. However, the car tested retained the standard Bentley ratio, which is the lower of the two available.

All Bentleys have automatic transmissions. In addition, the Continentals have special Rolls-Royce Girling drum brakes, those in front being of four-shoe design. Continentals are also fitted with 8·00 × 15in tyres in place of 8·20 × 15 on standard models. The engine is the Rolls-Royce aluminium vee-8, fully described in *The Autocar* of 25 September 1959.

A light alloy four-door body, designed and built by James Young Ltd., of Bromley, Kent, is fitted to the test car; its lavish equipment is included in the model price quoted; only the white-wall tyres are extras.

In subtle ways, difficult to identify, this Continental is pleasanter to drive than the Rolls-Royce Silver Cloud tested last May. In particular, after an hour or two of familiarization, it gives the impression of being one of the smallest and most handleable large cars we have ever driven. As tested, it is only a matter of pounds lighter that the Silver Cloud and S2 Bentley, so the weight cannot have a significant effect. Part of the answer lies in the rather greater quietness and smoothness of the engine, perhaps resulting from more effective body sound damping materials.

Regarding the type of automatic transmission fitted, it should be sufficient to remind readers that its design is of American origin and that it comprises basically a fluid coupling and trains of epicyclic gears. The selector quadrant allows, in addition to fully automatic operation in position 4, 3rd to be held up to the maximum permissible speed in that ratio, and 2nd to be held for ascending or descending long and steep hills.

Engine braking is slight in top but more pronounced in 3rd. On this car, the adjustment is such as to make kickdown into 3rd quite reluctant unless the accelerator is fully depressed. Kickdown into 2nd, a marked change in ratio, also calls for full depression and does not occur above about 22 m.p.h. This is not altogether convenient in some circumstances; for example, when commencing an ascent immediately after a sharp turn. There is then an accompanying jerk and some engine roar. For this reason, the instruction manual recommends down changes into 2nd only on a light throttle. Maximum speed in 2nd is approximately 50 m.p.h., and there is no guard to prevent over-speeding of the engine, if 2nd hold is selected. Upward changes from 2nd to 3rd occur at a maximum of about 40 m.p.h. in the automatic range.

A great deal of torque is produced at low r.p.m. by the vee-8 engine and 3rd gear engages very sweetly if the lever is lightly flicked into position 3 on the quadrant. This seems to be the best technique for check braking into corners and

Of greater capacity than it appears, the boot, fore-shortened by the camera, is neatly trimmed. The spare wheel is under the floor

115

Bentley S2 Continental...

This Continental four-door has very pleasing lines, in no way interrupted by the sensibly massive bumper overriders. Note the small parking lamp provided on the centre door pillar

to obtain lively acceleration coming out. In all normal circumstances, out of town and city, driving is almost entirely in top gear.

Position R on the quadrant provides, in addition to reverse, a positive lock forward or backward for parking on an incline. In addition, if the car is stopped on a slope when in 4, another lock prevents it from rolling back.

Since the pressure lubrication system of the transmission depends on the rotation of the power input shaft, coasting in neutral must be avoided as must towing—other than for a very short distance for starting should the battery fail. For a tow-start Neutral is first selected and then at about 20 m.p.h. the lever is moved to position 4.

In spite of the size of the Bentley, the components and fittings are so numerous that there is little latitude in positioning the pedals or steering assemblies. This, no doubt, accounts in part for the steering column being angled slightly to the right, for the proximity of the two pedals and for the accelerator being placed close under the massive guide for the push-pull handbrake. The pedals themselves are small and of uneven height from the floor; the brake pedal cannot be operated conveniently by the left foot, and the welt of the driver's right shoe is apt to catch under it if a quick movement has to be made across from the lower-placed throttle pedal.

Exceptional Brakes

Few braking systems, disc or drum, are as effective as those of the Bentley, or give greater confidence. A mechanical servo giving instant response is provided, the hydraulic systems are duplicated for insurance against possible pipe fracture and the front drums have a special four-shoe arrangement as already mentioned. Frequent hard braking generated considerable heat but there was no fade and only a small increase in pedal effort. Check braking is always smooth, even and powerful in response to light pedal pressures; maximum retardation occurs at only 70lb pressure (the test track surface was damp at the time). When inching forward in a traffic stream there is negligible servo action, so the brake pedal must be pressed harder.

Bentley (and Rolls-Royce) steering is hydraulic power assisted. If the engine is stopped, and with it the power pump, the steering still operates quite normally, simply requiring more effort at the wheel. According to requirements, more or less power assistance is provided—the greatest amount for manœuvrability at walking pace and the least when guiding the car at speed. Assistance is proportional to the effort of the steering wheel, which all makes for a very light-feeling and controllable car which may be thrown around like a small roadster should the driver so wish. Even if the tail is induced to slide, it does so progressively and predictably and may be checked at once. There is no impression of under- or oversteer, but the car corners more readily under power than on the overrun.

A slight shortcoming of the steering, which probably only a few owners would detect, may be noted when an unexpected demand is made on it. Examples of such circumstances during our test were correction at speed of the effect of a sudden cross-wind gust; steering the wheels out of tram tracks with which they coincided exactly in Sheffield and Glasgow; and holding course at certain times when the road had heavy camber or an uneven pitching surface. In these rather extreme conditions our drivers found themselves correcting (or over-correcting) frequently and clumsily, and felt justified in blaming the car. For all normal driving the steering is exceptionally good. It is almost effortless, real feel is retained, yet road reaction at the steering wheel never exceeds a tickle in the drivers' palms. The thin-rimmed wheel itself is plain, slightly dished and of conveniently small diameter. In the large, almost flat boss is mounted the horn button.

With the exception of the slightly smaller section tyres, the Continental Bentley has no feature different from other models in the range which would affect the ride. A hard-soft switch controlling the rear hydraulic dampers is provided for suspension adjustments, and a distinctly firmer ride does follow the selection of Hard. This setting was found useful, in particular, for fast driving over the winding well-surfaced main roads of Scotland. With Soft selected the ride is still quite firm on this Bentley; there is practically no roll on corners, while vertical movements are damped out immediately.

Dunlop W.H.2 nylon tyres are fitted; they give good wet weather adhesion and are quiet and squeal-free. For maximum speeds tyre pressures were raised by 5 p.s.i. all round to 25 front and 30 rear.

Because the optional low-geared back axle was fitted to this car the maximum speed—a best figure of 114 m.p.h.—was not expected to be higher than those for the standard Bentley and Rolls-Royce. The overall fuel consumption figure for 1,440 miles—much of it fast driving—of 13·1 m.p.g., on the other hand, was particularly good. With a tank capacity of 18 gallons the green 3-gallon reserve tell-tale winked inconveniently often on long runs.

100 m.p.h. Cruising

On major roads, such as A1, the car cruised quietly and effortlessly between 90 and 100 m.p.h., and miles fell behind with remarkably little fatigue to the occupants. Engine noise was very slight indeed and the body was also silent, except for some wind roar which appeared to originate in the vicinity of the passenger's side screen pillar. The adjacent quarter light, which closed securely, was not the culprit.

At night the spread beams of the pass lamps proved to be very useful for showing up kerbs and obstructions in dimly lit residential areas, and in heavy traffic on the open roads. The main headlamps gave a powerful long-range beam, apparently of rather limited spread, since there were times when all four lamps would have been appreciated. The multiple light switch, however, does not permit this. On dipped headlamps, the cut-off is abrupt.

Workmanship of the highest order is seen in the James Young body and a minute search reveals nothing that is other than excellent. The fit and click-shut of the doors are a joy; the problems of body sealing have been mastered so that not a drop of water reached the interior during blinding rainstorms.

As already mentioned, the lavish equipment of the interior is almost all included in the price of the body, although this particular car had one or two personal extras, such as a pair of high-pitched wind horns and matching stop watch and chronometer on the panel. The normal Bentley radio had been replaced by a Motorola set (£7 for the change)

Exceptional quality of workmanship, as well as of materials, characterizes the luxurious interior of the James Young four-door body

which gave very pleasing reception through either front or rear speaker, or both together.

Only the front door windows are power operated on this car, but the two at the back may be, at an extra cost of £60. The rear window has built-in electric demisting which did not seem very effective; the quarter lights at the front swivel in response to small winders to give draught-free fresh air. Driving with main windows open is not pleasant because of air pulsation.

A very good view is obtained by all occupants and the well-curved (but not wrap-round) screen is plenty large enough, although it is not deep by the latest standards. The wipers are a little disappointing, both for the area they sweep and in the light blade pressures which do little to dispel screen smear. The rear view mirror, in conjunction with the wide rear window, gives an exceptionally clear view of following traffic.

Were we to order a car such as this Bentley, we should ask to have the main instrument dials turned through 180 deg, so that the most useful sector would appear at the top and so be easier to see at a glance. The r.p.m. dial on a car with automatic transmission is a traditional Continental feature of little value today. We should also ask for the subsidiary dials, particularly the fuel indicator, to register accurately in units, i.e., gallons, litres and degrees, rather than being marked only with sectors.

Among the luxuries of the Bentley are three cigar lighters —one in front and one at each side in the back—all accompanied by ashtrays. The front doors contain "pockets" with neat sliding doors, and there is a locker, with key, in the main panel.

On a car of this quality the driver's seat is usually made to suit the owner. The upholstery and soft leather covering are very comfortable indeed and the rake of the back rest, in addition to the fore and aft setting of the seat, can be adjusted with the aid of a knurled knob. Because of the attitude of the pedals, some drivers found that if the seat was set back for their comfort in relation to the steering wheel, its front edge roll supported their thighs too high. Between the front seats is a separate armrest, which swings up into position and contains another locker for small objects.

Heating, demisting and ventilation are provided by the basic dual system common to all the cars from Crewe, but no adjustable outlets are provided in the scuttle as there are in the case of, say, the Silver Cloud. For rear seat passengers, two ducts feed air from floor level beside the central body pillars. The heating system of this car needed attention, both warmth and strength of air flow being below average. In the engine compartment are two three-way heater taps, marked for winter or summer operation, or cut-off.

Under the instrument panel are two switches, one of which selects either twin horns or headlamps for operation by the horn button; the other cuts out one of the horns for softer warning in towns. Also beneath the instrument panel is a socket for an inspection lamp or battery charger.

In addition to the seats, the doors and some panels are tastefully trimmed in light fawn leather. The floors have several layers of covering, topped at the back by a deep silk pile carpet and, in front, by reinforced carpets. The instrument panel and top, and window sills, are finished in fine walnut veneer. On its lower edge the panel has a padded leather roll to give protection to the front passenger, but at its upper edge there is a narrow lip of wood. The doors proper extend to waist level and above this the windows have slim metal frames. Wide access is given to the front seats; the rear door openings are more restricted. We should have expected both front doors to carry locks.

Few owners would find the capacity of the luggage boot inadequate; the floor area is considerable, although at the forward end the height is rather restricted. Under the boot floor, beneath a cover, is the spare wheel, and let in at the left side, a tray of tools. Wheel-changing equipment is also stowed here. The boot lid is balanced so that it is very easy to lift; like the doors, it clicks shut under gentle pressure. Master and limited keys are provided, the one operating all locks, the other ignition and door only.

Bentley owners will seldom attempt their own maintenance, but some of the recommendations are of interest.

Many will recognize the great cairn on Culloden Muir, near Inverness, the site of the famous battle of 1746. The white-wall tyres set the car off in the dull surroundings

Front suspension and steering needs greasing at intervals of only 10,000 miles, which to many owners means annually. At the rear, the assembly is lubricated for life, the grease packed springs being leather gaitered. The engine itself should be drained and refilled every 2,500 miles and the gearbox every 2,000 miles.

This must be one of the few remaining designs, the bonnet of which (with excellent latches) is divided and hinged down the centre line. The engine compartment is not very easy to get at and is filled to capacity. However, those few items which might need attention are placed where they can be reached immediately—fuses, carefully labelled in the box lid, high on the bulkhead; brake fluid reservoirs high on the driver's side; filler cap for the pressure cooling system (for which a spanner is provided) and sump dipstick on the passenger side.

Without doubt the Continental Bentley lives up to the traditional associations of its name : few cars would provide as rapid, restful and satisfying transport from, say, Paris to Nice. For owners who place special value on maximum speed, there is the alternative high-geared final drive, giving about 120 m.p.h. On arrival at its destination this potent vehicle at once reverts to the exceptionally docile and distinguished town carriage.

BENTLEY S2 CONTINENTAL FOUR-DOOR

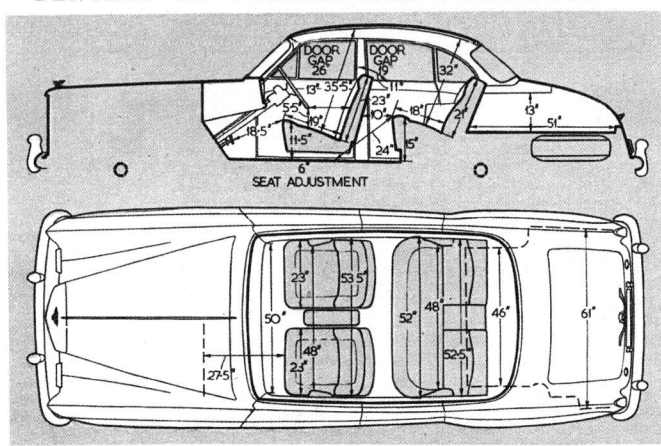

Scale ⅛in. to 1ft. Driving seat in central position. Cushion uncompressed.

PERFORMANCE

ACCELERATION TIMES (mean):

Speed range, m.p.h.	Gear Ratios and Time in Sec.			
	3.08 to 1	4.46 to 1	8.10 to 1	11.75 to 1
10—30	—	—	3.1	—
20—40	—	5.4	3.5	—
30—50	7.6	5.3	—	—
40—60	7.8	6.1	—	—
50—70	8.7	7.2	—	—
60—80	10.2	—	—	—
70—90	12.2	—	—	—
80—100	16.6	—	—	—

From rest through gears to:
- 30 m.p.h. .. 4.0 sec.
- 40 ,, .. 6.3 ,,
- 50 ,, .. 8.9 ,,
- 60 ,, .. 12.1 ,,
- 70 ,, .. 15.9 ,,
- 80 ,, .. 20.5 ,,
- 90 ,, .. 26.9 ,,
- 100 ,, .. 37.1 ,,

Standing quarter mile 18.6 sec.

MAXIMUM SPEEDS ON GEARS:

Gear	m.p.h.	k.p.h.
Top (mean)	112.7	181.3
(best)	114.5	184.2
3rd	70	113
2nd	50	80
1st	21	34

TRACTIVE EFFORT (by Tapley meter):

	Pull (lb per ton)	Equivalent gradient
Top	310	1 in 7.1
Third	463	1 in 4.8
Second	636	1 in 3.4

SPEEDOMETER CORRECTION: m.p.h.

Car speedometer:	10	20	30	40	50	60	70	80	90	100	110	120
True speed:	10	20	30	39	48	57	66	74	82	90	98	108

BRAKES (at 30 m.p.h. in neutral):

Pedal load in lb	Retardation	Equiv. stopping distance in ft
25	20	151
50	63	48
70	90	33.6

FUEL CONSUMPTION (at steady speeds in top gear):

30 m.p.h.	20.2 m.p.g.
40 ,,	19.9 ,,
50 ,,	19.0 ,,
60 ,,	18.3 ,,
70 ,,	16.6 ,,
80 ,,	14.4 ,,
90 ,,	12.3 ,,
100 ,,	9.5 ,,

Overall fuel consumption for 1,440 miles, 13.1 m.p.g. (21.5 litres per 100 km.).

Approximate normal range 11—17 m.p.g. (25.7—16.6 litres per 100 km.).

Fuel: Premium grade.

TEST CONDITIONS: Weather: Fair, gusty, damp surface. 10-30 m.p.h. wind. Air temperature, 52 deg. F.

STEERING: Turning circle.
Between kerbs, L, 45ft 0.5in., R, 43ft 1in.;
Between walls, L, 46ft 11.5in.; R, 45ft 0in.
Turns of steering wheel, lock to lock, 4.25.

DATA

PRICE (basic), with James Young four-door saloon body, **£6,150.**
British purchase tax, £2,563 12s 6d.
Total in Great Britain, £8,713 12s 6d.

ENGINE: Capacity, 6,230 c.c. (380 cu. in.).
Number of cylinders, 8.
Bore and stroke, 104.1 × 91.4 mm. (4.1 × 3.6in.).
Valve gear, o.h.v., self-adjusting tappets.
Compression ratio, 8 to 1.
M.p.h. per 1,000 r.p.m. in top gear, 27.0.

WEIGHT: (With 5 gal fuel) 39.8 cwt. (4,460 lb).
Weight distribution (per cent); F, 49.6; R, 50.4.
Laden as tested, 42.7 cwt (4,786 lb).
Lb per c.c. (laden), 0.77.

BRAKES: Type, Rolls-Royce Girling drum. 4 shoes front, 2 L. & T. rear.
Method of operation, Hydro-mechanical, servo assisted and duplicated hydraulic systems.
Drum dimensions: F & R 11.25in. diameter; 3.0in. wide.
Swept area: F, 212 sq. in; R, 212 sq. in. (196 sq. in. per ton laden).

TYRES: 8.00-15in. Dunlop C Road Speed W.H.2.
Pressures (p.s.i.); F, 20; R, 25 (normal); F, 25; R, 30 (fast driving).

TANK CAPACITY: 18 Imperial gallons.
Oil sump, 13 pints.
Cooling system, 21 pints.

DIMENSIONS: Wheelbase, 10ft 3in.
Track; F, 4ft 10.5in.; R, 5ft 0in.
Length (overall), 17ft 8in.
Width, 6ft 1in.
Height, 5ft 1in.
Ground clearance, 7in.
Frontal area, 23.5 sq. ft. (approximately).

ELECTRICAL SYSTEM: 12-volt; 67 ampère-hour battery.
Headlamps, 60-36 watt bulbs.

SUSPENSION: Front: Independent, coil springs, with anti-roll bar.
Rear: Live axle on asymmetric half-elliptic leaf springs; hydraulic dampers controlled by two-position switch on control column.

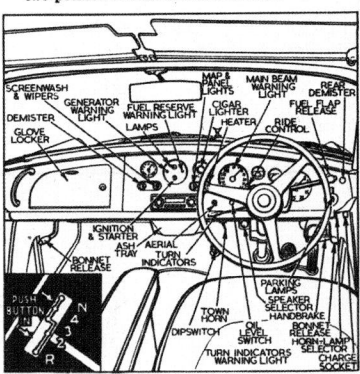

This is Hooper's only body for a Bentley S2 – and final Bentley body – on Continental chassis BC1AR. Though the design number was now 8570, the styling was essentially unchanged from the S1 Continental, design number 8512.

Above & opposite page: For the S2 Continental chassis James Young amended its two-door saloon with a more rounded rear quarter-light and wrap-around rear window. This is BC110AR.

R. G. McLeod's second Bentley Continental, supplied by H. J. Mulliner & Co. to his own shortened design, S2 chassis BC106AR. The off-side exhaust tailpipe was a dummy to give the impression of a dual system.

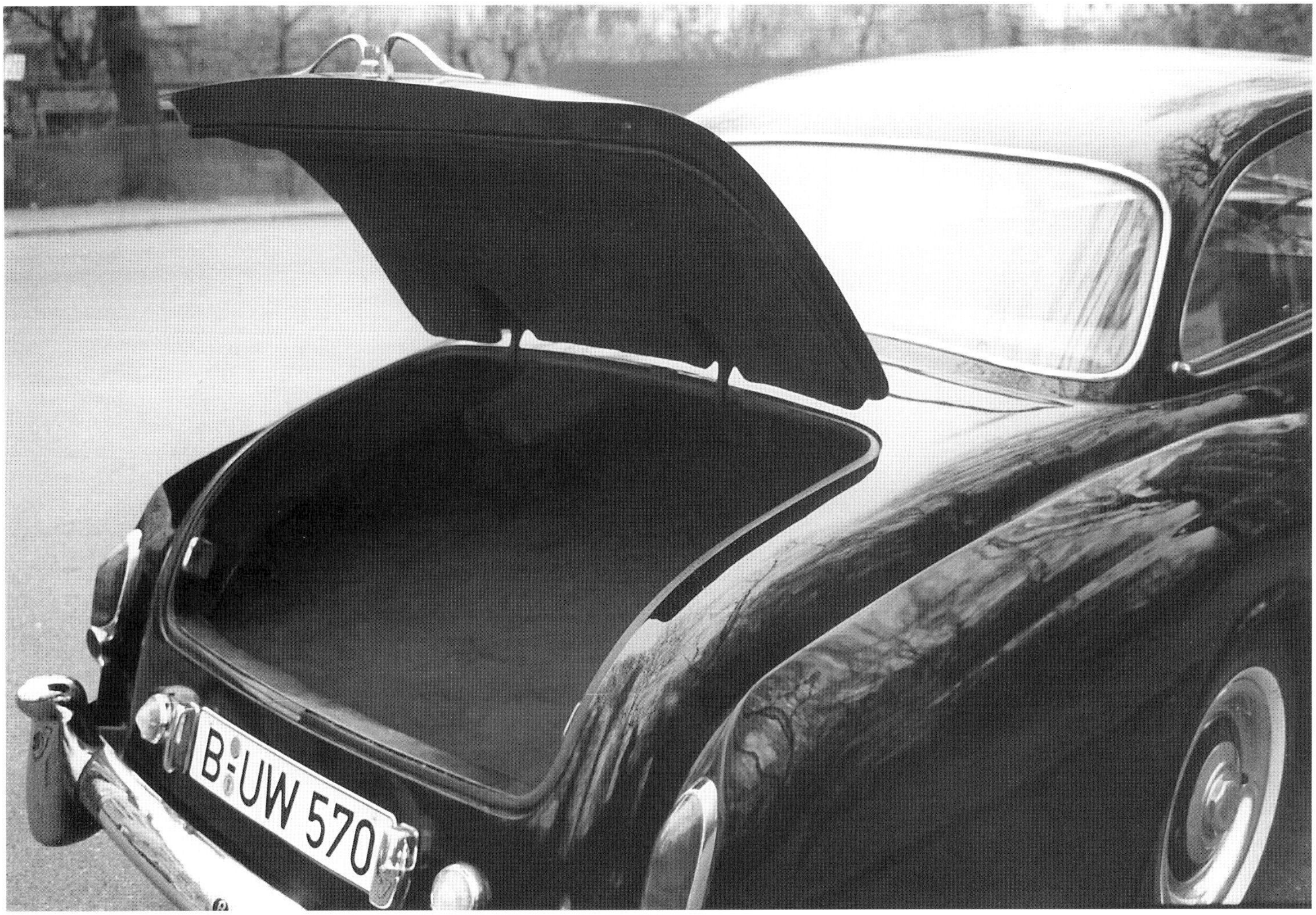
B-UW 570

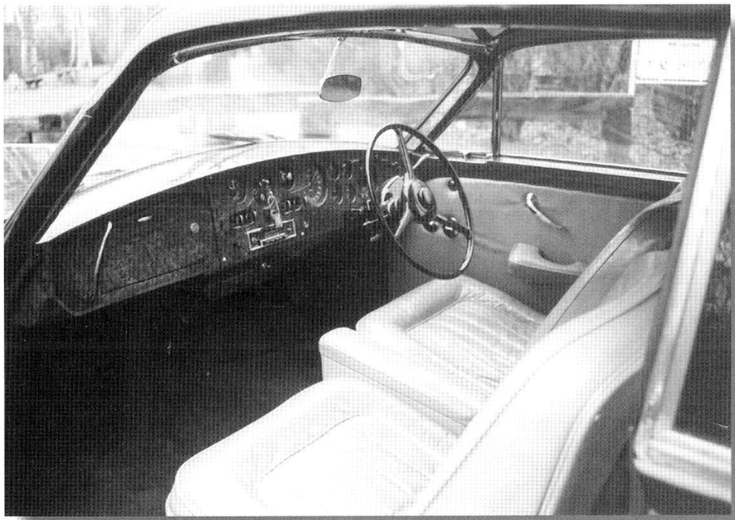

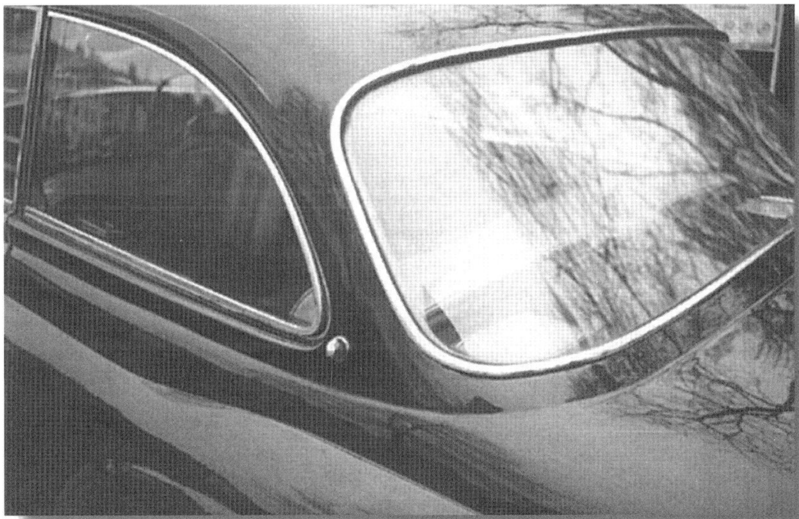

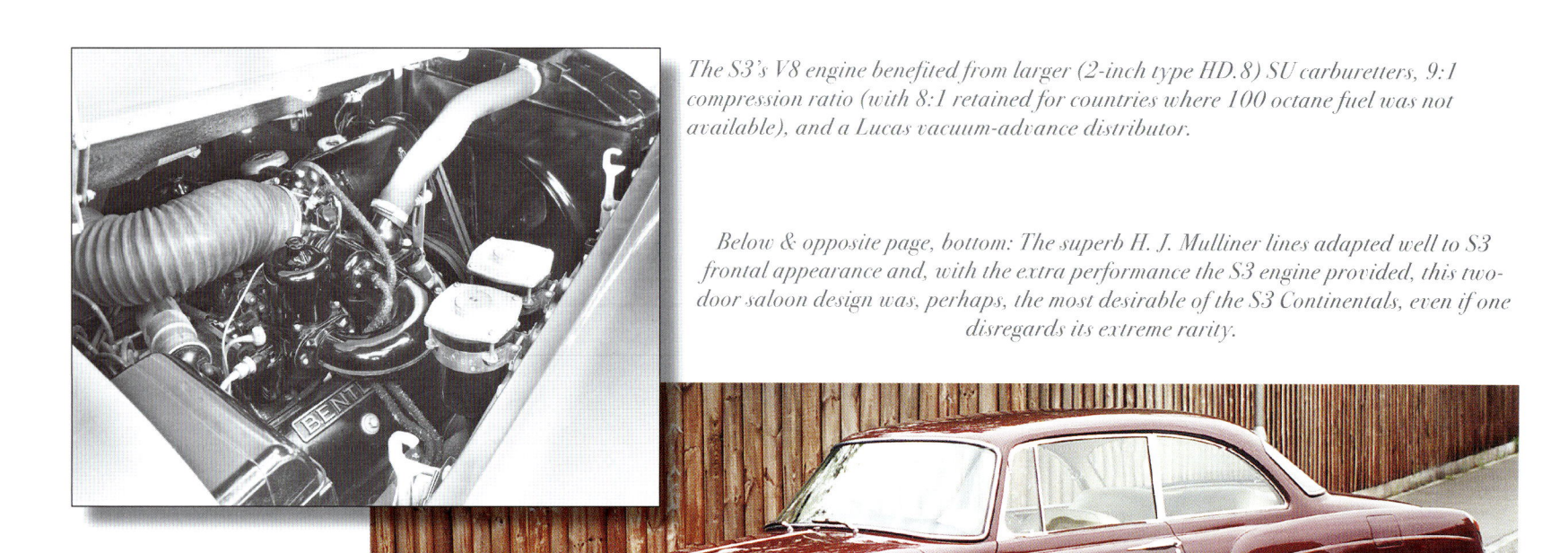

The S3's V8 engine benefited from larger (2-inch type HD.8) SU carburetters, 9:1 compression ratio (with 8:1 retained for countries where 100 octane fuel was not available), and a Lucas vacuum-advance distributor.

Below & opposite page, bottom: The superb H. J. Mulliner lines adapted well to S3 frontal appearance and, with the extra performance the S3 engine provided, this two-door saloon design was, perhaps, the most desirable of the S3 Continentals, even if one disregards its extreme rarity.

H. J. Mulliner's superb two-door saloon design was adapted to S3 guise, but only eleven examples were built on early S3 Continental chassis before the Koren-designed, Park Ward two-door saloon became the standard two-door offering. This is Peter Wharton's drawing of the H. J. Mulliner two-door car, which was given the H. J. Mulliner, Park Ward design number 2012. It is perhaps strange to see a Park Ward man's initials on a Mulliner coachwork design!

The interior view serves to illustrate the Bentley Continental instrumentation. The basic similarity of the facia to that of the original H. J. Mulliner Continental, including the deeply recessed instruments, is obvious. The large brake pedal and treadle-type accelerator, fitted to left-hand drive cars, may be glimpsed. Note how massive the front seats appear – a luxurious touch that would not have been countenanced for the lightweight R Type Continental.

The final changes to the Continental S Series cars took place with the introduction of the Bentley S3 in October 1962. As was customary, Continental chassis had been delivered to the coachbuilders during the previous month. This model could be dismissed as merely a face-lifted S2 but, in fact, represented a considerable advance compared to its outwardly more conservative predecessor. The most obvious change to the casual observer was of course the twin headlamp arrangement. The changes and improvements introduced for the S3 Continental went beyond mere external appearance, however, and may be summarized as follows:

- Four headlamp system for more illumination at a greater distance ahead and to more effectively light the sides of the road.
- Flashing indicators and sidelamps combined in a single unit mounted in the noses of the front wings of H. J. Mulliner and James Young designs.
- New, smaller bumper overriders (the older pattern remained available if specified and were normally fitted to export cars).
- A new Lucas distributor with vacuum advance.
- 9:1 compression ratio for the home market and other countries where 100 octane petrol was readily available.
- Larger (2-inch in lieu of 1¾-inch) SU carburetters.
- Improvements to the power-assisted steering which made the new cars even lighter to park and manoeuvre without robbing the driver of 'feel' at speed.

The use of 2-inch SU carburetters, similar to those of the late six-cylinder cars, together with the increase in compression ratio to 9:1, gave the new models a slight edge in acceleration, particularly above 60mph, and a slightly higher top speed. An improvement in fuel economy was attributed to better breathing and the new vacuum advance Lucas (previously Delco-Remy) distributor.

Peter Wharton's drawing of the S3 Continental Park Ward drophead coupé. H. J. Mulliner, Park Ward design numbers were in the 2000 series and this design was given the number 2006.

The Park Ward drophead coupé, design number 2006. The paired headlights, set at an angle in the extremities of the front wings, are the main feature distinguishing these cars from the earlier S2 Continentals. Though built by the combined firm of H. J. Mulliner, Park Ward, these cars were of Park Ward origin and continued to carry Park Ward stepsill plates until well into 1963, when the combined firm's plates began to appear on the designs of both companies.

Two views of early S3 design number 2006 dropheads. The lower picture shows that these had the same 'anatomically' designed front seats as the S2.

Specification for H. J. Mulliner, Park Ward Coachwork

to Design No. 2006.

Construction
Framework of special lightweight steel and alloy construction covered with steel and alloy panels. Wide vision screen pillars and the scuttle reinforced. Chromium plated superimposed moulding on lower edge of body and front wings. Non-tarnishable strip along body side.

Seating
Two persons in the front on sliding bucket type seats, the backs of which are adjustable for rake and tip forward to give access to the rear seat which accommodates two persons and incorporates a centre folding armrest. The rear seat backrest hinges forwards on to cushion to provide for additional luggage carrying capacity.

Doors
Two, hung on front pillars, fitted with best quality locks, striking plates and concealed hinges. Push button release type exterior door handles. Private lock with weathershield fitted to both doors and interior safety catches incorporated in remote control interior handles. Recessed pockets in each door. Adjustable armrest on each door recessed to serve as door pull.

Windows
Glasses to doors and quarters to drop flush and operated by mechanical lifts with winder handles. Swivelling ventilating windows with drip channels fitted to front of doors. Safety glass throughout.

Head
Power operated head fitting, covered with suitable available material to standard range of shades. Supplementary inner lining of cloth to tone with upholstery. Envelope cover of leather to match upholstery provided for hood when down and with bag for stowing when not in use.

Windscreen
Wrap round wide vision type made in one panel and permanently fixed, of laminated safety glass. Dual two-speed wipers fitted at base of screen.

Direction Indicators
Approved flashing type, and operated by lever on steering column.

Ventilation
Fresh air inlet to interior through frontal grilles.

Wings
Special rear wings of steel and front of aluminium integral with body, with stone shields and mud lips. Front wings incorporate 4-headlight system and combined direction indicator and side light unit. Access to petrol filler by means of hinged door in nearside rear wing, locked internally.

Instrument Board
All instruments and switches supplied with chassis fitted up thereon in approved manner. Cubby hole on passenger's side having a hinged door and fitted with lock. Cigar lighter fitted. Grab handle on passenger's side. Pull-out picnic table underneath board with combined ashtray.

Trimming Style
Of approved design.

Interior Fittings
One electric light at rear operated automatically with opening and closing of the doors. Switch provided also for independent operation.
Ashtrays in convenient positions for rear seat passengers.
Interior driving mirror.
Sun visors attached to screen rail with vanity mirror on passenger's visor.
Slip pocket provided at each side of scuttle.

Floor Covering
Floor to be covered with pile carpet, colour to tone with upholstery, suitably underlined. Heel pads fitted to front carpet.

Luggage and Tools
Luggage boot at rear, access being gained by means of counter balanced door hinged at the top and operated by push button release type handle incorporating lock. Road tools and small tools conveniently accommodated in rear boot. Light in rear boot operated automatically by opening and closing of boot lid.

Spare Wheel
One spare wheel and tyre supplied with chassis accommodated in compartment below luggage boot floor.

Other Equipment
Flasher lamp, stop-tail-reflector lamp and reverse lamp built into each rear wing. Bumpers as supplied with chassis fitted to front and rear. Heating, demisting and defrosting equipment as provided with chassis. Radio Set with speaker as provided with chassis with controls recessed in instrument panel facia. Windscreen spray equipment on scuttle controlled by switch on instrument board. Concealed and internally operated locks to bonnet. Connecting up lamp equipment supplied with chassis. Provision at front and rear for identification plates. Provision at front and rear for number plates.

Exterior Finish
In cellulose process, colour to standard range of shades.

Upholstery
In best quality Vaumol leather to standard range of shades.

Interior Woodwork
Door and quarter finishers and instrument board walnut veneered on face, incorporating soft padded cappings covered in leather on top and bottom edges.

Note :
For cars intended for use abroad, appropriate modifications would be made to such items as number plates, private door locks, and the like, to equip the car for the country concerned, and may be subject to an extra charge.

H. J. Mulliner, Park Ward Limited reserve the right to change this Specification and any other detail of the coachwork at any time without notice.

Specification, design number 2006, for the drophead coupé.

The styling of the drophead coupés on the previous pages was the basis of this S3 Continental two-door saloon, design number 2035, seen here in Peter Wharton's side elevation. This variant had already been designed with the S2 Continental in mind, but was not actually built until March 1963, as an S3. It superseded the H. J. Mulliner two-door saloon, becoming the standard two-door car in what had become a rationalised coachwork range now that Mulliner and Park Ward were combined under the Rolls-Royce Ltd umbrella.

The first design number 2035 two-door saloon, on chassis BC46XA. Construction was of steel, with front wings and all 'opening' panels in aluminium.

BC46XA, showing (above) the distinctive headlamp treatment and (below) the unusual rear aspect featuring 'fins' and a full-width, recessed, and slightly hooded rear window – neither of which were usually associated with Bentley cars but which somehow suited these designs. The bottom picture was taken in a park at Neasden; a convenient photographic location a short distance from the Park Ward works.

The sumptuously appointed interior of design number 2035, the S3 Continental Park Ward two-door saloon. The front seats are bulkier and of simplified design compared with those of the early drophead coupés. The narrow padded section between the front seats lifts up and back to form an armrest.

The rear quarter-lights of design number 2035 are hinged on their leading edges, and normally open manually and latch shut by means of an 'over-centre' catch as seen in the previous photograph. However, at the customer's request, the quarter-light could be electrically operated, as seen here on chassis BC14XE.

One hears opposing views of whether or not the revised frontal appearance was actually in keeping with the otherwise largely conservative body styles. From the maker's point of view, the change was almost certainly intended to subtly prepare customers for the radically new styling of the T Series (and Rolls-Royce Silver Shadow) that was to follow three years later. However, the fact that the cars sold well at the time, and the S3's comparatively bouyant value in today's market, strongly suggest that the frontal appearance was — and remains — an appealing feature. Other enthusiasts are attracted to the fact that these were the last Bentley cars with a body mounted on a separate chassis: they were also the last to have drum brakes and live rear axle. This attracted the criticism that cars made by Rolls-Royce were old-fashioned, though many other cars that were technically much more backward escaped such criticism. The fact that most other cars of the period were extremely unrefined in comparison seems to have been largely overlooked.

The Bentley Continental by now had neither a more powerful engine nor higher gearing than the standard car. Nor did it need to, for the standard specification was more than adequate to see off not only virtually all saloon cars of the period, but most sports cars, too! The differences that distinguished the Continental chassis were so few and of such a minor nature that, more than ever, it was now the coachwork that distinguished the Bentley Continentals, along with their special comprehensive instrumentation, complete with rev counter. Although four-shoe front brakes were inherited from the S2 Continental, standard two-shoe front brakes were reintroduced from chassis BC166LXA.

Any performance advantage that the Continental possessed over the standard S3 came from its sleeker, lighter coachwork.

In the early days of the Bentley Continental, the two-door sports saloon was the only body style and H. J. Mulliner the only coachbuilder. The situation from 1959, after H. J. Mulliner had joined Park Ward under the Rolls-Royce Ltd umbrella, was that Mulliner was the coachbuilder for closed cars and Park Ward for dropheads. This continued in the early months of S3 production, though, by this time, the two coachbuilders had become fully integrated as H. J. Mulliner, Park Ward Ltd with the combined firm's coachbuilding activities concentrated on the former Park Ward works in Willesden.

Although H. J. Mulliner's superb two-door saloon design was adapted to S3 guise, only eleven examples were built on early S3 Continental chassis before a decision was implemented that the Koren-designed, Park Ward two-door saloon was to be the standard two-door offering. After that (March/April 1963), the only remaining H. J. Mulliner design was the 'Flying Spur' four-door saloon. All coachwork styles offered by H. J. Mulliner, Park Ward Ltd were derived from the designs of the two constituent companies, and carried the individual Company's step-sill plates until well into 1963.

The only other coachbuilder offering body designs for the S3 Continental was James Young Ltd, a firm which was destined to remain in business for only another five years. The Bromley firm's S3 Continental two- and four-door saloons were derived from existing S2 designs.

The former Park Ward, Koren-designed drophead coupé continued to be offered by H. J. Mulliner, Park Ward Ltd. The four headlamp arrangement for this and the new two-door saloon was incorporated by the Crewe Styling Office in rather a novel way. During their retirements, both Styling Department head, John Blatchley, and his assistant, Bill Allen, who produced the drawings for the four headlamp front end for these cars, expressed misgivings about the

Specification for H. J. Mulliner, Park Ward Coachwork to Design No. 2035.

Construction
Framework of special lightweight steel and alloy construction covered with steel and alloy panels. Wide vision screen pillars and the scuttle reinforced. Chromium plated superimposed moulding on lower edge of body and front wings. Non-tarnishable strip along body side.

Seating
Two persons in the front on sliding bucket type seats, the backs of which are adjustable for rake and tip forward to give access to the rear seat which accommodates two persons and incorporates a centre folding armrest.

Doors
Two, hung on front pillars, fitted with best quality locks, striking plates and concealed hinges, etc.
Push-button release type exterior door handles. Private lock with weathershield fitted to both doors and interior safety catches incorporated in remote control interior handles.
Recessed pockets in each door.
Adjustable armrest on each door recessed to serve as door pull.

Windows
Glasses to doors to drop flush and operated by mechanical lifts with winder handles. Quarter light glasses to hinge outwards.
Swivelling ventilating windows with drip channels fitted to front of doors.
Safety glass throughout.
Full width backlight incorporating demister element.

Roof
Fixed and panelled.

Windscreen
Wrap round wide vision single panel fixed type of laminated safety glass.
Dual wipers fitted at base of screen.

Direction Indicators
Approved flashing type, operated by lever on steering column.

Ventilation
Fresh air inlet to interior through frontal grilles.

Wings
Special front wings of aluminium and rear wings of steel integral with body, with stone shields and mud lips.
Front wings incorporate 4-headlamp system together with combined direction indicator and side lamp unit.
Access to petrol filler by means of hinged door in nearside rear wing, locked internally.

Instrument Board
All instruments and switches supplied with chassis fitted up thereon in approved manner.
Cubby on passenger's side having a hinged door and fitted with lock.
Cigar lighter fitted.
Grab handle on passenger's side.
Pull-out picnic table underneath board with combined ashtray.

Trimming Style
Of approved design.

Interior Fittings
One electric light to centre of roof operated automatically with opening and closing of the doors. Switch provided also for independent operation.
Ashtrays in convenient positions for rear seat passengers.
Interior driving mirror.
Sun visors attached to screen rail with vanity mirror on passenger's visor.
Slip pocket provided at each side of scuttle.

Floor Covering
Floor to be covered with pile carpet, colour to tone with upholstery, suitably underlined. Heel pads fitted to front carpet.

Luggage and Tools
Luggage boot at rear, access being gained by means of counter-balanced door hinged at the top and operated by push-button release type handle incorporating lock.
Road tools and small tools conveniently accommodated in rear boot.
Light in rear boot operated automatically by opening and closing of boot lid.

Spare Wheel
One spare wheel and tyre supplied with chassis accommodated in compartment below luggage boot floor.

Other Equipment
Flasher lamp, stop-tail-reflector lamp and reverse lamp built into each rear wing.
Bumpers as supplied with chassis fitted to front and rear.
Heating, demisting and defrosting equipment as provided with chassis.
Radio Set with speaker as provided with chassis with controls recessed in instrument panel facia. Windscreen spray equipment on scuttle controlled by switch on instrument board.
Concealed and internally operated locks to bonnet.
Provision at front and rear for number plates.

Exterior Finish
In cellulose process, colour to standard range of shades.

Upholstery
In best quality Vaumol leather to standard range of shades.

Interior Woodwork
Door and quarter panels and instrument board walnut veneered on face, incorporating soft padded cappings covered in leather on top and bottom edges.

H. J. Mulliner Park Ward Ltd. reserve the right to alter this Specification without notice if the materials are not available or for any other reasons.

Specification for design number 2035.

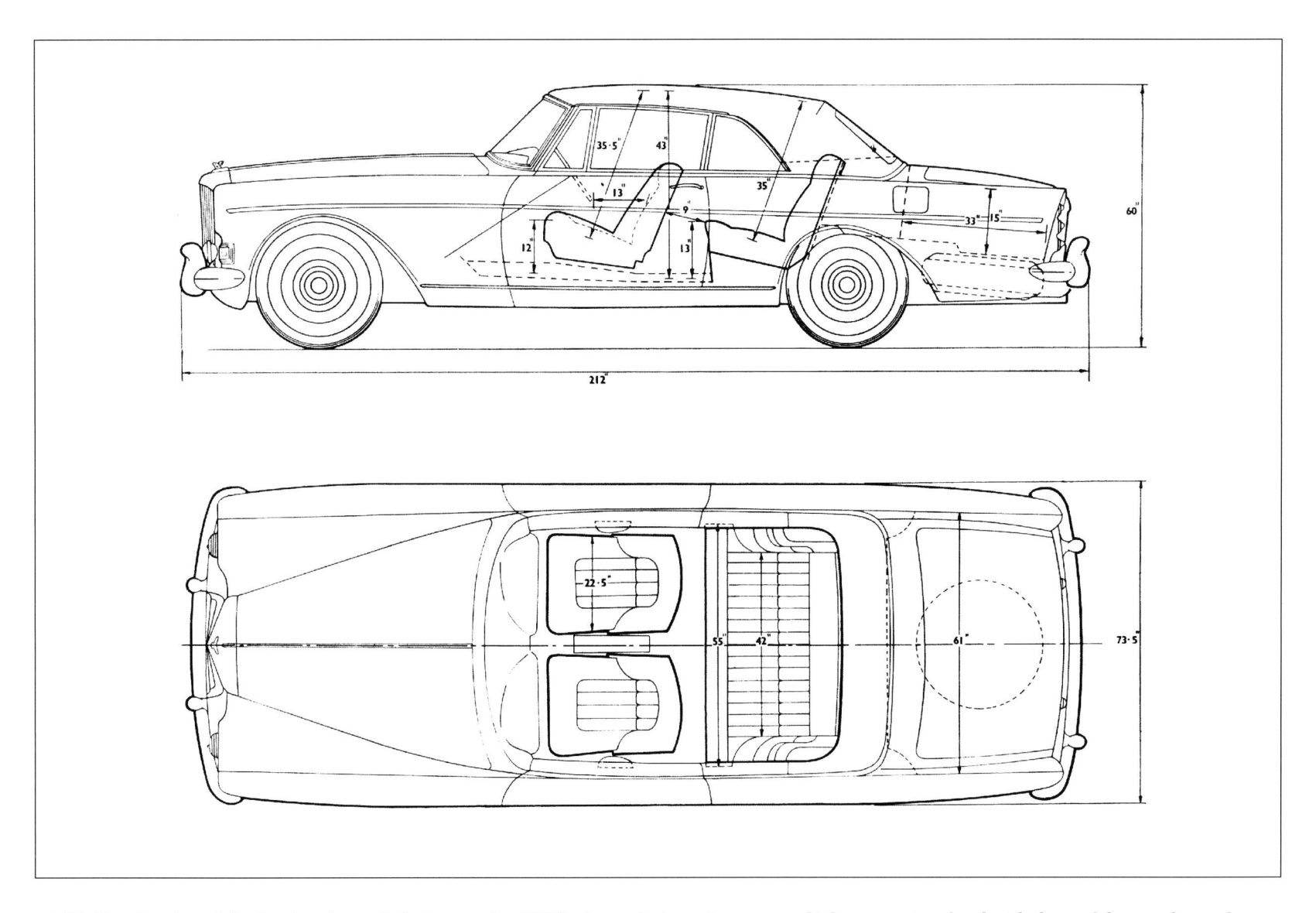

This line drawing of the drophead coupé, design number 2006, shows the later front seats which were rationalised with those of the two-door saloon, and the chrome strip across the lower panels. The added chrome was intended to break up the otherwise unrelieved mass of panel surface below the waistline.

sloping pairs of headlamps. At the time, however, it was the only practical solution other than vertical pairs, as seen on the contemporary Alvis (which also had coachwork by H. J. Mulliner, Park Ward).

The two-door saloon with this styling, designed by Koren for the S2 but not actually built, was offered on the Continental S3 chassis — displacing the H. J. Mulliner two-door car in what had become a rationalised coachwork range — and proved extremely popular.

Rationalisation of the range of special coachwork offered, which began in 1963, together with pressure from the Sales Department, resulted in Bentley Continental body styles being offered on Rolls-Royce chassis. Special Silver Cloud III chassis, conforming to Bentley Continental specification to the extent that they had the lower steering column and other details necessary to make the bodies fit, were built at Crewe. Aside from the radiator shell and badging, and simplified instrumentation for the driver, these coachbuilt Silver Cloud IIIs were identical to the Bentley S3 Continentals. This marked the beginning of what could easily have been the end for the Bentley Continental name and, indeed, for the Bentley marque as a whole. The Bentley Continental model name died out after the last S3s were built early in 1966 and was not revived until 1984.

Even four-and-a-half decades on, few cars are as ideally suited to fast, fatigue-free, long distance motoring as a Bentley S3, particularly in Continental guise. The lofty driving position, beautifully finished interior furnishings and fittings, the commanding view over the elegant bonnet, excellent handling and road-holding, smooth but firm ride and effortless, long-legged power all contribute to the pleasure of driving these superb motor cars.

This later example of design number 2006, BC176XC, is fitted with the chrome side strip. This was initially fitted at the request of a customer and was subsequently adopted as standard. The stylist, Vilhelm Koren, disapproved of this, believing it an unnecessary embellishment that adversely affected the inherent smoothness of his design. Also in evidence are the mouldings over the wheelarches that appeared on these later cars.

Also displaying the chrome side strip, 1964 S3 Continental Park Ward drophead coupé, BC84XC. Though built by the combined firm H. J. Mulliner, Park Ward Ltd, the design is nevertheless of Park Ward derivation, with styling by Vilhelm Koren of the Crewe Styling Department.

This page & opposite, top: Vilhelm Koren's misgivings notwithstanding, it is difficult to escape the impression that the chrome side strip did improve the appearance of the otherwise unrelieved mass below the waistline. It was perhaps at its most 'right' in side elevation, but in the three-quarter front view tends to cut across the headlights and therefore perhaps was not wholly satisfactory. This is chassis BC98LXA, probably the first to be fitted with the chrome strip. It lacks the wheelarch mouldings seen on later cars. The 'S3' motif on the boot-lid was fitted to all but the first few cars. Merrington Road, London, again, on the company drivers' delivery route to Lillie Hall, May 1963.

Line drawing of the Park Ward two-door saloon, design number 2035. This is the later version with chrome side strip and mouldings over the wheelarches.

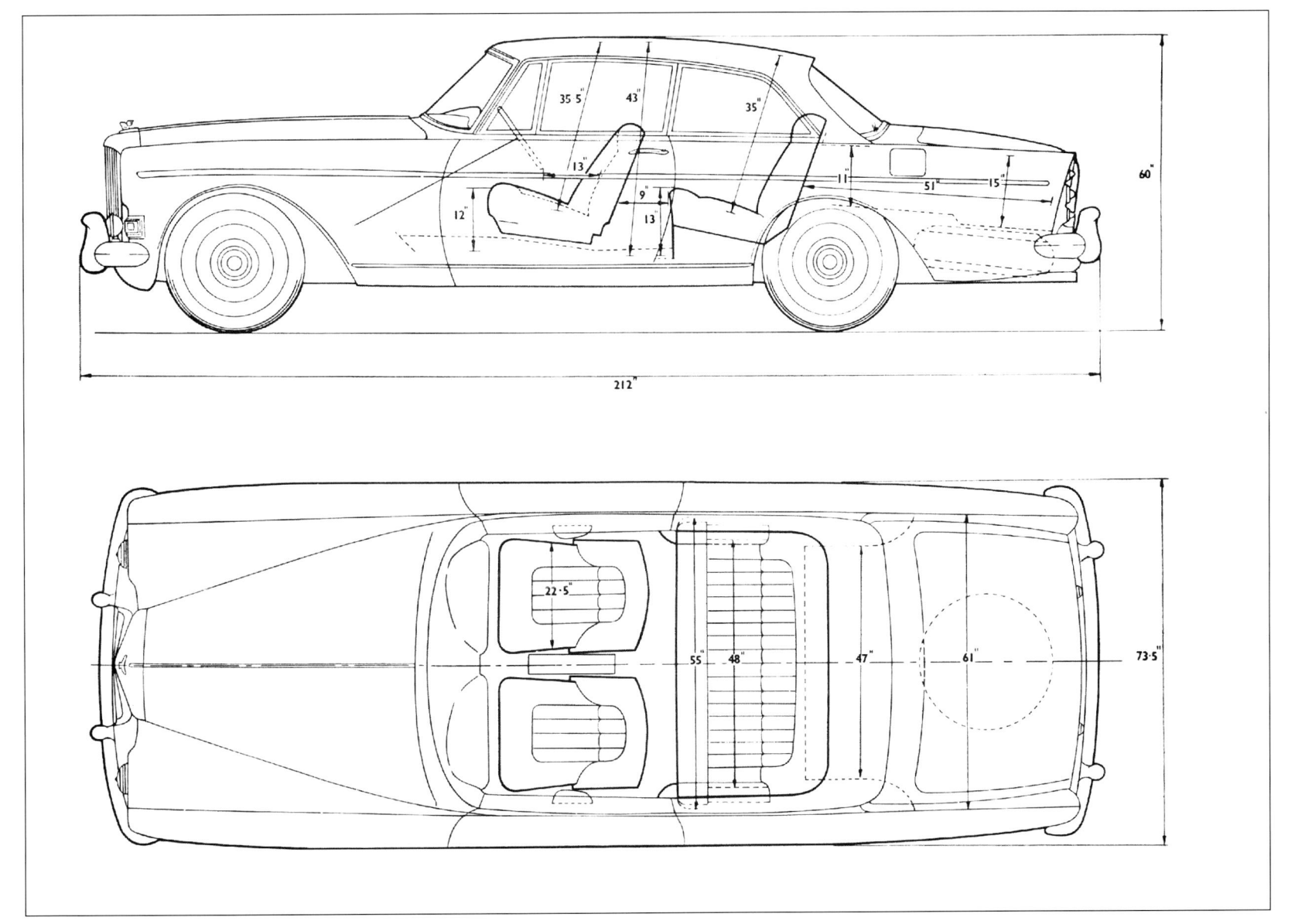

135

Wider than standard front seats, with built-in folding centre armrests, were fitted to BC22XE, a two-door saloon, design number 2035.

Another design number 2035 two-door saloon, on chassis BC14XE, fitted with the standard front seats that had electrical operation of the driver's seat.

Above & opposite, top: A special, one-off variant of design number 2035 was design number 2035/F, specially designed and built for R. G. McLeod on S3 Continental chassis BC38XC. In this instance, truncating the coachwork has given it a distinct BMC 1100 air.

Above, left: BC38XC: front interior. Standard apart from the Reutter seat reclining mechanisms, high-vision roof panel and heavy-duty floor covering.

Above, right: BC38XC: the chassis was shortened just aft of the tubular crossmember behind the rear spring shackles. Note the ends of the chassis rails are plated over, and the dummy tail-pipe on the right of the car to give the impression of a dual exhaust system. The top of McLeod's personal registration number 'H1' can just be glimpsed.

BC16XD, a design number 2006 drophead coupé for HM The King of Denmark, was fitted with a split, bench-type front seat with folding centre armrests. Note the combination of hide and Phantom V type cloth for the upholstery.

BC120XE, a design number 2006 drophead coupé, had leather coverings throughout in place of polished wood. Even the steering column and horn button were leather-covered, and a leather-covered steering wheel was fitted at Lillie Hall before delivery.

BC8XD, a design number 2006 drophead coupé, was fitted with fully reclining Reutter front seats, with both centre and side armrests built into the seats and no armrests on the doors. Note the front passenger's head restraint and the reading light stowed on the back of the seat squab.

BC60XC, a design number 2006 drophead coupé for the Earl of Inchcape, besides having fully reclining Reutter front seats, was fitted with Irvin safety belts, only one of which is visible in this photograph.

BC136LXC, a design number 2006 drophead coupé, fitted with a Philips 45rpm record player below its standard pull-out picnic table.

Close-up of 'Flying Spur' front seats. The knurled knob at the base of the squab adjusts the rake.

Left & below: H. J. Mulliner's 'Flying Spur' saloon was continued by H. J. Mulliner, Park Ward for the S3 Continental, though with the revised frontal appearance which, it is felt, suited it particularly well. An extremely handsome car with performance to match. This is BC18XA, the Conduit Street Trials car.

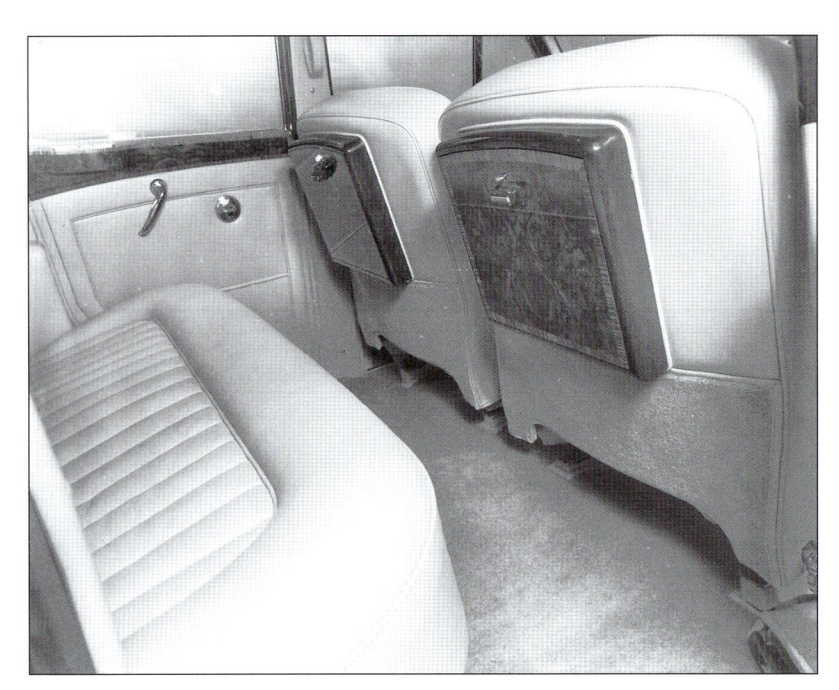

Above, left: 'Flying Spur' rear compartment, showing the optional picnic tables.

Above, right: 'Flying Spur' facia. The speedometer reads to 140mph and the revolution counter is 'red-lined' at 4500rpm. The two lower gauges in front of the driver are less than readily visible in a normal seating position, and therefore the two critical engine function gauges are given priority at the top of the facia. The veneer is typical H. J. Mulliner 'flame' pattern with boldly striped crossbanding.

1964 S3 Continental 'Flying Spur' saloon by H. J. Mulliner, chassis BC134XC. Again, by that time, the coachbuilder was in fact the combined firm H. J. Mulliner, Park Ward Ltd, but the design is, of course, quintessentially Mulliner.

Above left: This is a very rare 'Flying Spur' variant with small rear quarter-lights, in this instance still a six-light body, unlike the four-light 'Flying Spur' seen earlier.

Above, right: Like the H. J. Mulliner and Park Ward designs, the James Young coachwork for the S3 Continental remained unchanged from the S2 designs, apart from frontal appearance, as did the design number, CV.100.

S3 Continental saloon by James Young, design number CV.100. Note the distinctive door handles, with their characteristic James Young square push-buttons. There was also a very rare two-door variant.

JACK BARCLAY
LIMITED

Announce

THE NEW S.2 TYPE

CONTINENTAL BENTLEY

WITH SPECIAL COACHWORK BY

JAMES YOUNG

James YOUNG LTD
BROMLEY, KENT Tel. RAVensbourne 3434

The sole remaining privately owned coachbuilders for Rolls-Royce and Bentley, a subsidiary of Jack Barclay Ltd., offer the most distinguished and elegant coachwork, designed for the new Continental Bentley chassis.

JACK BARCLAY LTD., *The Largest Official Retailers of* ROLLS-ROYCE *and* BENTLEY
BERKELEY SQUARE, LONDON, W.1 MAYfair 7444

TECHNICAL SPECIFICATIONS – BENTLEY CONTINENTAL S2 & S3

ENGINE

Dimensions
Eight cylinders in 90-degree vee formation. Bore 4.1in (104.14mm), stroke 3.6in (91.44mm), cubic capacity 380in^3 (6230cc). Compression ratio 8:1. S3: 9:1 standard, 8:1 for countries where 100 octane fuel not available.

Cylinder block/crankcase
High silicon content aluminium alloy block with cast iron wet cylinder liners.

Crankshaft
Nitride hardened chrome molybdenum steel, with integral balance weights, running in five main bearings.

Pistons
Aluminium alloy. Three compression rings and one oil control ring.

Cylinder heads
Aluminium alloy with austenitic steel valve seats.

Valve gear
Overhead valves. Monikrom cast iron camshaft driven by helical gears, four bearings. Hydraulic tappets.

Carburetters
S2: Two SU type HD.6 (1¾in) carburetters with automatic choke. Acoustic air intake silencer incorporating micronic air filter. S3: two SU type HD.8 (2in) carburetters with paper or oil wetted wire mesh air filter element.

Ignition system
Ignition by high tension coil and Delco-Remy distributor with twin contact breaker points. S3: Lucas distributor with vacuum advance. Firing order A1, B1, A4, B4, B2, A3, B3, A2.

Lubrication system
Helical gear oil pump in crankcase driven by skew gear from crankshaft. Oil pick-up in sump incorporating gauze strainer. Full-flow filter on side of crankcase. Pressure relief valve regulates oil pressure at approximately 40lb/sq.in. Sump capacity 12 pints (14.4 US pints, 6.8 litres).

Cooling system
Pressurised system operating at 7lb/in². Temperature control by thermostat at the front of engine. Belt driven centrifugal coolant pump and fan.

CHASSIS

Dimensions
Overall length, 17ft 7¾in (5378mm). Wheelbase, 10ft 3in (3124mm). Front track 4ft 10½in (1486mm). Rear track 5ft 0in (1524mm). Note: for overall lengths of S3s fitted with the smaller overriders, subtract 1in (25mm) from the overall length.

Frame
Closed box section frame of welded steel construction with cruciform centre bracing and crossmembers.

Suspension
Front: independent by coil springs and rubber bushed wishbones, double acting hydraulic dampers and anti-roll bar. Rear: semi-elliptic leaf springs protected by leather gaiters. Controllable hydraulic dampers by solenoid operated by switch on left side of steering column. 'Z' type axle control rod.

Steering
Power-assisted cam and roller, Hobourn Eaton belt driven pump. Three-piece track linkage. Turns lock to lock 4¼.

Transmission
Rolls-Royce automatic gearbox and fluid coupling with selector mounted on the right of the steering column. Four forward speeds and reverse. Ratios: Top 1:1, Third 1.45:1, Second 2.63:1, First 3.82:1, Reverse 4.3:1. Divided propeller shaft with Detroit type front universal joint, needle roller bearing Hardy-Spicer type rear universal joint and flexibly mounted centre bearing. Rear axle: semi-floating type with hypoid bevel gears. Ratio, 2.92:1. S2 from chassis BC100BY onwards and S3: 3.08:1.

Brakes
Hydraulic front, hydraulic and mechanical rear, drum brakes. Operation by means of friction disc servo on the offside of the gearbox, which applies the brakes through two master cylinders and dual hydraulic circuits and assists the mechanical application of the rear brakes. Handbrake on rear wheels by pull-and-twist handle under facia through a cable and mechanical linkage. Cast iron drums. S2 and early S3: four-shoe front brakes. S3 from chassis BC166LXA: two-shoe front brakes.

Exhaust system
Single system with three expansion boxes, each tuned to absorb a different range of frequencies.

Lubrication system
Long-life grease lubrication by nipples at 21 points.

Fuel system
Rear mounted petrol tank, capacity 18 gallons (21.6 US gallons, 81.8 litres.) Twin SU electric fuel pump mounted in the frame.

Electrical system
12 volt negative earth system. Lucas special equipment dynamo and starter motor with pre-engagement pinion. Lucas built-in headlamps (S3: twin headlamps). Twin Lucas fog-lamps. Medium wave/Long wave or Medium wave/Short wave Radiomobile radio with push-button tuning and three speakers. An electrically operated wing-mounted aerial was available at extra cost. Direction indicators built into fog-lamps (S2 with Park Ward coachwork and S3: in noses of front wings combined with sidelamps), operated by switch mounted on left of steering column, which doubled as a headlamp flasher on S2 from chassis BC70CZ and S3 (except cars for North America). Electrically operated windscreen washer. Triplex heated rear window. Refrigerated air conditioning and electric windows available at extra cost.

Road wheels and tyres
15in steel disc wheels on five studs, carrying 8.00x15 tyres.

COACHWORK

All S2 and S3 Continental cars were coachbuilt by the following coachbuilders:

Continental S2		*Continental S3*	
Hooper	1	H. J. Mulliner	98*
H. J. Mulliner	222*	Park Ward	192*
Park Ward	125*	James Young	20
James Young	40	Graber	1
Total	388	Total	311

*H. J. Mulliner, Park Ward Ltd was formed in 1961 and some of these bodies were, strictly speaking, built by that firm. However, these figures are for the two constituent company's designs.

PERFORMANCE DATA

The following results were obtained by *The Autocar* when road testing Bentley S2 Continental (BC28AR) in December 1960. For comparison purposes figures obtained by the same journal for the S2 and S3 standard saloons (actually Rolls-Royce Silver Clouds II & III) are also given.

Acceleration through gears (seconds)	*S2*	*S2 Continental*	*S3*
0-30mph	3.4	4.0	3.5
0-60mph	10.9	12.1	10.8
0-100mph	40.1	37.1	34.2
Best maximum speed (mph):	113.9	114.5	117.0
Petrol consumption (mpg):	12.0	13.1	12.3

CHASSIS AND ENGINE NUMBERS

Bentley Continental S2

Chassis and engines are numbered consecutively, omitting 13.

Series	*Chassis numbers*	*Engine numbers*
A	BC1AR to BC151AR	A1BC to A150BC
B	BC1BY to BC101BY	B1BC to B100BC
C	BC1CZ to BC139CZ	C1BC to C138BC

Total: 388 cars

Bentley Continental S3

All chassis series start with 2 and use even numbers only. Engines are numbered consecutively.

Series	*Chassis numbers*	*Engine numbers*
A	BC2XA to BC174XA	1ABC to 87ABC
B	BC2XB to BC100XB	1BBC to 50BBC
C	BC2XC to BC202XC	1CBC to 101CBC
D	BC2XD to BC28XD	1DBC to 14DBC
E	BC2XE to BC120XE*	1EBC to 60EBC*

Total: 311 cars

*Omitting chassis BC56XE and engine 28EBC (car completed and delivered as Rolls-Royce Silver Cloud III chassis LCSC83C).

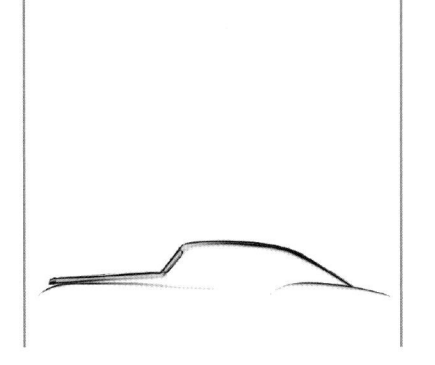

5. BENTLEY CONTINENTAL DESIGNERS & COACHBUILDERS

There have always been – and long may there continue to be – those who crave and are prepared to pay for a motor car with individuality. Even when standardised bodies became firmly established there were many who would have none of it; these were the discerning people who, in the 1950s and early '60s, purchased coachbuilt cars like the Bentley Continentals. Bentley customers continued to select their motor car coachwork from designs offered by coachbuilders, sometimes ordering significant changes to otherwise 'standard' designs, and the various coachbuilding companies that offered magnificent creations on Bentley Continental chassis are worthy of closer examination.

Before the war coachbuilders built bodies on chassis for which (at least, in the case of Rolls-Royce and Bentley), there was no standard factory alternative. In the post-war period, with the advent of the standard steel saloon,

Clay, or wax, modelling came into use at H. J. Mulliner in the 1950s. This is a quarter-scale model of the famous 'fastback' styling, for want of a better term, for the S1 Continental, design number 7400. Note that there are no rear lamps in evidence, probably because a design had not yet been decided, and the absence of boot-lid hardware perhaps indicates that the lid was intended to be released remotely from inside the car.

H. J. Mulliner & Co. Ltd Bedford Park Works circa 1960 with H. J. Mulliner two-door and 'Flying Spur' S2 Continental saloons at various stages of construction. Some (left and centre) have been mounted on their chassis while others (right) are being constructed on subframes for mounting on the actual chassis later. A newly arrived chassis may be glimpsed at the far left of the picture.

this situation changed. The surviving coachbuilders now had a new objective: to offer 'something different' which distinguished the coachbuilt car from the standard factory offering. This was achieved with varying degrees of success and, increasingly, the trend was to offer standardised designs, with the customer choosing the paint and upholstery colours and, perhaps, some minor interior changes. This did not entirely preclude one-off bodies, but significant departures from standard designs became increasingly rare as the 1950s progressed.

Post-war coachwork was, at first, built by methods that remained largely unchanged from before the war. Ironically though, in the 1950s when the coachbuilding trade was in decline, construction methods and materials used improved enormously. Most coachbuilders were using less wood and more metal in the body framework, with the result that bodies were stronger and potentially longer-lasting.

Since well before World War II, most of the coachwork offered by the larger coachbuilding houses had been built in batches to standardised designs, rather than on an exclusive 'one-off' basis. However, this is not to say that one-offs were not built, and, in any case, a customer's requirement for a two-door saloon or drophead coupé, for example, could only be met by specialist coachbuilders.

The position of the Bentley radiator shell and height and width of the scuttle were fixed, so limiting the coachbuilder's scope to depart from the general outline intended by Rolls-Royce Ltd. It was also a condition of supply of the chassis that the eventual body design should meet Company approval, and the work of the British coachbuilders and, indeed, that of most of the foreign ones, was tasteful and elegant.

The leisurely, unhurried methods employed by even the most progressive and innovative coachbuilders meant that there could be a delay of up to many months between receipt of the chassis by the coachbuilder and delivery of the completed car to the customer. Given the continuous nature of chassis development, including the introduction of major changes such as automatic gearbox, power-assisted steering, and the like, coachbuilt cars, when delivered, often had mechanical specifications that had been overtaken by improvements, or had even been superseded by an entirely new model. This caused problems for the coachbuilders and, in at least one instance, for Rolls-Royce Ltd, when power-assisted steering was first offered as an option in 1956 and a considerable number of S Type Continental customers opted for the new feature when earlier specification chassis had already been with the coachbuilders for some weeks. Such problems were at least minimised by building coachwork on a dummy chassis and ordering the actual chassis only when the structurally complete body was ready.

The vast majority of Bentley Continentals were bodied by one of three major surviving post-war coachbuilders. H. J. Mulliner & Co. Ltd and Park Ward & Co. Ltd were located within a short distance of each other in west

Cars at a later stage of construction at H. J. Mulliner, with a completed S2 Continental in the foreground with trade plate attached ready for road testing. Most of the cars here are Bentley Continentals, though there is a Rolls-Royce Silver Cloud drophead coupé on the right and, intriguingly, the one-off Hooper Phantom V (5AS19) on the left.

London, whilst James Young Ltd, which built far fewer bodies than either of the above two concerns, was in south-east London. Hooper & Co., also in west London, only built a very small number of Bentley Continental bodies in the late 1950s. Freestone & Webb ceased coachbuilding in 1958 without ever building a Bentley Continental body, so that firm need not concern us.

H. J. Mulliner & Co. Ltd Bedford Park Works, Bath Road, Chiswick, London W4

The Mulliner family coachbuilding business was founded in Northampton in 1760. The firm of H. J. Mulliner & Co. dates from 1900, when Henry Jervis Mulliner purchased the coachbuilding business, Mulliner London Ltd, from his cousins Arthur Mulliner of Northampton and A. G. Mulliner of Liverpool, though the H. J. Mulliner letterhead claimed 1897. H. J. Mulliner was born in 1870 and was apprenticed at his father's Liverpool coachbuilding factory from 1888 to 1891, after which he spent two years in Paris studying the application of coachbuilding to the then new motor car, his chief interest.

The new coachbuilding firm established a close association with Rolls-Royce Ltd from early in the Company's history. H. J. Mulliner and C. S. Rolls were close friends and business associates, and part of H. J. Mulliner's Brook Street premises was leased to C. S. Rolls & Co. Mr Mulliner was co-founder of the Automobile Club of Great Britain and Ireland (later the Royal Automobile Club). Claude Johnson, a major driving force behind Rolls-Royce Ltd and the Company's General Manager, was the Club's first Secretary.

H. J. Mulliner's Brook Street business premises were quite close to the famous Rolls-Royce Ltd offices and showrooms in Conduit Street, Mayfair (alas, now vacated by the Company after more than 90 years). Mulliner later acquired larger premises in Grafton Street, Mayfair and in 1906 a factory was established in Bedford Park, Chiswick – London's first 'garden suburb.' The office building in Bath Road was, like many of the houses hereabouts, the work of celebrated architect R. Norman Shaw, and was built in 1880 in Tudor style. The factory was behind the offices, in Flanders Road.

In 1908, after only eight years in business, H. J. Mulliner sold his business to the old coachbuilding firm of John Croall and Sons Ltd of Edinburgh. Though some bodies were transported to John Croall for painting, trimming and finishing, H. J. Mulliner & Co. continued to operate independently at Chiswick, with Croall retaining a financial interest until the 1959 purchase of Mulliner by Rolls-Royce Ltd.

Like most coachbuilders, during World War II Mulliner was engaged in war related work, which included the manufacture of aircraft components such as engine cowls for Mosquitos. Meanwhile, the firm's handsome coachwork awaited its chance to re-emerge when Rolls-Royce and Bentley motor car production resumed, and additional factory space was acquired after the war at 212 New King's Road, Fulham.

Like many commodities in the immediate post-war period, seasoned hardwood was in short supply. This led to the traditional timber body framework being replaced by 'composite' construction, with extensive use of metal in the framework. In 1950, Managing Director Arthur Johnstone and Technical Director Stanley Watts visited Italy to study the coachbuilding trade's use of tubular steel body framework. From this, H. J. Mulliner & Co. developed their all-metal 'Lightweight' mode of construction, with extensive use of light alloy ('Reynolds Metal') extrusions for the framework, but still using aluminium for the panels.

The best known early application of this construction method was the Bentley (R Type) Continental, structural coachwork design and final styling details for which were developed by Stanley Watts and George Moseley. As Mulliner's Technical Director, Watts was responsible for the distinctive look of H. J. Mulliner coachwork. Moseley had been recruited from Harold Radford Ltd specifically to work on the Bentley Continental. H. G. R. (Herbert) Nye, who had worked for two years under Osmond Rivers at Hooper just after the war, was draughtsman, styling designer and technical representative. He joined H. J. Mulliner & Co. at the end of 1947.

Mulliner dominated coachwork production for Bentley Continentals and, in 1957, actually persuaded Rolls-Royce to allow four-door coachwork (something the Company had always resisted) on the Continental chassis. Thus, the very beautiful – and, today, highly sought-after – 'Flying Spur' saloon was born and Mulliner somehow cleverly contrived to build these four-door cars with absolutely no weight penalty compared to their two-door counterparts. The Flying Spur was styled by George Moseley, who had taken over as Chief Designer from Stanley Watts who died in 1956.

The end for H. J. Mulliner & Co. – at least as a separate and independent concern – came in 1959 when the firm was acquired by Rolls-Royce Ltd. By that time, Park Ward had been part of the Rolls-Royce empire for twenty years and the two coachbuilders were merged into the combined firm of H. J. Mulliner, Park Ward Ltd soon after, though the creations of the two coachbuilders continued to be built in separate works under their individual names until 1962. Operations were then concentrated on the Park Ward works in Willesden, though H. J. Mulliner step-sill plates continued to appear on cars of their design for a further year or so.

Henry Jervis Mulliner, having retired after he sold his company to John Croall in 1908, enjoyed an amazingly long retirement and died on October 8th

Below & overleaf: Motor Car Division Managing Director, 'Doc' Llewellyn Smith (LS), and Chief Stylist, John Blatchley (JPB), 'discovered' Vilhelm Koren after visiting the Turin Motor Show and admiring an Alfa-Romeo coupé he had designed. Koren was persuaded to go to Crewe to work in JPB's department, specifically to style the forthcoming S2 Continental. These pictures, taken in July 1958, show the quarter-scale clay model of Koren's design for a two-door saloon. Note the differing treatment of the front and rear lamps on the left and right sides.

1967, aged 97. He was the last surviving founder member of the Automobile Club of Great Britain and Ireland (later the RAC). He must have been very proud of the elegant and superbly built coachwork which bore his name.

Although the famous old coachbuilding name of H. J. Mulliner & Co. survived into the 1990s in the Mulliner Park Ward Division of Rolls-Royce Ltd, latterly incorporated into the Crewe factory complex, from 1996 Rolls-Royce began a process of separating the two names, which were again used individually for a time, with Mulliner being the 'coachbuilder' for Bentley cars.

Park Ward & Co. Ltd 473 High Road, Willesden, London NW10

The coachbuilding house of Park Ward was formed after W. M. Park and C. W. Ward met while employed by Sizaire Berwick. Park had been apprenticed to A. C. Penman and Ward to the South London Gas Company. Park Ward & Co. was formed in 1919 and a factory established in High Road, Willesden, to build high-class coachwork on various makes of chassis such as Daimler, Mors, Lanchester and Sunbeam. The Company first occupied a small smith's shop then, as business grew, took over the stables of the London General Omnibus Company, which had been rendered redundant by the advent of the motor bus. It was from this address that Park Ward – and, from 1962, the combined firm of H. J. Mulliner, Park Ward – built their fine coachwork.

Park Ward built the firm's first bodies for Rolls-Royce cars within a year of the firm being founded, albeit on second-hand chassis. In an innovative move, former World War I staff cars and limousines were purchased from the government and the old bodies were removed. The chassis were returned to Rolls-Royce Ltd in Derby for reconditioning and modifications to the steering column rake. Park Ward then fitted new open tourer bodies. The first order on a new Rolls-Royce chassis was in 1921 and, by the end of the 1920s, some ninety per cent of its work was on Rolls-Royce chassis.

In the early 1930s, Rolls-Royce Ltd entrusted Park Ward with research and development work for its new 3½-litre Bentley project and, in 1933, acquired a substantial financial interest in the coachbuilder. The increased resources available to Park Ward helped the firm develop advanced engineering techniques in metalworking, resulting in Patent No. 470698 being obtained in 1935 to cover the all-steel body framework. This not only made for great strength, rigidity and immunity from dry-rot, it also helped Park Ward to produce bodies of standardised designs in comparatively large numbers. A

S3 Continental Park Ward drophead coupé, design number 2006, in the early stages of construction at H. J. Mulliner, Park Ward's Willesden works, circa 1963. Traditional coachbuilding was beginning to give way to more sophisticated body engineering, though the degree to which highly skilled handwork was called upon remained undiminished. The extremely strong steel structure made for greater rigidity than one normally expects from a separate chassis drophead coupé, but the box sections, particularly around the boot area, ultimately proved somewhat rust-prone, causing a headache for many a restorer! Note the Rolls-Royce Phantom V limousine at body frame stage in the background.

When Koren's Bentley Continental styling was adapted to S3 guise, a serious difficulty arose in incorporating the paired headlamps into the design, which did not lend itself to horizontal pairs at the front of the 'catwalk' between the bonnet and wings, as on the other body styles. Whilst the headlamps could have been arranged in vertical pairs, like those of the Park Ward-bodied Alvis, that possibility was not pursued. The scheme eventually settled on was to arrange the headlamps in sloping pairs, with the outer lamps in the extremities of the wings. After the first ten cars the headlamps were less deeply recessed than on this front end mock-up, pictured in H. J. Mulliner, Park Ward's experimental area at Willesden.

This page & opposite: A two-door saloon, design number 2035, at a similar stage of construction.

standard saloon body was offered on the 3½-litre and later 4¼-litre Bentleys. In the case of the Bentley Mk V, with the added stresses of independent front suspension, the all-steel frame construction really came into its own.

In 1939, when the Bentley Mk V was about to replace the 4¼-litre, Rolls-Royce Ltd purchased the remaining equity in Park Ward & Co., which then became a wholly-owned subsidiary. However, the outbreak of war curtailed, for the time being at least, any plans Rolls-Royce may have had for the newly-acquired coachbuilding subsidiary. In any case, being essentially a small-scale producer of coachbuilt bodies, Park Ward could never have built bodies in the numbers then being envisaged. Nevertheless, the patent steel-framed body meant valuable economies of scale, increased strength and durability, as well as weight-savings.

The war years saw Park Ward engaged in a new kind of activity when skills acquired in coachbuilding were directed to new channels. Precision engineering and a high standard of quality control were at a premium throughout the country, and the Ministry of Aircraft Production sought out those companies already geared to meet the most exacting technical specifications. Aircraft components of many kinds were manufactured, including bomb doors and cowlings for the de Havilland Mosquito, and cowlings for Hurricane and Spitfire fighters and Lancaster bombers. Engine mountings and air intakes were supplied to all major British aircraft builders.

After the war, standard steel saloon bodies, supplied by the Pressed Steel Company, severely limited the roles of Park Ward and other specialist coachbuilders. The Bentley Continental chassis, however, was never fitted with standard steel coachwork and, from 1954, two-door saloon and drophead coupé bodies for Bentley Continental chassis were increasingly important to Park Ward.

Until 1952, Park Ward stylists and designers were responsible for their own designs, both exterior and interior. In that year, Charlie Ward Snr and Jack Scott, 'Doc' Llewellyn Smith and John Blatchley of the parent Company, had tried, at several meetings, to address what were perceived as certain failings of Park Ward styling. The men compared Park Ward and H. J. Mulliner coachwork side-by-side, inside and out, with Blatchley pointing out the shortcomings of Park Ward styling to a none-too-pleased Ward! They were also anxious to ensure that future Park Ward coachwork should share a certain 'family resemblance' with the Crewe standard saloons, rather than developing in a different direction, though it must be said that this ideal was not always possible.

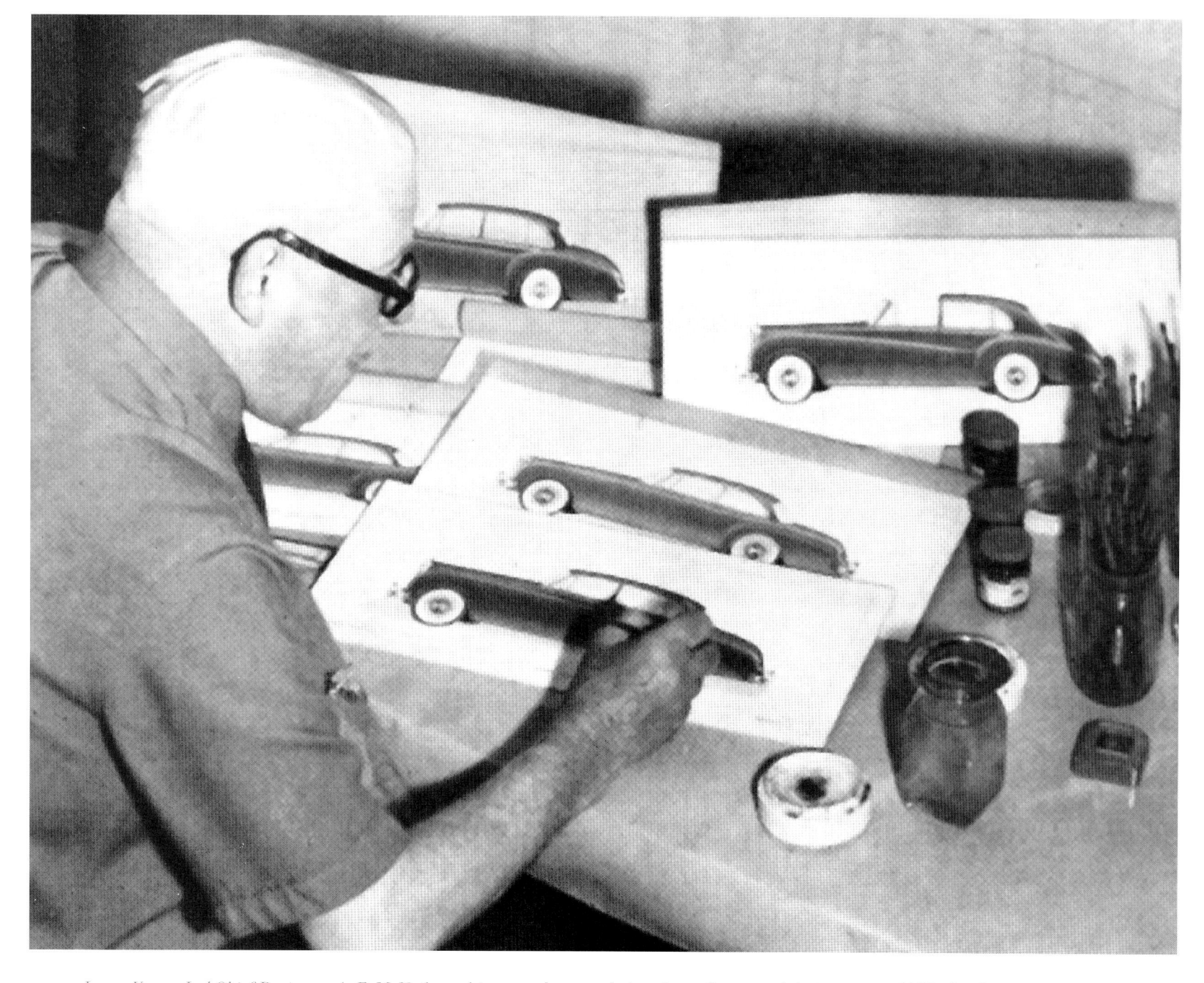

James Young Ltd Chief Designer, A. F. McNeil, working on colour wash drawings of proposed designs, circa 1958, for the then forthcoming Silver Cloud II and Bentley Continental S2 range.

A decision was reached that the Crewe Styling Office take over the external styling of the Park Ward coachbuilt bodies, and this became the responsibility of John Blatchley. Park Ward's High Road, Willesden, styling office under its Senior Stylist, Peter Wharton, retained control over interior design, whilst structural design and detailing continued to be carried out by Park Ward's design and drawing office.

The first Park Ward designs styled by John Blatchley under this policy were the rare two-door saloon and drophead coupé for the Bentley Continental (R Type) chassis. These were later successfully adapted for the S Type Continental, which was three inches longer in the wheelbase than the original Continental chassis.

In 1959, H. J. Mulliner & Co. joined Park Ward under the umbrella of Rolls-Royce Ltd and, in 1961, the Park Ward factory was reorganised to accommodate H. J. Mulliner coachwork production. It is said that, for many years after this amalgamation, there existed considerable resentment about the influx of 'Mulliner men,' some of whom were placed at foreman level, displacing Park Ward men. Despite the difficulties, however, by 1962 the two firms were fully integrated as H. J. Mulliner, Park Ward Ltd.

Park Ward's expertise in all-steel coachwork construction and aircraft construction techniques stood the new Company in good stead when Rolls-Royce adopted monocoque (chassisless) construction for the Bentley T Series (and Rolls-Royce Silver Shadow) range in 1965.

Incredibly, the post-war Park Ward drawings, which had been stored above the Joiners' Shop at High Road, Willesden, were deemed a fire hazard and incinerated at Hythe Road as recently as 1980.

James Young Ltd 37 London Road, Bromley, Kent

James Young Ltd was the last independent coachbuilding firm to build bodies on Rolls-Royce and Bentley chassis, as the other two surviving companies (Park Ward and H. J. Mulliner) had already been acquired by Rolls-Royce Ltd.

James Young was established in coachbuilding in 1863 when Mr Young took over the London Road, Bromley coachbuilder, J. K. Hunter. The new Company quickly became famous for the lightweight Bromley Brougham – a speciality product – and also for its high quality landaus, wagonettes, double Victorias, dog-cart phaetons, panel carts, governess carts and even a horse-drawn omnibus.

Around the turn of the century, all forward-looking coachbuilders, including James Young, looked to the new and exciting field of motor car body building. Within a few years, the skill and craftsmanship of these firms had produced motor car coachwork of unmatched style and beauty. James Young's first motor car body, on a 1908 Wolseley chassis, was built for the then MP for Bromley, Mr W. Smithers. Further orders quickly followed and a wide variety of chassis types passed through the works in those early days, including marques such as Alfa-Romeo, Austro Daimler, Bugatti, Hispano-Suiza, Isotta Fraschini, Lanchester, Mercedes and, of course, the earliest examples of Rolls-Royce (and later Bentley) which foreshadowed the magnificent creations produced when coachbuilding ceased in 1968.

James Young Ltd became a member of the Society of British Motor Manufacturers in 1922 and began exhibiting its products at the annual Motor Show in 1925. In 1937, the firm was acquired by Jack Barclay Ltd and the brilliant A. F. McNeil was tempted away from Gurney Nutting (later also to be acquired by Jack Barclay Ltd) to become Chief Designer at James Young.

Over the years, James Young Ltd was responsible for innovations that later became integral features of quantity-produced cars. As long ago as 1925, at its first official appearance at a London Motor Show, a James Young-bodied car featured a new method of roof construction which, in order to reduce drumming, employed light wire in place of wood or metal. The other many distinctive features of design initiated and developed at Bromley have included the All weather head, the Beatonson Rol Visor and the abortive Parallel Action Door.

Like other coachbuilders, during both world wars, James Young Ltd was called upon to play its part in the national effort. In World War I, the Company built lorry, armoured car and ambulance bodies on Darracq and Hudson chassis. When war came again in 1939, the craftsmen used their skills to build items of war material such as 45 gallon jettison tanks for Spitfires, shells, inflatable rafts, ammunition boxes and feed necks for Hurricane fighters, Air Ministry tarpaulins, gun covers and mobile canteens. In the 1941 blitz on London, the works was completely burnt out and a Bentley Mk V and all records were lost. The premises were rebuilt, only to be damaged again by a V1 flying bomb. Nevertheless, work continued until the end of the war, when production of coachwork on Rolls-Royce and Bentley chassis was immediately resumed.

By the early 1960s, James Young coachwork was being built at the rate of fifty to sixty bodies per year, some sixty per cent of which went for export. By that time, the only Bentley chassis regularly fitted with the firm's coachwork was the S3 Continental. A. F. McNeil was still Chief Designer and it is with him that the credit for these exceptionally beautiful and graceful designs belongs. He died in November 1965. His Bentley Continental coachwork designs outlived him in application for only a few months, the last S3 Continentals being delivered early in 1966. Towards the end of 1967, the Company was winding down its coachbuilding activities following the advent of the chassisless Silver Shadow and Bentley T Series. The standard bodies adapted by James Young into two-door saloons could not compete with the much shapelier H. J. Mulliner, Park Ward version, which had behind it the full resources of Rolls-Royce Ltd.

Hooper & Co. (Coachbuilders) Ltd, Western Avenue, Park Royal, London W3

The history of Hooper & Co. (Coachbuilders) Ltd can be traced to 1807, when the coachbuilding firm of J. & G. Adams was formed.

In 1830, George Hooper became a partner in the firm, which then became known as Adams & Hooper, with premises at 28, Haymarket, London. In 1846, following a long illness, George Adams withdrew from the business and, following his subsequent death, the firm became known as Hooper & Co. and additional premises were established at 4 & 5, Little Windmill Street. In 1896, the name Hooper & Co. (Coachbuilders) Ltd was registered and new showrooms established the following year at 54, St. James's Street, London SW1, together with a factory at 75, Kings Road, Chelsea.

Also in 1830 the firm was awarded its first Royal Warrant of Appointment as coachbuilder to King William IV. Royal Warrants were granted to Hooper continuously throughout the following 130 years, spanning seven reigns.

George Northgate Hooper, son of the original George Hooper, joined the business in the 1840s.

With the advent of the motor car, Hooper & Co., like other coachbuilders, turned their attention to building custom bodies for automobiles, mainly on British-made chassis and principally for Daimler and Rolls-Royce. One of the first motor car bodies built by Hooper was for HRH The Prince of Wales, in 1903, followed soon after by another for the same royal customer when he was HM King Edward VII. Both were on Daimler chassis, the marque then most favoured by royalty.

In 1933, a modern new factory was built in the popular art deco style in Western Avenue, Acton, although the old factory in Chelsea was kept until 1947. The few Bentley Continental bodies by Hooper were built at Western Avenue.

During World War II, Hooper, like other coachbuilders, was engaged in aero and other war related work. The firm was acquired by Daimler in 1940 which, in turn, was acquired at the end of the war by the Birmingham Small Arms Company (BSA).

In the post-war period, Hooper's Chief Draughtsman and Designer was the talented and innovative Osmond Rivers, who joined the firm in 1911, ultimately becoming Managing Director as well as Chief Designer. He died in 1982, at the age of 87.

By late 1950, Hooper coachbuilding work was exclusively on Rolls-Royce and Bentley chassis. In 1958, the Hooper directors were made aware of Rolls-Royce Ltd plans for a monocoque (chassisless) car and a decision to discontinue coachbuilding was reached. The famous showroom in St. James's Street closed its doors on September 30th that year.

Construction of motor car bodies came to an end in October 1959 with the completion of body number 10294, the only Bentley S2 to be bodied by the firm, on the first S2 Continental chassis, BC1AR. This, and two Rolls-Royce cars, were exhibited on Stand 163 (the last Hooper motor show stand) at the 1959 Earls Court Motor Show. Though its final body was a Bentley Continental, in fact, Hooper & Co. bodied only a handful of Continental chassis.

On New Year's Eve, 1959, Hooper & Co. (Coachbuilders) Ltd closed and a new company, Hooper Motor Services Ltd, was formed to look after the maintenance and coachwork repair requirements of owners of cars with Hooper coachwork.

This 1966 photograph was taken in the Park Ward experimental department at Willesden. It shows the prototype monocoque drophead coupé, design number 3020, under construction. This was a Rolls-Royce Silver Shadow, but the Bentley equivalent eventually became, in 1984, the Bentley Continental. In the background, a Silver Shadow saloon is being lengthened for HRH Princess Margaret.

The Corniche (and Continental) two-door cars were built by Mulliner Park Ward on special underframes supplied by Pressed Steel Fisher. This is a convertible underframe; that for the two-door saloon, which was built until the end of 1980, was similar except for the roof structure which was added prior to panelling (inset).

H. J. Mulliner, Park Ward Ltd, 473, High Road, Willesden, London NW10 (until 1981) then Hythe Road, Scrubs Lane, Willesden, London NW10

After H. J. Mulliner Ltd joined Park Ward in the Rolls-Royce fold in 1959, the two constituent companies continued to operate separately for a while. In 1961, in order to streamline coachbuilding and other resources within the Company, it was decided the two would merged. A new company, H. J. Mulliner, Park Ward Ltd, was formed and H. J. Mulliner vacated the Chiswick factory soon after. The Park Ward factory at Willesden was reorganised to accommodate Mulliner coachwork production. For the time being, Mulliner's Bedford Park site remained open as a Repair and Service Depot.

The Senior Stylist at H. J. Mulliner, Park Ward was Peter J. Wharton (PJW), who had started in Park Ward's drawing office in 1934. However, in practice, the responsibility for H. J. Mulliner, Park Ward external styling fell to John P. Blatchley (JPB), Chief Styling Engineer at Rolls-Royce Ltd, Crewe.

For a few months after the 1965 introduction of the chassisless

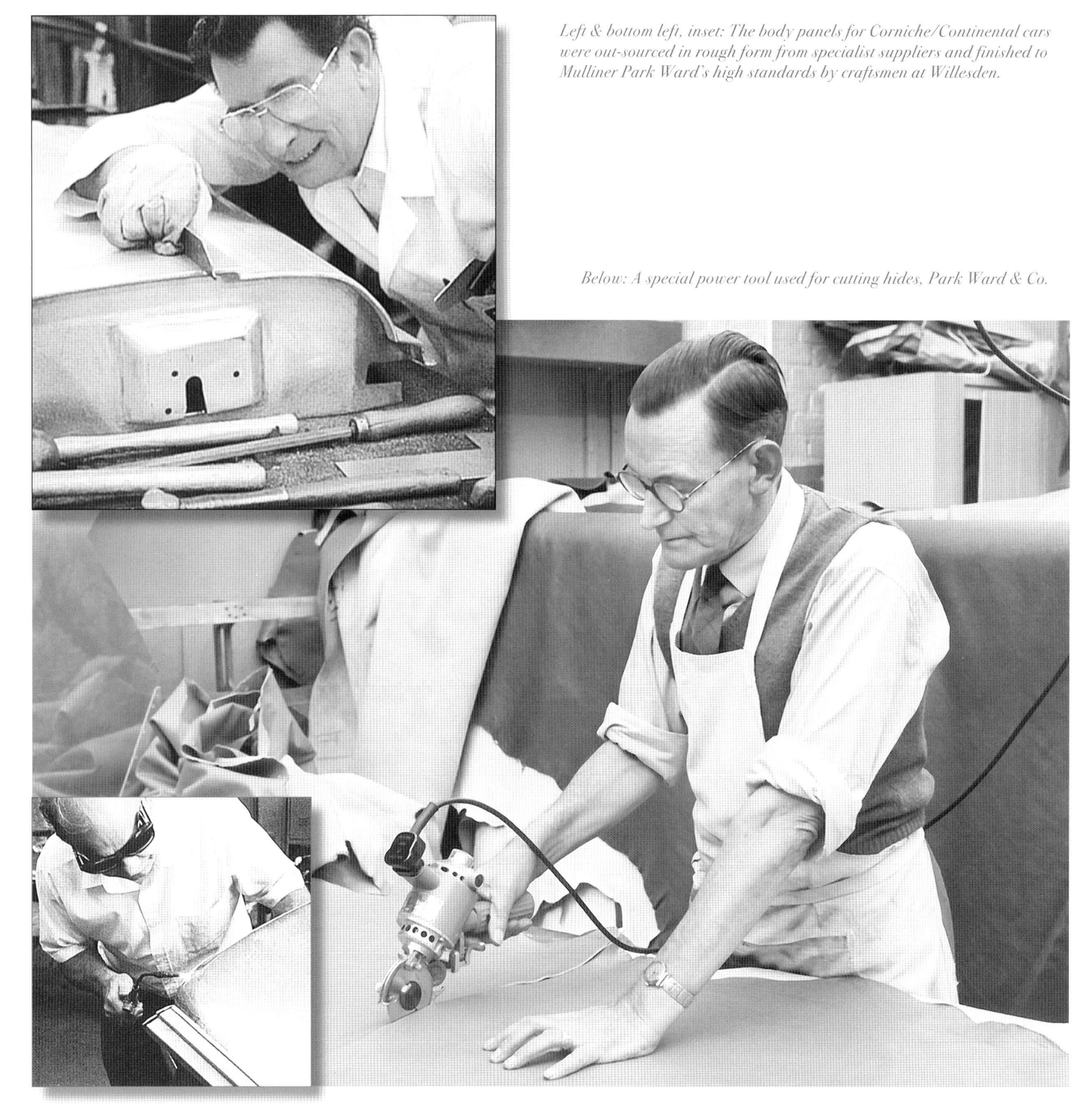

Left & bottom left, inset: The body panels for Corniche/Continental cars were out-sourced in rough form from specialist suppliers and finished to Mulliner Park Ward's high standards by craftsmen at Willesden.

Below: A special power tool used for cutting hides, Park Ward & Co.

A wood polisher examining his work, H. J. Mulliner, Park Ward Ltd.

Rolls-Royce Silver Shadow and Bentley T Series, H.J. Mulliner, Park Ward continued to build coachwork on the tail-end production of Bentley S3 Continental chassis. The advent of the monocoque cars meant that H. J. Mulliner, Park Ward needed to modify its skills, which, in effect, became body engineering rather than coachbuilding in the traditional sense, though strong elements of hand work and craftsmanship remained.

In 1981, following an appraisal of all the London manufacturing and servicing operations, the old Park Ward factory in High Road, Willesden, was closed and what had, by then, become the Mulliner Park Ward Division, moved into premises occupied by Servicing and Repairs in Hythe Road, Willesden, where suitable empty sites were available.

Construction of bodies was undertaken on a basic 'body-in-white' (complete but unpainted body shell) line, which necessitated hoisting the bodies from each stage of construction to the next. In the early 1970s, with the Rolls-Royce Camargue on the horizon, it was decided to adopt a more modern approach to body production, using build stations through which the bodies passed on trolleys and were located by hydraulic clamps. This new line was placed in the adjacent former Triplex building and, being oval in shape, was known as 'the carousel.' It took some time to bring the carousel into full production and, in the meantime, body build continued at the main site. In its straightened form, this line continued to produce Rolls-Royce Corniche IV and Bentley Continental bodies-in-white until 1992, after which the operation

John Polwhele Blatchley (JPB), Chief Styling Engineer, Rolls-Royce Ltd. Blatchley joined Rolls-Royce during World War II from Gurney Nutting, where he had been Chief Designer from 1937 until the outbreak of war stopped coachwork production. His aero engine cowling designs were his contribution to the war effort. After the war he went to work for Ivan Evernden in the Experimental Department at Belper, where he added flare and styling finesse to the Bentley Mk VI standard steel saloon then being made ready for production. He was responsible for all the standard saloon body styling from then, up to and including the Silver Shadow/Bentley T Series, as well as all Park Ward styling from 1952. He retired on March 21st 1969.

A craftsman working on Corniche front seat squabs in the trim shop at Willesden.

was transferred to Crewe. The original pits, which occupied the whole of one wing, were filled in to make way for Camargue finishing operations.

These arrangements lasted only a short time, until late 1982, when a dramatic slump in sales (especially in the normally strong Corniche market of North America) prompted a decision to relocate the Service Centre and consolidate all body production on the old Service Centre site. A new site for the servicing operations, comprising three industrial units, was found at School Road, North Acton. This was adapted as necessary, and the equipment transferred from Hythe Road in April 1983.

Various changes were made to the old Hythe Road site to accommodate all aspects of Corniche and Bentley Continental production. The School of Instruction, for so long a London institution, was transferred to Crewe and its place taken by the Car Finishing Centre (CFC). In turn, the CFC and Spares building became the new paint shop, opened in 1990.

The dramatic downturn in sales in 1991 led to a severe curtailing of Mulliner Park Ward's activities and closure of the Mulliner Park Ward main site was announced on May 15th 1991. By early 1992, the 540 strong workforce had been reduced to fewer than 50, building Rolls-Royce Corniche and Bentley Continental bodies-in-white. All painting, interior trimming, convertible hood construction and finishing operations were transferred to Crewe and undertaken in designated Mulliner Park Ward areas there. True to the Rolls-Royce tradition of using code-names, this operation was called 'Project Alexandra.' Some forty Mulliner Park Ward craftsmen spent several months at Crewe assisting the workforce there in the ways of London finishing operations. Most were subsequently made redundant.

For a short time, in its greatly reduced role, the Hythe Road site was dubbed 'H. J. Mulliner Coachworks.' By mid-1993, the workforce had been reduced to just 40 craftsmen and staff, and, by the following year, the site was empty and for sale. Incredibly, it is now a used car lot.

J. P. Blatchley and the Crewe Styling Department

It is to John P. Blatchley (JPB) that we owe the styling of some of the most defining of all Rolls-Royce and Bentley body designs, but – contrary to widespread belief – not that of the original Bentley Continental.

A boyhood fascination with cars – and particularly their styling – developed into a firm ambition to become a motor car stylist. After failing his entrance exams to Jesus College, Cambridge, JPB attended the Chelsea School of Engineering in London and, later, the Regent Street Polytechnic.

However, it was not so much this formal training as his impressive portfolio of car drawings that prompted Gurney Nutting's Chief Designer, A. F. ('Mac') McNeil to offer JPB a position with that highly respected firm of coachbuilders. This was 1935, and the Chelsea firm of J. Gurney Nutting had already earned considerable renown for exceptionally stylish coachwork; in 1931, the firm had been entrusted with the task of building the streamlined bodywork for Sir Malcolm Campbell's Land Speed Record-breaking Bluebird. Members of the Royal Family were counted among Gurney Nutting's customers and, from the early 1930s, the firm held the Royal Warrant. This was fertile ground for John Blatchley to develop his natural talents.

'Mac' McNeil was a brilliant stylist who produced many superb designs for Gurney Nutting. He saw great potential in the young Blatchley, becoming his teacher, mentor and friend for many years. Blatchley worked on concept drawings which were shown to customers for approval before being passed to the works for construction. Within two years, McNeil had moved on to James Young Ltd and John Blatchley found himself, at the age of 23, Chief Designer at Gurney Nutting. It seems almost superfluous to add that, during this period, many superlatively elegant designs emerged from Gurney Nutting, which was a relatively small scale producer of truly bespoke coachwork.

World War II put a stop to this, as it did to all normal life in England's green and pleasant land. John Blatchley worked for the war effort at the Rolls-Royce Ltd Aero Design Headquarters at Hucknall in Nottinghamshire, where he designed aircraft engine cowlings. He yearned for the peacetime world of motor car body styling, and, whilst at Hucknall, heard rumours of a new, post-war Rolls-Royce and Bentley model range. When war finally ended, he stayed on with Rolls-Royce and, in 1946, moved to Clan Foundry at Belper, north of Derby, where the Experimental Department was.

His opinion was sought on the prototype that had, by then, reached the stage where Belper personnel considered it to be all but ready to pass over to the Pressed Steel Company of Oxford, for series production of the new standard steel saloon. Evernden had designed the new body with a 'play it safe' philosophy in mind, but Blatchley was bemused by what he saw as the prototype's lack of elegance and detail sophistication. However, he had arrived on the scene too late to change matters very much beyond adding a touch of Gurney Nutting finesse to some of the details, transforming the prototype into a more attractive design that, whilst scarcely beautiful, was at least acceptable to the Company's post-war clientele. Bill Allen (Aln), with whom John Blatchley worked under Ev, recalls that Blatchley even designed the chrome horn grilles behind which the horns of the early post-war cars were concealed under the wings. He also designed the entire interior of the standard steel saloon, ensuring that it was in every way the equal of the best coachbuilders' work.

In 1950, when work began on the 'Corniche II' (Bentley Continental) project, John Blatchley worked on some early styling suggestions, but in retirement disclaimed any credit for the design as it ultimately emerged. As we have read in earlier chapters, it was Ivan Evernden, inspired by the pre-war Embiricos Bentley, who conceived the Continental's styling, and worked with Stanley Watts and George Moseley of H. J. Mulliner Ltd on the final styling details.

In September 1951, the Styling Department was moved to Crewe and John Blatchley appointed to the newly created position of Chief Styling Engineer, taking the cypher 'JPB.' Soon after Park Ward coachwork styling was transferred from Willesden to Crewe in 1952, John Blatchley began work on the two-door saloon and drophead coupé for the Bentley Continental chassis. These designs were completed in time to appear on a small number of late R Type Continentals.

Before the end of 1951, work had begun on an entirely new standard saloon. A proposed Bentley VIII was stillborn, though a working prototype styled by JPB had been built and tested. Bentley IX, known by the code-name 'Siam,' was chosen to replace Bentley VII (now known as the R Type).

John Blatchley styled Siam superbly. Once the shape was decided, two prototype bodies were built in aluminium by Park Ward, working from the quarter-scale wax model which JPB had made, and the Styling Office drawings, and mounted on an Experimental chassis. It was an exceptionally beautiful design when viewed from absolutely any angle. Once the fine new chassis was ready for production, and JPB had attended to a few last-minute

'Project 90' was a concept car mock-up exhibited at the 1985 Geneva Motor Show, marking the start of the project which eventually produced the Bentley Continental R.

details, fine-tuning the body style to absolute perfection, Siam was passed to the Pressed Steel Co. for building of the bodies in steel with aluminium bonnet, doors and boot lid. It was announced, to considerable acclaim, in April 1955 as the Bentley S Type (and Rolls-Royce Silver Cloud). JPB's Park Ward R Type Continental designs were successfully adapted for the Continental version of the new chassis, which was three inches longer in the wheelbase than the R Type.

In the late 1950s, the Crewe styling team was joined by Vilhelm Koren (VKN), who worked with JPB to style the drophead coupé coachwork for the Bentley Continental S2. Koren also worked on other, secret body styles for various Experimental projects, none of which ever saw production. John Blatchley recalls that, when he retired in 1969, he tried to convince Koren that he was the right man to replace him as Chief Styling Engineer, and encouraged him to apply for the position. However, Koren was unwilling to sacrifice his London lifestyle for life in Crewe, and turned down this opportunity, opting instead for a modern furniture design teaching post at the Royal College of Art in London.

Before Siam was even launched, work had already begun on a new generation of monocoque (chassisless) cars, code-named 'Tibet' (Rolls-Royce) and 'Burma' (Bentley). It was intended that the Bentley would be a smaller car than the Rolls-Royce, but, as development work progressed, this idea was dropped and the two projects were merged to become SY – or the Rolls-Royce Silver Shadow and Bentley T Series, as they were ultimately called.

In order to smooth the transition between the look of these new cars and that of their predecessors, some styling changes were introduced on the Bentley S Type, and its Rolls-Royce stablemate, in October 1962. These included paired, sealed-beam headlamps, re-styled front wings with new combined sidelights/direction indicators mounted in the wing noses, Silver Shadow pattern bumper overriders (except for North America) and a 1½-inch lower grille shell. This was the Bentley S3 (and Rolls-Royce Silver Cloud III).

The SY styling brief included coachbuilt versions, to be built in two-door saloon and drophead coupé variants by the now combined London coachbuilding subsidiary H. J. Mulliner, Park Ward Ltd. These were the last cars to be styled under John Blatchley's influence and supervision.

Of JPB's leadership qualities, Bill Allen recalls: "I had only five bosses during my career of 49 years, and John was the best. He had that quality of leadership which tends to defy analysis; once I saw this described as `the art that conceals the art'. Whatever problems he had with those superior in rank to him were never allowed to disturb the even temperament and quiet confidence with which he dealt with us."

John Blatchley retired, at the age of 55, on March 21st 1969. The styling of Rolls-Royce and Bentley cars was moving in a direction that had diminished in appeal to him and he opted for early retirement. He was succeeded as Chief Stylist by Fritz Feller (FF), an Austrian-born engineer whose project at Rolls-Royce had been abandoned, rendering him redundant. Despite Feller's engineering, rather than styling background, he successfully applied for JPB's job and presided over the styling aspects of the SZ project, the new generation of Rolls-Royce and Bentley cars introduced in October 1980 as the Silver Spirit and Bentley Mulsanne.

Design and construction of Bentley Continental coachwork

Coachbuilt bodies began life as sketches, followed by more accurate working drawings, in the coachbuilder's drawing office. These drawings would be approved by Rolls-Royce Ltd at this stage and, in the case of non-standard designs, by the customer too. Often they were changed into water colour wash drawings, in order for a customer to approve the proposed body style and colour scheme. After comment and modification, fully detailed, large-scale drawings were prepared and, in many cases, full-size working drawings were hung on the workshop wall. From these the body was built.

In the Crewe Styling Department – where Park Ward coachwork was styled after 1952, as well as H. J. Mulliner, Park Ward coachwork after the two coachbuilders were combined – the wax or 'clay' model was used to create the essential three dimensional impression of how the car would look. The initial styling sketches were usually followed by one eighth-scale drawings, then the wax model was made. This was invariably quarter-scale, built up on a plywood armature, or 'coffin', as it was colloquially known at Crewe, shaped from the scale drawings, but a little undersize to accommodate the layer of modelling wax. The model supplemented, rather than replaced, drawings in the styling process. Sometimes the model was different side-to-side so that alternative styling features could be evaluated.

From the model, scale working drawings were produced. There was usually also a full-size model or mock-up, the main purpose of which was to test the interior layout and ensure that door apertures and the like were practicable in actual use. From here, the design normally progressed to actual working prototype cars. Then came tooling, production planning and, at last, actual production. Small wonder that this process invariably took at least two – and, in some cases, up to four – years.

From the drawings, the wooden jigs, or 'bucks,' used to form the wings, doors and other panels were constructed in the setting-out shop and body framing took shape. Although Park Ward had developed and patented all-steel body framing before the war, seasoned ash remained the preferred frame material of most coachbuilders in the early post-war period. Composite construction, in which steel and aluminium alloy frame components were used in conjunction with timber, later became the norm with most firms. Park Ward was an early user of all-metal body framework and, from 1950, H. J. Mulliner began using framework with no structural timber and extensive use of extrusions of light aluminium alloy. Hooper adopted all-metal construction in the same year, also using aluminium alloy framework and no steel. As well as improving strength and durability, this method of construction gave useful weight-savings; by the close of the 1950s, timber and composite body frames had passed into history.

The body panels were almost exclusively of aluminium sheet, shaped on the aforementioned wooden patterns in the case of the more complex parts such as wings, or on a wheeling machine in the case of more gently curved panels. Flatter panels were formed over the actual framework.

The chassis, which were transported from Crewe to the coachbuilder, came complete with engine compartment rear bulkhead and side panels, bonnet, radiator shell, bumpers, wheel discs, instruments, tools, all front, rear and interior lighting and steel pressings for the passenger compartment floors, boot platform and spare wheel compartment. The body was attached to the chassis by way of special rubber mountings.

In the case of S Series chassis (except when open coachwork was fitted), the body was mounted in accordance with a procedure evolved by Rolls-Royce Ltd With the body in position on Silentbloc bushes along the chassis side members, an air cylinder connected to each bracket 'floated' the body at a pressure of 50psi. This ensured that the weight was supported uniformly on the mountings before spacing washers were inserted and the mounting bolts tightened to a pre-determined torque.

After the body was mounted on the chassis, the doors and boot lid were hung with great care, and skilled, individual attention ensured even gaps and accurate fit. The doors were increasingly of the 'half-frame' variety on

This 1986 colour rendering by Chief Stylist Graham Hull was the turning point in the styling of the Continental R. The headlamp treatment eventually adopted was quite different, but essentially the styling had been decided. The interior design drawing (following page) shows that radical departures from traditional Bentley interior styling were under consideration.

bodies other than the largest seven-seater limousines. That is, the actual door structure extended to only just above the waist rail, with the door window frame brazed from slim, brass channel strip. Along with the waist mouldings, door handles, windscreen surrounds and the like, these components were plated with copper, then nickel, followed by a heavy deposit of chromium. Park Ward mainly used standard exterior and interior door handles, window winders, grab handles and other interior fittings, supplied by Crewe, but other coachbuilders used their own distinctive items. The identity of the coachbuilder of most post-war bodies could usually be readily determined by door handles alone.

Cabinet makers in the woodshop made and fitted all interior woodwork, including instrument panels, door cappings, picnic tables and rear 'companions,' where fitted. These were built up on a plywood base and veneered, usually with walnut, in either burr or flame pattern, but always carefully selected for their beautiful grain patterns and colouring. The veneers were 'book matched' either side of the centre line of each main panel, and sometimes the figuring was arranged to radiate in four directions from the centre of a panel, in each case creating a unique pattern. The main areas of veneer were usually edged with 'cross-banding' – a narrow fillet of straight-grained veneer with the grain at right angles to the edge of the panel. This was especially attractive when carried out by James Young Ltd, who used boldly striped 'zebranno' veneer for this purpose, although each coachbuilder had its own distinctive and readily recognizable style of interior woodwork. The natural beauty of the wood was highlighted by lacquering and polishing to a finish that looked like glass and was nearly as hard.

In the paintshop, at least twenty coats of primer, filler, stopper, gunglaze undercoat and cellulose colour were applied by spray-gun and rubbed down by hand between each coat. Superlative finishes were achieved, and fine-lining was applied by hand to the waist rail and wheel discs using a long-haired, sharply pointed artist's brush called a fitch, a steady hand and lots of skill.

In the finishing shop the car was glazed and all exterior lights, fittings and chrome mouldings attached. Highly skilled interior trimmers made seat cushions and backrests, armrests and door trim panels, and fitted the headlining after sound and heat insulation had been fixed in place. Carpets were fitted over a felt underlay. High quality, top grain hide was the usual upholstery material, with West of England cloth for the headlining.

The completed Bentley Continental was handed over to Rolls-Royce Ltd inspectors, who subjected it to a critical and searching road test. The car was returned to the coachbuilder for rectification of any small faults revealed by this test after which, groomed to perfection, it was ready to hand over to the customer or retailer. The usual three year Bentley guarantee was issued and dated the day the car was delivered to its fortunate owner.

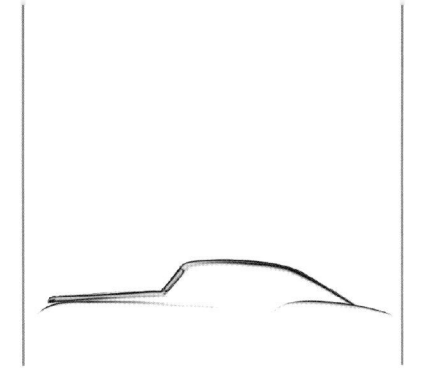

6. THE CORNICHE – & RETURN OF THE CONTINENTAL

Though the Bentley S3 Continental continued to be built into the first few months of 1966, due to the lead time required for the construction of coachwork, the end for the Bentley S3 really came in October 1965, when the culmination of the SY project, the Rolls-Royce Silver Shadow and its Bentley counterpart, the T Series, were announced.

These new models were introduced by the Company as "the most radically new Rolls-Royce cars for 59 years." Monocoque (chassisless) construction, all-independent, self-levelling suspension, disc brakes, high-pressure hydraulic system for brakes and levelling and electrically operated seat adjustment and gear range selection were the principle new features that characterised this entirely new range of cars. Never before had so many new features been introduced at once.

When SY was being developed, its external appearance was influenced as much by the Engineering and Sales people as by the Styling Department. The engineers had determined that the car would be of monocoque construction with independent rear suspension. The Sales Department wanted a car that was externally smaller and lower, but roomier inside, with much greater luggage capacity in a boot of more practical shape, and longer touring range (a larger fuel tank). All this had to be translated into styling that, though unmistakably Rolls-Royce and Bentley, had modern looks that would endure for at least ten years.

That these cars remained fundamentally unchanged for a fifteen year model run, with the Corniche derivative running a further fifteen years, amply testifies to the 'rightness' of the original concept and styling. Though it is, perhaps, debatable to what extent the outstanding success of these models was due to the underlying affluence of the times and other economic factors, rather than any increased appeal of the actual cars, the fact remains that the Silver Shadow and its derivatives were far more widely accepted than, and handsomely outsold, all previous models. The only possible negative aspect was the sad but inescapable fact that the Bentley marque was allowed to come perilously close to extinction, and for a short time at least an observer could have been forgiven for believing this to be deliberate Company policy.

There was no Bentley Continental in this new range, though a very limited range of 'coachbuilt' cars was offered.

Among the most important considerations in the styling of the Silver Shadow and Bentley T Series (which, from this point, I shall refer to simply as the T Series), was that it should withstand the ravages of time. Obviously, a firm such as Rolls-Royce, with a relatively modest output, cannot afford the luxury of frequent styling changes. Therefore, styling features that are liable to date quickly need to be avoided. As a result, the fifteen years of T Series production saw only minimal changes to the standard saloon body,

Above & opposite: To have announced a new model, just after Rolls-Royce Ltd had been placed in the hands of the official receiver over financial difficulties with the RB.211 jet engine project, demonstrated that the Car Division remained confident and forward-looking. The Division was solvent and profitable, so this confidence was well-founded. Also, instructions from the receiver were quite specific – business as usual in the Car Division. So, early in March 1971, the Corniche was unveiled. It was not so much a new model as a significantly revised existing one. With a new, low-loss exhaust system, new facia and new spun stainless steel wheel trims, the H. J. Mulliner, Park Ward coachbuilt cars were given a new lease of life that, though it could scarcely have been predicted at the time, was to extend a further 24 years (at least in convertible form). For the first time, a model designation was shared by Rolls-Royce and Bentley versions. The Bentley Corniche is a rare variant in both closed and open guises, as most buyers specified the Rolls-Royce version. This is the Bentley Corniche two-door saloon, a 1974 example without the standard painted roof finish, CBH16177. The car on the opposite, and previous page, has the optional 'Everflex' roof covering.

with the most obvious of the few cosmetic changes being confined almost entirely to the interior. The body style that resulted from these aims and constraints was conservative and timeless, and this is particularly true of the coachbuilt cars, the styling of which remained current for nearly 30 years without ever looking unduly dated.

Beneath this conservative – not to say ordinary – exterior lay a wealth of technical sophistication and innovation. It is all too easy to overlook the fact that, when first introduced in 1965, these cars were conspicuously the most technically advanced in the world. With few major changes having been made, there is little risk of contradiction when stating that, in many ways, they still held this distinction when the four-door cars were discontinued in 1980. In fact, the same design concept formed the basis of the succeeding range of cars that appeared in 1980, some derivatives of which were still being built in the opening years of the 21st century, while the T series two-door styling had remained in production for nearly three decades.

Unlike its predecessors, the T Series had no separate chassis and the extremely rigid monocoque body was mounted on a front subframe (virtually a half-chassis) that carried the engine, gearbox, front suspension and steering equipment, and two substantial crossmembers at the rear of the car to which the rear suspension and final drive were attached.

Suspension was all-independent with front anti-dive and rear anti-lift characteristics to resist nose-diving under heavy braking. Superimposed on the suspension, but playing no part in the actual springing or damping, was a sophisticated, high pressure, hydraulic, self-levelling – or height control – system to maintain optimum ride height and attitude regardless of load and load distribution. This system, certain features of which were covered by Citroën patents, operated at two speeds with fast levelling taking effect when 'Park' was selected. The hydraulic pressure for the levelling and brakes, at 2500 pounds per square inch, was supplied by a pair of camshaft-driven piston pumps and stored in spherical accumulators. Rams above each coil spring were supplied by hydraulic fluid under pressure by height control valves, or sensors; one for the front pair of rams and two for the rear pair. In May 1969, the front height control valve and levelling rams were deleted, with automatic height control remaining on the rear only, where experience had shown it had been doing nearly all the effective levelling work. The Corniche, with which we are concerned here, had the simplified height control system from the outset.

The four-wheel disc brake system incorporated two independent powered circuits, using high pressure hydraulics from the same pump and accumulator that supplied the height control system for one circuit and the second pump and accumulator for the second circuit, with a third, conventional master cylinder circuit connected directly to the pedal. One powered circuit provided 46 per cent of the total braking, operating one caliper on each front disc and part of the rear braking, while the other powered circuit provided 31 per cent of the total braking, operating the second caliper of each front disc. The direct master cylinder circuit provided the remaining 23 per cent of braking and served the same purpose as the direct mechanical linkage in the old brake system; introducing positive 'feel' into the pedal. A deceleration-conscious, pressure-limiting valve, or 'G-valve,' was provided to prevent premature wheel locking.

Power-assisted steering was by Saginaw (US) recirculating ball steering box with integral ram – as opposed to the external ram of the S Series system – supplied with hydraulic pressure by a belt-driven pump. For the first time on a Rolls-Royce or Bentley, the steering column was collapsible for safety, and the steering wheel was a new, two-spoke design with central horn button.

The engine used for the early T Series was, at first, basically the same 6230cc unit first introduced in October 1959, though with redesigned cylinder heads which gave a more efficient combustion chamber shape and brought the sparking plugs up to a more readily accessible position above the redesigned exhaust manifolds. Likewise, the automatic gearbox, at least on right-hand drive cars, was still the four-speed Rolls-Royce 'box with fluid coupling as first introduced in 1952. The Corniche, like the later standard saloons, had the 'stroked' 6750cc engine, and a three-speed automatic transmission with torque converter (bought-in complete from General Motors in Detroit) was now standard. The GM transmission was fitted unmodified – such was the state of the art of automatic transmission manufacture in the US. Range selection was electrically operated, thus eliminating a possible noise path and allowing light finger-tip action.

The opportunity for the remaining coachbuilders to express their traditional art was severely curtailed by the monocoque mode of construction of the T Series, though this did not discourage James Young Ltd from embarking on a series of two-door cars based on standard T Series body shells. These cars were, it must be said, somewhat plain-looking, but, apart from a solitary car from Pininfarina, they represented the only effort by a coachbuilder for the T Series outside the Rolls-Royce Ltd empire. There was still no Bentley Continental, and James Young, a modest contributor to the previous tally of Bentley Continental coachwork and the last independent coachbuilder for Rolls-Royce and Bentley cars, bowed out soon after the two-door conversion exercise.

As a subsidiary of Rolls-Royce Ltd, H. J. Mulliner, Park Ward was better placed to fulfil the demand for coachbuilt cars (even if they were no longer really coachbuilt in the previously accepted sense), and the task of turning out a truly distinctive two-door car fell to that firm. After S3 Continental coachwork construction ceased, sleek new two-door saloon and drophead coupé designs for the new models were introduced. These cars, like the standard saloon, were styled by John Blatchley's talented team at Crewe and were built in a manner more accurately described as body engineering rather than coachbuilding, though there was still a great deal of hand work and the interior trimming and finishing remained traditional coachbuilding tasks. The cars were built on part completed standard four-door underframes supplied by Pressed Steel Fisher which removed these underframes from their build line at an agreed stage. They were then modified in London to suit two-door construction and the bodies were built using panels and components sourced from outside suppliers such as Albany Jig & Tool, Airflow Streamlines and Dowty, Boulton & Paul.

On February 4th 1971, Rolls-Royce Ltd went into receivership following an unmanageable blow-out in the development costs of the RB211 jet engine – a new, larger engine which the Company was developing for the new generation of wide-bodied jets, notably the Lockheed Tristar. Motor car production, however, continued without interruption on the specific instructions of the Receiver, E. R. Nicholson, who subsequently separated the motor car and diesel engine divisions from the aero engine business. In May 1973, a new public Company, Rolls-Royce Motors Ltd, was formed.

Within two weeks of Rolls-Royce Ltd going into receivership, a new model was announced: more accurately, two variants of the existing model had been significantly revised and given a distinctive new model name. In a bold move, given the circumstances of only two weeks earlier, the H. J. Mulliner, Park Ward coachbuilt Rolls-Royce Silver Shadow and T Series cars became the Corniche – the only instance of a model name being shared by the Rolls-Royce and Bentley variants of a model. This was the start of a policy of giving model names to body styles rather than to chassis types, which was, perhaps, inevitable given the absence of a separate chassis under the modern Rolls-Royce and Bentley cars. This soon evolved to the point at which each body style and wheelbase had its own model name.

Corresponding with the new model appellation was a new technical specification, a revised interior, new wheel covers and Corniche badging. The technical upgrades included a 10 per cent power output increase over that of the standard four-door car (and of the earlier two-door cars), which effectively meant that there was now a compelling case for the Bentley Corniche to be regarded as a Continental. Though the name Corniche has strong Bentley associations, in retrospect it is difficult to escape the conclusion that an opportunity was missed by not applying the evocative Continental name to the Bentley from the outset, to distinguish it from its much more abundant Rolls-Royce cousin. This sad situation was not corrected until 1984 when the Continental name was belatedly revived for the Bentley version of the Corniche.

The choice of the model designation Corniche was not a difficult one for the Company. As related in Chapter One, Corniche was a name first registered by Rolls-Royce Ltd in 1939, when it was applied to a high-performance derivative of the Bentley Mk V which, due to the outbreak of World War II, never saw production. As we have also read, the prototype post-war Bentley Continental was known within the Experimental Department as 'Corniche II'. Despite the clear Bentley connotations of the

The Bentley Corniche in its popular Convertible guise. The hood was electro-hydraulically operated, which required that the car be stationary with the transmission in 'Park' and the handbrake applied.

name Corniche, the Rolls-Royce version of the new model was the one that was shown off to the news media. Moreover, many people were entirely unaware of the existence of a Bentley Corniche, and customers specifying that unsung variant were outnumbered twenty to one by those preferring the Rolls-Royce. Thus, the Bentley Corniche was assured of a place as a rare and desirable collector's item. The Company announced at the time that "the name Corniche has been chosen for the latest coachbuilt models because it symbolizes their high cruising speeds and ability to cover great distances with the minimum of fatigue for driver and passengers".

By means of modifications to the valve and ignition timing, a more efficient air intake silencer, and a low-loss exhaust system increased in bore from two to two and a quarter inches, Corniche performance was better than that of standard models. Traditionally, as already mentioned, for many decades Rolls-Royce did not disclose the power output of its motor car engines, preferring to describe it as 'adequate' or 'sufficient'. However, in the case of the Corniche it was announced, somewhat tongue-in-cheek, that the new model's engine power was "adequate plus ten per cent." It was sufficiently adequate, in fact, to give the big coupés a top speed in excess of 120mph, with acceleration capabilities, particularly from speeds above 50mph, considerably better than those of the standard four-door car – itself no sluggard – and even better than those of the average 'sports car' of the period! The engine modifications did not apply to the Corniche for export to the United States, due to the overriding requirement to comply with emission regulations there.

Visually, the Corniche differed from the coachbuilt T Series from which it was derived by having new, distinctive, spun stainless steel wheel trims, which were designed to allow better air flow around the brakes, and a new facia with comprehensive instrumentation, which included a rev counter and a fifteen inch diameter, wood-rimmed steering wheel with leather-covered spokes (soon deleted on safety grounds in favour of the standard sixteen inch, black plastic wheel). A 'Corniche' badge on the boot lid identified the new model.

The Corniche was fitted with an elegant model name badge, designed by Martin Bourne of the Crewe Styling Department.

The Corniche facia was all-new, with the comprehensive instrumentation, including a tachometer, to which Bentley Continental owners were accustomed. The 15-inch, wood-rimmed steering wheel with leather covered spokes was a shortlived casualty of the emerging safety regulations, soon replaced by the 16-inch black plastic wheel of the standard T Series.

Corniche rear seat, in this instance the two-door saloon with its individual squabs. The Convertible's rear seat was a bench-type, and was narrower due to the intrusion of the hood bows into the interior space.

The engine installation in the monocoque cars was a tight fit and visually impressive. Due to the lower bonnet (in comparison with the S3), the air filter was positioned in the off-side wing. The large container at the bottom right of the picture is the hydraulic fluid reservoir, divided into two compartments. Note the very large SU type HD.8 carburetters, which had a polished finish rather than the black enamel of the S3 and earlier models. Like the automatic transmission, the air conditioning compressor was a General Motors product.

An interesting technical innovation, first introduced on the Corniche but later standardised on all models, was automatic speed control, or 'cruise control.' The controls for this were mounted on the facia below the rev counter, and maintained any desired speed, regardless of gradient, to within 1mph or so. The system could be overridden by pressing the accelerator, or disengaged by using the brake pedal, after which the selected cruising speed could be resumed by pressing a 'Resume' button. Similar systems are fairly commonplace today, even on relatively low-priced cars, but it was practically unknown on other British cars in the early 1970s.

The Corniche drophead coupé, marketed as the Convertible using American terminology, was surely the ultimate in high-performance, open-air motoring, and so successful it was still being made for appreciative buyers as recently as 1995, though, naturally, with greatly updated technical specification and the model name Continental restored to the Bentley version. The car's body styling dates from September 1967, when it was introduced as the T Series drophead coupé. In two-door saloon form it dates from eighteen months before that, but that variant was discontinued at the end of 1980.

During the fifteen year production run of the T Series, over 2000 individual technical and coachwork changes were introduced, many of which were mere details. Perhaps the most important change, apart from those that came with the T2, of which more anon, was an increase in engine capacity from 6230cc to 6750cc, made possible by lengthening the stroke from 3.6 to 3.9 inches, which took place in July 1970 and was therefore applicable to all Corniche cars. Also applicable to all Corniche cars (until the 1992 model year) was the three-speed GM automatic transmission, which was fitted to left-hand drive cars from the outset and had become standard on right-hand drive models by November 1968.

Regarding the styling evolution of the Corniche, Crewe Styling Chief, John Blatchley (JPB), recalls that he "took quite a lot of 'flack' over the Koren (S2 and S3) Continentals." This came from Grylls, Llewellyn Smith and others in the Company hierarchy, who were a little sceptical of Koren's styling of the Park Ward S2 and S3 Continentals, despite their undoubted commercial success. JPB was determined that the styling of the two-door T Series (which in 1971 became the Corniche) "should much more closely follow the 'Cloud' theme – retrogressive, maybe, but in an updated form."

Therefore, these new two-door coachbuilt cars were deliberately 'retro'-styled rather than attempting to be styling leaders as earlier coachbuilt cars had (particularly the Koren coupés). The task of shaping the quarter-scale wax model fell to JPB's assistant, Bill Allen (Aln). This task, begun in January 1964, was completed in six weeks, during much of which time JPB had been absent from the department due to illness and other circumstances. However, when the model was completed exactly in accordance with his requirements, JPB passed it without amendment. The shapely wingline, with distinctly 'separate' rear wings, embodied unmistakable echoes of JPB's earlier styling for the Silver Cloud and Bentley S Type, while nonetheless looking thoroughly modern. The design of the complete car was coded SY20, while the coachwork design numbers allocated by their makers, H. J. Mulliner, Park Ward Ltd, were 3010 (two-door saloon) and 3020 (drophead coupé).

In October 1974, a Solex four-barrel downdraught carburetter installation first appeared on the Corniche for all markets other than North America, Japan and Australia. Together with the Lucas Opus breakerless electronic ignition introduced at the same time, this made for considerably enhanced performance, particularly at the higher end of the rev range.

At this point, mention should be made of the Camargue, introduced in 1975. This Pininfarina-styled coupé was produced only in Rolls-Royce guise, save for a solitary Bentley example. The Experimental prototypes, code-named 'Delta,' had been Bentleys, and a turbocharged Bentley Camargue had been tested and considered for production before the decision was made that the Bentley Turbo would be a standard four-door saloon. Though it seems that the opportunity for a truly great Bentley in the Continental mold was squandered, the mores of the period did not favour such a project.

When the Rolls-Royce Silver Shadow II and Bentley T2 cars appeared in February 1977, the Corniche remained just that and did not take on the Series II appellation. However, the visual and mechanical changes applied equally to the Corniche. Note, for example, the polyurethane-faced bumpers and front air dam. This Bentley Corniche Convertible, carrying one of Crewe's 'cherished' registration numbers, is fitted with the headlamp wash/wipe feature introduced in mid-1978, and the very high-backed front seat design that appeared on the Corniche for a short time.

This Bentley Corniche Saloon sports the black polyurethane-faced bumpers but, being a US-specification car, lacks the air dam normally fitted below the bumper. For the United States, with its 55mph speed limits, this was deemed unnecessary.

It was a time when Bentley production had fallen to a derisory 4 per cent of total output at Crewe. Conversions of Bentleys to take on Rolls-Royce appearance – unthinkable today – were rife. So it was that a car with many Bentley Continental attributes was built and sold as a Rolls-Royce, and the projected high performance variant not produced at all.

Other than the early loss of the 15-inch wood-rim steering wheel which, for safety reasons, was changed for the standard 16-inch black plastic wheel, and the later loss of the rev counter, the Corniche changed little until the 1976 model year, when a new facia and highly sophisticated, automatic, bi-level air conditioning system, first used on the Rolls-Royce Camargue, was adopted for the Corniche, a year ahead of the standard four-door car. This was in-line with an established Rolls-Royce pattern of introducing such innovations on the top-of-the-range coachbuilt models first, then following up with their incorporation in standard cars once larger-scale production could be reliably achieved. For the Corniche, the controls for the automatic air conditioning were redesigned to give a neater appearance. The new facia had been designed by Crewe for the then forthcoming Rolls-Royce Silver Shadow II and Bentley T2 four-door saloons.

The most significant changes to the T Series range of cars occurred in February 1977, and were considered sufficient to justify revised model designations – Rolls-Royce Silver Shadow II and Bentley T2. The changes for these Series II cars, introduced in a single package, affected external appearance, interior, mechanical specification and handling characteristics of the car. The changes most obvious to the casual observer were the adoption as standard of American-style, wrap-around, black polyurethane-faced bumpers, and the fitting of an 'air dam' below the front bumper.

The most immediately noticeable interior change was the T2's full set of instruments and the suitably impressive facia in which they were displayed, which appeared without fanfare a year or so earlier on the 20A series Corniche.

More important than the cosmetic changes were the new technical features, perhaps the most significant of which, from the point of view of the enthusiastic driver, was the rack-and-pinion steering. The T Series and Corniche had always suffered from rather vague steering; although smooth,

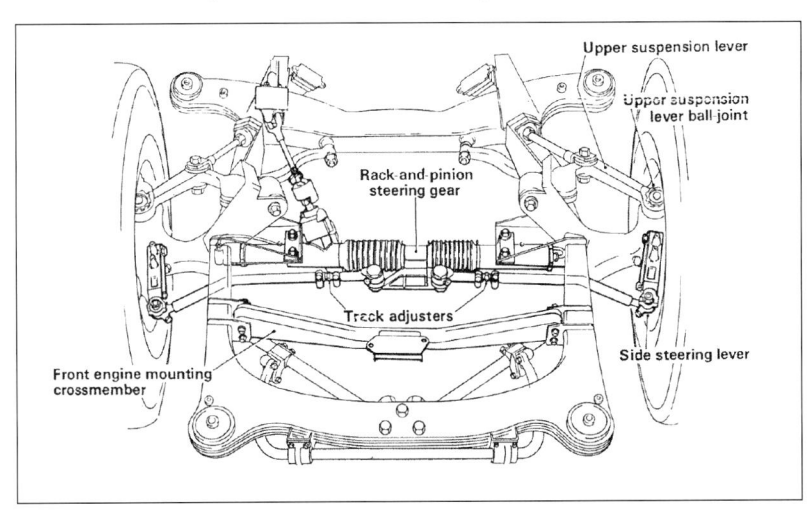

The revised front end design for the T2 range incorporated rack-and-pinion steering with highly refined power-assistance for precise, sensitive steering with more positive 'feel'. Modifications to the front suspension geometry kept the front wheels more upright when cornering, improving responsiveness and reducing roll angles.

The T2 style of facia, as well as automatic air conditioning, had actually been quietly introduced for 1976 on the Corniche. Note the leather-covered steering wheel fitted to this example. This series was known within the factory as CY20A.

In May 1979, commencing with serial number 50001, the Corniche facia was again revised to incorporate a central digital display for outside temperature, time of day, and elapsed journey time indicator. At the same time, a revised rear suspension arrangement and mineral oil hydraulic system were introduced. These changes anticipated the Rolls-Royce Silver Spirit and Bentley Mulsanne range of cars which followed in October 1980, and were a manifestation of the policy of introducing major changes on the low volume coachbuilt cars ahead of the four-door saloons.

light, progressive and accurate to a nicety, it nevertheless felt vague. Even with the benefit of higher gearing and smaller (16-inch) steering wheel from August 1971, it was anything but sporting. Now, at speed, the new rack-and-pinion steering, with its highly refined power-assistance, as well as being more precise and sensitive, provided the positive 'feel' that experienced drivers expect. A still smaller (15-inch) steering wheel went with the new rack-and-pinion steering. Modifications to the front suspension geometry, designed to keep the front wheels more upright when cornering, improved responsiveness still further, as well as reducing roll angles, with consequent reductions in noise and scrub and beneficial effects on tyre life.

There were also some power unit changes, mainly in the cooling and carburation areas. A smaller, but more efficient, seven-bladed plastic fan, driven through a viscous coupling, was assisted by a thermostatically controlled electric fan mounted forward of the radiator. The large SU HD.8 carburetters, which had served on several models, were replaced with the much more technically advanced but slightly smaller HIF.7s, though, for certain countries, Corniche cars were by now fitted with a large downdraught Solex instrument. The advanced design of the HIF.7 carburetter, featuring linear ball-race dashpots, meant much more efficient maintenance of exhaust emission control standards than both the old SUs and the Solex and, in conjunction with the lower power absorption characteristics of the revised cooling arrangements, and a new, low-loss twin exhaust system, helped improve fuel economy. The twin exhaust system, of stainless steel, also compensated for the slight loss of power incurred by the smaller carburetters. The alternator was of increased capacity and the oil filter the disposable, spin-on type in lieu of the earlier separate element type.

It needs to be clearly understood that the name of the Corniche was not amended to Corniche II at this stage.

A further manifestation of the policy of introducing new features first on the coachbuilt cars occurred from May 1979, when some of the technical features of the coming new Silver Spirit range of cars were quietly introduced on the Corniche. Briefly, these features were: the use of mineral oil in lieu of conventional brake fluid for the hydraulic systems, revised rear suspension

Though the Corniche two-door saloon was discontinued at the end of 1980, the Convertible was retained in the Silver Spirit/Mulsanne model range, its appeal completely undiminished. Serious consideration had been given to re-styling the car to give it a family resemblance to the four-door models. This proceeded to a full-size mock-up before being abandoned in favour of retaining the existing, more traditional shape.

As part of the overall strategy to renew interest in the Bentley marque, in August 1984 the Bentley Corniche was renamed the Continental – a name which, arguably, it should have received at the outset and certainly from 1971, if not 1966 when the body styling made its debut. New features for this model included new front seats with adjustable lumbar supports, and a redesigned facia with traditional Continental-type individual gauges in lieu of the previous four-in-one instrument. External recognition points included finishing the bumpers, side mirrors and radiator grille vanes in the body colour.

Rolls-Royce Motors' Chief Executive Richard Perry (right) and Managing Director, Sales and Marketing Peter Ward, with the new Bentley Continental in 1984. The re-naming of the Bentley Corniche re-established a priceless model name that had gone unexploited since 1966. Mr Ward went on to become Chief Executive of the Company in 1986.

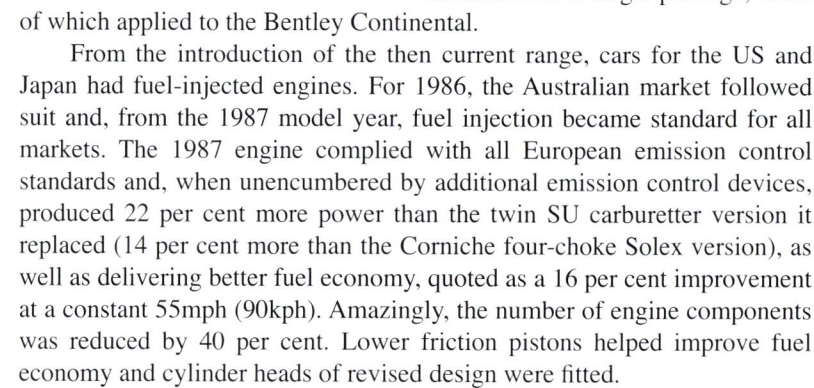

incorporating gas springs and a digital display in the centre of the facia for outside ambient temperature, journey elapsed time indicator and clock.

The model code of the Corniche had been changed from SY20 to CY20 in the mid-1970s. Whilst the four-door saloon code changed from SY20 to SY20AB with the change to the Series II cars, that of the coachbuilt cars changed in two stages – to CY20A for the 1976 model year cars with automatic ACU and the new facia, and then to CY20AB for the other changes coinciding with the Silver Shadow II for 1977.

In 1984, as part of a new policy to revitalise the Bentley marque, the name Continental was revived – after an absence of eighteen years – for the drophead coupé formerly marketed as the Bentley Corniche Convertible. This latter-day Continental featured colour-keyed bumpers, external mirrors and radiator grille vanes, redesigned front seats incorporating adjustable lumbar support and a restyled facia.

The 1987 model year saw a range of significant improvements introduced as a single package, some of which applied to the Bentley Continental.

From the introduction of the then current range, cars for the US and Japan had fuel-injected engines. For 1986, the Australian market followed suit and, from the 1987 model year, fuel injection became standard for all markets. The 1987 engine complied with all European emission control standards and, when unencumbered by additional emission control devices, produced 22 per cent more power than the twin SU carburetter version it replaced (14 per cent more than the Corniche four-choke Solex version), as well as delivering better fuel economy, quoted as a 16 per cent improvement at a constant 55mph (90kph). Amazingly, the number of engine components was reduced by 40 per cent. Lower friction pistons helped improve fuel economy and cylinder heads of revised design were fitted.

The Pininfarina-styled Camargue was only ever intended to be a Rolls-Royce car, its introduction in 1975 coinciding with a period in which the Bentley marque was being conspicuously neglected. However, the Experimental Camargues always wore Bentley radiator shells for road testing purposes and the Experimental Camargue Turbo (above) was a Bentley. Also, there was a solitary production Bentley Camargue, SCBYJ00 0XFCH10150 (left). It was delivered to its fortunate owner in 1985.

180

This page: The 1986 model year Bentley Continental benefited from a handsome variant of the distinctive alloy wheels previously only fitted to the

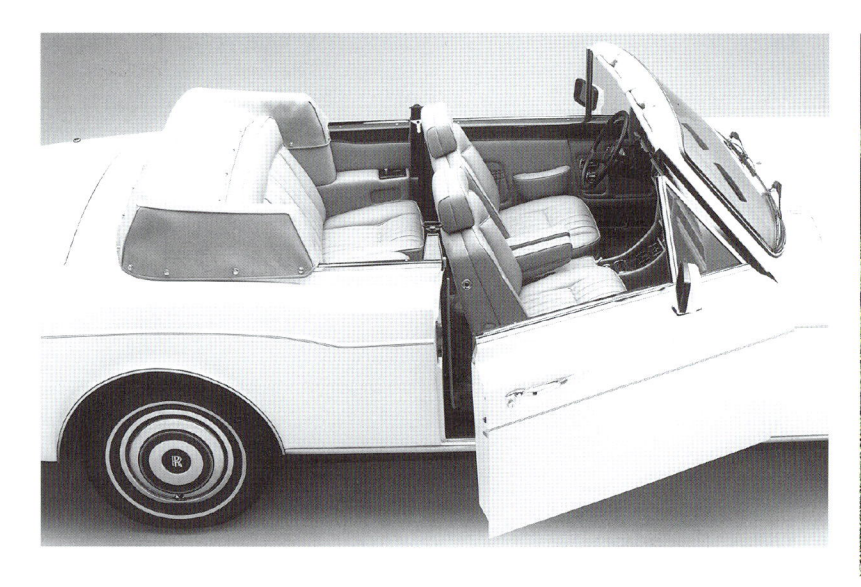

The interior of the 1986 Continental shows the revised seats and facia introduced in August 1984. The front centre armrests were changed for 1986 to the type shown here. These formerly folded out of the seat squabs and were slimmer.

Below: 1988 Bentley Continental, SCBZD00AXJCH23168, again showing the handsome alloy wheels introduced for the 1986 model year and (above) the interior.

The 1992 Bentley Continental convertible acquired the Automatic Ride Control fitted to the four-door saloon models since 1990, together with a new hood with heated glass rear window. In 1994, the hood was further revised, with the heated rear window repositioned to improve rearward view, while the hood and its tensioning system were improved to assist in hood operation.

Electrical equipment changes included a higher capacity alternator and a new, smaller, quieter but more powerful (Japanese) starter motor. Anti-locking (ABS) brakes were fitted to all cars for markets other than North America. This electronically-controlled system measures wheel speed and modulates braking pressure when wheel slip exceeds a determined limit. A great deal of research and development work was carried out at Crewe, aimed at avoiding the 'wooden' pedal feel that all too often characterizes ABS braking systems.

Interior changes included the addition of power squab rake control and four position memory switches to the electrically-operated seats.

On June 14th 1988, several significant changes were announced for the 1989 model year. Visual changes affecting the Bentley Continental were redesigned seat trim with lateral pleating, a fixed centre armrest between the front seats incorporating a stowage compartment, an illuminated cassette storage drawer, a return to all-analogue instruments and a more powerful in-car entertainment system. More significant, perhaps, were the power train developments designed to provide all models in the range with increased refinement and even more power. The engine crankcase was ribbed and cross-bolted adjacent to the three centre main bearings to increase stiffness for better noise and vibration suppression. The stiffened, heavy-duty-type THM400 transmission was fitted.

In October 1989, further significant improvements were announced as a single package at the Frankfurt Motor Show. The most important of these was the introduction of automatic ride control, though this was not fitted to the coachbuilt cars until 1992. However, a K-Motronic engine management system, and an automatic parking brake release electrically linked to the gear range selector, were among the changes introduced for all models for 1990.

The computer activated automatic ride control system was developed over a four year period in the Experimental Department at Crewe and set new standards of ride comfort and handling. This was introduced on the Bentley Continental for the 1992 model year and continued the evolution of the self-levelling system which, in one form or another, has been a feature of Rolls-Royce and Bentley cars since 1965, as well as recalling the 'ride control' fitted to all models before 1966, right back to the 1930s.

If good handling is to be achieved in any motor car, conventional single-setting damper systems must inevitably represent a compromise between the stiffness needed to limit roll when cornering, and softness required for comfortable ride quality. With the introduction of this new suspension system, the self-levelling feature remained as before, but the need to compromise damper settings was eliminated by adopting the automatic ride control system which adapts to changes in road conditions in one hundredth of a second, automatically selecting the appropriate 'comfort,' 'normal' or 'hard' ride mode. This is achieved by an electronically controlled system comprising a micro-processor and vertical, longitudinal and lateral accelerometers which monitor acceleration, deceleration, road surface condition and steering changes. The mode changes occur so quickly and unobtrusively that the driver and passengers are unaware that, on entering a tight corner, the suspension has moved imperceptibly from 'comfort' to 'firm.' Unlike the pre-1966 ride control systems, the driver has no manual control over the settings.

The styling of these magnificent convertibles remained essentially unchanged since 1967, when this fine design was first introduced as the Bentley T Series (and Rolls-Royce Silver Shadow) drophead coupés, based on the slightly earlier two-door saloon. Consideration had been given to re-styling the Corniche to give it a close family resemblance to the Mulsanne saloon, possibly using the four-door car's front wings and bonnet. Former Park Ward draughtsman, Peter Wharton, prepared drawings and a colour wash painting of the proposed car, and a full-size mock-up was built (page 177.) However, a decision was taken to continue with the more traditional styling for the convertible models. In retrospect, this was undoubtedly the commercially correct decision, given the strong demand for traditionally-styled convertibles that continued until the last examples were built in 1995.

The Corniche two-door saloon was discontinued at the end of 1980, and a 1986 proposal, dubbed 'CZS,' for a revival of this model using a fixed, fibre-glass 'hard-top' turret was not proceeded with.

A little known variant of the Bentley Continental appeared in 1992. This was the Continental Turbo, of which three examples were built to the special order of the Sultan of Brunei. Fitting the turbocharged engine to the Convertible car presented some difficulties: the bodies needed to be modified to fit the intercooler and ducting, and the standard sills were replaced by stiffened structures to cope with the extra power. Turbo R exhaust system and 16-inch Continental R wheels and tyres were fitted. It was decided not to make this model generally available and the three Brunei cars are thought to be the only Continental Turbo convertibles built.

This & following page: Car specification sheets for SCBZD04D6NCH40091, the first of three Bentley Continental Turbo Convertibles built to the special order of the Sultan of Brunei.

```
                            CAR SPECIFICATION
Order No: BD5076100                  Vin : SCBZD04D6NCH40091
Car Type: BENTLEY       CONTINENTAL TURBO              RHD
                         ───CUSTOMER/MARKET───
Dealer :R-RMC LTD - PACIFIC OPERATIONS  Car Family: BDLNC  /NON-CATALYST
Ship To:CONDUIT STREET            Built For : BRUNEI

                            ─── RECORD ───
Engine   :              Wheel Key :                Radio :
Body     :              Lock      :                BIB Nα

                            ─── EXTERIOR ───
Main Body        :ROYAL BLUE (C/B)             9531002

Sec. Body        :ROYAL BLUE (C/B)             9531002

Hood             :DARK BLUE EVERFLEX           5470 DH

Fine Line Type   :NO FINE LINES
Fine Line Colour :

                            ─── MISC ───
Radio            :RADIO/TAPE+POWER AMP.-RF2
Tyres - Type     :AVON 255/60/ZR16 TYRES
Tyres - Colour   :BLACK TYRES

                       ─── OPTIONS AND EXTRAS ───
   NON OPENING REAR SEAT ARMREST      AIR BAG SYSTEM
   HEAD RESTS TO REAR SEAT            FIRE EXTINGUISHER TO FOOTWELL
   OPEN COMPARTMENT - LH DOOR         OPEN COMPARTMENT - RH DOOR
   FIXED REAR SEAT                    INDIVIDUAL CUSHION - REAR SEAT
   INDIVIDUAL SQUAB - REAR SEAT       TINTED WINDSCREEN - "SUNDYM"
   RAD.SHELL-CHROME-PAINTED VANES     RHS BOOT BADGE - CONTINENTAL
   LHS BOOT BADGE - BLACK BENTLEY     AIR HORNS

                       ─── FEATURES NOT FITTED ───
   NO ASHTRAYS TO WAISTRAILS          NO PICNIC TABLES
   NO COCKTAIL CABINET CTR STOW       NO FIRE EXTINGUISHER TO BOOT
   NO LOOSE FOOT RESTS                NO GRAB HANDLES TO FR. SEATS
   NO BADGE BAR                       NO REAR QUARTER BADGES
   NO FRONT WING BADGES               NO MASCOT ALARM
   NO WHEEL FINISHER                  NO RADIO TELEPHONE
   NO SECOND R.T. HANDSET             NO FRONT FOGLAMPS




              DEVIATIONS AND SPECIAL FEATURES EXIST

Issued : 01/05/92   By : Stf      PAGE 1     Date required :31/08/92
                                                       CONTINUED........
```

```
                              CAR  SPECIFICATION
Order No: BD5076100                    Vin : SCBZD04D6NCH40091

Car Type: BENTLEY         CONTINENTAL TURBO            RHD
                         ─CUSTOMER/MARKET─
Dealer :R-RMC LTD - PACIFIC OPERATIONS Car Family: BDLNC  /NON-CATALYST

Ship To:CONDUIT STREET             Built For : BRUNEI
                              ─INTERIOR─
```

Main Trim	: SLATE HIDE	A4137
Piping	: WHITE HIDE	A4169
Inserts	: SLATE HIDE	A4137
Headlining	: BARODA BLUE HEADL. CLOTH 18 OZ	TRA45
Carpet	: GRANITE	89
Carpet Binding	: SLATE HIDE	A4137
Top Roll	: DARK BLUE HIDE	A4133
Underdash	: SLATE HIDE	A4137
Centre Console	: SLATE HIDE	A4137
Centre Stowage Bin	: SLATE HIDE	A4137
Front Header Trim	: SLATE HIDE	A4137
Steering Wheel	: STEERING WHEEL - BLACK HIDE	
Lambswool Rugs	: GRANITE	89
Woodwork	: BURR WALNUT+CB + BOXWOOD INLAY	
A Post Trim	: SLATE HIDE	A4137
Armrest Tops	: SLATE HIDE	A4137
Draught Welts	: SLATE HIDE	A4137
Door Kickpad Binding	: SLATE HIDE	A4137
ACU Cover/Coat Hook	:	

─ADDITIONAL COLOURED FEATURES─

SUNVISORS TO CUST. COL. CHOICE	SLATE HIDE	A4137
PIPING TO DOOR ARMRESTS	SLATE HIDE	A4137

─PRODUCTION DEVIATIONS─

CAR TO BE BUILT NON CATALYST WITH TURBO-CHARGED ENGINE
SEE ATTACHMENT
.
FIT PROVISION FOR UK SPECIFICATION RADIO-TELEPHONE
.
FIT FULLY REFLECTIVE TYPE GLASS ALL ROUND IF POSSIBLE

─CAR TO GO TO SFD FOR THE FOLLOWING─

FIT PIONEER 900 RADIO/CD WITH BOOT MOUNTED DISC STACKER

DEVIATIONS AND SPECIAL FEATURES EXIST

Issued : 01/05/92   By : Stf   PAGE 2   Date required : 31/08/92

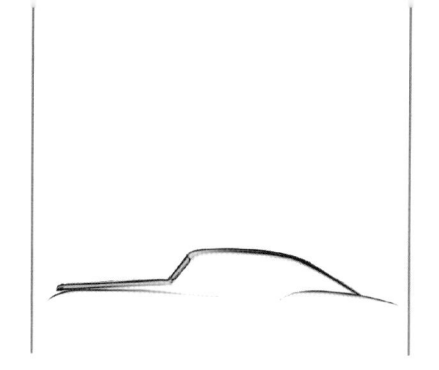

TECHNICAL SPECIFICATIONS – BENTLEY CORNICHE (1971-84) & CONTINENTAL (1984-95)

ENGINE

Dimensions
Eight cylinders in 90-degree vee formation. Stroke 3.9in (99.1mm), cubic capacity 412in^3 (6750cc). Compression ratio 9:1 (8:1 for countries where 100 octane fuel not available). From October 1975: compression ratio 8:1 (7.3:1 for Australia, Japan and USA).

Cylinder block/crankcase
High silicon content aluminium alloy block with cast iron wet cylinder liners.

Crankshaft
Nitride hardened chrome molybdenum steel, with integral balance weights, running in five main bearings.

Pistons
Aluminium alloy. Three compression rings and one oil control ring.

Cylinder heads
Aluminium alloy with austenitic steel valve seats.

Valve gear
Overhead valves. Monikrom cast iron camshaft driven by helical gears, four bearings. Hydraulic tappets.

Carburetters
Two SU type HD.8 (2in) carburetters with paper air filter element. From serial number 19741 (home market): Solex type 4A1 four barrel downdraught. From serial number 30001: two SU type HIF.7 (1⅞in) carburetters. From serial number 40194 (California): Lucas K-Jetronic fuel injection, subsequently phased in for all of North America and Japan. From 1987 model year: fuel injection standard all markets. From 1989 model year: MK Motronic fuel injection and engine management system.

Ignition system
Ignition by high tension coil and Lucas distributor with vacuum retard. From serial number 22118: Lucas 'Opus' electronic ignition. From serial number 23059: for Australia, Japan and USA): vacuum advance distributor. From 1981: Lucas DM8 Constant Energy Electronic Ignition. Firing order A1, B1, A4, B4, B2, A3, B3, A2. From 1987 model year: A1, A3, B3, A2, B2, B1, A4, B4.

Lubrication system
Helical gear oil pump in crankcase driven by skew gear from crankshaft. Oil pick-up in sump incorporating gauze strainer. Full-flow filter on side of crankcase. Pressure relief valve regulates oil pressure at approximately 40lb/in^2. Sump capacity 12.5 pints (15 US gallons, 7.1 litres.)

Cooling system
Pressurised system containing a solution of 50 per cent anti-freeze, or inhibited glycol, and 50 per cent water. Temperature control by thermostat at the front of engine. Belt-driven centrifugal coolant pump and fan. From serial number 30001 (specification CY20AB): plastic fan and supplementary thermostatic electric fan.

CHASSIS

Monocoque construction with separate front and rear subframes: front – steel box-section construction mounted to car underframe by resilient metal mounts; rear – comprises the final drive crossmember mounted to the underframe by two resilient metal mounts and connected by a torque reaction arm to the rear subframe. Short telescopic damper fitted to each front mount to dampen fore and aft movement.

Dimensions
Overall length, 16ft 11½in (5169mm), Overall length, with neoprene-type bumpers, 17ft ½in (5194mm), Wheelbase, 9ft 11½in (3035mm), Track, front and rear, 4ft 9½in (1460mm).

Suspension
Front: independent by coil springs and rubber bushed wishbones, double acting hydraulic telescopic dampers and anti-roll bar. Rear: independent by coil springs and trailing arms, hydraulic telescopic dampers. From serial number 12734: compliant front suspension. From 1992 model year: Electronic 3-position automatic ride control system.

Hydraulic system
Two camshaft-driven hydraulic pumps delivering brake fluid under pressure (up to 2500psi) to a pair of hydraulic accumulators mounted on the side of the crankcase. Hydraulic pressure stored in the accumulators is used for the braking and height control systems. Two low pressure warning lights on the facia, one for each hydraulic circuit.

Brakes
11in disc brakes on all four wheels. Each front wheel fitted with two twin-cylinder calipers and each rear wheel with one four-cylinder caliper. Three separate and independent hydraulic circuits, two from the high pressure hydraulic system operated by distribution valves connected to the brake pedal and a direct master cylinder circuit. Deceleration-conscious, pressure limiting valve ('G' valve) incorporated in one of the power circuits to prevent premature rear wheel locking. Separate brake pads for handbrake. From serial number 22118: master cylinder circuit deleted.

Height control system
Fully automatic hydraulic height control system to maintain the standing height of the car under all load conditions, by means of height control valves and hydraulic rams over the coil spring of rear each wheel. This system was designed to operate at two speeds – slow levelling when driving and fast levelling with the gear selector lever in neutral or a door opened.

Steering
Power-assisted recirculating ball, Saginaw belt-driven pump. Three-piece track linkage. From serial number 11501: steering ratio increased. From serial number 30001: power-assisted rack-and-pinion steering with centre take-off.

Transmission
General Motors GM.400 three-speed automatic transmission and torque converter. Ratios: Top 1:1, Third 1.5:1, First 2.5:1, Reverse 2:1. From 1992 model year: General Motors 4L80-E four-speed automatic transmission. One-piece propeller shaft. Final drive: hypoid bevel rigidly mounted on a crossmember which, in turn, is mounted to the body underframe by resilient metal mounts. Drive transmitted to the rear wheels by two driveshafts. The inner end of each shaft is connected to the final drive by a Detroit-type ball and trunnion joint and the outer end by a Hardy-Spicer type universal joint. Ratio 3.08:1.

Exhaust system
Single system with three expansion boxes, each tuned to absorb a different range of frequencies.

Lubrication system
Long-life grease lubrication.

Fuel system
Rear mounted petrol tank, capacity 24 gallons (29 US gallons, 109 litres). Twin SU electric fuel pump mounted in the body underframe.

Electrical system
12 volt negative earth system. Lucas alternator and starter motor with pre-engagement pinion. Radiomobile Medium wave/Long wave or Medium wave/Short wave radio with push-button tuning and two speakers. An electrically operated wing mounted aerial standard. Electrically-operated seat adjustments. Electrically-operated windscreen washer. Triplex heated rear window. Electric windows. Refrigerated air conditioning. From serial number 21998 (other than America), 22583 (Convertible, all markets) and 22648 (two-door saloon, all markets): automatic air conditioning unit in revised facia.

Road wheels and tyres
15in steel disc wheels on five studs, carrying 205x15 radial ply tyres, later 235/70x15.

COACHWORK

Monocoque construction two-door saloon or Convertible by H. J. Mulliner, Park Ward Ltd (later Mulliner Park Ward.)

PERFORMANCE DATA

The following results were obtained by *The Autocar* when road-testing a (Rolls-Royce) Corniche two-door saloon in 1974. For comparison purposes, figures obtained by the same journal for the 6.75-litre Silver Shadow four-door saloon are also given.

Acceleration through gears (seconds)	Four-door saloon	Corniche
0-30mph	3.8	3.2
0-60mph	10.6	9.6
0-100mph	36.5	30.0
Best maximum speed (mph):	120.0	122.0
Petrol consumption(mpg):	13.6	11.9

CHASSIS NUMBERING SYSTEM

(see Appendix 2)

First car serial numbers, Bentley Corniche

	Chassis No.
Bentley Corniche two-door Saloon	CBH10420
Bentley Corniche Convertible	DBH10122
CY20A Bentley Corniche two-door Saloon (1976)	CBH24209
CY20A Bentley Corniche Convertible (1976)	DBH24505
CY20AB Bentley Corniche two-door Saloon (1977)	CBH31226
CY20AB Bentley Corniche Convertible (1977)	DBH31219
CYZ Bentley Corniche two-door Saloon (1979)	CBK50037
CYZ Bentley Corniche Convertible (1979)	DBK50042

Lasts:
Car Serial Numbers commencing 50001 were used for Corniche with HSMO (Hydraulic Systems Mineral Oil) hydraulic system and Silver Spirit-type rear suspension package. Within the factory these cars were code-named CYZ. The last numbers in this 'half-way house' series, prior to the introduction of the 17-digit Vehicle Identification Number (VIN) system, were:

Corniche two-door Saloon	50614 (then discontinued)
Corniche Convertible	50756 (then to 17-digit VIN system)

First Vehicle Identification Numbers, Bentley Corniche from 1981 and Continental Convertibles:

	17-digit No.
Corniche (1981)	SCBYD42A7BCX02499
CZ underframe Corniche (1982)	SCBZD0009CCH05822
Continental (1984)	SCBZD42A8GCX13412
1990 model year Continental (1989)	SCBZD02A4LCX30002
1992 model yearContinental (1991)	SCBZD02A2NCH40002
1993 model year Continental (1992)	SCBZD02DXPCX40503
1994 model year Continental (1993)	SCBZD02C4RCX50003
Bentley Camargue (1985)	SCBYJ000XFCH10150
Continental Turbo convertibles (Brunei, 1992)	SCBZD04D6NCH40091
	SCBZD04D8NCH40092
	SCBZD04DXNCH40093

Note: the Corniche Saloon was discontinued just prior to the introduction of the 17-digit VIN system. The first 17-digit Corniche Convertible is a 1981 car, due to production of the previous 50001 series extending into that year.

Number of cars built, 1966-1995

Bentley T Series two-door saloon*	98
Bentley T Series drophead coupé*	41
Bentley Corniche two-door saloon	63
Bentley Corniche Convertible	77
Bentley Camargue	1
Bentley Continental Convertible	405

* These early H. J. Mulliner, Park Ward coachbuilt cars are included for interest's sake. Though they are the predecessors of the Corniche and 1984 Continental they are not strictly within the scope of this book and do not necessarily conform to the above specification in all details.

7. A SUPERCAR FOR THE NINETIES & BEYOND

On March 5th 1991, Rolls-Royce Motor Cars Ltd launched the Bentley Continental R, describing it as "the first new style Bentley since 1952." The obvious inaccuracy aside, this was an exciting development, and it was at least true that this was the first Bentley since 1963 not to share body styling with a Rolls-Royce. As a sleek and stylish two-door car, it filled a gap in the Rolls-Royce and Bentley model range left by the 1986 departure of the Camargue – only this time the Bentley Continental name and image were essential features and a Rolls-Royce variant was not offered.

The pricing of this model, too, recalled the Camargue, whose price tag was, upon introduction, a staggering 50 per cent more than the Corniche's. This was because it was intended to keep the model ultra-exclusive, and to make the point that, in the troubled times of 1975, Rolls-Royce was moving forward and intended to remain at the very pinnacle of the luxury car pyramid. In an initial press release, the Continental R was priced at £160,000 in the UK, inclusive of all taxes. However, this was revised in a slightly later release to £175,000, partly as a result of an increase in the VAT rate announced in the UK budget.

With the resurgent interest from the early 1980s in the Bentley marque, came thoughts of returning to exclusively Bentley body styles, an approach favoured by the Company's then Chief Executive, Peter Ward. The 1985 'Project 90,' a full-size, glass-fibre mock-up exhibited at the 1985 Geneva Motor Show, was a step in this direction and the Continental R was an obvious derivation of that concept. The subtleties of the body styling were, however, quite different. The number of people seeking to place orders for a 'Project 90' type car, following the 1985 Geneva showing, together with acclaim in the press, left no doubt about the strength of appeal of such an individual Bentley, and the decision to proceed with an exclusive Bentley model that would further enhance the marque's sporting image was taken.

By 1986, the design team had advanced a number of proposals, all benefiting from Turbo R developments and other exclusively Bentley features, such as the 7-inch round headlamps. After considering – and rejecting – the idea of a two-door version of the standard saloon, a dedicated body style, designed with the aid of styling consultants John Heffernan and Ken Greenley of International Automotive Design, was settled on. Radical departures from tradition were incorporated into the design, including cut-into-roof doors and sophisticated use of new composite materials for the integrated bumper system. The traditional skills of the coachbuilder were complimented by the latest computer technology to create a shape appropriate to the marque, with a distinctive appearance, high speed stability and low wind noise in sufficient measures to do justice to the Continental appellation.

The Continental R, which was code-named 'Nepal' in a long-standing Experimental Department tradition of using Far Eastern names for new projects, was designed to be built entirely at Crewe. However, the Mulliner Park Ward London Coachbuilding Division (since closed) had a hand in the design and development work, and Heffernan and Greenley worked from a design studio adjacent to Mulliner Park Ward's Hythe Road, Willesden works in a building that later became the Metrology Department.

The Continental R was the first Bentley Continental to have an all-steel body. The pressed steel body panels were supplied by Park Sheet Metal, who also supplied the pressings for the Camargue body. In the case of the Continental R, however, the highest quality tooling was specified to minimise hand-work and, unlike on the Camargue, no lead was used to size apertures.

As had been the case with the original Bentley Continental in 1951, the Continental R body shape was wind-tunnel proven, the well contoured form and carefully raked windscreen proving their worth with notably lower Cd (drag co-efficient) than the then current saloon cars. This also brought benefits in reduced fuel consumption and enhanced performance. It is worth recording that when the Continental R was unveiled at Geneva, to the strains of Handel's Zadok the Priest and Elgar's Pomp and Circumstance, it was one of the few occasions on which the assembled throng has broken into a spontaneous round of applause at the first sight of a new car.

The Continental R as introduced was the first model since the original Continental to have 16-inch wheels, in this instance carrying low profile 255/60ZR16 Avon tyres of a type that could scarcely have been dreamt of in

'Project 90' was a concept car mock-up exhibited at the 1985 Geneva Motor Show, marking the start of the project which eventually produced the Bentley Continental R. The number of people seeking to order such a car left no doubt about the appeal of an individual Bentley. In the background is a Continental S1 of around 1956, with H. J. Mulliner coachwork.

1951. Like its contemporary Bentleys, the Continental R was fitted with alloy wheels of distinctive and handsome appearance with, for this model only, a recessed winged 'B' insignia on the wheel centres.

Although Heffernan's and Greenley's design drawings show that they had something rather more radical in mind, the interior styling was reassuringly familiar, with similar seating to that of the Turbo R saloon and a basically similar layout to the instruments and controls, except that the centre console was extended into the rear compartment. The electric gear range selector was mounted in the centre console – the first time this had been anywhere other than on the steering column on an automatic Bentley. The automatic transmission was also new, having four forward speeds with the direct drive in third and an overdrive fourth speed for even more effortless, low rpm cruising and improved fuel economy.

The turbocharged engine, which had acquitted itself so convincingly in the Turbo R saloon, provided the Continental R with scorching performance. With top speed turbo-boost regulated to 145mph (233kph) and 0-60mph in a mere 6.6 seconds, the earliest Continental R left little room for improvement. Nevertheless, later versions were good for 155mph (250kph) with 60mph attainable in under six seconds!

It is difficult to imagine a preferable car for driving between, say, London

Winter trials in Sweden were part of the Continental R development programme, using this experimental car. The Continental R was code-named 'Nepal' at the experimental stage.

and Monte Carlo. Though somewhat heavier than its four-door stablemates, the 'barn-storming' performance, impressive handling, splendidly elegant looks and good luggage capacity meant that the Continental R in every way lived up to its revered appellation. This was an extraordinarily refined Bentley Continental that took the marque into a challenging new era with conspicuous success.

Requiring the greatest investment ever by the Company in the improvement of an existing model range, the significant changes announced in August 1993 mainly affected the 1994 model year Continental R in respect of the engine – and therefore performance – which was already remarkable by any standard. Redesigned cylinder heads and manifolding and combining a proven layout with state-of-the-art technology were largely responsible for a 20 per cent increase in power output across the speed range. Performance and responsiveness of the Continental R were further enhanced by the introduction of Electronic Transient Boost Control, which temporarily overrides the normal maximum turbo boost when full load acceleration is required, effectively over-boosting the engine during initial stages of heavy acceleration, such as when overtaking. Occupant safety was further improved by the introduction of airbags as standard for driver and front seat passenger.

The years 1991 to 1994 were difficult ones for the Company, with sales of cars falling alarmingly due to the world-wide recession. As is again proving to be the case, such downturns always affect luxury car sales far more seriously than most other goods. A clever ploy which enabled the Company to keep sales up as much as possible during those difficult years was the introduction of a number of 'niche' models, one of which was the Bentley Turbo S saloon. This was an even more powerful version of the Turbo R, but which is outside the scope of this book. However, the same more powerful engine was installed in a small run of Continental Rs, which were sold as the Continental S. Later, the 385bhp 'S' engine became standard for the Continental R.

On March 7th 1995, at the Geneva Motor Show, the Company unveiled

This page & overleaf: On March 5th 1991, at the Geneva Motor Show, the Bentley Continental R was launched, for deliveries commencing in the 1992 model year. In these photographs of one of the three prototypes, it can be clearly discerned that the new, squatter radiator shell (painted in body colour like that of the Turbo R saloon) has a slight rearward lean. With no front quarter-lights, the traditional stainless steel door window frames would not have been sufficiently stiff for good sealing at the speeds of which the car is so effortlessly capable, so the doors are one-piece steel structures with heavy window frames extending into the roof, and slim stainless steel finishers to preserve the traditional appearance. For the first time there is no chrome moulding down the centreline of the bonnet and no provision for a radiator mascot.

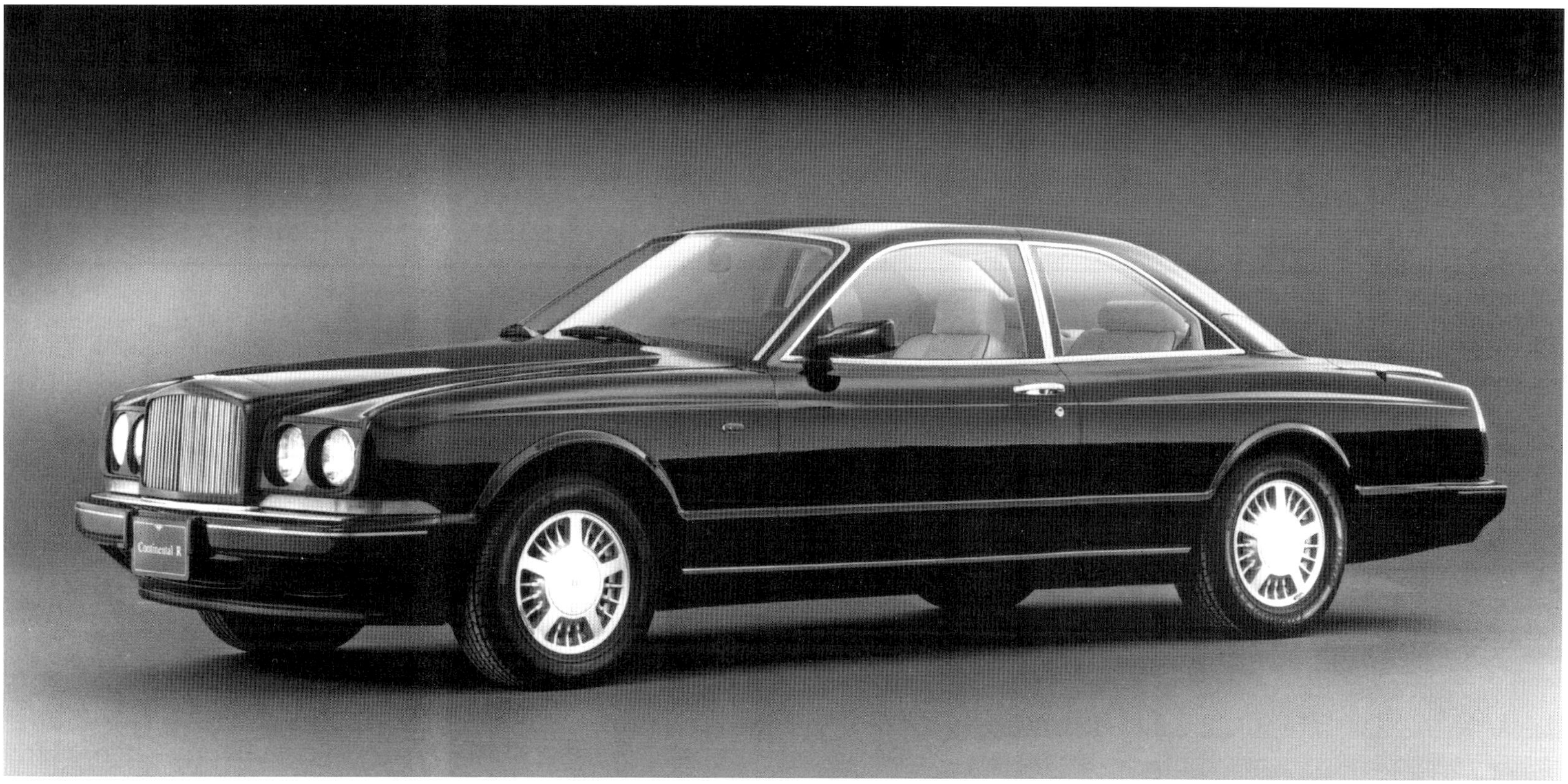
Continental R

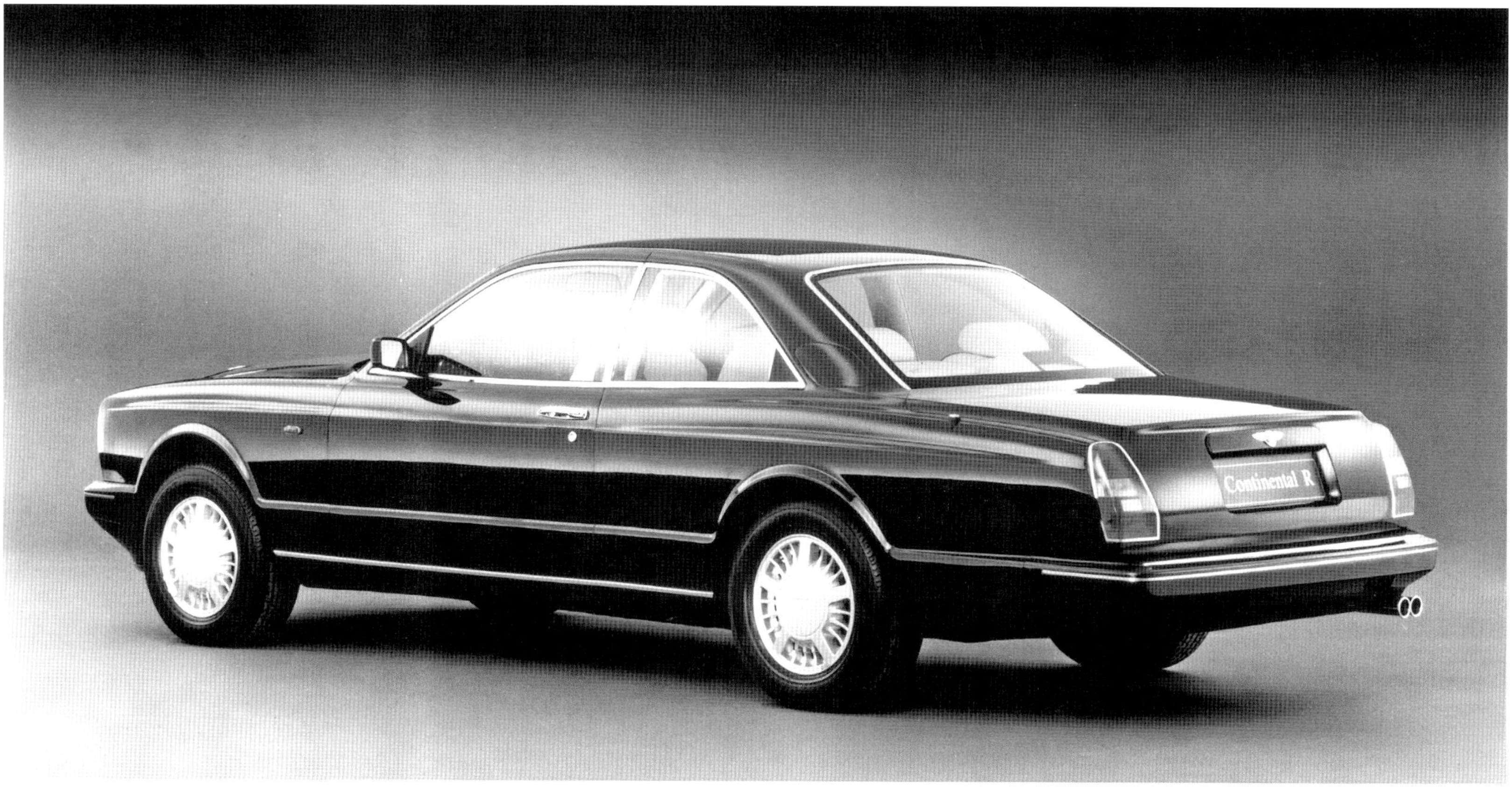
Continental R

The Continental R's interior is traditional yet thoroughly modern, remaining familiar in appearance, but with a new, full-length centre console and fixed centre armrests. The instrumentation is the most comprehensive of any Bentley, and like the R Type Continental of 1952, the gauges include an oil temperature gauge. The front centre armrest houses a compact disc player unit, a telephone and the owner's handbook. If the need arises to carry a third rear-seat passenger, the rear centre console and armrest can be lifted out and stowed in the boot. Note the electric selector in the centre console for the four-speed, overdrive-top automatic gearbox. A switch at the outside top of each front seat squab motors the seat forward for access to the rear seats.

a convertible version of the Continental R. Called the Bentley Azure, this was the first entirely new convertible since 1967. The much acclaimed Continental R lines were superbly adapted to convertible form with the assistance of Pininfarina, unquestionably a world leader in convertible styling. Chris Woodwark, then the recently-appointed Chief Executive of Rolls-Royce Motor Cars, was delighted with this, the first new model since his appointment. "We have shown how we continue to develop new models that exceed the highest expectations of our customers and set new standards at the peak of the luxury and performance car market. Great credit is due to the Bentley design team at Crewe and our colleagues at Pininfarina. We believe this to be the most exciting product announcement in recent years. It represents another major step forward for this Company, and one in which we can all take great pride."

The advent of the Azure, and the dropping of the old Continental Convertible soon after, meant that the Company was well and truly back in the very high performance convertible sector of the market. This is not to say that the old Corniche and Continental convertibles were anything other than high performance cars, but the Azure represented a return to the original

An October 1992 advertisement for the Continental R, from The Spectator, *contains a message about the qualities of the car — and its price!*

The Bentley Continental R. Two cars for the price of four.

The Continental R became a classic motor car the moment it swept onto the highways and by-ways, reintroducing connoisseurs to the real meaning of 'gran turismo': a motor car that provides the epitome of comfort over long distances and, when requested, performs like a whole stable of thoroughbreds.

At the merest press of a button, the gears are held for longer, the suspension responds to the change in pace and the Continental R is transformed from a luxurious tourer into something altogether more sporting.

You will find no single other car will ever capture the essence of the Continental R.

No matter how many you buy.

BENTLEY MOTORS

A WHOLLY OWNED SUBSIDIARY OF ROLLS-ROYCE MOTOR CARS LIMITED

Continental ideal of a higher performance car than the standard models of the range, in convertible form. There were now two cars – a coupé and a convertible – which more than lived up to the Bentley Continental name and ideals.

As Pininfarina had played a vital rôle in developing the Azure, participation in its construction was also appropriate. The bodies were fitted with the hood mechanism and painted by Pininfarina in Italy, before being returned to Crewe for mounting on their mechanical units, trimming and finishing.

New cylinder heads, throttle body, low-loss intake system, liquid charge-air cooling and Zytek engine management system for the 1996 model year Continental R and Azure (announced in June 1995) benefited those models to the tune of 8 per cent in performance and 7 per cent in fuel economy.

In June 1996, a very special derivative of the Continental R made its appearance. With a wheelbase four inches shorter than standard, this was the shortest wheelbase Bentley ever, but, at 400bhp, (later 420bhp) it was also the most powerful and certainly more than 'adequate'!

Shortening the body aft of the doors, with smaller rear quarter-lights and, inevitably, rather less rear seat legroom, lent the Continental T a distinctive stance, more dramatically reflecting the thoroughbred attributes of the Bentley marque. Special 18-inch alloy wheels with very wide, ultra-low profile tyres added to the aggressively powerful look. The cockpit, with its 'engine-turned' aluminium facia and straight-grained mahogany waistrails, recalled the indomitable racing cars built by W. O. Bentley's original Company. Another retro-feature – and a nice touch – was the red engine start button alongside the gear selector.

The special relationship between Rolls-Royce Motor Cars Ltd and the famous Berkeley Square, London Rolls-Royce & Bentley dealer Jack Barclay Ltd, facilitated the production of limited runs of two very special cars. The first of these, the Jack Barclay Continental, was based on the Continental R and was produced in close collaboration with Mulliner Park Ward at Crewe. Only ten were built. These special cars are illustrated in this chapter. The unique exterior stance of the Jack Barclay Continental was enhanced by 18-inch alloy wheels similar to those of the Continental T, flared wheelarches and chrome-plated radiator shell and vanes. The cockpit-like interior featured Azure-type front seats with 'ruched' leather flutes, burr elm woodwork, a 'chunky' steering wheel and an additional gauge for turbo boost pressure.

A 1995 Continental R.

The second Jack Barclay limited edition appeared at the end of 1996 and marked the 70th anniversary of Jack Barclay Ltd, as well as rounding off an outstanding year for Rolls-Royce and Bentley sales around the world. This was the Platinum Anniversary Azure and, again, only ten were built.

A number of external and interior styling changes were announced at the 1997 Geneva Salon. The most obvious of these was a new 'matrix' grille described as "a modern interpretation of the 1920s racing Bentleys, created by hand with the latest materials and laser technology." The front and rear bumpers were re-styled to present softer, more flowing lines, while a new style of 17-inch wheel became standard on both the Continental R and Azure. 18-inch wheels, like those of the Continental T, were offered as an option on the Continental R for even greater emphasis on handling and striking appearance.

The Azure's front seats became standard on the Continental R to enable that model to benefit from the integral seatbelt, for increased comfort and ease of access to the rear seats.

The Continental R was a sensation and a huge success for the Company from the time it first stole the limelight at Geneva in 1991, and deservedly so. It was certainly the ultimate genuine four-seater, grand touring coupé. Even disregarding, for a moment, its ultra-high performance and superb handling characteristics, looks alone would guarantee it a place as a classic in its own lifetime. Overuse and misuse of the word 'classic' has tended to devalue its meaning and impact, but in this instance, it is entirely apt.

The same comments apply equally to the Continental R's derivatives, and particularly to the highly desirable convertible version – the Azure. What other convertible motor car could possibly hope to compete with this one? Since introduction in 1995, its popularity steadily increased in northern Europe, including in the UK, as well as in the traditional convertible markets of California and Florida.

The tradition of subjecting one engine in every hundred to an even more vigorous and exhaustive test procedure than normal continued at Crewe, until engine build was contracted out to fellow Vickers group company Cosworth in mid-1997. Here, a Crewe engineer carefully reassembles one of the one per cent so tested in 1992.

Under the bonnet the 1994 model year cars were visually improved by smart new engine covers. Gone is the old cat's cradle appearance in favour of the 'clean' look seen in this photograph of the Bentley Turbo engine, as fitted to the Continental R. However, the improvements were by no means confined to enhanced appearance: new heads and manifolding allowed the 6.65-litre V8 engine to deliver 20 per cent more power, with improved fuel economy and cleaner emissions.

The 1994 model year Continental R acquired completely re-styled 17-inch wheels and benefited from new Electronic Transient Boost Control, which temporarily overrides the turbocharger's normal maximum boost when full acceleration is called for, such as when overtaking. Despite weighing in at 2.4 tonnes, this ultimate supercar is capable of accelerating smoothly from standstill to 60mph in an amazing 6.2 seconds.

In March 1995, the Company's first entirely new convertible since 1967 was announced. This was a convertible version of the by now legendary Continental R. Originally intended to be called the Continental R Convertible, the name Azure was decided upon a matter of weeks before its announcement. Azure is defined as the colour of clear skies, and is suggestive of the soft and comfortable climate in which the unique pleasures of open air motoring really come into their own.

For the Bentley Azure Pininfarina of Italy assisted with the task of adapting the Continental R's superb lines to this exceptionally elegant convertible form. Performance is, of course, comparable to that of the Continental R.

The Bentley Azure's superb interior is similar to that of the Continental R. The front seats have a built-in seatbelt arrangement.

The unique exterior stance of the Jack Barclay Continental, based on the Continental R, is enhanced by special 18-inch alloy wheels with ultra-low profile tyres, flared wheelarches, special paint colours unique to Jack Barclay and a distinctive frontal appearance with bright chrome finish to the radiator shell and vanes.

The exclusive cockpit-like interior of the Jack Barclay Continental featured Azure-pattern seats with 'ruched' leather pleating, burr elm woodwork, and a 'chunky' steering wheel and gear knob. An additional gauge for turbo boost pressure complements the already comprehensive Continental R instrumentation. Only ten were built.

No Parking
Hunt Thompson Associates
JB 2001
NO PARKING PLEASE

JB 2001

Opposite page: The Jack Barclay Platinum Anniversary Azure. This special limited edition of ten Bentley Azure convertibles marked the 70th Anniversary of Jack Barclay Ltd – the famous Berkeley Square Rolls-Royce & Bentley dealer. Note the special 'ruched' seat pleats and 'starburst' burr walnut veneers.

This page: A 4-inch shorter wheelbase and 18-inch wheels with ultra-low profile tyres give the Continental T an even more distinctive sporting stance than the Continental R, of which this 'niche' model is an obvious derivative. Introduced in June 1996, the Continental T's styling, engineering and appointments were designed to more dramatically reflect the thoroughbred attributes of the Bentley marque. Engine power is a lusty 400bhp, with more than 500lb/ft of torque.

Above left: The Continental T's cockpit reflects the dynamic exterior, with hand-worked 'engine-turned' polished aluminium facia finish and straight-grain mahogany waistrails (though burr walnut veneered waistrails as seen here were available). These features might be regarded as departures from tradition but in fact are redolent of 1920s Le Mans-winning Bentleys. Note the extraordinarily comprehensive instrumentation, even by Bentley Continental standards, with chrome bezel surrounds to the individual gauges. This was the first Bentley Continental since the last of the R Types in 1955 to have an engine start button, which can be seen in the console beside the gear selector.

Above right & below: A later version of the Continental T featured the 'matrix' grille and revised cockpit features. The last remnant of traditional woodwork has gone from the door cappings and perforated leather is used for the pleated parts of the seat upholstery. The gear selector knob is chrome, and the red engine start button has been relocated from the console onto the centre panel of the facia. Note the amazingly comprehensive instrumentation.

The 1997 Continental R factory demonstrator. External styling changes for the 1998 model year included a new 'matrix' grille and re-styled bumpers contributing to softer, more flowing lines. Revised alloy wheels completed the new look.

The interiors of the 1998 model year Continental R (left) and Azure (right) showing the revised upholstery style with curved pleats and partially 'ruched' leather. If the two-tone steering wheel was not to your liking, you could opt for a black leather finish, or it could tone with your car's paintwork or upholstery. In fact, you could have whatever you wanted when ordering a Bentley Continental R or Azure!

The 1998 model year Azure featured similar styling amendments to the Continental R.

Soon after Carlo Talamo acquired his Italian Rolls-Royce & Bentley dealership, Gialloquaranta, Bentley sales soared from three per cent of total sales per year to thirty-three per cent. Sr Talamo's own Continental R was extremely unusual. Built to his own specification, this very special Continental R used the Continental T engine, but with a more sporting camshaft, a larger turbocharger, gas-flowed heads, and ram air intake to boost the power output to an incredible 425bhp. The interior was characterised more by what was left out than by what was added, with little by way of the luxury surroundings normally associated with Bentley Continentals. There was no rear seat in the conventional sense, though there was a roll cage and full racing harnesses. The facia was turned aluminium, like that of the Continental T.

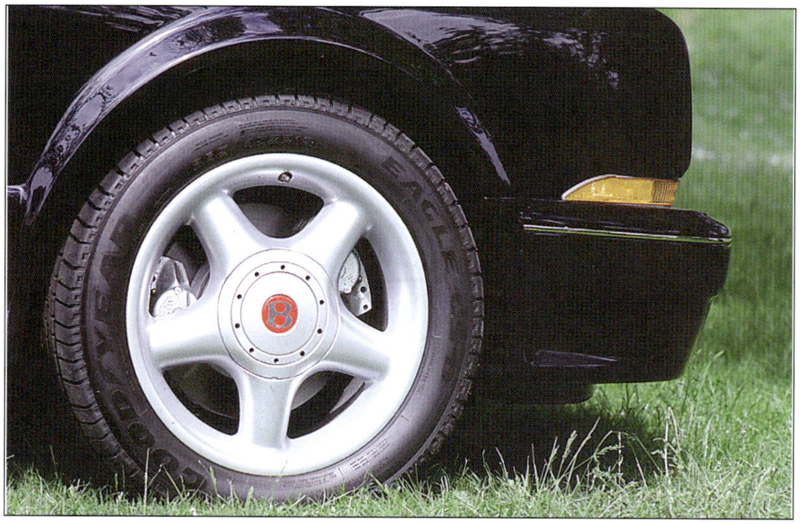
EAGLE

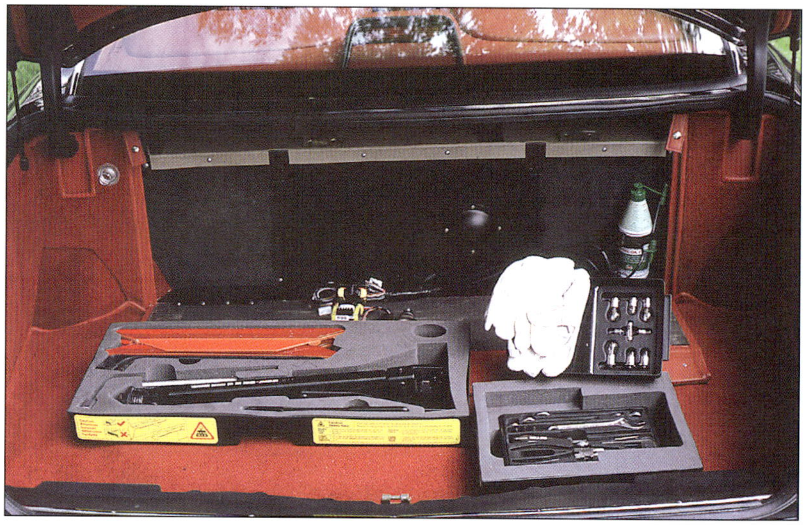

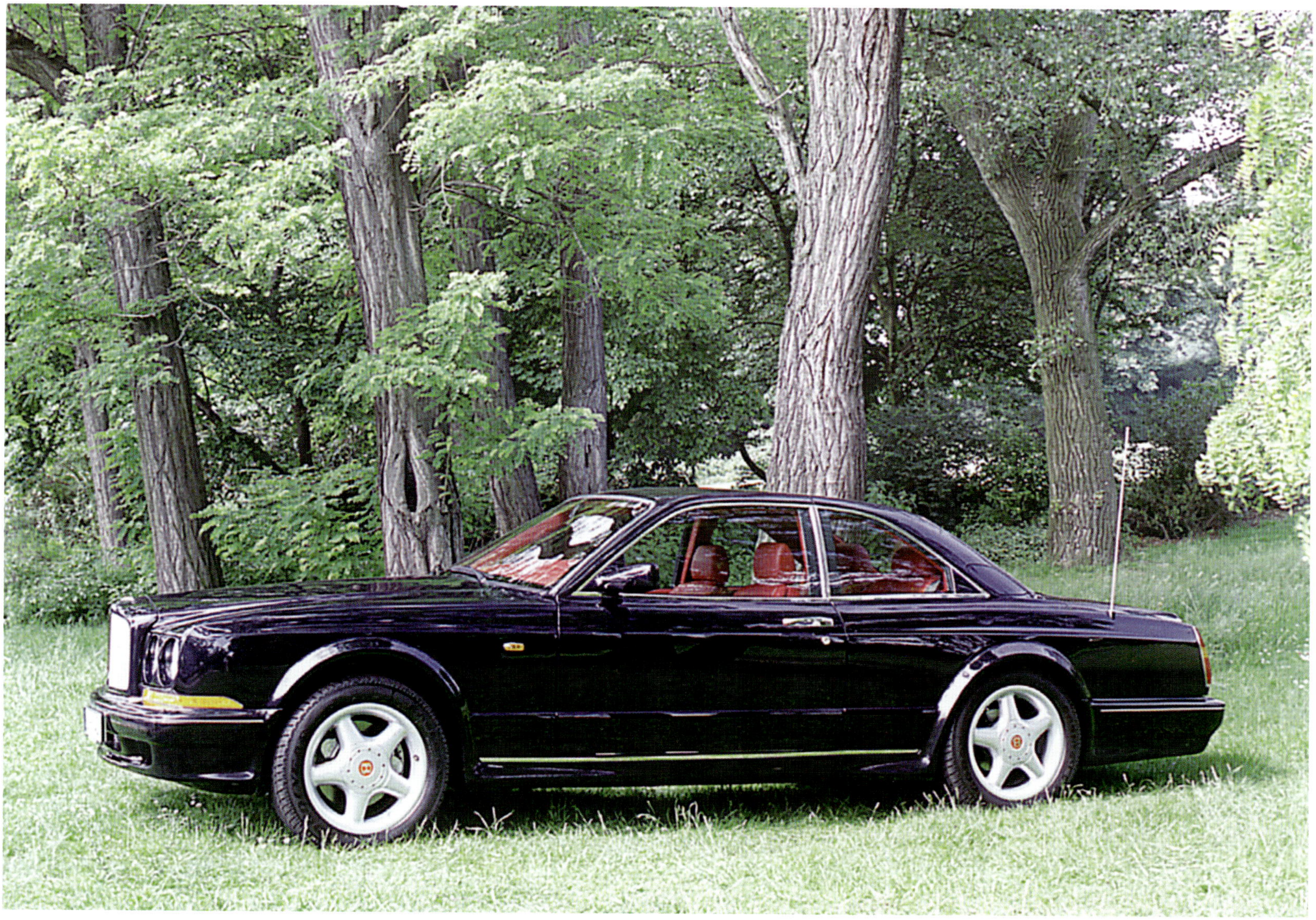

Both pages: 1997 Continental T SCBZU23CXVCX53458. The best-performing Bentley up to that time, and as superbly styled as any of its predecessors. The under-bonnet installation is both visually impressive and tidy, while the boot is equally luxuriously carpeted as the passenger compartment. The tools, normally stowed behind a panel in the front of the boot, are seen here with the bottle of spare Hydraulic System Mineral Oil.

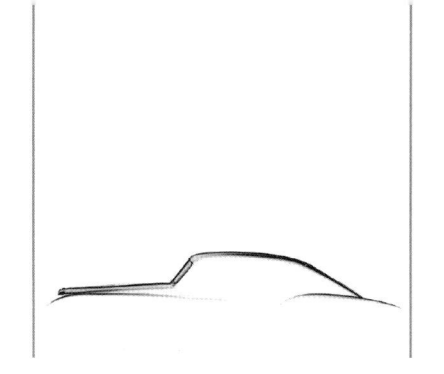

TECHNICAL SPECIFICATIONS – CONTINENTAL R & DERIVATIVES

ENGINE

Dimensions
Eight cylinders in 90-degree vee formation. Bore 4.1in (104.1mm), stroke 3.9in (99.1mm), cubic capacity 412in^3 (6750cc). Compression ratio 8:1.

Cylinder block/crankcase
Aluminium alloy monobloc casting with 'wet' cylinder liners. Cross-bolted crankcase.

Crankshaft
Nitride hardened chrome molybdenum steel. Integral balance weights. Five main bearings.

Pistons
Aluminium alloy with four rings.

Cylinder heads
Aluminium alloy with austenitic steel valve seat inserts.

Valve gear
Overhead valves operated through hydraulic tappets and push-rods. Monikrom cast iron camshaft driven by helical gears.

Fuel injection
Electronic fuel injection with Zytek EMS3 engine management system.

Ignition system
Constant Energy Electronic. Knock-sensing automatic retard system.

Cooling system
Coolant solution of 50 per cent anti-freeze, 50 per cent water pressurised at 15psi, circulated by belt-driven centrifugal pump. Temperature regulation by thermostat.

Power output
1998 Continental T: 420bhp (312kw) and 650lb/ft (875Nm) of torque.

CHASSIS

Monocoque construction with separate front and rear subframes: front – steel box-section construction mounted to car underframe by rubber mounts; rear – comprises the rear suspension and final drive crossmembers connected by tubular members to form a rigid structure. Attached to car underframe by cylindrical rubber mounts. Short telescopic damper fitted to each front mount to dampen fore and aft movement.

Dimensions
Overall length: 17ft 6.3in (5342mm). Overall length, Continental T: 17ft 2.3in (5241mm). Wheelbase, standard: 10ft ½in (3061mm). Wheelbase, Continental T: 9ft 8 ½in (2959mm). Front track: 5ft 1in (1549mm). Rear track: 5ft 2¼in (1581mm). Kerbside weight of car: 5401lb (2450kg).

Suspension
Front – independent by coil springs with lower wishbones, compliant controlled upper levers, telescopic dampers and anti-roll bar mounted on the front subframe. Rear – independent by coil springs with semi-trailing arms, gas springs in conjunction with suspension struts acting as integral dampers and height control rams. Anti-roll bar. Electronic 3-position automatic ride control system.

Hydraulic system
Two camshaft-driven hydraulic pumps delivering Hydraulic Systems Mineral Oil under pressure (up to 2500psi) to a pair of hydraulic accumulators mounted on either side of the crankcase. Hydraulic pressure stored in the accumulators is used for the braking and height control systems. Warning lights on the facia to indicate low pressure or fluid level for each hydraulic circuit.

Brakes
Anti-lock (ABS) disc brakes on all four wheels. Each front wheel fitted with two twin-cylinder calipers and each rear wheel with one four-cylinder caliper. Two separate and independent hydraulic circuits from the high pressure hydraulic system operated by distribution valves connected to the brake pedal. Foot applied, hand released parking brake. Separate brake pads for parking brake.

Height control system
Fully automatic hydraulic height control system to maintain the standing height of the car under all load conditions, by means of height control rams integral with the rear gas springs.

Steering
Power-assisted rack-and-pinion steering with centre take-off. Power assistance by hydraulic pressure from Saginaw engine-driven pump. Energy-absorbing collapsible steering column. Turns lock to lock: 2.7.

Transmission
General Motors 4-speed electronically controlled automatic transmission with overdrive top gear and torque converter lock-up, electronically linked to the engine management system. Electrically operated gear selection by control lever in centre console with sport/standard gearchange pattern selector.
Propeller shaft: dynamically balanced, single straight tube with rubber jointed coupling at front and rear.
Viscous control differential for optimum traction and control. Final drive ratio: 2.69:1.

Exhaust system
Cars not fitted with catalytic converter: Twin pipe system with six silencer boxes. Cars fitted with catalytic converter: Twin downtake pipes from the engine merge into a single pipe prior to the catalytic converter, after which the system reverts to a dual system with twin intermediate and rear silencer boxes.

Road wheels and tyres
At introduction: 16in aluminium alloy wheels with 255/60 ZR16 low profile radial ply tyres. 1994 model year: 17in aluminium alloy wheels with 255/55 ZR17 low profile radial ply tyres. 1998 model year Continental T: 18in aluminium alloy wheels with Pirelli 285/45 ZR18 asymmetrical tyres developed specifically for the Continental T.

COACHWORK

Two-door saloon, coupé, or drophead coupé coachwork built entirely in steel at Crewe.

PERFORMANCE DATA

The following performance figures are quoted for the Continental R, Azure, and Continental T.

Acceleration through gears (seconds)	*Continental R*	*Azure*	*Continental T*
0-60mph	6.0	6.3	5.7
Maximum speed (mph):	155.0	150.0	170.0
Petrol consumption (mpg):	16.0	15.9	15.1

CHASSIS NUMBERING SYSTEM

(See Appendix 2.)

First Vehicle Identification Numbers

Continental R (prototype)	SCBZB03D5NCX42001
Continental R (1993 model year)	SCBZB03DXPCX42501
Continental R (1994 model year)	SCBZB03C4RCX52001
Azure	SCBZK03C3SCH50801

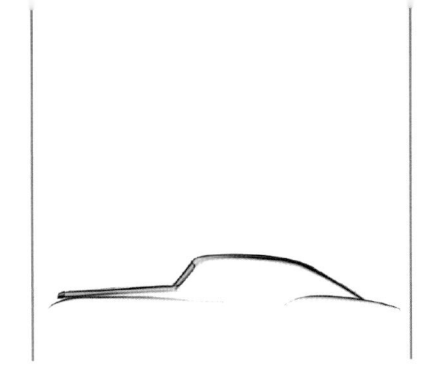

APPENDIX 1
CHASSIS & ENGINE NUMBERING SYSTEMS EXPLAINED

R Type to S3 1952-66

Chassis numbering system

Bentley Continentals – from R Type to S3 inclusive – had chassis numbers with a 'BC' prefix ahead of one, two or three numerals, followed by another letter denoting the series (R Type), or two letters (S1, S2 and S3), the first of which denoted the series. Chassis were numbered consecutively, omitting 13, with the exception of the Continental S3 which used even numbers only. In all cases, left-hand drive cars were distinguished by the addition of the letter 'L' ahead of the regular series letters, as in the following randomly chosen examples:

Model	Sample rhd chassis number	Sample lhd chassis number
R	BC7A	BC8LA
S1	BC14AF	BC15LAF
S2	BC1AR	BC2LAR
S3	BC2XA	BC4LXA

Engine numbering system

The engine numbers of Bentley Continentals R Type to S3 were closely related to their chassis numbers, incorporating the letters 'BC' and the main series letter, with the positions of these elements of the engine numbering differing between the four models concerned. In the case of consecutively numbered chassis (R Type, S1, S2), the numerical part of the engine number was the same as that of the chassis number, up to and including 12. After that, due to the traditional omission of 13 from chassis numbering, the engine number fell one behind the chassis number. In the case of the Continental S3, which had even numbers only, the numerical part of the engine number was the chassis number halved. All of this is made clear by the following examples:

Model	Sample chassis number	Corresponding engine number
R	BC10A	BCA10
	BC20A	BCA19
S1	BC12AF	BC12A
	BC14AF	BC13A
S2	BC12AR	A12BC
	BC30AR	A29BC
S3	BC10XA	5ABC
	BC40XA	20ABC

213

T Series and Corniche 1966-80

Chassis numbering system

In October 1965, when the Rolls-Royce Silver Shadow and Bentley T Series cars were introduced, a changed system of numbering was adopted. Within these Car Serial Numbers, each digit of the three-letter prefix has a specific meaning, explained below. This prefix is followed by a four- or five-digit number. This Silver Shadow numbering system included the derivative Bentley Corniche, and the explanation below only includes digits applicable to that model. The sample Car Serial Number shown is that of the first Bentley Corniche.

C B H 1 0 4 2 0
1 2 3 4 5 6 7 8

1. Body type
   C – Two-door Saloon
   D – Convertible

2. Marque
   B – Bentley

3. Steering position/year
   H – home (right-hand drive)
   X – export (left-hand drive)

On North American specification cars, commencing with the 1972 model year, X was replaced by a year code letter, as follows:
   A – 1972
   B – 1973
   C – 1974
   D – 1975
   E – 1976
   F – 1977
   G – 1978
   K – 1979
   L – 1980

4-7. Sequential identification number
   Cars for California with fuel injection (from 1980) had a 'C' suffix.

The numbers used for coachbuilt T Series and Corniche cars were allocated from the Silver Shadow numbering system, as follows:
   1149-4548
   5001-5603
   6001-8861
   9001-26708
   30001-41686 (CY20AB spec. cars)
   50001-50776 (with mineral oil hydraulic system)

Engine numbering system

Except in the case of an engine change prior to a car leaving the factory, the engine number was the same as the car serial number, without the prefix.

First and last car serial numbers, coachbuilt Bentley T and Bentley Corniche:

Firsts:	Chassis no: (prefix omitted)
Bentley T HJMPW two-door saloon	1149
Bentley T HJMPW drophead coupé	3049
Bentley Corniche two-door Saloon	10420
Bentley Corniche Convertible	10122

Car serial numbers commencing 50001 were used for Corniche with HSMO (Hydraulic Systems Mineral Oil) hydraulic system and Silver Spirit-type rear suspension package. Within the factory these cars were code-named CYZ. The last numbers in this 'half-way house' series, prior to the introduction of the 17-digit Vehicle Identification Number (VIN) system, were:

Lasts: *Chassis no: (prefix omitted)*

Corniche 2-door Saloon   50614 (then discontinued)

Corniche Convertible   50756 (then to 17-digit VIN system)

From October 1980

Chassis numbering system (Vehicle Identification Number)

In October 1980, when the Rolls-Royce Silver Spirit and Bentley Mulsanne range of cars was introduced, an entirely new system of numbering was adopted. This was the 17-digit Vehicle Identification Number (VIN), an American device adopted by the International Standards Organisation for world use. The coachbuilt cars were integrated into this system early in 1981. Each of the first twelve digits has a specific meaning, detailed below. The remaining five digits made up the car's number. The sample VIN below is that of the first 17-digit numbered Bentley Corniche, followed by an explanation of the meaning of the 17 digits.

S	C	B	Y	D	4	2	A	7	B	C	X	0	2	4	9	9
1	2	3	4	5	6	7	8	9	10	11	12	13	14	15	16	17

1 & 2   World Manufacturer Identifier (country):
       S – Europe C – England

3   World Manufacturer Identifier (marque)
       B – Bentley

4   Chassis or underframe type:
       Y – early Corniche and Camargue VINs*
       Z – later Corniche, Continental, Continental R and derivative VINs
       * Early 17-digit Corniche cars used a different underframe code because they had a 'half-way house' underframe, basically Silver Shadow (SY) but with Silver Spirit (SZ) type 'Rear Suspension Package,' which had been developed for the 1979/80 (50001 series) Corniche. When the Corniche eventually progressed from CYZ underframe to the full Silver Spirit specification (CZ) underframe, the 4th digit of the VIN was changed to Z.

5   Body type:
       D – Convertible (the two-door saloon was discontinued before the 17-digit numbering system began)
       J – Camargue (only one Bentley Camargue built)
       B – Continental R and S
       K – Azure
       U – Continental T

6   US requirement. Indicates engine type.
       Cars for all other markets initially had 0000 for the unused digits 6 to 9. Later, these digits came into use for all markets.
       4 – type L410 engine
       0 – other than America

7   Carburetters or fuel injection
       1 – carburetters
       2 – fuel injection
       T – Turbo
       0 – other than America

      From the 1987 model year the following engine type codes were phased in for digits 6 and 7:
      00 – naturally aspirated, fuel injected

02 – naturally aspirated, fuel injected, catalyst equipped
03 – turbocharged, catalyst equipped
04 – turbocharged

8 Occupant restraint system
A – Active belts
B – Passive belts - front (USA only)
C – Airbags
D – Driver-only airbag, passenger active belts
0 – other than America (prior to 1987 model year)

9 Check digit
AUS requirement. Used to ensure VIN is correct and to foil would-be VIN forgers. If the VIN is incorrect at any one digit, the check digit will show this. The check digit is 0 to 9 or X.

10 Year
Indicates the model year for which, and not necessarily in which, a car was built.

A – 1980	M – 1991
B – 1981	N – 1992
C – 1982	P – 1993
D – 1983	R – 1994
E – 1984	S – 1995
F – 1985	T – 1996
G – 1986	V – 1997
H – 1987	W – 1998
J – 1988	X – 1999
K – 1989	Y – 2000
L – 1990	

11 Factory
C – Crewe

12 Steering position
H – right-hand drive
X – left-hand drive

13-17 Sequential identification number
These commenced at 01001 in 1980.

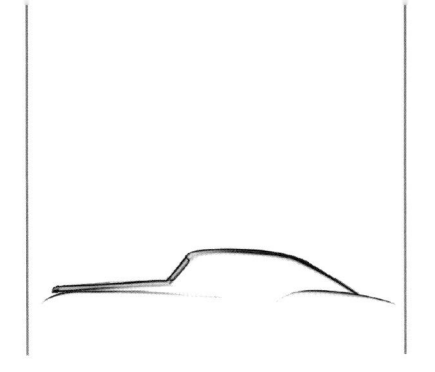

APPENDIX 2
BENTLEY CONTINENTAL MODIFICATION DATA, R TYPE TO S3, 1952-1966

The chassis numbers indicated are those from which the listed modifications were continuously embodied in production, except where otherwise mentioned. For clarity, 'L' for left-hand drive has been omitted from chassis numbers.

R Type Continental

BC19A	Reduced compression height pistons
BC1B	Revised (R Type) chassis frame
BC4C	Commonised cylinder head
BC18C	Non-opposed springs in side steering tube deleted
BC21C	All welded chassis frame
BC30C	Deletion of reduced friction modifications on steering connections
BC50C	Introduction of B.VI type gearbox tie rod
BC52C	Centre bar in radiator shell
BC70C	Flywheel inertia rings (automatic cars)
BC78C	Thicker third motion shaft thrust washer
BC1D	3¾in bore engine. Compensator pipe between front and rear servo
BC5D	Strengthened jaws on front brake operating links
BC12D	Elimination of chromium-plated servo pressure plate
BC35D	Flexibox seal in water pump
BC37D	Long stroke starter pinion
BC43D	Improved cold starting device
BC47D	2nd speed start (in selector position '2', automatic gearbox)

S1 Continental

BC11AF	Load of fulcrum bracket bolt spread over larger area; modified butterfly valve and countersunk screws in cold starting device
BC12AF	Strengthened rear axle tube
BC16AF	Setscrews for main bearing caps; improved servo sealing
BC19AF	Increased bearing surface to steering ball-joint nuts
BC21AF	Increased friction on brake shakeback stops; increased load on servo return spring
BC69AF	Brake wheel cylinder material changed from aluminium to cast iron; stronger rear anti-roll bar clamps
BC70AF	Provision of brake fluid reservoir filter
BC79AF	Revised rear engine mounting
BC81AF	Drag links with greater resistance to kinking under compression

BC88AF	Aluminium brake master cylinder
BC96AF	Modified rear engine mounting bracket and larger bolts; strengthened front spring support plates
BC1BG	Increased number of fixing holes in rear axle tube
BC2BG	Roller bearings in steering lever
BC3BG	Strengthened front suspension fulcrum bracket
BC6BG	Modified brake shakeback stops
BC16BG	Dual brake master cylinders and fluid reservoirs
BC21BG	8:1 compression cylinder head with 2in diameter inlet valves; modified dynamo and regulator
BC23BG	Modified sealing ring on centre steering lever (power-assisted steering cars)
BC27BG	Welded stiffeners to jacking brackets
BC28BG	Copper petrol pipes; uphill run pipes from master cylinders to fluid reservoirs; reach nut and washer to suit spot facing of ball-joint and trunnion body, output shaft to propeller shaft
BC30BG	New radiator and drain tap to suit revised chassis frame
BC37BG	Revised chassis frame with splayed front ends
BC62BG	Increased number of fixing holes in rear axle centre casing
BC70BG	Power steering mounting bolt reversed
BC92BG	Oil deflector plates for rear shock dampers
BC96BG	Voltage regulator with swamp resistance
BC1CH	Strengthened front shock damper body and sleeve in mounting bolt bore
BC7CH	Stronger front shock damper casing
BC31CH	Combined inertia and starter ring; modified starter drive; stiffened clutch casing
BC41CH	Stronger axle yoke fulcrum pin
BC1DJ	Improved propeller shaft seal
BC8DJ	Modified stub axle yoke seal
BC10DJ	Modified rear axle shaft flange
BC36DJ	Stronger drag link
BC42DJ	'Roto' finished pulleys
BC44DJ	Strengthened steering cam adjusting sleeve
BC47DJ	Larger shock damper end cover studs
BC1EL	Type DR.3 windscreen wiper motor
BC3EL	Stronger rear shock damper link bushes
BC1FM	Idler lever lubrication pipe deleted; modified rear silencer mounting; improved rear brake expander wedges; final type modified stub axles; centrally mounted twin-jet windscreen washer; grease lubricated track rods; larger diameter axle shaft splines; grease lubrication of centre steering link; intermediate heater and demister controls; wire type clips on propeller shaft grease seals; extended lower triangle lever outer bearing blocks; increased capacity boot type air conditioning refrigeration unit; increased side clearance on rear brake expander wedges; larger ($5/16$in) valance plate bolts; modified handbrake cable run
BC11FM	Enlarged shakeback stop in brake shoe web
BC14FM	Strengthened front hubs
BC31FM	Plain washer at ends of pivot distance piece on braking system direct and indirect linkage
BC44FM	Brake fluid supply pipe check valve deleted
BC1GN	Simplified starter relay mounting
BC9GN	Thermal conductor type coolant temperature gauge
BC16GN	Seal between bearing housing body and front shock damper
BC25GN	Extended neck on propeller shaft seal
BC28GN	Modified front brake shoe link
BC30GN	Purolator air filter (cars with refrigerated air conditioning)

S2 Continental

BC2AR	Improved throttle controls, left-hand drive cars
BC11AR	Sealed thermal delay switch
BC38AR	Solid camshaft

BC45AR	First improvement to crown wheel bolts
BC52AR	Second improvement to crown wheel bolts
BC66AR	Seamless propeller shaft
BC106AR	Otter switch in automatic choke
BC112AR	Lagged air pipes in automatic choke
BC114AR	New automatic choke butterfly valve
BC137AR	New automatic choke bi-metal strip cover
BC139AR	Modified hydraulic tappets
BC1BY	Modified starter motor; new front shock damper mounting plate; brake pedal gap plate
BC3BY	Change to fast idle cam bracket
BC10BY	Shorter fan mounting extension cone; extended radiator bottom outlet pipe; new bottom coolant hose
BC16BY	Reversion to S1 Type front silencer with modified pipes and flanges
BC21BY	New radiator filler cap seal
BC40BY	New starter motor
BC51BY	New dynamo mounting bracket; revised cylinder head assembly and valves, etc.
BC72BY	New switching arrangement for instrument and capping rail lights; new map lamp; cigar lighter with amber glow ring
BC74BY	Crankcase modified to raise oil level in camshaft trough (except BC97BY)
BC76BY	New silencer assemblies
BC78BY	Revised valve shaft and rockers
BC90BY	York Shipley air conditioning compressor replaced Tecumseh compressor
BC92BY	New front shock damper body
BC93BY	47-degree servo cams to reduce front to rear braking ratio
BC99BY	Accelerator pedal stop and gearbox throttle valve control, right-hand drive cars
BC100BY	Final drive ratio changed from 2.92:1 to 3.08:1
BC28CZ	Petrol tank breather
BC37CZ	Heatsink in automatic choke
BC43CZ	Waterproof sparking plug adaptor
BC66CZ	Blue instrument lighting
BC70CZ	Headlamp flashing facility (except North America)
BC78CZ	Handbrake warning light; new rear lamps (except Park Ward cars)
BC85CZ	New starter ring gear
BC109CZ	Modified water connections
BC112CZ	Increased capacity fuel pump
BC134CZ	Improved valve rockers
BC135CZ	Brake pedal ball crank lever; lighter steering, left-hand drive cars
BC137CZ	Reversion to original starter ring gear
BC139CZ	New method of cam wheel lubrication

S3 Continental

BC24XA	Longer starter relay cable
BC72XA	Improved radiator pressure relief valve
BC144XA	New top and bottom radiator hoses; stainless steel wheel trim discs
BC152XA	Modified steering box to allow trapped air to be bled
BC166XA	Two-shoe front brakes
BC12XB	Modified carburetter float chamber lid and needle valve; steering hose re-routed and heatshield fitted to steering box mounting arm, left-hand drive cars
BC74XB	Automatic gearbox torus cover
BC68XC	New voltage regulator
BC100XC	Revised handbrake cable system, right-hand drive cars
BC116XC	Heatshield on right-hand exhaust manifold
BC122XC	Choke in reversing light circuit
BC124XC	Carburetter vent pipe bore increased

BC148XC	New dynamo bracket
BC152XC	Bellhousing undertray fitted (except BC154XC and cars for tropical or dusty countries)
BC156XC	New steering box spool valve and housing
BC158XC	Link strip replaced starter solenoid cable; modified power steering cylinder
BC172XC	Improved copper battery cable
BC182XC	Power steering hoses re-routed, right-hand drive cars
BC184XC	New high tension resistive core ignition cables
BC22XD	Ventilation holes in flywheel bellhousing
BC6XE	New camshaft (except BC8XE)
BC34XE	Standard S3 demister blower; electrically operated valves and taps in heating/demisting system; increased capacity windscreen wiper motor (Park Ward coachwork)
BC64XE	Interference fit cylinder liners
BC68XE	New SU type AUF 400 fuel pump

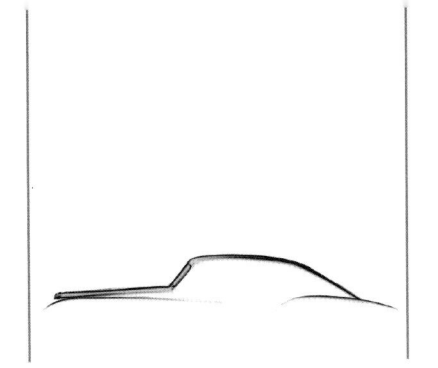

APPENDIX 3
GEARBOX & GEARCHANGE ANALYSIS, R TYPE CONTINENTAL

Right-hand drive cars:

Manual, right-hand change	126*
Manual, centre change	6**
Automatic	33
Total right-hand drive cars	165

* including the prototype BC26A, formerly 9-B-VI.
** including BC20B, built with centre gearchange but later changed to standard right-hand change.

Left-hand drive cars:

Manual, column change	11
Manual, centre change	23
Automatic	9
Total left-hand drive cars	43

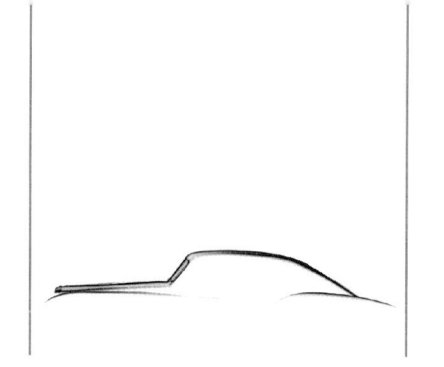

APPENDIX 4 –
CAR LISTINGS: R TYPE & S TYPE CONTINENTALS

Chassis number
In accordance with Bentley Continental chassis numbering, all chassis numbers listed here commence with the 'BC' suffix, and the letter 'L' ahead of the series letter(s) indicates a left-hand drive car (see also Appendix 2.) The number 13 was always omitted from chassis numbering.

Engine number
Engine numbers were allocated in strict sequence (see Appendix 2.)

Coachbuilder
All Bentley Continentals were coachbuilt and the name of the coachbuilder responsible for the coachwork on each chassis is given here. After H. J. Mulliner & Co. Ltd. was acquired by Rolls-Royce Ltd. in 1959, that firm and Park Ward & Co. Ltd. (acquired by Rolls-Royce in 1939) became progressively integrated, eventually becoming H. J. Mulliner, Park Ward Ltd. in 1961. For a further two years or so, the designs of the two constituent companies continued to carry individual step-sill plates. In order to avoid confusion between the two constituent companies' designs, they are attributed here to the individual coachbuilders, even where, strictly speaking, they were built by the combined firm.

Body style
Coachwork types are listed here in accordance with generic body style designations. For example, a 2-door saloon is listed as such even where the records indicate 'fixed head coupé,' 'saloon coupé,' 'sports saloon,' or some other description. However, any true fixed head coupé is listed as such. All 4-door saloons are listed simply as 'Saloon,' with the exception of H. J. Mulliner's 'Flying Spur' saloon, which is listed as just that.

Delivery date
Delivery dates of complete cars. These are listed numerically, showing the month and year. For example: 6-63 means June 1963.

Country
This is the country of original delivery. Some dilemmas arose here. For example, a left-hand drive car delivered (and registered) in the UK to an American customer who subsequently shipped the car to the USA – should this be listed as UK or USA? In such cases I have shown that the UK was the country of original delivery. What about a right-hand drive car delivered to the Netherlands for the use of one of Her Majesty's Ambassadors, and which was obviously intended to be repatriated at the end of the tour of duty? Again, the Netherlands is listed as the country of original delivery.

UK registration number
Where known, the original registration mark of each car delivered new in the UK is listed here.

Original owner
The name of the person to whom, or organisation to which, each car was delivered when new is listed here.

Remarks
Some of the Motor Show exhibits, Trials cars and the like are shown as such in this column, where known.

R TYPE CONTINENTAL

Chassis no.	Eng. no.	Coachbuilder	Body style	Del.	Country	UK reg. no.	Original owner	Remarks
BC1A	BCA1	H. J. Mulliner	2-door saloon	6-52	France		J. Simon	
BC2A	BCA2	H. J. Mulliner	2-door saloon	6-52	France		H. Sentet	
BC3A	BCA3	H. J. Mulliner	2-door saloon	7-52	USA		W. Spear	
BC4A	BCA4	H. J. Mulliner	2-door saloon	7-52	USA		Briggs Cunningham	
BC5A	BCA5	H. J. Mulliner	2-door saloon	8-52	USA		C. Moran	
BC6A	BCA6	H. J. Mulliner	2-door saloon	9-52	France		H. Lafond	1952 Paris Salon
BC7A	BCA7	H. J. Mulliner	2-door saloon	11-52	France		L. Sanielevici	1952 Earls Court Show
BC8LA	BCA8	H. J. Mulliner	2-door saloon	9-52	USA		H. Kizer	
BC9A	BCA9	H. J. Mulliner	2-door saloon	10-52	Belgium		C. Lang	
BC10A	BCA10	H. J. Mulliner	2-door saloon	12-52	Switzerland		G. Filipinetti	
BC11A	BCA11	H. J. Mulliner	2-door saloon	11-52	France		Mrs Guiness	
BC12A	BCA12	H. J. Mulliner	2-door saloon	12-52	Italy		A. Agnielli	
BC14LA	BCA13	H. J. Mulliner	2-door saloon	10-52	USA		Dr W. Burden	
BC15A	BCA14	H. J. Mulliner	2-door saloon	1-53	France		André Embiricos	
BC16LA	BCA15	H. J. Mulliner	2-door saloon	1-53	USA		S. Magnus Swenson	
BC17A	BCA16	H. J. Mulliner	2-door saloon	1-53	Switzerland		R. Habisreutinger	
BC18LA	BCA17	H. J. Mulliner	2-door saloon	5-53	Portugal		C. Ferreira	
BC19A	BCA18	H. J. Mulliner	2-door saloon	2-53	Switzerland		A. Frey	
BC20A	BCA19	H. J. Mulliner	2-door saloon	2-53	Switzerland		L. Schneiter	1953 Geneva Show
BC21A	BCA20	H. J. Mulliner	2-door saloon	3-53	Switzerland		G. Luginbuhl	1953 Geneva Show
BC22A	BCA21	H. J. Mulliner	2-door saloon	3-53	Switzerland		C. Gillet	
BC23A	BCA22	H. J. Mulliner	2-door saloon	3-53	France		J. Foussier	
BC24A	BCA23	H. J. Mulliner	2-door saloon	3-53	France		Sir Duncan Orr-Lewis	
BC25A	BCA24	H. J. Mulliner	2-door saloon	4-53	France		Aristotle Onassis	
BC26A	BH11	H. J. Mulliner	2-door saloon	8-51	UK	OLG 490	Rolls-Royce Ltd	Experimental prototype, originally 9-B-VI
BC1LB	BCB1	H. J. Mulliner	2-door saloon	4-53	USA		J. Gordon Mack	
BC2LB	BCB2	H. J. Mulliner	2-door saloon	3-53	USA		R. Parish	1953 New York Show
BC3B	BCB3	H. J. Mulliner	2-door saloon	4-53	France		R. Faye	
BC4B	BCB4	H. J. Mulliner	2-door saloon	5-53	France		Franco-Britannic Autos	Paris Trials car
BC5B	BCB5	H. J. Mulliner	2-door saloon	5-53	France		W. Zietz	
BC6B	BCB6	H. J. Mulliner	2-door saloon	7-53	UK	NRU 111	F. McInnes	
BC7B	BCB7	H. J. Mulliner	2-door saloon	6-53	UK	BEN 900	W. Street	
BC8LB	BCB8	H. J. Mulliner	2-door saloon	6-53	Canada		N. Monsarrat	
BC9B	BCB9	H. J. Mulliner	2-door saloon	7-53	UK	HRX 990	M. Collier	
BC10LB	BCB10	H. J. Mulliner	2-door saloon	5-53	USA		J. Bryce	
BC11LB	BCB11	H. J. Mulliner	2-door saloon	6-53	USA		Briggs Cunningham	
BC12B	BCB12	H. J. Mulliner	2-door saloon	6-53	Switzerland		M. Ras	
BC14B	BCB13	H. J. Mulliner	2-door saloon	5-53	UK	JM 1	J. Moores	
BC15B	BCB14	H. J. Mulliner	2-door saloon	6-53	UK	NYF 575	W. Riley	
BC16B	BCB15	H. J. Mulliner	2-door saloon	8-53	UK	IJ 1	C. Lord	
BC17LB	BCB16	H. J. Mulliner	2-door saloon	5-53	USA		L. Gilmour	
BC18B	BCB17	H. J. Mulliner	2-door saloon	6-53	Cuba		J. Tarafa	
BC19B	BCB18	H. J. Mulliner	2-door saloon	8-53	UK		S. McCrudden	
BC20B	BCB19	H. J. Mulliner	2-door saloon	9-53	UK	OGF 905	Rolls-Royce Ltd	Trials car
BC21B	BCB20	H. J. Mulliner	2-door saloon	7-53	UK	XMG 1	R. Holmes	
BC22B	BCB21	H. J. Mulliner	2-door saloon	1-54	UK	NXY 2	T. Burn	
BC23B	BCB22	H. J. Mulliner	2-door saloon	8-53	UK	MBM 777	B. Mavroleon	
BC24B	BCB23	H. J. Mulliner	2-door saloon	9-53	UK		G. Lambert	
BC25B	BCB24	H. J. Mulliner	2-door saloon	10-53	UK	A 3727	J. Sears	

R TYPE CONTINENTAL

Chassis no.	Eng. no.	Coachbuilder	Body style	Del.	Country	UK reg. no.	Original owner	Remarks
BC1C	BCC1	H. J. Mulliner	2-door saloon	12-53	UK	DVV 696	S. Sears	
BC2LC	BCC2	H. J. Mulliner	2-door saloon	8-53	USA		W. Kemble Carpenter	
BC3C	BCC3	H. J. Mulliner	2-door saloon	9-53	UK	FRD 444	H. Coriat	
BC4C	BCC4	H. J. Mulliner	2-door saloon	1-54?	UK	GR 77	G. Rotinoff	
BC5C	BCC5	H. J. Mulliner	2-door saloon	10-53	UK		J. Archdale	
BC6C	BCC6	H. J. Mulliner	2-door saloon	10-53	UK	RWB 704	K. Lee	
BC7C	BCC7	H. J. Mulliner	2-door saloon	11-53	UK	OLA 796	Stavros Niarchos	
BC8C	BCC8	H. J. Mulliner	2-door saloon	10-53	UK	NYF 7	L. Green	
BC9C	BCC9	H. J. Mulliner	2-door saloon	2-54	UK	MLT 3	P. Scrutton	
BC10C	BCC10	H. J. Mulliner	2-door saloon	2-54	USA		Maharajah of Indore	
BC11C	BCC11	H. J. Mulliner	2-door saloon	2-54	UK	SMA 410	Rolls-Royce Ltd	Conduit Street Trials car
BC12C	BCC12	H. J. Mulliner	2-door saloon	1-54	UK	439 BRE	C. Bowers	
BC14C	BCC13	H. J. Mulliner	2-door saloon	1-54	Switzerland		H. Martin	
BC15C	BCC14	H. J. Mulliner	2-door saloon	1-54	UK	HCX 404	R. Brown	
BC16C	BCC15	H. J. Mulliner	2-door saloon	12-53	Switzerland		R. Guenin	
BC17C	BCC16	H. J. Mulliner	2-door saloon	2-54	Switzerland		H. Brolliet	1954 Geneva Show
BC18C	BCC17	H. J. Mulliner	2-door saloon	1-54	UK	STC 200	C. Burrell	
BC19C	BCC18	H. J. Mulliner	2-door saloon	1-54	UK	OLO 1	S. Harris	
BC20C	BCC19	H. J. Mulliner	2-door saloon	1-54	UK	EUK 378	E.P. Jenks Ltd	
BC21LC	BCC20	H. J. Mulliner	2-door saloon	9-53	France		Emporer of Bao-Dai	1953 Paris Salon
BC22C	BCC21	H. J. Mulliner	2-door saloon	11-53	UK	LYS 515	D. Graham	1953 Earls Court Show
BC23C	BCC22	H. J. Mulliner	2-door saloon	11-53	UK	NYX 647	R. Wilkins	1953 Earls Court Show
BC24C	BCC23	H. J. Mulliner	2-door saloon	10-53	UK		M. Fergusson	
BC25C	BCC24	H. J. Mulliner	2-door saloon	9-53	France		P. Bernard	
BC26C	BCC25	H. J. Mulliner	2-door saloon	2-54	UK		P. Hall	
BC27C	BCC26	H. J. Mulliner	2-door saloon	3-54	UK	MJW 340	J. Salem	
BC28C	BCC27	H. J. Mulliner	2-door saloon	3-54	UK	OLX 36	Taylor Woodrow Plant Ltd	
BC29C	BCC28	H. J. Mulliner	2-door saloon	3-54	UK	OXK 826	V. Sangster	
BC30C	BCC29	H. J. Mulliner	2-door saloon	3-54	UK	MAD 1	T. Simmonds	
BC31C	BCC30	H. J. Mulliner	2-door saloon	2-54	UK	OLN 180	Princess of Berar	
BC32C	BCC31	H. J. Mulliner	2-door saloon	2-54	France		M. Cuny	
BC33LC	BCC32	H. J. Mulliner	2-door saloon	11-53	USA		C. Wrightsman	
BC34C	BCC33	H. J. Mulliner	2-door saloon	12-53	France		Comte de Villapadierna	
BC35LC	BCC34	H. J. Mulliner	2-door saloon	1-54	USA		W. Brewster	
BC36C	BCC35	H. J. Mulliner	2-door saloon	6-54	UK	888 CRE	W. Harrison	
BC37LC	BCC36	H. J. Mulliner	2-door saloon	2-54	NL		J. Simons	
BC38LC	BCC37	H. J. Mulliner	2-door saloon	2-54	USA		W. Spear	
BC39LC	BCC38	H. J. Mulliner	2-door saloon	1-54	Belgium		E. Zurstrassen	Brussels Show
BC40LC	BCC39	H. J. Mulliner	2-door saloon	3-54	USA		J. Mack	
BC41LC	BCC40	H. J. Mulliner	2-door saloon	3-54	France		Count Mario Pinci	
BC42LC	BCC41	H. J. Mulliner	2-door saloon	4-54	USA		A. Schumann	
BC43C	BCC42	H. J. Mulliner	2-door saloon	2-54	Switzerland		C. Gossweiter	1954 Geneva Show
BC44LC	BCC43	H. J. Mulliner	2-door saloon	2-54	France		Major E. Loder	
BC45C	BCC44	H. J. Mulliner	2-door saloon	4-54	UK	OYE 682	H. Bentley	
BC46LC	BCC45	H. J. Mulliner	2-door saloon	1-54	France		Baron Bich	
BC47LC	BCC46	H. J. Mulliner	2-door saloon	2-54	Switzerland		Major E. Loder	1954 Dutch Show
BC48LC	BCC47	H. J. Mulliner	2-door saloon	3-54	France		P. Avot	
BC49C	BCC48	Pininfarina	Fixed head coupé	7-54	UK	OUK 999	Charles Attwood Ltd	
BC50LC	BCC49	H. J. Mulliner	2-door saloon	4-54	USA		H. Kizer	
BC51LC	BCC50	Franay	2-door saloon	5-54	France		Vandendriesche et Fils	

R TYPE CONTINENTAL

Chassis no.	Eng. no.	Coachbuilder	Body style	Del.	Country	UK reg. no.	Original owner	Remarks
BC52C	BCC51	H. J. Mulliner	2-door saloon	4-54	UK	OXR 858	R. Weatherell	
BC53C	BCC52	H. J. Mulliner	2-door saloon	5-54	Denmark		K. Abildgaard	
BC54C	BCC53	H. J. Mulliner	2-door saloon	4-54	Spain		J. Bulto-Marques	
BC55C	BCC54	Graber	Drophead coupé	3-54	Switzerland		G. Filipinetti	1954 Geneva Show
BC56LC	BCC55	H. J. Mulliner	2-door saloon	7-54	USA		R. Moreland	
BC57C	BCC56	H. J. Mulliner	2-door saloon	5-54	UK		F. Button	
BC58C	BCC57	H. J. Mulliner	2-door saloon	4-54	UK	888 BMC	J.A. Prestwich	
BC59C	BCC58	H. J. Mulliner	2-door saloon	4-54	UK	ECN 231	N. Turner	
BC60C	BCC59	H. J. Mulliner	2-door saloon	5-54	UK	MJW 606	James Gibbons Ltd	
BC61C	BCC60	H. J. Mulliner	2-door saloon	5-54	UK		L. Hudson	
BC62LC	BCC61	H. J. Mulliner	2-door saloon	4-54	USA		L. Rockefeller	
BC63LC	BCC62	H. J. Mulliner	2-door saloon	7-54	Portugal		A. de Carvalho E. Silva	Converted to drophead coupé by Chapron, 1960
BC64C	BCC63	H. J. Mulliner	2-door saloon	5-54	UK	MGE 1	P. McDonald	
BC65C	BCC64	H. J. Mulliner	2-door saloon	6-54	UK	STO 88	R. Byrom	
BC66LC	BCC65	H. J. Mulliner	2-door saloon	4-54	USA		J. Dimick	
BC67C	BCC66	H. J. Mulliner	2-door saloon	5-54	Switzerland		N. Fuchs	
BC68C	BCC67	H. J. Mulliner	2-door saloon	5-54	UK	OYN 3	A. Atlas	
BC69C	BCC68	H. J. Mulliner	2-door saloon	5-54	UK	OYE 690	Capt. E. Bailey	
BC70C	BCC69	H. J. Mulliner	2-door saloon	6-54	UK	ECX 1	J. Hanson	
BC71C	BCC70	H. J. Mulliner	2-door saloon	6-54	UK	OLU 1	R. Way	
BC72C	BCC71	H. J. Mulliner	2-door saloon	6-54	UK	GAG 71	A. Cockburn	
BC73C	BCC72	Park Ward	Drophead coupé	12-54	UK	TMA 376	S.S. Downing (Birmingham) Ltd	
BC74C	BCC73	H. J. Mulliner	2-door saloon	6-54	UK	OYO 519	J.D. Alston Ltd	
BC75C	BCC74	H. J. Mulliner	2-door saloon	6-54	UK	OYO 512	E. Parry	
BC76C	BCC75	H. J. Mulliner	2-door saloon	7-54	UK	OYV 4	Lord Carnegie	
BC77C	BCC76	Graber	Drophead coupé	7-54	Switzerland		O. Ruegg	
BC78C	BCC77	H. J. Mulliner	2-door saloon	7-54	Switzerland		P. Baumgartner	
BC1LD	BCD1	H. J. Mulliner	2-door saloon	7-54	USA		F. Graupner	
BC2LD	BCD2	H. J. Mulliner	2-door saloon	9-54	USA		Miss M. Horn	
BC3D	BCD3	H. J. Mulliner	2-door saloon	8-54	UK	MCA 300	Sir Alfred McAlpine	
BC4D	BCD4	H. J. Mulliner	2-door saloon	10-54	Canada		W. McConnell	
BC5LD	BCD5	H. J. Mulliner	2-door saloon	9-54	USA		K. Merrill	
BC6D	BCD6	H. J. Mulliner	2-door saloon	8-54	Switzerland		K. Marx	
BC7LD	BCD7	H. J. Mulliner	2-door saloon	9-54	France		L. Paulet	
BC8D	BCD8	Park Ward	Drophead coupé	9-54	France		Baron de la Rochette	1954 Paris Salon
BC9D	BCD9	H. J. Mulliner	2-door saloon	9-54	UK	RU 1	A. Clark	
BBC10LD	BCD10	H. J. Mulliner	2-door saloon	9-54	Switzerland		G. Filipinetti	
BC11D	BCD11	H. J. Mulliner	2-door saloon	9-54	UK	DEG 1	J. Mitchell	
BC12D	BCD12	H. J. Mulliner	2-door saloon	11-54	Switzerland		Mme J. Amstutz	1954 Earls Court Show
BC14D	BCD13	H. J. Mulliner	2-door saloon	3-55	UK	UTU 3	W. Headlam	
BC15D	BCD14	H. J. Mulliner	2-door saloon	10-54	UK	FD 8	R. Hughes	
BC16LD	BCD15	H. J. Mulliner	2-door saloon	2-55	USA		E. Williamson	
BC17LD	BCD16	H. J. Mulliner	2-door saloon	11-54	Switzerland		R. de Romero	
BC18D	BCD17	H. J. Mulliner	2-door saloon	9-54	France		André Embiricos	
BC19D	BCD18	H. J. Mulliner	2-door saloon	11-54	Switzerland		S. Tricerri	
BC20D	BCD19	Franay	2-door saloon	11-54	France		B. Emery	
BC21D	BCD20	Franay	2-door saloon	2-55	France		C. Perroud	
BC22LD	BCD21	H. J. Mulliner	2-door saloon	2-55	USA		P. van Gerbig	

R TYPE CONTINENTAL

Chassis no.	Eng. no.	Coachbuilder	Body style	Del.	Country	UK reg. no.	Original owner	Remarks
BC23LD	BCD22	H. J. Mulliner	2-door saloon	10-54	France		Franco-Britannic Autos	Paris Trials car
BC24D	BCD23	Park Ward	2-door saloon	9-54	France		Brig. Gen. Gilbert-Berthier	
BC25D	BCD24 Shows	Park Ward	Drophead coupé	1-55	UK	PYN 701	Rolls-Royce Ltd	1954 Brussels & Turin
BC26D	BCD25	H. J. Mulliner	2-door saloon	11-54	UK	LMG 1	G. Vandervell	1954 Earls Court Show
BC27D	BCD26	H. J. Mulliner	2-door saloon	3-55	UK	PYP 255	I. Sanderson	
BC28D	BCD27	Park Ward	Drophead coupé	12-54	UK	FXT 4	Prince Frederick of Prussia	1954 Earls Court Show
BC29D	BCD28	Park Ward	2-door saloon	1-55	UK	PXD 84	Jack Dunfee	1954 Earls Court Show
BC30D	BCD29	H. J. Mulliner	2-door saloon	11-54	Australia		Mrs D. Lewis	1954 Melbourne Show
BC31LD	BCD30	H. J. Mulliner	2-door saloon	11-54	USA		Dr G. Westgate	
BC32D	BCD31	H. J. Mulliner	2-door saloon	11-54	UK	UTB 55	Barton Motors	
BC33D	BCD32	H. J. Mulliner	2-door saloon	11-54	UK		F. Morris	
BC34D	BCD33	H. J. Mulliner	2-door saloon	11-54	UK	CU 7777	J. Sangster	
BC35D	BCD34	H. J. Mulliner	2-door saloon	11-54	UK	OLM 7	Countess of Suffolk & Berkshire	
BC36D	BCD35	H. J. Mulliner	2-door saloon	1-55	UK	PUW 6	R. Dennis	
BC37D	BCD36	H. J. Mulliner	2-door saloon	1-55	UK	PXY 3	Jack Barclay	
BC38D	BCD37	H. J. Mulliner	2-door saloon	1-55	UK	YY 1	S. Harris	
BC39D	BCD38	H. J. Mulliner	2-door saloon	2-55	UK		C. Dracoulis	
BC40D	BCD39	H. J. Mulliner	2-door saloon	12-54	UK	OLY 1	A. Freedman	
BC41D	BCD40	H. J. Mulliner	2-door saloon	1-55	UK	PN 1	J. Holland	
BC42D	BCD41	H. J. Mulliner	2-door saloon	12-54	UK	ULG 663	J. Higham	
BC43D	BCD42	H. J. Mulliner	2-door saloon	1-55	UK	AST 1	Major H. Wood	
BC44D	BCD43	H. J. Mulliner	2-door saloon	1-55	UK		M. Kuhn	
BC45D	BCD44	H. J. Mulliner	2-door saloon	12-54	UK	PLL 3	H. Lipman	
BC46D	BCD45	H. J. Mulliner	2-door saloon	2-55	UK	OWU 10	Mrs J. Jacobson	
BC47D	BCD46	H. J. Mulliner	2-door saloon	1-55	UK	PXM 921	R. Robertson	
BC48D	BCD47	H. J. Mulliner	2-door saloon	1-55	Ireland		F. Svejdar	
BC49D	BCD48	H. J. Mulliner	2-door saloon	3-55	UK	PXT 900	Hon. A. Morton Weir	
BC50D	BCD49	H. J. Mulliner	Fixed head coupé	7-55	UK	H 1	R. McLeod	Specially shortened
BC51D	BCD50	H. J. Mulliner	2-door saloon	2-55	UK	PXM 926	R. Huggett	
BC52D	BCD51	H. J. Mulliner	2-door saloon	2-55	UK	PXU 291	G. Dawson	
BC53D	BCD52	H. J. Mulliner	2-door saloon	12-54	France		J. Ortiz-Linares	
BC54D	BCD53	H. J. Mulliner	2-door saloon	2-55	UK	PXD 98	G.C. Grundy Ltd	
BC55D	BCD54	H. J. Mulliner	2-door saloon	4-55	UK		A. Butler	
BC56D	BCD55	H. J. Mulliner	2-door saloon	2-55	UK	PXC 163	H. Carrington	
BC57D	BCD56	H. J. Mulliner	2-door saloon	3-55	UK	RND 780	S. Holt	
BC58D	BCD57	H. J. Mulliner	2-door saloon	3-55	UK	RMB 1	R. Montague Burton	
BC59D	BCD58	H. J. Mulliner	2-door saloon	3-55	UK	PYL 699	Hon. Lady Hogg	
BC60D	BCD59	H. J. Mulliner	2-door saloon	4-55	UK	PYL 698	G. Bartlett	
BC61D	BCD60	H. J. Mulliner	2-door saloon	3-55	UK	OJW 300	R. Whitehead	
BC62D	BCD61	H. J. Mulliner	2-door saloon	2-55	UK	UKL 109	R. Houchin	
BC63D	BCD62	H. J. Mulliner	2-door saloon	2-55	Switzerland		Mme M. Quilhot-Montalva	1955 Geneva Show
BC64D	BCD63	H. J. Mulliner	2-door saloon	3-55	UK	PYN 7	E. Webster	
BC65D	BCD64	H. J. Mulliner	2-door saloon	3-55	UK	DEL 393	S. Montgomery	
BC66LD	BCD65	Franay	2-door saloon	3-55	France		Marquis du Vivier	
BC67LD	BCD66	H. J. Mulliner	2-door saloon	4-55	France		J. Guiness	
BC68D	BCD67	Graber	Drophead coupé	3-55	Switzerland		A. Frey	Converted to 2-door saloon by W. Kong, 1957
BC69D	BCD68	H. J. Mulliner	2-door saloon	3-55	Cyprus		T. Dupree	
BC70D	BCD69	H. J. Mulliner	2-door saloon	3-55	UK		Capt. A. Wilson-Filmer	

R TYPE CONTINENTAL

Chassis no.	Eng. no.	Coachbuilder	Body style	Del.	Country	UK reg. no.	Original owner	Remarks
BC71D	BCD70	H. J. Mulliner	2-door saloon	4-55	UK	TZ 5675	S. McCrudden	
BC72D	BCD71	H. J. Mulliner	2-door saloon	2-55	Switzerland		A. Orsat	1955 Geneva Show
BC73D	BCD72	H. J. Mulliner	2-door saloon	3-55	Iran		Shah of Iran	
BC74LD	BCD73	H. J. Mulliner	2-door saloon	1-55	France		R. Grog	
BC1E	BCE1	H. J. Mulliner	2-door saloon	4-55	UK	PDA 200	West Midlands Erection Co. Ltd	
BC2E	BCE2	H. J. Mulliner	2-door saloon	4-55	UK	ROK 888	A. Dennis	
BC3E	BCE3	H. J. Mulliner	2-door saloon	4-55	UK	PYR 1	A. Schuster	
BC4E	BCE4	H. J. Mulliner	2-door saloon	4-55	UK	CWF 39	H. Farnsworth	
BC5E	BCE5	H. J. Mulliner	2-door saloon	4-55	UK	PYP 261	Major J. Kay	
BC6E	BCE6	H. J. Mulliner	2-door saloon	4-55	UK	PYP 265	W. Harrower	
BC7E	BCE7	H. J. Mulliner	2-door saloon	4-55	UK	DON 700	G. Brittain	
BC8E	BCE8	H. J. Mulliner	2-door saloon	4-55	UK	1 EMT	S. Gilbey	
BC9LE	BCE9	Franay	2-door saloon	5-55	France		M. Choumart	

S1 CONTINENTAL

Chassis no.	Eng. no.	Coachbuilder	Body style	Del.	Country	UK reg. no.	Original owner	Remarks
BC1AF	BC1A	Park Ward	Drophead coupé	9-55	UK	HES 182	J. Scott	
BC2AF	BC2A	Park Ward	Drophead coupé	10-55	UK	422 JKK	Sir J. Dean	
BC3AF	BC3A	H. J. Mulliner	2-door saloon	9-55	UK	LLH 1	M. Ferguson	
BC4AF	BC4A	Park Ward	Drophead coupé	12-55	UK	FLO 768	Mrs F. Cooke	
BC5AF	BC5A	Park Ward	Drophead coupé	10-55	UK	UUW 626	R. Gregory	
BC6AF	BC6A	H. J. Mulliner	2-door saloon	10-55	UK	HCH 950	C. Grant	
BC7AF	BC7A	Park Ward	Drophead coupé	10-55	UK	VTU 915	S. Norman	
BC8AF	BC8A	H. J. Mulliner	2-door saloon	10-55	UK		E. Parry	
BC9AF	BC9A	H. J. Mulliner	2-door saloon	10-55	UK		R. Way	
BC10AF	BC10A	Park Ward	2-door saloon	10-55	UK	LRV 330	W. Lutyens	
BC11AF	BC11A	H. J. Mulliner	2-door saloon	10-55	France		H. Bao Dai	
BC12AF	BC12A	H. J. Mulliner	2-door saloon	12-55	Switzerland		C. Gillet	
BC14AF	BC13A	H. J. Mulliner	2-door saloon	12-55	UK	JFX 777	The Hon. M. Portman	
BC15LAF	BC14A	Park Ward	Drophead coupé	9-55	USA		F. Dupont	
BC16LAF	BC15A	Park Ward	2-door saloon	10-55	USA		Jack Warner	
BC17LAF	BC16A	Franay	2-door saloon	11-57	France		F. Feriel	
BC18AF	BC17A	H. J. Mulliner	2-door saloon	11-55	UK	RYV 474	R. Harris	
BC19AF	BC18A	Park Ward	Drophead coupé	10-55	Belgium		A Davis	
BC20AF	BC19A	H. J. Mulliner	2-door saloon	10-55	UK	RYH 372	R. Robertson	
BC21AF	BC20A	Park Ward	2-door saloon	10-55	UK	OKJ 777	A. Johnson	
BC22AF	BC21A	Park Ward	Drophead coupé	10-55	UK		J. Chaplin	
BC23LAF	BC22A	Park Ward	Drophead coupé	12-55	USA		R. Parish	
BC24AF	BC23A	Park Ward	2-door saloon	7-56	UK	JRN 777	M. Marsh	
BC25AF	BC24A	Park Ward	2-door saloon	1-56	USA		Gary Cooper	
BC26LAF	BC25A	Park Ward	2-door saloon	1-56	UK	PLU 345	V. Bensaude	
BC27LAF	BC26A	Park Ward	2-door saloon	12-55	Italy		Marquis Luca Ferrero	
BC28AF	BC27A	Park Ward	Drophead coupé	4-56	UK	RXK 6	G. Rothschild	
BC30AF	BC29A	Park Ward	2-door saloon	2-56	UK	GJV 300	A. Butt	
BC31LAF	BC30A	Park Ward	2-door saloon	4-56	UK	RXC 465	E. Herzog	
BC32LAF	BC31A	H. J. Mulliner	2-door saloon	12-55	USA		P. Riffert	
BC33AF	BC32A	Park Ward	2-door saloon	3-56	UK	SLB 865	T. Westbrook	
BC34AF	BC33A	Park Ward	Drophead coupé	2-56	UK	SLH 993	J. Shatzow	
BC35AF	BC34A	Park Ward	2-door saloon	3-56	UK		R. Travis	

S1 CONTINENTAL

Chassis no.	Eng. no.	Coachbuilder	Body style	Del.	Country	UK reg. no.	Original owner	Remarks
BC36LAF	BC35A	H. J. Mulliner	2-door saloon	12-55	USA		D. Whitman	
BC37AF	BC36A	Park Ward	2-door saloon	5-56	UK	NOM 3	H. Tipper	
BC38AF	BC37A	H. J. Mulliner	2-door saloon	12-55	UK	RXY 620	Capt. O. Gross	
BC39AF	BC38A	Park Ward	2-door saloon	2-56	UK	EGT 5	H. Laing	
BC40AF	BC39A	H. J. Mulliner	2-door saloon	3-56	UK		D. McLean McDonald	
BC41AF	BC40A	H. J. Mulliner	2-door saloon	1-56	UK	MVY 100	A. Voorsanger	
BC42AF	BC41A	Park Ward	Drophead coupé	5-56	UK	RTR 860	W. Milne	
BC43AF	BC42A	H. J. Mulliner	2-door saloon	2-56	Switzerland		Dr. R. Kappeli	
BC44AF	BC43A	Park Ward	2-door saloon	3-56	UK	GMN 777	N. Robertson	
BC45AF	BC44A	H. J. Mulliner	2-door saloon	1-56	UK	YPL 100	J. Jameson	
BC46AF	BC45A	Park Ward	2-door saloon	5-56	UK		J. Townley	
BC47LAF	BC46A	H. J. Mulliner	2-door saloon	1-56	USA		J. Thomson	
BC48LAF	BC47A	Park Ward	2-door saloon	4-56	UK		D. Niven	
BC49AF	BC48A	H. J. Mulliner	2-door saloon	1-56	UK	SGT 790	F. Nield	
BC50AF	BC49A	H. J. Mulliner	2-door saloon	2-56	UK	RU 1	A. Clark	
BC51LAF	BC50A	H. J. Mulliner	2-door saloon	1-56	Switzerland		M. Dubuis	
BC52AF	BC51A	Park Ward	2-door saloon	4-56	UK	YBH 60	T. Sole	
BC53AF	BC52A	H. J. Mulliner	2-door saloon	1-56	UK	RBT 450	H. Hall	
BC54LAF	BC53A	Park Ward	Drophead coupé	4-56	USA		T. Neelands	
BC55AF	BC54A	H. J. Mulliner	2-door saloon	5-56	UK	OLM 7	Countess of Suffolk & Berkshire	
BC56LAF	BC55A	Park Ward	2-door saloon	3-56	Sweden		S. Salen	
BC57AF	BC56A	Park Ward	Drophead coupé	3-56	UK	VLK 933	James Lilley	
BC58AF	BC57A	H. J. Mulliner	2-door saloon	2-56	UK	KUU 1	S. Norman	
BC59LAF	BC58A	Park Ward	2-door saloon	3-56	UK	RXC 467	L. Wasserman	
BC60AF	BC59A	H. J. Mulliner	2-door saloon	3-56	UK	NM 7	N. Miles	
BC61AF	BC60A	Park Ward	2-door saloon	7-56	UK	SDA 789	Saunders Valve Co. Ltd	
BC62AF	BC61A	H. J. Mulliner	2-door saloon	3-56	UK	WKO 999	W. Powell	
BC63AF	BC62A	Park Ward	Drophead coupé	5-56	UK	SXL 406	Brevitt Shoe Ltd	
BC64AF	BC63A	H. J. Mulliner	2-door saloon	4-56	UK	SUV4	Cmdr. B. Russell	
BC65AF	BC64A	H. J. Mulliner	2-door saloon	3-56	UK	371 KRE	G. Wood	
BC66AF	BC65A	H. J. Mulliner	2-door saloon	2-56	UK	YY 1	S. Harris	
BC67AF	BC66A	Park Ward	2-door saloon	6-56	UK	HGS 918	B. McGowan	
BC68AF	BC67A	Park Ward	2-door saloon	7-56	UK	XKO 800	G. Percy Trentham Ltd	
BC69AF	BC68A	H. J. Mulliner	2-door saloon	4-56	UK	PCE 992	A. Marshall	
BC70AF	BC69A	Park Ward	2-door saloon	6-56	UK	SUL 324	W. Lawson	
BC71AF	BC70A	H. J. Mulliner	2-door saloon	4-56	UK		E. Hall	
BC72AF	BC71A	Park Ward	2-door saloon	6-56	UK	SKU 545	Sir F. Layland Barret Bt	
BC73AF	BC72A	H. J. Mulliner	2-door saloon	3-56	UK	RJW 757	P. Gibbons	
BC74AF	BC73A	Park Ward	2-door saloon	6-56	UK	YTF 999	B. Townley	
BC75AF	BC74A	Park Ward	Drophead coupé	4-56	UK	RGB 2	Mrs. M. Scott-Paine	
BC76AF	BC75A	Park Ward	Drophead coupé	6-56	UK	SYE 543	H. Lever	
BC77AF	BC76A	H. J. Mulliner	2-door saloon	4-56	UK	JW 8	J. Walton	
BC78AF	BC77A	Park Ward	2-door saloon	3-56	UK	HCS 620	H. Stenhouse	
BC79AF	BC78A	H. J. Mulliner	2-door saloon	6-56	UK	JF 1000	J. Frye	
BC80AF	BC79A	Park Ward	2-door saloon	5-56	UK	VAL 222	C. Evinson	
BC81AF	BC80A	H. J. Mulliner	2-door saloon	5-56	UK	SXB 31	B. Lindsay-Fynn	
BC82AF	BC81A	H. J. Mulliner	2-door saloon	6-56	UK	SXA 435	N. Turner	
BC83LAF	BC82A	Park Ward	Drophead coupé	2-56	Switzerland		Dr. I. Eweis	
BC84AF	BC83A	H. J. Mulliner	2-door saloon	4-56	UK	CEH 1	P. Hall	
BC85AF	BC84A	H. J. Mulliner	2-door saloon	5-56	UK	SLU 223	M. Samuel & Co. Ltd	

S1 CONTINENTAL

Chassis no.	Eng. no.	Coachbuilder	Body style	Del.	Country	UK reg. no.	Original owner	Remarks
BC86AF	BC85A	Park Ward	Drophead coupé	7-56	UK	SYE 550	P. Harker	
BC87LAF	BC86A	H. J. Mulliner	2-door saloon	3-56	France		R. Grey	
BC88AF	BC87A	H. J. Mulliner	2-door saloon	10-56	UK	SXW 1	A. Atlas	
BC89AF	BC88A	Park Ward	2-door saloon	5-56	UK	XMA 958	J. Bernes	
BC90AF	BC89A	H. J. Mulliner	2-door saloon	7-56	UK	GM 7	G. Martineau	
BC91AF	BC90A	Park Ward	2-door saloon	7-56	UK	555 MRE	M. Carding	
BC92AF	BC91A	H. J. Mulliner	2-door saloon	9-56	UK	TGW 565	T. Roberts	
BC93AF	BC92A	H. J. Mulliner	2-door saloon	8-56	UK	SYE 554	H. Lindsay	
BC94AF	BC93A	H. J. Mulliner	2-door saloon	7-56	UK	SYE 545	J. Alston	
BC95AF	BC94A	Park Ward	Drophead coupé	7-56	UK	DEG 1	J. Mitchell	
BC96LAF	BC95A	H. J. Mulliner	2-door saloon	3-56	Belgium		T. Vercoutere	
BC97AF	BC96A	H. J. Mulliner	2-door saloon	7-56	UK	SYE 541	E. Marsh	
BC98AF	BC97A	H. J. Mulliner	2-door saloon	9-56	UK	OHR 414	F. Readhead	
BC99AF	BC98A	H. J. Mulliner	2-door saloon	7-56	UK	SXU 33	H. Bannister	
BC100AF	BC99A	H. J. Mulliner	2-door saloon	6-56	UK		J. Mitchell	
BC101AF	BC100A	H. J. Mulliner	2-door saloon	9-56	UK	VOD 1	J. Day	
BC102AF	44X	H. J. Mulliner	2-door saloon	10-56	UK	VTU 524	Rolls-Royce Ltd	Experimental prototype, originally 27-B
BC1BG	BC1B	H. J. Mulliner	2-door saloon	6-56	UK	RXK 10	H. Madi	
BC2BG	BC2B	H. J. Mulliner	2-door saloon	11-56	UK	TLA 419	L. Gale	
BC3BG	BC3B	Park Ward	2-door saloon	6-56	UK	100 BPC	Wilmot Taylor Ltd	
BC4LBG	BC4B	H. J. Mulliner	2-door saloon	5-56	France		S.A. des Autos Peugeot	
BC5LBG	BC5B	H. J. Mulliner	2-door saloon	5-56	France		S.C.A.R.P. (Parfums Carven)	
BC6BG	BC6B	H. J. Mulliner	2-door saloon	11-56	UK	TLB 189	H. Vickery	
BC7LBG	BC7B	Park Ward	Drophead coupé	6-56	USA		Mrs M. Baird	
BC8BG	BC8B	Park Ward	2-door saloon	7-56	UK	KUD 155	D. Mackinnon	
BC9BG	BC9B	H. J. Mulliner	2-door saloon	9-56	UK	HN 8888	H. Needler	
BC10BG	BC10B	H. J. Mulliner	2-door saloon	10-56	UK	TLD 3	A. Gooda	
BC11BG	BC11B	H. J. Mulliner	2-door saloon	8-56	UK	VKD 460	R. Silcock	
BC12BG	BC12B	H. J. Mulliner	2-door saloon	4-56	UK	SNM 3	D. Robinson	
BC14BG	BC13B	H. J. Mulliner	2-door saloon	7-56	UK	VPO 669	M. Smithers	
BC15LBG	BC14B	H. J. Mulliner	2-door saloon	6-56	UK	BSK 454	N. Cac	
BC16BG	BC15B	H. J. Mulliner	2-door saloon	11-56	UK	200 ABH	J. Jacobs	
BC17BG	BC16B	H. J. Mulliner	2-door saloon	7-56	UK	SVM 1	F. Nield	
BC18BG	BC17B	Park Ward	2-door saloon	8-56	UK	SYE 612	L. Wallis	
BC19LBG	BC18B	H. J. Mulliner	2-door saloon	7-56	USA		Mrs W. Day	
BC20LBG	BC19B	Park Ward	2-door saloon	5-56	USA		F. Graupner	
BC21BG	BC20B	H. J. Mulliner	2-door saloon	3-57	UK	PFS 333	P. Scrutton	
BC22LBG	BC21B	Park Ward	Drophead coupé	8-56	USA		E. Gould	
BC23LBG	BC22B	Park Ward	2-door saloon	9-56	France		Soc. Bergere Lorraine	
BC24LBG	BC23B	Park Ward	Drophead coupé	8-56	Switzerland		K. Gertsche	
BC25BG	BC24B	Graber	Drophead coupé	3-57	Switzerland		H. Frey	
BC26LBG	BC25B	Park Ward	Drophead coupé	7-56	UK	SYP 701	A. Challe	
BC27BG	BC26B	Park Ward	Drophead coupé	9-56	UK	ND 5	Lady Docker	
BC28BG	BC27B	H. J. Mulliner	2-door saloon	9-56	UK	10 JML	D. Letts	
BC29BG	BC28B	H. J. Mulliner	2-door saloon	11-56	UK	TGW 564	T. Roberts	
BC30BG	BC29B	Park Ward	2-door saloon	9-56	UK	ENU 456	P. Tailby	
BC31BG	BC30B	Park Ward	2-door saloon	3-57	UK		S. Norman	
BC32BG	BC31B	Park Ward	2-door saloon	9-56	UK	TGK 300	T. Pick	

S1 CONTINENTAL

Chassis no.	Eng. no.	Coachbuilder	Body style	Del.	Country	UK reg. no.	Original owner	Remarks
BC33BG	BC32B	Park Ward	Drophead coupé	9-56	UK	MCA 301	Sir Alfred McAlpine	
BC34BG	BC33B	Park Ward	2-door saloon	10-56	UK		Jones (Aldbridge) Ltd	
BC35BG	BC34B	Park Ward	Drophead coupé	10-56	UK	SYN 72	N. Butler	
BC36BG	BC35B	Park Ward	2-door saloon	9-56	UK	TGH 895	Mrs D. Daly	
BC37BG	BC36B	H. J. Mulliner	2-door saloon	1-57	UK	ND 5	Sir Bernard Docker	
BC38BG	BC37B	H. J. Mulliner	2-door saloon	1-57	UK	SYX 716	Sir Duncan Orr-Lewis	
BC39BG	BC38B	H. J. Mulliner	2-door saloon	1-57	UK	281 SKE	D. Buller	
BC40BG	BC39B	Park Ward	Drophead coupé	11-56	UK		Mrs F. Bourner	
BC41BG	BC40B	H. J. Mulliner	2-door saloon	1-57	UK		J. Rawlings	
BC42BG	BC41B	H. J. Mulliner	2-door saloon	11-56	UK	TLA 936	Sir C. Brice-Gardner Bt	
BC43BG	BC42B	Park Ward	2-door saloon	11-56	UK	EIF 940	W. Barbour	
BC44BG	BC43B	Park Ward	2-door saloon	10-56	UK	TGO 207	Bowmaker Ltd	
BC45BG	BC44B	Park Ward	2-door saloon	11-56	UK		Sir Ralph Rickardson	
BC46BG	BC45B	H. J. Mulliner	2-door saloon	4-57	UK	TYF 333	E. Ostler	
BC47BG	BC46B	Park Ward	2-door saloon	1-56	UK	SYX 708	I. Fierro	
BC48LBG	BC47B	Park Ward	2-door saloon	10-56	France		F.B.A. Ltd	
BC49LBG	BC48B	Park Ward	2-door saloon	10-56	UK	SYK 304	D. Tuttle	
BC50BG	BC49B	Park Ward	2-door saloon	1-57	UK	TLP 437	L. Locan	
BC51BG	BC50B	H. J. Mulliner	2-door saloon	1-57	UK	JPB 20	J. Prideaux-Brune	
BC52BG	BC51B	Park Ward	Drophead coupé	11-56	UK	3 JMT	Behrens Trusted & Co.	
BC53BG	BC52B	H. J. Mulliner	2-door saloon	12-56	UK	OYV 4	Lord Carnegie	
BC54BG	BC53B	H. J. Mulliner	2-door saloon	4-57	Switzerland		O. Steicher	
BC55BG	BC54B	H. J. Mulliner	2-door saloon	3-57	UK	OLP 739	R. Hambro	
BC56BG	BC55B	H. J. Mulliner	2-door saloon	2-57	UK	TLC 389	R. Asquith	
BC57BG	BC56B	Park Ward	2-door saloon	12-56	Belgium		Mme L. Laumers-Jacqmotte	
BC58BG	BC57B	H. J. Mulliner	2-door saloon	2-57	Switzerland		Dr R. Buhler	
BC59BG	BC58B	Park Ward	2-door saloon	6-57	UK	SYN 67	F. du Pont	
BC60BG	BC59B	H. J. Mulliner	2-door saloon	2-57	UK	SFK 520	M. Ferguson	
BC61BG	BC60B	Park Ward	2-door saloon		UK	1 LMB	J. Shatzou	
BC62BG	BC61B	H. J. Mulliner	2-door saloon	2-57	UK	WKB 100	E. Bemrose	
BC63BG	BC62B	Park Ward	2-door saloon	1-57	UK	TLC 396	Vandervell Products Ltd	
BC64BG	BC63B	H. J. Mulliner	2-door saloon	2-57	UK	TLP 767	Guest, Keen & Nettlefolds Ltd	
BC65BG	BC64B	H. J. Mulliner	2-door saloon	7-57	UK	RW 100	R. Way	
BC66BG	BC65B	H. J. Mulliner	2-door saloon	4-57	UK	TUL 210	J. Archdale	
BC67BG	BC66B	Park Ward	2-door saloon	1-57	UK	100 NRF	Metal Products Co. Ltd	
BC68BG	BC67B	Park Ward	2-door saloon	11-56	UK	RC 12	Hon. H. Cayzer	
BC69BG	BC68B	H. J. Mulliner	2-door saloon	2-57	UK	MGE 1	P. McDonald	
BC70LBG	BC69B	H. J. Mulliner	2-door saloon	4-57	France		Agente Francaise de Propogande	
BC71BG	BC70B	H. J. Mulliner	2-door saloon	1-57	UK	DON 700	G. Brittain	
BC72BG	BC71B	H. J. Mulliner	2-door saloon	3-57	UK	DG 175	J. Evan Cook	
BC73BG	BC72B	Park Ward	2-door saloon	1-57	UK		Countess of Suffolk & Berkshire	
BC74BG	BC73B	H. J. Mulliner	2-door saloon	5-57	UK	OLM 7	Countess of Suffolk & Berkshire	
BC75BG	BC74B	H. J. Mulliner	2-door saloon	4-57	UK	WKD 777	G. & W. Collins Ltd	
BC76BG	BC75B	H. J. Mulliner	2-door saloon	12-57	UK	UUL 900	Capt. D. Mackinnon	
BC77BG	BC76B	Park Ward	Drophead coupé	2-57	UK	PLG 123	Hon. J. Astor	
BC78BG	BC77B	Park Ward	Drophead coupé	2-57	UK	DS 3975	Major E.G. Thomson	
BC79BG	BC78B	H. J. Mulliner	2-door saloon	6-57	UK	TXF 106	A.W. Berner	
BC80BG	BC79B	Park Ward	2-door saloon	5-57	UK	2 DPA	G. Albertini	
BC81BG	BC80B	H. J. Mulliner	2-door saloon	3-57	UK	MAD 1	J. Simmonds	
BC82BG	BC81B	Park Ward	2-door saloon	3-57	UK	PXK 2	J. Goulandris	

S1 CONTINENTAL

Chassis no.	Eng. no.	Coachbuilder	Body style	Del.	Country	UK reg. no.	Original owner	Remarks
BC83BG	BC82B	H. J. Mulliner	2-door saloon	7-57	UK	ARG 8	C. Echaque	
BC84BG	BC83B	Park Ward	2-door saloon	3-57	UK	TUC 840	Wallis & Co. (Costumiers) Ltd	
BC85BG	BC84B	Park Ward	2-door saloon	3-57	UK	MA 20	Hon. M. Astor	
BC86BG	BC85B	H. J. Mulliner	2-door saloon	4-57	UK	RCE 777	A. Marshall	
BC87BG	BC86B	H. J. Mulliner	2-door saloon	5-57	UK	DN 123	D. Deeprose	
BC88BG	BC87B	H. J. Mulliner	2-door saloon	2-57	Sweden		Kilafors Jernverks AB	
BC89BG	BC88B	H. J. Mulliner	2-door saloon	3-57	France		H. Lafond	
BC90BG	BC89B	H. J. Mulliner	2-door saloon	2-57	UK	10 CMK	H. J. Mulliner & Co. Ltd	
BC91LBG	BC90B	Park Ward	Drophead coupé	12-56	USA		F. Brewster	
BC92BG	BC91B	H. J. Mulliner	2-door saloon	4-57	UK	TUL 204	I Sanderson	
BC93BG	BC92B	Park Ward	Drophead coupé	5-57	UK	TSS 1	P. Swain	
BC94LBG	BC93B	Park Ward	2-door saloon	4-57	Belgium		Baron C. Janssen	
BC95BG	BC94B	H. J. Mulliner	2-door saloon	4-57	UK	JCS 105	G. Sleight	
BC96LBG	BC95B	H. J. Mulliner	2-door saloon	4-57	USA		W. Brewster	
BC97LBG	BC96B	H. J. Mulliner	2-door saloon	2-57	Switzerland		Mme J. Amstutz	
BC98BG	BC97B	Park Ward	Drophead coupé	2-57	UK	TXP 1	J. Gibson	
BC99BG	BC98B	H. J. Mulliner	2-door saloon	5-57	UK		J. Bamford	
BC100BG	BC99B	Park Ward	Drophead coupé	4-57	UK	SYN 73	Gen. P. Wakeham	
BC101LBG	BC100B	H. J. Mulliner	2-door saloon	3-57	UK		F. Dutton	
BC1CH	BC1C	Park Ward	2-door saloon	4-57	UK	EML 1	Belling & Lee Ltd	
BC2CH	BC2C	H. J. Mulliner	2-door saloon	8-57	UK	ULP 728	K. Keith	
BC3LCH	BC3C	Park Ward	2-door saloon	6-57	UK	SYX 961	H. Day	
BC4LCH	BC4C	H. J. Mulliner	2-door saloon	7-57	USA		A. Gross	
BC5LCH	BC5C	Park Ward	Drophead coupé	4-57	USA		C. Cummings	
BC6LCH	BC6C	H. J. Mulliner	2-door saloon	7-57	UK	TXF 902	L Gilmour	
BC7LCH	BC7C	H. J. Mulliner	2-door saloon	8-57	USA		F. McMahon	
BC8LCH	BC8C	H. J. Mulliner	Flying Spur saloon	9-57	USA			
BC9LCH	BC9C	H. J. Mulliner	Flying Spur saloon	9-57	UK	UGH 452	H. Cushing	
BC10LCH	BC10C	Park Ward	Drophead coupé	4-57	USA		D. Gallahue	
BC11LCH	BC11C	Park Ward	2-door saloon	4-57	UK	SYX 956	R. Sumpf	
BC12CH	BC12C	Park Ward	Drophead coupé	5-57	UK		Parkland Manufacturing Co. Ltd	
BC14CH	BC13C	H. J. Mulliner	2-door saloon	6-57	UK	500 CTC	B. Townley	
BC15CH	BC14C	H. J. Mulliner	Flying Spur saloon	9-57	UK	NG 1000	W. Glover	
BC16CH	BC15C	H. J. Mulliner	2-door saloon	7-57	UK	ULP 729	G. Palmer	
BC17CH	BC16C	James Young	Saloon	11-57	UK	ULX 645	Sir B. Mountain	
BC18LCH	BC17C	Park Ward	Drophead coupé	7-57	Belgium		H. Germeau	
BC19CH	BC18C	H. J. Mulliner	2-door saloon	6-57	UK	EXC 1	J. Hanson	
BC20CH	BC19C	Park Ward	Drophead coupé	5-57	UK	TYW 470	J. Irwin	
BC21LCH	BC20C	Park Ward	Drophead coupé	7-57	USA		Baroness N. de Koenigswarter	
BC22LCH	BC21C	Park Ward	2-door saloon	6-57	UK	TXF 108	S. Niarchos	
BC23LCH	BC22C	Park Ward	2-door saloon	7-57	UK		C. Sfezzo	
BC24CH	BC23C	H. J. Mulliner	Flying Spur saloon	9-57	UK	1 BMM	B. Mavroleon	
BC25CH	BC24C	James Young	Saloon	2-58	UK	TVM 2	F. Nield	
BC26CH	BC25C	James Young	2-door saloon	6-58	UK	VGU 206	W. Harrower	
BC27CH	BC26C	Park Ward	2-door saloon	6-57	UK	TYF 555	J. Dew	
BC28CH	BC27C	H. J. Mulliner	Flying Spur saloon	5-58	UK	VGU 210	E. Marsh	
BC29LCH	BC28C	H. J. Mulliner	2-door saloon	8-57	UK		S. Swenson	
BC30LCH	BC29C	Park Ward	Drophead coupé	8-57	UK	TXF 917	G. Embiricos	
BC31LCH	BC30C	Park Ward	2-door saloon	7-57	UK		Mme Periere	

S1 CONTINENTAL

Chassis no.	Eng. no.	Coachbuilder	Body style	Del.	Country	UK reg. no.	Original owner	Remarks
BC32LCH	BC31C	H. J. Mulliner	Flying Spur saloon	10-57	USA		E. Simmons	
BC33CH	BC32C	H. J. Mulliner	2-door saloon	9-57	UK		V. Sangster	
BC34CH	BC33C	H. J. Mulliner	Flying Spur saloon	11-57	UK	JR 9	S. Wagner	
BC35LCH	BC34C	Park Ward	2-door saloon	9-57	UK	UGH 453	H. Eiteljorg	
BC36LCH	BC35C	H. J. Mulliner	2-door saloon	11-57	USA		N. Oppenheimer	
BC37LCH	BC36C	H. J. Mulliner	2-door saloon	9-57	UK	TXF 926	HRH Prince Heritier	
BC38LCH	BC37C	Park Ward	2-door saloon	7-57	USA		Dr H. Salter	
BC39LCH	BC38C	Park Ward	2-door saloon	7-57	China			
BC40LCH	BC39C	Park Ward	Drophead coupé	7-57	Canada		T. Eaton	
BC41LCH	BC40C	Park Ward	Drophead coupé	7-57	USA		E. Nisbet	
BC42CH	BC41C	Park Ward	Drophead coupé	8-57	UK	TWF 382	G. Field	
BC43LCH	BC42C	Park Ward	Drophead coupé	8-57	USA		L. Beeke	
BC44LCH	BC43C	Park Ward	2-door saloon	8-57	USA		Karl's Shoe Stores	
BC45CH	BC44C	H. J. Mulliner	Flying Spur saloon	11-57	UK		H. Martineau	
BC46CH	BC45C	H. J. Mulliner	2-door saloon	11-57	UK	700 CPT	G. Stephenson	
BC47CH	BC46C	H. J. Mulliner	2-door saloon	11-57	UK	UXD 2	J. Irvin	
BC48LCH	BC47C	Park Ward	2-door saloon	10-57	W. Germany		C. Matthiesson	
BC49CH	BC48C	Park Ward	2-door saloon	11-57	UK	UXF 100	A. Beatty	
BC50LCH	BC49C	H. J. Mulliner	2-door saloon	7-57	Switzerland		Major E. Loder	
BC51CH	BC50C	Park Ward	Drophead coupé	11-57	UK	UXF 686	Mrs W. Liley	
BC1LDJ	BC1D	Park Ward	2-door saloon	9-57	France		L. Paulet	
BC2LDJ	BC2D	Park Ward	Drophead coupé	12-57	UK	UGK 12	American Flange Mfg. Co. Ltd	
BC3LDJ	BC3D	Park Ward	Drophead coupé	10-57	USA		Karl's Shoe Stores Ltd	
BC4LDJ	BC4D	H. J. Mulliner	2-door saloon	10-57	UK	UGH 664	Miss J. Tarafa	
BC5DJ	BC5D	Park Ward	2-door saloon	11-57	UK	RGD 999	James Robertson	
BC6DJ	BC6D	H. J. Mulliner	Flying Spur saloon	11-57	UK	JMT 1	J. Turner	
BC7DJ	BC7D	H. J. Mulliner	2-door saloon	11-57	Australia		Sir Tom Barr-Smith	
BC8DJ	BC8D	Park Ward	Drophead coupé	1-58	UK		Lawrence & Hilton Ltd	
BC9DJ	BC9D	Park Ward	Drophead coupé	11-57	UK	MDW 1	G. Latham	
BC10DJ	BC10D	Park Ward	Drophead coupé	1-58	UK	DM 65	Lt. Cdr. D. Miller	
BC11DJ	BC11D	James Young	Saloon	6-58	UK	VLC 3	P. Harker	
BC12DJ	BC12D	H. J. Mulliner	2-door saloon	12-57	UK		J. Trigg	
BC14DJ	BC13D	H. J. Mulliner	Flying Spur saloon	12-57	UK	KLL 125	Mrs M. Mackinnon	
BC15LDJ	BC14D	Park Ward	Drophead coupé	10-57	UK	UUC 457	J. Hutton	
BC16DJ	BC15D	H. J. Mulliner	Flying Spur saloon	1-58	UK	UXX 10	J. Lorant	
BC17DJ	BC16D	James Young	Saloon	2-58	UK	VXN 2	Delapena & Son Ltd	
BC18DJ	BC17D	Hooper	Saloon	7-59	UK	DM 65	Hooper & Co. (Coachbuilders) Ltd	
BC19LDJ	BC18D	Park Ward	2-door saloon	12-57	France		J. Politis	
BC20LDJ	BC19D	Park Ward	Drophead coupé	2-58	USA		W. Glazier	
BC21DJ	BC20D	James Young	Saloon	10-58	UK		G. Brittain	
BC22DJ	BC21D	H. J. Mulliner	Flying Spur saloon	2-58	UK	UXF 690	A. Holmes	
BC23LDJ	BC22D	H. J. Mulliner	2-door saloon	11-57	UK	UGH 670	Horizon American Pictures Inc.	
BC24DJ	BC23D	H. J. Mulliner	Flying Spur saloon	1-58	Switzerland		G. Filipinetti	
BC25LDJ	BC24D	Park Ward	Drophead coupé	3-58	Iraq		Crown Prince of Iraq	
BC26LDJ	BC25D	Park Ward	2-door saloon	3-58	Switzerland		R. Montgomery	
BC27LDJ	BC26D	Park Ward	Drophead coupé	10-57	Belgium		J. Van Zuylen	
BC28LDJ	BC27D	H. J. Mulliner	2-door saloon	6-58	UK	UGU 965	J. Harrison	
BC29LDJ	BC28D	H. J. Mulliner	2-door saloon	7-58	UK	WGH 320	Mrs R. Leather	
BC30DJ	BC29D	H. J. Mulliner	Flying Spur saloon	3-58	UK	RSF 919	J. Fleming & Co. Ltd	

S1 CONTINENTAL

Chassis no.	Eng. no.	Coachbuilder	Body style	Del.	Country	UK reg. no.	Original owner	Remarks
BC31DJ	BC30D	H. J. Mulliner	Flying Spur saloon	1-58	UK	SGV 309	W. Knott	
BC32LDJ	BC31D	H. J. Mulliner	2-door saloon	4-58	UK	UGK 732	H. Sears	
BC33DJ	BC32D	H. J. Mulliner	2-door saloon	2-58	UK	REV 58	Rev. A. Cole	
BC34DJ	BC33D	H. J. Mulliner	2-door saloon	2-58	UK	MCH 606	Wing Cdr. J. Aiton	
BC35LDJ	BC34D	Park Ward	2-door saloon	10-58	Venezuela			
BC36DJ	BC35D	Park Ward	2-door saloon	3-58	SA		D. Ovenstone	
BC37DJ	BC36D	H. J. Mulliner	2-door saloon	4-58	UK		E. Bateman	
BC38DJ	BC37D	Park Ward	2-door saloon	2-58	UK	UGK 20	J. Ovenstone	
BC39DJ	BC38D	H. J. Mulliner	Flying Spur saloon	3-58	UK	DEL 393	S. Montgomery	
BC40DJ	BC39D	H. J. Mulliner	2-door saloon	3-58	SA		J. McWilliams	
BC41DJ	BC40D	H. J. Mulliner	2-door saloon	1-58	SA		R. Hunt	
BC42LDJ	BC41D	Park Ward	Drophead coupé	2-58	Belgium		Mme S. Mayne	
BC43DJ	BC42D	H. J. Mulliner	Flying Spur saloon	1-58	UK	KGS 222	G. Sanderson	
BC44DJ	BC43D	Park Ward	Drophead coupé	1-58	SA		G. Carruthers	
BC45DJ	BC44D	H. J. Mulliner	2-door saloon	3-58	UK		Sir E. Cadbury	
BC46DJ	BC45D	James Young	Saloon	6-58	UK	VXO 798	M. Ferguson	
BC47DJ	BC46D	James Young	2-door saloon	6-58	UK	RA 3	W.M. Asquith Ltd	
BC48DJ	BC47D	Park Ward	Drophead coupé	3-58	UK	GRK 8	G. Kennerley	
BC49DJ	BC48D	H. J. Mulliner	Flying Spur saloon	3-58	UK	UYW 549	M. Rayne	
BC50DJ	BC49D	Park Ward	Drophead coupé	2-58	UK	UXK 351	J. Abrahams (Diamonds) Ltd	
BC51DJ	BC50D	H. J. Mulliner	Flying Spur saloon	5-58	UK	213 NTW	Balfour Marine Eng. Co. Ltd	
BC1EL	BC1E	H. J. Mulliner	Flying Spur saloon	8-58	UK		Aladdin Industries Ltd	
BC2EL	BC2E	H. J. Mulliner	Flying Spur saloon	3-58	UK	HLD 111	H. Dowsett	
BC3EL	BC3E	H. J. Mulliner	Flying Spur saloon	3-58	UK	ULY 6	Theydon & Tresanton Ltd	
BC4EL	BC4E	Park Ward	Drophead coupé	3-58	UK	600 CMB	M. Summers	
BC5EL	BC5E	H. J. Mulliner	2-door saloon	3-58	France		H. Ortiz-Linares	
BC6EL	BC6E	H. J. Mulliner	2-door saloon	4-58	UK	UYU 328	A. Parkinson	
BC7EL	BC7E	Park Ward	Drophead coupé	5-58	UK	RG 1	A. Lewis	
BC8EL	BC8E	H. J. Mulliner	Flying Spur saloon	5-58	UK	VCR 100	A. Agg	
BC9EL	BC9E	Park Ward	Drophead coupé	2-58	UK	WGH 327	Major D. Vaughan	
BC10EL	BC10E	H. J. Mulliner	2-door saloon	11-57	UK	SER 777	A. Marshall	
BC11LEL	BC11E	H. J. Mulliner	Flying Spur saloon	2-58	USA		R. Reiger	
BC12LEL	BC12E	H. J. Mulliner	2-door saloon	2-58	UK		E. Chamay	
BC14LEL	BC13E	H. J. Mulliner	Flying Spur saloon	7-58	USA		P. Shields	
BC15LEL	BC14E	Park Ward	2-door saloon	2-58	Switzerland		A. Another	
BC16EL	BC15E	Park Ward	2-door saloon	4-48	UK	UGK 734	Mrs A. Mauze	
BC17EL	BC16E	H. J. Mulliner	Flying Spur saloon	4-58	UK	XWS 357	J. Menzies & Co. Ltd	
BC18LEL	BC17E	Park Ward	Drophead coupé	7-58	USA		Mrs J. Dreyfus	
BC19EL	BC18E	H. J. Mulliner	2-door saloon	10-58	UK	WGT 343	Sir Duncan Orr-Lewis	
BC20EL	BC19E	Park Ward	Drophead coupé	4-58	UK	AD 33	Lord Sherborne	
BC21EL	BC20E	Park Ward	2-door saloon	3-58	UK	UYU 327	P. Swiffen	
BC22LEL	BC21E	H. J. Mulliner	Flying Spur saloon	7-58	USA		J. Dimick	
BC23LEL	BC22E	James Young	2-door saloon	8-58	USA		C. Waterman	
BC24EL	BC23E	Park Ward	2-door saloon	4-58	UK	WS 17	Swiffen & Sons Ltd	
BC25EL	BC24E	James Young	Saloon	5-58	UK	JB 1	Jack Barclay	
BC26EL	BC25E	H. J. Mulliner	2-door saloon	5-58	UK	GS 25	Lt. Col. G. Sinclair	
BC27EL	BC26E	Park Ward	Drophead coupé	7-58	UK	WGH 324	Mrs F. Ewald	
BC28LEL	BC27E	H. J. Mulliner	Flying Spur saloon	8-58	USA		Gary Trust & Savings Bank	
BC29EL	BC28E	James Young	Saloon	12-58	UK	DAG 22	T. Daglish	

S1 CONTINENTAL

Chassis no.	Eng. no.	Coachbuilder	Body style	Del.	Country	UK reg. no.	Original owner	Remarks
BC30EL	BC29E	James Young	Saloon	10-58	UK	VXO 840	Mrs E. Snagge	
BC31EL	BC30E	H. J. Mulliner	Flying Spur saloon	9-58	UK	VXA 294	P. Hill & Partners Ltd	
BC32LEL	BC31E	Park Ward	Drophead coupé	5-58	UK	UGU 931	The Butler Co.	
BC33LEL	BC32E	H. J. Mulliner	Flying Spur saloon	9-58	UK	WGN 402	R. Salant	
BC34LEL	BC33E	H. J. Mulliner	Flying Spur saloon	7-58	USA		Alfred Hitchcock	
BC35EL	BC34E	H. J. Mulliner	Flying Spur saloon	6-58	UK	56 WE	A. Laver	
BC36EL	BC35E	H. J. Mulliner	Flying Spur saloon	9-58	UK	NVY 1	D. Lycett Green	
BC37EL	BC36E	H. J. Mulliner	Flying Spur saloon	7-58	UK		L. Brown	
BC38LEL	BC37E	H. J. Mulliner	2-door saloon	1-59	USA		P. Roebling	
BC39EL	BC38E	Park Ward	Drophead coupé	6-58	UK	VLB 112	Vernons Mail Order Stores Ltd	
BC40EL	BC39E	Park Ward	Drophead coupé	5-58	UK	ELM 9	Mather & Crowther Ltd	
BC41EL	BC40E	Park Ward	Drophead coupé	7-58	Switzerland		Baronne M. de Rothschild	
BC42EL	BC41E	H. J. Mulliner	Flying Spur saloon	7-58	UK	VLF 333	Lord Inverforth	
BC43EL	BC42E	Hooper	Saloon	11-58	UK	7 AVW	Sir Lindsay Parkinson & Co. Ltd	
BC44EL	BC43E	H. J. Mulliner	Flying Spur saloon	8-58	UK	JD 11	Beecham Group Ltd	
BC45EL	BC44E	H. J. Mulliner	Flying Spur saloon	10-58	UK		J. Delaney	
BC46LEL	BC45E	H. J. Mulliner	Flying Spur saloon	2-59	USA		E. Macdonald	
BC47LEL	BC46E	James Young	Saloon	10-58	UK	WGT 909	Stavros Niarchos	
BC48LEL	BC47E	Park Ward	2-door saloon	7-58	France		J. Dunbaugh	
BC49EL	BC48E	James Young	Saloon	1-59	UK	VE 25	Cabinet Industries Ltd	
BC50EL	BC49E	Park Ward	Drophead coupé	7-58	UK	EYT 192	Mrs H. Jenkins	
BC51LEL	BC50E	H. J. Mulliner	Flying Spur saloon	10-58	UK	WGU 2	R. Stoney	
BC1FM	BC1F	Park Ward	Drophead coupé	9-58	UK	VXH 335	Kemsley Newspapers Ltd	
BC2FM	BC2F	H. J. Mulliner	Flying Spur saloon	11-58	UK	VXO 824	R. Macready	
BC3LFM	BC3F	Park Ward	2-door saloon	9-58	France			
BC4FM	BC4F	Park Ward	2-door saloon	8-58	UK	WOK 21	Dunlop Rubber Co. Ltd	
BC5FM	BC5F	Park Ward	2-door saloon	9-58	UK	900 DTU	D. Crowther	
BC6FM	BC6F	James Young	Saloon	1-59	UK	VYW 672	J.T. Cook & Son Ltd	
BC7FM	BC7F	Hooper	Saloon	4-59	UK	WLE 671	C. Mathes	
BC8FM	BC8F	H. J. Mulliner	2-door saloon	11-58	UK	NUP 1	G. Stephenson	
BC9FM	BC9F	H. J. Mulliner	Flying Spur saloon	11-58	UK	VEX 853	G.K.N. Ltd	
BC10FM	BC10F	Park Ward	Drophead coupé?	1-59	UK	WGT 907	Rex Harrison	
BC11FM	BC11F	Park Ward	2-door saloon	11-58	UK	MAD 1	Samuel Simmonds & Son Ltd	
BC12LFM	BC12F	Park Ward	Drophead coupé	12-58	USA		S. Goodman	
BC14FM	BC13F	H. J. Mulliner	2-door saloon	11-58	UK	WAR 11	W. Reynolds	
BC15FM	BC14F	Park Ward	Drophead coupé	9-58	UK	100 FKX	J. Smith	
BC16FM	BC15F	H. J. Mulliner	2-door saloon	10-58	UK	G 34	P. Mcdonald	
BC17FM	BC16F	H. J. Mulliner	2-door saloon	1-59	UK	HSU 438	S. Tippetts	
BC18FM	BC17F	James Young	Saloon	6-59	UK		Jack Barclay Ltd	
BC19FM	BC18F	H. J. Mulliner	Flying Spur saloon	11-58	UK		W. Swiffen	
BC20FM	BC19F	Park Ward	2-door saloon	11-58	France		M. Matos	
BC21FM	BC20F	H. J. Mulliner	Flying Spur saloon	11-58	UK	JBU 488	J. Upton	
BC22FM	BC21F	Park Ward	Drophead coupé	11-58	UK	VXO 834	Boult Bros. Ltd	
BC23FM	BC22F	James Young	Saloon	8-59	UK		I. Hillman	
BC24FM	BC23F	H. J. Mulliner	2-door saloon	1-59	UK		Sir D. Bevan Evans	
BC25LFM	BC24F	Park Ward	Drophead coupé	12-58	UK	WGU 13	M. von Ritter	
BC26FM	BC25F	H. J. Mulliner	Flying Spur saloon	3-59	UK	KUU 1	Balfour Marine Engineering Co. Ltd	
BC27FM	BC26F	H. J. Mulliner	Flying Spur saloon	12-58	UK	JCS 105	G. Sleight	
BC28FM	BC27F	H. J. Mulliner	Flying Spur saloon	1-59	UK		C. Miller	

S1 CONTINENTAL

Chassis no.	Eng. no.	Coachbuilder	Body style	Del.	Country	UK reg. no.	Original owner	Remarks
BC29FM	BC28F	Park Ward	Drophead coupé	1-59	UK		C. Walker	
BC30FM	BC29F	H. J. Mulliner	2-door saloon	1-59	UK	VYW 667	Capo Bora Esperanza SA	
BC31FM	BC30F	H. J. Mulliner	2-door saloon	2-59	UK	TVM 1	F. Nield	
BC32LFM	BC31F	H. J. Mulliner	2-door saloon	5-59	USA		L. Packard	
BC33LFM	BC32F	Park Ward	2-door saloon	2-59	USA		A. Haskell	
BC34FM	BC33F	Park Ward	Drophead coupé	2-59	UK	WLB 1	Cdr B. Preston	
BC35FM	BC34F	H. J. Mulliner	2-door saloon	1-59	UK	DON 700	G. Brittain	
BC36FM	BC35F	James Young	Saloon	9-59	UK		J. Gallimore	
BC37FM	BC36F	H. J. Mulliner	2-door saloon	3-59	UK		B. Townley	
BC38FM	BC37F	Park Ward	2-door saloon	1-59	UK	SD 147	S. Docherty	
BC39FM	BC38F	Park Ward	Drophead coupé	2-59	UK		Lady Crane	
BC40LFM	BC39F	Park Ward	Drophead coupé	5-59	USA		Mrs R. Dimond	
BC41LFM	BC40F	H. J. Mulliner	Flying Spur saloon	3-59	USA		V. Shea	
BC42LFM	BC41F	James Young	Saloon	6-59	USA		J. Thouron	
BC43LFM	BC42F	H. J. Mulliner	Flying Spur saloon	4-59	UK	WGT 905	J. Ohrbach	
BC44LFM	BC43F	H. J. Mulliner	Flying Spur saloon	4-59	USA		L. Voorhees	
BC45FM	BC44F	H. J. Mulliner	Flying Spur saloon	4-59	UK		S. McCrudden	
BC46FM	BC45F	H. J. Mulliner	2-door saloon	4-59	UK		Arthur Lee & Sons Ltd	
BC47FM	BC46F	H. J. Mulliner	Flying Spur saloon	5-59	UK	WXV 615	W. Pegley	
BC48FM	BC47F	James Young	Saloon	8-59	UK		D. Davis	
BC49LFM	BC48F	Park Ward	2-door saloon	4-59	Canada		I. Hollway	
BC50FM	BC49F	H. J. Mulliner	2-door saloon	4-59	UK	WXP 777	P. Sellars	
BC51LFM	BC50F	H. J. Mulliner	Flying Spur saloon	5-59	UK	XGF 9	A. Jergens	
BC1GN	BC1G	H. J. Mulliner	2-door saloon	3-59	UK	UCE 777	A. Marshall	
BC2LGN	BC2G	H. J. Mulliner	2-door saloon	2-59	Switzerland		J. J. Hegnauer	
BC3LGN	BC3G	H. J. Mulliner	Flying Spur saloon	6-59	USA		Economy Blue Print & Supply Co.	
BC4GN	BC4G	Park Ward	Drophead coupé	3-59	UK	FT 1	F. Thrush	
BC5LGN	BC5G	Hooper	Saloon	6-59	USA		B. Ridder	
BC6GN	BC6G	Hooper	Saloon	7-59	UK	HF 53	H. Fraser	
BC7GN	BC7G	Park Ward	2-door saloon	4-59	UK	WGA 1	J. Mclaren Ltd	
BC8GN	BC8G	H. J. Mulliner	Flying Spur saloon	5-59	UK	GBW 149	G. Watson	
BC9GN	BC9G	Park Ward	2-door saloon	5-59	UK	PC 649	P. Cadbury	
BC10GN	BC10G	Park Ward	Drophead coupé	6-59	UK	XLO 1	J. Payne	
BC11GN	BC11G	H. J. Mulliner	Flying Spur saloon	6-59	UK	S 60	T. Stewart	
BC12LGN	BC12G	Park Ward	2-door saloon	6-59	USA		R. Salant	
BC14LGN	BC13G	Park Ward	Drophead coupé	4-59	UK	XGF 7	W. Hales	
BC15GN	BC14G	Park Ward	Drophead coupé	5-59	UK	VXC 852	Berry's Electric Ltd	
BC16GN	BC15G	Hooper	Saloon	6-59	UK	818 HKX	E. Prestwick	
BC17GN	BC16G	H. J. Mulliner	Flying Spur saloon	5-59	UK	WXM 44	Vernon's Pools Ltd	
BC18GN	BC17G	Park Ward	Drophead coupé	5-59	UK	776 RPE	C. Neale	
BC19GN	BC18G	H. J. Mulliner	Flying Spur saloon	5-59	UK	VAX 100	P. Stephens	
BC20LGN	BC19G	Park Ward	Drophead coupé	5-59	USA		Mrs W. Brewster	
BC21GN	BC20G	H. J. Mulliner	Flying Spur saloon	8-59	UK		F. Craddock	
BC22GN	BC21G	H. J. Mulliner	Flying Spur saloon	7-59	UK	PXE 6	C. Lake	
BC23GN	BC22G	Park Ward	2-door saloon	5-59	UK	NF 12	N. Field	
BC24GN	BC23G	Park Ward	2-door saloon	7-59	UK	MEE 59	Mrs M. Dixon	
BC25GN	BC24G	H. J. Mulliner	2-door saloon	6-59	UK	WYO 700	Crowden & Reeves Ltd	
BC26GN	BC25G	H. J. Mulliner	2-door saloon	6-59	UK	JEH 1	Hanson Buses Ltd	
BC27GN	BC26G	H. J. Mulliner	2-door saloon	7-59	UK	GJW 36	Winnets Investments Ltd	

S1 CONTINENTAL

Chassis no.	Eng. no.	Coachbuilder	Body style	Del.	Country	UK reg. no.	Original owner	Remarks
BC28GN	BC27G	Park Ward	Drophead coupé	6-59	UK	UD 2	H. Wills	
BC29GN	BC28G	H. J. Mulliner	Flying Spur saloon?	7-59	UK	WYX 443	W. Turniff	
BC30LGN	BC29G	H. J. Mulliner	Flying Spur saloon	12-60?	UK	497 AGF	Fuerzas Electricas de Cataluna SA	
BC31GN	BC30G	Park Ward	Drophead coupé	6-59	UK	GS 33	G. Southall	

S2 CONTINENTAL

Chassis no.	Eng. no.	Coachbuilder	Body style	Del.	Country	UK reg. no.	Original owner	Remarks
BC1AR	A1BC	Hooper	Saloon	12-59	UK	VLU 132	Rank Organisation Ltd	Hooper stand '58 Earls Court Show
BC2LAR	A2BC	H. J. Mulliner	2-door saloon	2-60	USA		P. Sinclaire	
BC3LAR	A3BC	H. J. Mulliner	2-door saloon	12-59	NL		H. Smeets	
BC4LAR	A4BC	H. J. Mulliner	Flying Spur saloon	12-59	France		P. Bernard	
BC5LAR	A5BC	H. J. Mulliner	Flying Spur saloon	2-60	UK	XGW 513	L. Gilmour	
BC6LAR	A6BC	James Young	Saloon	12-59	UK	XGW 740	C. Wrightsman	
BC7LAR	A7BC	H. J. Mulliner	Flying Spur saloon	11-59	France		S. Millikin	
BC8AR	A8BC	Park Ward	Drophead coupé	3-60	Iran		Mecanin Development Corporation	
BC9LAR	A9BC	Park Ward	Drophead coupé	12-59	USA		A. Chaney	
BC10AR	A10BC	Park Ward	Drophead coupé	9-59	UK	603 HMB	Rolls-Royce Ltd	Conduit St. Trials car
BC11AR	A11BC	H. J. Mulliner	2-door saloon	1-60	UK	JLM 204	J. Mackinlay	
BC12AR	A12BC	H. J. Mulliner	Flying Spur saloon	5-60	USA		A. Shaw	
BC14AR	A13BC	H. J. Mulliner	Flying Spur saloon	1-60	UK	YLN 1	Hammer Films Ltd	
BC15LAR	A14BC	Park Ward	Drophead coupé	2-60	USA		Holiday Groves Inc.	
BC16AR	A15BC	H. J. Mulliner	2-door saloon	1-60	Belgium		E. Blaton	
BC17LAR	A16BC	Park Ward	Drophead coupé	2-60	USA		L. Moore	
BC1L8AR	A17BC	H. J. Mulliner	Flying Spur saloon	1-60	Belgium		W. Burden	
BC19LAR	A18BC	H. J. Mulliner	Flying Spur saloon	2-60	USA		J. Thouron	
BC20LAR	A19BC	H. J. Mulliner	Flying Spur saloon	3-60	USA		S. Goodman	
BC21AR	A20BC	H. J. Mulliner	Flying Spur saloon	2-60	UK	GB 666	G. Sandersen	
BC22LAR	A21BC	H. J. Mulliner	Flying Spur saloon	8-60	USA		H. Shuttleworth	
BC23AR	A22BC	Park Ward	Drophead coupé	2-60	UK		Emu Wine Co. Ltd	
BC24LAR	A23BC	H. J. Mulliner	Flying Spur saloon	3-60	France		E. da Silva Ramos	
BC25AR	A24BC	Park Ward	Drophead coupé	3-60	UK	JRB 300	J. Bateman	
BC26AR	A25BC	H. J. Mulliner	2-door saloon	2-60	UK	YLY 150	Aladdin Industries Ltd	
BC27AR	A26BC	James Young	Saloon	4-60	UK	YYN 382	Stauss Turnbull & Co.	
BC28AR	A27BC	James Young	Saloon	4-60	UK	100 ELB	Jack Barclay Ltd	Jack Barclay Trials car
BC29LAR	A28BC	H. J. Mulliner	Flying Spur saloon	2-60	USA		L. Rockefeller	
BC30AR	A29BC	Park Ward	Drophead coupé	3-60	UK	RCT 123	R. Dennis	
BC31LAR	A30BC	H. J. Mulliner	Flying Spur saloon	4-60	UK	YGN 632	H. Davis	
BC32AR	A31BC	H. J. Mulliner	Flying Spur saloon	2-60	UK	FC 77	Copeland & Jenkins	
BC33LAR	A32BC	H. J. Mulliner	2-door saloon	7-60	UK	XGX 520	D. Feldman	
BC34AR	A33BC	Park Ward	Drophead coupé	3-60	UK	MS 48	M. Summers	
BC35AR	A34BC	James Young	Saloon	3-60	UK	YXE 859	Sir E. Cadbury	
BC36AR	A35BC	H. J. Mulliner	2-door saloon	2-60	UK	3 ABM	D. Robinson	
BC37AR	A36BC	Park Ward	Drophead coupé	4-60	UK	YYH 337	G. Palmer	
BC38LAR	A37BC	James Young	Saloon	3-60	Switzerland		Dr C. Gossweiler	
BC39LAR	A38BC	H. J. Mulliner	2-door saloon	3-60	W. Germany		A. Schwitler	
BC40AR	A39BC	H. J. Mulliner	2-door saloon	4-60	UK	1 AFC	E. Stanning	
BC41LAR	A40BC	H. J. Mulliner	2-door saloon	5-60	France		M. Mathet	
BC42AR	A41BC	H. J. Mulliner	2-door saloon	3-60	UK	BMM 66	Counties Ship Management Ltd	
BC43LAR	A42BC	H. J. Mulliner	Flying Spur saloon	3-60	UK	YGN 636	R. Parish	

S2 CONTINENTAL

Chassis no.	Eng. no.	Coachbuilder	Body style	Del.	Country	UK reg. no.	Original owner	Remarks
BC44LAR	A43BC	H. J. Mulliner	Flying Spur saloon	4-60	USA		H. Fischback	
BC45LAR	A44BC	James Young	2-door saloon	5-60	USA		People's Express Co.	
BC46AR	A45BC	James Young	Saloon	6-60	UK		H. Martineau	
BC47AR	A46BC	H. J. Mulliner	2-door saloon	5-60	UK		Hanson Haulage Ltd	
BC48AR	A47BC	H. J. Mulliner	2-door saloon	4-60	UK	MW 7	W. Wallis	
BC49AR	A48BC	H. J. Mulliner	2-door saloon	5-60	UK	777 AXB	W. Morton	
BC50AR	A49BC	H. J. Mulliner	2-door saloon	4-60	Switzerland		A. Berner	
BC51AR	A50BC	H. J. Mulliner	2-door saloon	4-60	UK	YYH 332	I. Sanderson	
BC52LAR	A51BC	H. J. Mulliner	2-door saloon	4-60	USA		E. McIntosh	
BC53AR	A52BC	James Young	2-door saloon	5-60	UK	TBF 855	G. Farrow	
BC54AR	A53BC	Park Ward	Drophead coupé	5-60	UK	XGH 942	J. Neal	
BC55LAR	A54BC	H. J. Mulliner	2-door saloon	9-60	W. Germany		Consul Gen. J. Hagarder	
BC56AR	A55BC	H. J. Mulliner	2-door saloon	5-60	UK	1 EMM	E. Miller	
BC57AR	A56BC	Park Ward	Drophead coupé	5-60	UK	KUU 1	Balfour Engineering Co. Ltd	
BC58AR	A57BC	H. J. Mulliner	2-door saloon	5-60	UK	8777 DA	J. Morgan	
BC59AR	A58BC	H. J. Mulliner	2-door saloon	5-60	UK	717 APG	Major E. Cliff McCulloch	
BC60AR	A59BC	Park Ward	Drophead coupé	5-60	UK	MC 98	John Peters Furnishing Stores Ltd	
BC61AR	A60BC	Park Ward	Drophead coupé	5-60	UK	FD 8	R. Hughes	
BC62AR	A61BC	James Young	Saloon	5-60	UK	787 AXA	P. Harker	
BC63AR	A62BC	H. J. Mulliner	Flying Spur saloon	5-60	UK	DOL 40	Sir Duncan Orr-Lewis	
BC64AR	A63BC	Park Ward	Drophead coupé	5-60	UK	GRK 8	G. Kennerley	
BC65AR	A64BC	H. J. Mulliner	Flying Spur saloon	2-60	Switzerland		A. Gemuseus	
BC66LAR	A65BC	H. J. Mulliner	Flying Spur saloon	5-60	USA		Dr G. Westgate	
BC67LAR	A66BC	Park Ward	Drophead coupé	6-60	Lichtenstein		Yul Brynner	
BC68AR	A67BC	James Young	Saloon	5-60	UK		Redvales Ltd	
BC69AR	A68BC	H. J. Mulliner	Flying Spur saloon	5-60	UK	YYP 747	J. Billmeir	
BC70AR	A69BC	H. J. Mulliner	2-door saloon	6-60	UK	WER 777	A. Marshall	
BC71LAR	A70BC	H. J. Mulliner	2-door saloon	4-60	France		R. Grog	
BC72LAR	A71BC	Park Ward	Drophead coupé	6-60	UK	782 AXA	J. Shellim	
BC73AR	A72BC	Park Ward	Drophead coupé	2-60	Switzerland		A. Heumann	
BC74AR	A73BC	Park Ward	Drophead coupé	7-60	UK	797 AXA	B. Jenks	
BC75AR	A74BC	Park Ward	Drophead coupé	7-60	UK	DW 4	Richard Thomas & Baldwins Ltd	
BC76AR	A75BC	H. J. Mulliner	Flying Spur saloon	2-60	UK	785 AXA	P. Hill & Partners Ltd	
BC77LAR	A76BC	Park Ward	Drophead coupé	10-60	Argentina		J. Vacarezza	
BC78AR	A77BC	James Young	Saloon	6-60	UK		Keith Prowse & Co. Ltd	
BC79AR	A78BC	James Young	Saloon	6-60	UK		R. Clifford-Turner	
BC80LAR	A79BC	Park Ward	Drophead coupé	5-60	UK	YGP 127	I. Geist	
BC81AR	A80BC	H. J. Mulliner	Flying Spur	6-60	UK	1564 BZ	G. Brittain	
BC82AR	A81BC	Park Ward	Drophead coupé	6-60	UK	GEE 1	C. Neale	
BC83AR	A82BC	H. J. Mulliner	Flying Spur saloon	6-60	UK		R. Carter	
BC84LAR	A83BC	H. J. Mulliner	Flying Spur saloon	6-60	UK	AJ 6	A. Jergens	
BC85AR	A84BC	H. J. Mulliner	2-door saloon	6-60	UK	123 LTU	Rolls-Royce Ltd	
BC86AR	A85BC	H. J. Mulliner	2-door saloon	7-60	UK	884 AYF	J. Archdale	
BC87AR	A86BC	H. J. Mulliner	2-door saloon	7-60	UK	OLM 7	Countess of Suffolk & Berkshire	
BC88AR	A87BC	Park Ward	Drophead coupé	11-60	UK	570 BYS	H. Stenhouse	
BC89AR	A88BC	H. J. Mulliner	Flying Spur saloon	6-60	UK	KRN 7	Moy, Davis, Smith, Vandervell & Co.	
BC90AR	A89BC	H. J. Mulliner	2-door saloon	6-60	UK	RMB 1	M. Burton Ltd	
BC91AR	A90BC	Park Ward	Drophead coupé	7-60	UK	2190 AZ	S. McCrudden	
BC92LAR	A91BC	H. J. Mulliner	Flying Spur saloon	7-60	UK	NV 1	Prince Veranund of Siam	
BC93AR	A92BC	Park Ward	Drophead coupé	8-60	UK	DEG 1	J. Mitchell	

S2 CONTINENTAL

Chassis no.	Eng. no.	Coachbuilder	Body style	Del.	Country	UK reg. no.	Original owner	Remarks
BC94AR	A93BC	James Young	Saloon	6-60	UK	788 AXA	M. Brown	
BC95AR	A94BC	James Young	Saloon	7-60	UK	AXA 798	Miss J. Burton	
BC96AR	A95BC	James Young	Saloon	7-60	UK	SS 33	Major J. Collins	
BC97AR	A96BC	James Young	Saloon	7-60	UK	AYF 888	C. Forte	
BC98AR	A97BC	H. J. Mulliner	Flying Spur saloon	7-60	UK	9 BOP	Guest, Keen & Nettlefolds Ltd	
BC99AR	A98BC	H. J. Mulliner	Flying Spur saloon	7-60	UK	BK 600	Bluebird Caravans Ltd	
BC100AR	A99BC	H. J. Mulliner	2-door saloon	7-60	UK	SG 30	S. Gilbey	
BC101AR	A100BC	James Young	Saloon	10-60	UK	VR 5	W. Radford	
BC102LAR	A101BC	H. J. Mulliner	Flying Spur saloon	4-61	UK	489 AGF	Mrs C. Kocens	
BC103LAR	A102BC	James Young	Saloon	9-60	USA		Gary Cooper	
BC104AR	A103BC	H. J. Mulliner	2-door saloon	7-60	UK	4666 NB	S. de Ferranti	
BC105AR	A104BC	James Young	Saloon	9-60	UK	EWR 1	E. Ross	
BC106AR	A105BC	H. J. Mulliner	2-door saloon	7-60	UK	H 1	R.G. McLeod Tools Ltd	Specially shortened
BC107LAR	A106BC	Park Ward	Drophead coupé	6-60	USA		A. Williams	
BC108LAR	A107BC	Park Ward	Drophead coupé	8-60	UK	FLB 121	S. Brody	
BC109AR	A108BC	Park Ward	Drophead coupé	8-60	Australia		C. Lloyd Jones	
BC110AR	A109BC	James Young	2-door saloon	2-61	UK	WNT 779	M. Rollason	
BC111AR	A110BC	Park Ward	Drophead coupé	10-60	UK	28 BGX	Empire Stores (Bradford) Ltd	
BC112AR	A111BC	Park Ward	Drophead coupé	10-60	UK	1600 JW	F. Hanson	
BC113AR	A112BC	James Young	2-door saloon	11-60	UK		R. Wilkins	
BC114AR	A113BC	Park Ward	Drophead coupé	9-60	UK	GG 11	Sir Giles Guthrie	
BC115AR	A114BC	H. J. Mulliner	2-door saloon	9-60	UK	726 AYW	D. Letts	
BC116LAR	A115BC	H. J. Mulliner	Flying Spur saloon	10-60	USA		R. Sinclaire	
BC117AR	A116BC	Park Ward	Drophead coupé	12-60	UK	JM 101	Marcus Construction Ltd	
BC118AR	A117BC	H. J. Mulliner	Flying Spur saloon	8-60	UK	FYF 452	Duke of Fife	
BC119AR	A118BC	Park Ward	Drophead coupé	9-60	UK	LEL 532	L. Lawrie	
BC120AR	A119BC	Park Ward	Drophead coupé	11-60	UK	JL 11	Lilley & Skinner Ltd	
BC121AR	A120BC	James Young	Saloon	1-61			Calgary & Edmonton Land Co. Ltd	
BC122AR	A121BC	H. J. Mulliner	2-door saloon	8-60	UK	YB 4	Mrs F. Bourner	
BC123LAR	A122BC	Park Ward	Drophead coupé	12-60	USA		E. Wallach	
BC124AR	A123BC	H. J. Mulliner	Flying Spur saloon	8-60	UK	SVH 669	A. Lee & Sons Ltd	
BC125AR	A124BC	Park Ward	Drophead coupé	12-60	UK	HRW 363	H. Whitty	
BC126AR	A125BC	H. J. Mulliner	Flying Spur saloon	7-60	UK	999 LKE	W. Powell	
BC127AR	A126BC	H. J. Mulliner	2-door saloon	8-60	UK	EGT 5	McVitie & Price Ltd	
BC128AR	A127BC	James Young	Saloon	1-61	UK	391 BLA	Daily Mirror Newspapers Ltd	
BC129AR	A128BC	H. J. Mulliner	Flying Spur saloon	8-60	UK	HCS 1	H. Stenhouse	
BC130LAR	A129BC	H. J. Mulliner	Flying Spur saloon	8-60	UK	463 AGF	D. Brostrom	
BC131AR	A130BC	H. J. Mulliner	Flying Spur saloon	8-60	UK	KLL 125	Mrs A. MacKinnon	
BC132AR	A131BC	H. J. Mulliner	Flying Spur saloon	11-60	UK	170 BGW	Vernon's Pools Ltd	
BC133AR	A132BC	H. J. Mulliner	Flying Spur saloon	11-60	UK		W. Morris	
BC134AR	A133BC	H. J. Mulliner	2-door saloon	9-60	UK	690 AXV	Sir C. Bruce-Gardner	
BC135LAR	A134BC	H. J. Mulliner	2-door saloon	3-61	France		Mlle L. Chantrell	
BC136AR	A135BC	H. J. Mulliner	2-door saloon	11-60	UK	DSC 44	Dart Spring Co. Ltd	
BC137LAR	A136BC	H. J. Mulliner	Flying Spur saloon	10-60	Sweden		I. Christensen	
BC138AR	A137BC	H. J. Mulliner	Flying Spur saloon	11-60	UK	GM 7	G. Martineau	
BC139AR	A138BC	H. J. Mulliner	Flying Spur saloon	1-61	UK		P. Cadbury	
BC140LAR	A139BC	H. J. Mulliner	Flying Spur saloon	10-60	France		P. Bernard	
BC141AR	A140BC	H. J. Mulliner	2-door saloon	10-60	UK	973 CGD	P. McDonald Ltd	
BC142LAR	A141BC	H. J. Mulliner	Flying Spur saloon	12-60	UK	684 BGH	King Hussein of Jordan	
BC143AR	A142BC	H. J. Mulliner	2-door saloon	10-60	UK	JKJ 6	Times Furnishing Co. Ltd	

S2 CONTINENTAL

Chassis no.	Eng. no.	Coachbuilder	Body style	Del.	Country	UK reg. no.	Original owner	Remarks
BC144AR	A143BC	H. J. Mulliner	2-door saloon	12-60	UK	784 BGK	E. Parry	
BC145AR	A144BC	H. J. Mulliner	Flying Spur saloon	12-60	UK	786 BGK	Macready's Metal Co. Ltd	
BC146AR	A145BC	H. J. Mulliner	2-door saloon	12-60	UK	HBH 1	A Hewitt	
BC147AR	A146BC	H. J. Mulliner	2-door saloon	12-60	UK	GM 20	J. Anderson MBE	
BC148LAR	A147BC	H. J. Mulliner	Flying Spur saloon	3-61	UK	953 AGF	L. Knight	
BC149AR	A148BC	Park Ward	Drophead coupé	12-60	UK	J 184	J. Scrase	
BC150AR	A149BC	H. J. Mulliner	2-door saloon	12-60	UK	NUP 1	G. Stephenson & Co. Ltd	
BC151AR	A150BC	Park Ward	Drophead coupé	6-61	UK	569 BYT	E. Prestwick	
BC1LBY	B1BC	H. J. Mulliner	Flying Spur saloon	1-61	UK	907 AGF	M. Jonklow	
BC2BY	B2BC	Park Ward	Drophead coupé	11-60	UK		Lord Greville	
BC3BY	B3BC	H. J. Mulliner	Flying Spur saloon	12-60	UK	450 ABP	Mrs F. Nagle	
BC4LBY	B4BC	Park Ward	Drophead coupé	9-60	UK	100 AGF	R. Lang	
BC5LBY	B5BC	James Young	Saloon	2-61	Switzerland		Ervin Piqueres Industriel	
BC6LBY	B6BC	Park Ward	Drophead coupé	10-60	USA		Mrs E. Du Pont Riegel	
BC7BY	B7BC	H. J. Mulliner	Flying Spur saloon	1-61	UK	JS 333	J. Stenhouse	
BC8BY	B8BC	Park Ward	Drophead coupé	11-60	UK	GH 82	G. Hochschild	
BC9BY	B9BC	H. J. Mulliner	Flying Spur saloon	2-61	Switzerland		P. Fluckiger	
BC10BY	B10BC	Park Ward	Drophead coupé	2-61	UK	99 PMA	Mrs F. Cooke	
BC11LBY	B11BC	H. J. Mulliner	2-door saloon	12-60	USA		J. Merrick	
BC12LBY	B12BC	Park Ward	Drophead coupé	10-60	UK	481 AGF	A. Clapham	
BC14LBY	B13BC	H. J. Mulliner	2-door saloon	12-60	Switzerland		A. Clafisch	
BC15LBY	B14BC	H. J. Mulliner	2-door saloon	12-60	USA		G. Brothers	
BC16BY	B15BC	H. J. Mulliner	Flying Spur saloon	2-61	UK	PN 1	F. Nelson	
BC17BY	B16BC	James Young	2-door saloon	4-61	UK		Cayzer Irvine & Co.	Subsequently changed to four-door saloon
BC18BY	B17BC	H. J. Mulliner	Flying Spur saloon	1-61	UK	MCA 11	Sir Robert McAlpine & Sons Ltd	
BC19LBY	B18BC	H. J. Mulliner	Flying Spur saloon	12-60	UK	906 AGF	Stavros Niarchos	
BC20LBY	B19BC	Park Ward	Drophead coupé	12-60	UK	496 AGF	N. Monsarrat	
BC21BY	B20BC	H. J. Mulliner	Flying Spur saloon	12-60	UK	WJ 90	W. Jarratt	
BC22LBY	B21BC	Park Ward	Drophead coupé	12-60	UK	908 AGF	W. Schweitzer	
BC23LBY	B22BC	H. J. Mulliner	2-door saloon	3-61	Switzerland		C. Haimoff	
BC24LBY	B23BC	Park Ward	Drophead coupé	10-60	UK	KWS 88	R. Salant	
BC25BY	B24BC	H. J. Mulliner	2-door saloon	1-61	UK	BOM 600	P. Levy	
BC26BY	B25BC	James Young	Saloon	3-61	UK		W. Turner	
BC27BY	B26BC	Park Ward	Drophead coupé		UK		J. Milles	
BC28LBY	B27BC	H. J. Mulliner	Flying Spur saloon	3-61	France		Prince S. Aga Khan	
BC29BY	B28BC	James Young	Saloon	3-61	UK	DAG 131	T. Daglish	
BC30BY	B29BC	Park Ward	Drophead coupé	4-61	UK		Mrs M. Joseph	
BC31BY	B30BC	H. J. Mulliner	2-door saloon	4-61	UK	G 34	P.A.J. McDonald Ltd	
BC32BY	B31BC	Park Ward	Drophead coupé	11-60	UK	CWH 34	C. Hutley	
BC33LBY	B32BC	H. J. Mulliner	2-door saloon	12-60	UK	909 AGF	W. Schweitzer	
BC34LBY	B33BC	Park Ward	Drophead coupé	1-61	USA		Holiday Groves Inc.	
BC35BY	B34BC	H. J. Mulliner	Flying Spur saloon	2-61	UK	XMR 333	Col. B. Ivory	
BC36BY	B35BC	Park Ward	Drophead coupé	2-61	UK		H. Bailey	
BC37BY	B36BC	H. J. Mulliner	Flying Spur saloon	3-61	UK	NXH 777	F. Smithson	
BC38BY	B37BC	Park Ward	Drophead coupé	3-61	UK	DSE 822	A. Thomson	
BC39BY	B38BC	H. J. Mulliner	Flying Spur saloon	3-61	UK	1 EMM	E. Miller	
BC40BY	B39BC	H. J. Mulliner	2-door saloon	1-61	UK	HCM 1	H. Martineau	
BC41BY	B40BC	James Young	Saloon		Switzerland		Mme M. Colombo	
BC42BY	B41BC	H. J. Mulliner	2-door saloon	1-61	UK	KFC 36	K. Craggs	

S2 CONTINENTAL

Chassis no.	Eng. no.	Coachbuilder	Body style	Del.	Country	UK reg. no.	Original owner	Remarks
BC43BY	B42BC	H. J. Mulliner	Flying Spur saloon	5-61	UK	R 800	Enden Plant Hire Co. Ltd	
BC44LBY	B43BC	H. J. Mulliner	Flying Spur saloon	3-61	Switzerland		R. Schasseur	
BC45BY	B44BC	James Young	Saloon	4-61	UK	DOL 40	Sir Duncan Orr-Lewis	
BC46BY	B45BC	H. J. Mulliner	Flying Spur saloon	4-61	UK	FWP 430	Pontins Ltd	
BC47LBY	B46BC	H. J. Mulliner	Flying Spur saloon	4-61	UK	518 CGF	F. Galvao	
BC48BY	B47BC	H. J. Mulliner	Flying Spur saloon	6-61	UK	JMM 331	J. Menzies & Co. Ltd	
BC49BY	B48BC	H. J. Mulliner	2-door saloon	2-61	UK	382 BLU	A. Parkinson MBE	
BC50LBY	B49BC	Park Ward	Drophead coupé	1-61	USA		H. Karl	
BC51BY	B50BC	Park Ward	Drophead coupé	1-61	UK	500 BXK	Wilkins & Mitchell Ltd	
BC52BY	B51BC	H. J. Mulliner	2-door saloon	3-61	UK	J 2666	J. Trigg	
BC53BY	B52BC	Park Ward	Drophead coupé	5-61	UK	926 AGF	W. Dugger	
BC54LBY	B53BC	H. J. Mulliner	2-door saloon	2-61	Switzerland		M. Dubuis	
BC55LBY	B54BC	Park Ward	Drophead coupé	2-61	Switzerland		R. Von Hirsch	
BC56LBY	B55BC	H. J. Mulliner	2-door saloon	3-61	USA		H. Coleman	
BC57LBY	B56BC	Park Ward	Drophead coupé	3-61	Austria		R. Van Sickle	Trials car
BC58BY	B57BC	H. J. Mulliner	2-door saloon	4-61	UK	YAM 444	F. Readhead	
BC59LBY	B57BC	Park Ward	Drophead coupé	2-61	Switzerland		J. Koerfer	
BC60LBY	B59BC	H. J. Mulliner	Flying Spur saloon	3-61	USA		S. Currier	
BC61LBY	B60BC	Park Ward	Drophead coupé	5-61	Italy		R. Mambretti	
BC62BY	B61BC	H. J. Mulliner	Flying Spur saloon	5-61	UK		L. Knight	
BC63LBY	B62BC	Park Ward	Drophead coupé	4-61	USA		F. Larson	
BC64LBY	B63BC	H. J. Mulliner	Flying Spur saloon	5-61	UK	535 CGF	A. Lamborn	
BC65LBY	B64BC	Park Ward	Drophead coupé	5-61	UK	527 CGF	W. Snee	
BC66LBY	B65BC	Park Ward	Drophead coupé	5-61	USA		W. White	
BC67BY	B66BC	Park Ward	Drophead coupé	5-61	UK	JB 6	Rolls Razor Ltd	
BC68LBY	B67BC	H. J. Mulliner	Flying Spur saloon	6-61	USA		Mrs H. Alvarez-Hill	
BC69BY	B68BC	Park Ward	Drophead coupé	3-61	UK	FWS 50	F. Stenbridge	
BC70LBY	B69BC	H. J. Mulliner	Flying Spur saloon	6-61	USA		H. Johnson	
BC71BY	B70BC	H. J. Mulliner	2-door saloon	5-61	UK	9 CLK	Reid Bros. (Tailors) Ltd	
BC72BY	B71BC	Park Ward	Drophead coupé	3-61	UK	RGB 2	R. Bouralie	
BC73LBY	B72BC	H. J. Mulliner	Flying Spur saloon	6-61	UK	NR 800	Mrs N. Reisini	
BC74LBY	B73BC	Park Ward	Drophead coupé	3-61	Switzerland		H. Grether	
BC75BY	B74BC	H. J. Mulliner	Flying Spur saloon	4-61	UK	NF 80	Norman Field Investments Ltd	
BC76LBY	B75BC	H. J. Mulliner	Flying Spur saloon	5-61	UK	556 CGF	L. Johnson	
BC77BY	B76BC	Park Ward	Drophead coupé	5-61	UK	GM 13	G. Marcow	
BC78BY	B77BC	H. J. Mulliner	2-door saloon	5-61	UK	DRG 71	D. Greig	
BC79LBY	B78BC	Park Ward	Drophead coupé	4-61	UK	504 CGF	C. Stevenson	
BC80BY	B79BC	James Young	Saloon	6-61	UK		Major S. Cayzer	
BC81BY	B80BC	Park Ward	Drophead coupé	6-61	UK	NW 301	Sir N. Watson	
BC82LBY	B81BC	Park Ward	Drophead coupé	5-61	UK	508 CGF	R. Perkin	
BC83BY	B82BC	H. J. Mulliner	2-door saloon	6-61	UK	BJF 111	B. Forbes	
BC84BY	B83BC	Park Ward	Drophead coupé	4-61	UK	VN 2	Viscount Downe	
BC85BY	B84BC	H. J. Mulliner	2-door saloon	6-61	UK	YCE 777	A. Marshall	
BC86BY	B85BC	Park Ward	Drophead coupé	7-61	UK	550 CXO	J. Eisinger	
BC87LBY	B86BC	H. J. Mulliner	Flying Spur saloon	8-61	UK	549 CGF	P. Van Gerbig	
BC88BY	B87BC	H. J. Mulliner	2-door saloon	6-61	UK	567 SLG	E. Scragg & Sons Ltd	
BC89BY	B88BC	James Young	Saloon	7-61	UK	577 CGF	Mrs D. Herbert	
BC90LBY	B89BC	H. J. Mulliner	Flying Spur saloon	6-61	UK	APD 888	Mrs C. Davis	
BC91BY	B90BC	H. J. Mulliner	Flying Spur saloon	7-61	UK	GT 84	G. Trapani	
BC92BY	B91BC	Park Ward	Drophead coupé	6-61	UK	REE 100	A. Dixon	

S2 CONTINENTAL

Chassis no.	Eng. no.	Coachbuilder	Body style	Del.	Country	UK reg. no.	Original owner	Remarks
BC93BY	B92BC	H. J. Mulliner	2-door saloon	6-61	UK	HLV 36	H. Vickery Ltd	
BC94BY	B93BC	H. J. Mulliner	Flying Spur saloon	7-61	UK	9 CXE	S. Simpson Ltd	
BC95BY	B94BC	James Young	Saloon	3-61	UK	491 CYP	Reunion Properties Co. Ltd	
BC96LBY	B95BC	Park Ward	Drophead coupé	5-61	USA		W. Brewster	
BC97BY	B96BC	H. J. Mulliner	Flying Spur saloon	7-61	UK	110 CLU	Aladdin Industries Ltd	
BC98LBY	B97BC	Park Ward	Drophead coupé	4-61	UK	918 AGF	Ohrbach (London) Ltd	
BC99BY	B98BC	H. J. Mulliner	Flying Spur saloon	9-61	UK	3300 HA	Guest, Keen & Nettlefolds Ltd	
BC100LBY	B99BC	Park Ward	Drophead coupé	5-61	USA		R. Stolkin	
BC101LBY	B100BC	H. J. Mulliner	2-door saloon	8-61	Italy		W. Harrison	
BC1CZ	C1BC	Park Ward	Drophead coupé	7-61	UK	398 CLO	H. & J. Wilson Ltd	
BC2CZ	C2BC	H. J. Mulliner	2-door saloon	7-61	UK	389 CLO	Dolcis Ltd	
BC3CZ	C3BC	James Young	Saloon	9-61	UK	499 CXX	J. Brierley	
BC4LCZ	C4BC	Park Ward	Drophead coupé	3-62	France		Baron H. de Tenbossche	
BC5CZ	C5BC	H. J. Mulliner	2-door saloon	7-61	UK	RC 12	Cayzer Irvine & Co. Ltd	
BC6CZ	C6BC	Park Ward	Drophead coupé	7-61	UK	GT 84	G. Trapani	
BC7CZ	C7BC	H. J. Mulliner	Flying Spur saloon	9-61	UK	492 CXX	Truvox Engineering Co. Ltd	
BC8CZ	C8BC	James Young	Saloon	3-62	UK	ET 11	R. Tatham	
BC9LCZ	C9BC	Park Ward	Drophead coupé	8-61	UK	LH 7	Magla Productions	
BC10LCZ	C10BC	H. J. Mulliner	Flying Spur saloon	7-61	USA		E. Gengras	
BC11LCZ	C11BC	Park Ward	Drophead coupé	9-61	UK	43 CGT	N. Granz	
BC12CZ	C12BC	H. J. Mulliner	2-door saloon	8-61	UK	486 CYP	A. Holmes	
BC14LCZ	C13BC	Park Ward	Drophead coupé	7-61	Morocco		King Hassan II	
BC15CZ	C14BC	H. J. Mulliner	2-door saloon	12-61	UK	SXW 1	Brevitt Shoes Ltd	
BC16LCZ	C15BC	H. J. Mulliner	2-door saloon	9-61	Switzerland		C. Kunz	
BC17CZ	C16BC	H. J. Mulliner	Flying Spur saloon	9-61	UK		H. Cohen	
BC18CZ	C17BC	H. J. Mulliner	Flying Spur saloon	11-61	UK	SL 22	W. Lawson	
BC19LCZ	C18BC	H. J. Mulliner	Flying Spur saloon	8-61	Lichtenstein		Mme H. Beaumont	
BC20CZ	C19BC	H. J. Mulliner	2-door saloon	10-61	UK	RCK 8	F.S. Ratcliffe (Rochdale) Ltd	
BC21CZ	C20BC	H. J. Mulliner	Flying Spur saloon	7-61	UK	LSM 351	London & Scandinavian Metallurgical Co. Ltd	
BC22LCZ	C21BC	H. J. Mulliner	Flying Spur saloon	9-61	UK	593 CGF	L. Gilmour	
BC23CZ	C22BC	Park Ward	Drophead coupé	9-61	Switzerland		Societe Idylle	
BC24LCZ	C23BC	H. J. Mulliner	Flying Spur saloon	11-61	UK	50 CGT	D. Barton	
BC25CZ	C24BC	Park Ward	Drophead coupé	9-61	UK		C. Cooper	
BC26CZ	C25BC	H. J. Mulliner	2-door saloon	1-62	UK	2 DXN	J. Carreras	
BC27LCZ	C26BC	H. J. Mulliner	Flying Spur saloon	10-61	France		M. Lucas	
BC28LCZ	C27BC	Park Ward	Drophead coupé	8-61	USA		Mrs R. Greenewald	
BC29CZ	C28BC	H. J. Mulliner	2-door saloon	12-61	UK		C. Barker	
BC30LCZ	C29BC	H. J. Mulliner	Flying Spur saloon	10-61	Switzerland		R. Schappi	
BC31LCZ	C30BC	Park Ward	Drophead coupé	9-61	France		P. Bernard	
BC32LCZ	C31BC	Park Ward	Drophead coupé	9-61	UK	40 CGT	D. Cunningham	
BC33CZ	C32BC	H. J. Mulliner	Flying Spur saloon	10-61	UK	SC 11	J. Stewart-Clark	
BC34LCZ	C33BC	Park Ward	Drophead coupé	11-61	USA		G. Friedland	
BC35LCZ	C34BC	H. J. Mulliner	Flying Spur saloon	11-61	UK	76 CGT	P. Nelson	
BC36CZ	C35BC	H. J. Mulliner	Flying Spur saloon	12-61	UK	1200 KC	G. & W. Collins Ltd	
BC37CZ	C36BC	Park Ward	Drophead coupé	9-61	UK	290 CXX	S. Whitaker	
BC38CZ	C37BC	H. J. Mulliner	2-door saloon	8-62	Sweden		A. B. Svensk Bilkontrol Ltd	
BC39CZ	C38BC	H. J. Mulliner	Flying Spur saloon	2-62	UK	906 DAC	T. Bird	
BC40CZ	C39BC	Park Ward	Drophead coupé	4-62	UK	7700 LJ	A. Mantovani	

S2 CONTINENTAL

Chassis no.	Eng. no.	Coachbuilder	Body style	Del.	Country	UK reg. no.	Original owner	Remarks
BC41CZ	C40BC	H. J. Mulliner	Flying Spur saloon	11-61	UK	V 15	W. Black	
BC42LCZ	C41BC	H. J. Mulliner	Flying Spur saloon	11-61	UK	65 CGT	Mrs W. Alton Jones	
BC43LCZ	C42BC	H. J. Mulliner	2-door saloon	10-61	UK	600 CGT	Conte P. Orsi Mangelli	
BC44CZ	C43BC	James Young	Saloon	3-62	UK		Asquith Machine Tool Co. Ltd	
BC45LCZ	C44BC	Park Ward	Drophead coupé	11-61	UK	72 CGT	W. Dick	
BC46CZ	C45BC	H. J. Mulliner	2-door saloon	12-61	UK	3838 HA	Guest, Keen & Nettlefolds Ltd	
BC47CZ	C46BC	H. J. Mulliner	Flying Spur saloon	4-62	UK	2070 UK	C. Marshall	
BC48CZ	C47BC	H. J. Mulliner	Flying Spur saloon	12-61	UK	179 CYT	M. O. Lewis & Co. Ltd	
BC49LCZ	C48BC	H. J. Mulliner	Flying Spur saloon	10-61	UK	57 CGT	Mrs S. Harrah	
BC50CZ	C49BC	James Young	Saloon	1-62	UK	492 CYP	Cornbrook Brewery Co. Ltd	
BC51CZ	C50BC	James Young	Saloon	5-62	UK		Lt. Col. S. Pitman	
BC52LCZ	C51BC	Park Ward	Drophead coupé	12-61	USA		N. Barnes	
BC53LCZ	C52BC	H. J. Mulliner	2-door saloon	12-61	USA		Economy Blue Print & Supply Co.	
BC54CZ	C53BC	H. J. Mulliner	Flying Spur saloon	11-61	UK	2700 SR	Sir James Cayzer	
BC55CZ	C54BC	H. J. Mulliner	2-door saloon	9-62	UK	660 EXD	Mrs M. Herbert-Jenkins	
BC56CZ	C55BC	H. J. Mulliner	2-door saloon	3-62	UK	777 AVE	A. Marshall	
BC57LCZ	C56BC	Park Ward	Drophead coupé	11-61	USA		V. Shea	
BC58LCZ	C57BC	Park Ward	Drophead coupé	12-61	UK	73 CGT	H. Lauhoff	
BC59LCZ	C58BC	H. J. Mulliner	2-door saloon	1-62	USA		W. Schwindt	
BC60LCZ	C59BC	H. J. Mulliner	Flying Spur saloon	11-61	UK	78 CGT	H. Mudd	
BC61LCZ	C60BC	Park Ward	Drophead coupé	10-61	UK	64 CGT	Prince Moulay Abdullah	
BC62LCZ	C61BC	H. J. Mulliner	Flying Spur saloon	2-62	USA		Leonard Antiques	
BC63CZ	C62BC	H. J. Mulliner	Flying Spur saloon	1-62	UK	DON 700	G. Brittain	
BC64LCZ	C63BC	H. J. Mulliner	Flying Spur saloon	3-62	USA		R. Stoddart	
BC65CZ	C64BC	H. J. Mulliner	Flying Spur saloon	2-62	Australia		Sir Tom Barr-Smith	
BC66CZ	C65BC	H. J. Mulliner	2-door saloon	1-62	France		S. Geronimo Remorino	
BC67CZ	C66BC	H. J. Mulliner	2-door saloon	4-62	UK	768 XPK	W. Igoe	
BC68CZ	C67BC	H. J. Mulliner	Flying Spur saloon	12-61	UK	349 MTX	D. Martin	
BC69CZ	C68BC	H. J. Mulliner	Flying Spur saloon	2-62	UK	VCX 721	Hopkinsons Ltd	
BC70CZ	C69BC	Park Ward	Drophead coupé	1-62	UK		F. Craddock	
BC71CZ	C70BC	H. J. Mulliner	2-door saloon	2-62	Switzerland		O. Streicher	
BC72CZ	C71BC	H. J. Mulliner	2-door saloon	4-62	UK	150 EXL	Mrs E. Snagge	
BC73CZ	C72BC	H. J. Mulliner	Flying Spur saloon	3-62	UK	178 CYT	S. Docherty	
BC74CZ	C73BC	Park Ward	Drophead coupé	12-61	UK		A. J. Hines Ltd	
BC75CZ	C74BC	H. J. Mulliner	2-door saloon	2-62	UK	3 DUU	D. Robinson	
BC76LCZ	C75BC	H. J. Mulliner	Flying Spur saloon	2-62	Switzerland		E. Anderegg	
BC77LCZ	C76BC	James Young	Saloon	5-62	UK	743 CGT	E. MacDonald	
BC78LCZ	C77BC	Park Ward	Drophead coupé	12-61	USA		R. Erickson	
BC79LCZ	C78BC	Park Ward	Drophead coupé	1-62	UK	86 CGT	S. Tanaubaum	
BC80CZ	C79BC	H. J. Mulliner	2-door saloon	2-62	UK	GM 20	J. Anderson	
BC81CZ	C80BC	Park Ward	Drophead coupé	1-62	UK		Sir W. Carr	
BC82CZ	C81BC	H. J. Mulliner	Flying Spur saloon	3-62	UK	ABG 77	Allander Blending Co.	
BC83CZ	C82BC	H. J. Mulliner	Flying Spur saloon	2-62	UK		C. Miller	
BC84CZ	C83BC	Park Ward	Drophead coupé	3-62	UK	93 CGT	G. Sinclair Noble	
BC85CZ	C84BC	H. J. Mulliner	2-door saloon	4-62	UK	788 DYL	B. Jenks	
BC86LCZ	C85BC	Park Ward	Drophead coupé	1-62	USA		P. Riffert	
BC87CZ	C86BC	H. J. Mulliner	2-door saloon	2-62	UK	1600 WF	H. Watson Hall	
BC88CZ	C87BC	H. J. Mulliner	2-door saloon	3-62	UK	NUP 1	H. Stephenson	
BC89LCZ	C88BC	Park Ward	Drophead coupé	1-62	UK	92 CGT	R. Golseth	
BC90CZ	C89BC	H. J. Mulliner	Flying Spur saloon	3-62	UK	287 DUV	J. Bateman	

S2 CONTINENTAL

Chassis no.	Eng. no.	Coachbuilder	Body style	Del.	Country	UK reg. no.	Original owner	Remarks
BC91CZ	C90BC	H. J. Mulliner	Flying Spur saloon	3-62	UK	VOD 1	J. Day	
BC92LCZ	C91BC	Park Ward	Drophead coupé	2-62	Switzerland		Traub GMBH	
BC93CZ	C92BC	H. J. Mulliner	2-door saloon	3-62	UK	307 DXP	R. Silcock	
BC94CZ	C93BC	H. J. Mulliner	Flying Spur saloon	3-62	UK	WW 15	W. Whittingham Ltd	
BC95LCZ	C94BC	Park Ward	Drophead coupé	3-62	USA		E. Clayton Glengras	
BC96CZ	C95BC	Park Ward	Drophead coupé	3-62	UK		J. Hood	
BC97CZ	C96BC	H. J. Mulliner	Flying Spur saloon	3-62	UK	RF 19	Fell Construction Co. Ltd	
BC98CZ	C97BC	H. J. Mulliner	Flying Spur saloon	4-62	UK	601 CWA	F. Hearnshaw	
BC99LCZ	C98BC	Park Ward	Drophead coupé	4-62	UK	685 CGT	W. Chamberlain	
BC100CZ	C99BC	H. J. Mulliner	Flying Spur saloon	4-62	UK		Potts & Co. (Holdings) Ltd	
BC101LCZ	C100BC	H. J. Mulliner	2-door saloon	4-62	Switzerland		E. Schmidheiny	
BC102LCZ	C101BC	Park Ward	Drophead coupé	3-62	UK	689 CGT	H. Mee	
BC103LCZ	C102BC	H. J. Mulliner	2-door saloon	4-62	UK	706 CGT	G. Steel	
BC104CZ	C103BC	H. J. Mulliner	Flying Spur saloon	4-62	UK	FJS 100	F. Stratton	
BC105LCZ	C104BC	Park Ward	Drophead coupé	10-62	UK	JJF 113	Mrs G. Taylor	
BC106LCZ	C105BC	H. J. Mulliner	Flying Spur saloon	5-62	Argentina		G. Kosztelitz	
BC107CZ	C106BC	H. J. Mulliner	Flying Spur saloon	5-62	UK	KRN 7	Major J. Dewhurst	
BC108CZ	C107BC	Park Ward	Drophead coupé	4-62	UK	784 DYL	C. Manning	
BC109CZ	C108BC	H. J. Mulliner	Flying Spur saloon	5-62	UK	JOO 630	H. Green	
BC110CZ	C109BC	H. J. Mulliner	2-door saloon	5-62	UK	744 CGT	E. Morf	
BC111CZ	C110BC	Park Ward	Drophead coupé	4-62	UK	95 DXY	D. de Ferranti	
BC112LCZ	C111BC	H. J. Mulliner	Flying Spur saloon	1-62	UK	728 CGT	E. Jette	
BC113CZ	C112BC	Park Ward	Drophead coupé	5-62	UK	202 GYX	M. Price	
BC114LCZ	C113BC	Park Ward	Drophead coupé	5-62	UK	741 CGT	S. Tankoos	
BC115CZ	C114BC	Park Ward	Drophead coupé	4-62	UK	1 VPP	V. Cousin	
BC116LCZ	C115BC	Park Ward	Drophead coupé	5-62	USA		W. Walker	
BC117LCZ	C116BC	Park Ward	Drophead coupé	5-62	USA		Henslee Mobile Homes	
BC118LCZ	C117BC	Park Ward	Drophead coupé	5-62	USA		N. Sackheim	
BC119LCZ	C118BC	Park Ward	Drophead coupé	8-62	UK	814 CGT	G. Kelley	
BC120CZ	C119BC	Park Ward	Drophead coupé	6-62	UK	635 LRO	G. Saunders	
BC121LCZ	C120BC	H. J. Mulliner	Flying Spur saloon	5-62	USA		J. Wilson	
BC122LCZ	C121BC	H. J. Mulliner	2-door saloon	5-62	USA		H. Dietrich	
BC123CZ	C122BC	H. J. Mulliner	Flying Spur saloon	5-62	UK	WTV 1	P. Cadbury	
BC124CZ	C123BC	H. J. Mulliner	2-door saloon	5-62	UK	EVA 10	Mrs E. Denny	
BC125CZ	C124BC	H. J. Mulliner	Flying Spur saloon	8-62	UK	123 CBL	J. Edwards	
BC126CZ	C125BC	H. J. Mulliner	Flying Spur saloon	6-62	UK	BK 600	Bluebird Caravan Co. Ltd	
BC127LCZ	C126BC	Park Ward	Drophead coupé	2-62	UK	756 CGT	H. Burns	
BC128LCZ	C127BC	Park Ward	Drophead coupé	6-62	UK	738 CGT	J. Constant van Rijn	
BC129LCZ	C128BC	H. J. Mulliner	2-door saloon	6-62	Switzerland		J. Piasio	
BC130CZ	C129BC	James Young	Saloon	6-62	UK		Westfield Transport Ltd	
BC131LCZ	C130BC	Park Ward	Drophead coupé	7-62	UK	740 CGT	M. Boyer	
BC132CZ	C131BC	H. J. Mulliner	Flying Spur saloon	6-62	UK	877 ELH	A. Sherman	
BC133LCZ	C132BC	H. J. Mulliner	Flying Spur saloon	6-62	UK	761 CGT	Dr M. Bernstein	
BC134CZ	C133BC	H. J. Mulliner	2-door saloon	7-62	USA		R. Griffin	
BC135LCZ	C134BC	H. J. Mulliner	Flying Spur saloon	8-62	UK	821 CGT	L. MacNaughton	
BC136LCZ	C135BC	Park Ward	Drophead coupé	8-62	UK	823 CGT	E. Williams	
BC137LCZ	C136BC	H. J. Mulliner	2-door saloon	7-62	UK	835 CGT	Trezza SPA	
BC138CZ	C137BC	James Young	Saloon	7-62	UK	7 ELT	W. Matlock	
BC139CZ	C138BC	H. J. Mulliner	Flying Spur saloon	8-62	UK	291 EXD	D. Tyzack	

S3 CONTINENTAL

Chassis no.	Eng. no.	Coachbuilder	Body style	Del.	Country	UK reg. no.	Original owner	Remarks
BC2XA	1ABC	James Young	Saloon	11-62	UK		Lady R. Guthrie	
BC4LXA	2ABC	Park Ward	Drophead coupé	3-63	USA		V. Cronin	
BC6LXA	3ABC	H. J. Mulliner	2-door saloon	1-63	USA		Beverly Leasing Co.	
BC8LXA	4ABC	Park Ward	Drophead coupé	10-62	USA		E. Fisher	
BC10XA	5ABC	H. J. Mulliner	Flying Spur saloon	11-62	UK	V 28	P. Hall	
BC12XA	6ABC	James Young	Saloon	11-62	UK		Sir E. Cadbury	
BC14XA	7ABC	Park Ward	Drophead coupé	12-62	UK	311 EXV	D. Howitt	
BC16XA	8ABC	H. J. Mulliner	Flying Spur saloon	1-63	USA		H. Carson	
BC18XA	9ABC	H. J. Mulliner	Flying Spur saloon	10-62	UK	502 EXW	Rolls-Royce Ltd	Conduit St. Trials car
BC20XA	10ABC	H. J. Mulliner	2-door saloon	12-62	UK	900 EYN	Strauss Turnbull & Co.	
BC22LXA	11ABC	Park Ward	Drophead coupé	11-62	USA		R. Firestone	
BC24LXA	12ABC	H. J. Mulliner	Flying Spur saloon	11-62	USA		R. Salant	
BC26LXA	13ABC	Park Ward	Drophead coupé	10-62	UK	861 CGT	M. Ras	
BC28XA	14ABC	H. J. Mulliner	2-door saloon	11-62	UK	1400 RU	S. Macey	
BC30LXA	15ABC	Park Ward	Drophead coupé	1-63	USA		G. Marston	
BC32XA	16ABC	H. J. Mulliner	Flying Spur saloon	12-62	UK		F. Lawrence Knight	
BC34LXA	17ABC	Park Ward	Drophead coupé	12-62	USA		Dr H. Axelrod	
BC36LXA	18ABC	H. J. Mulliner	Flying Spur saloon	11-62	USA		R. Parish	
BC38LXA	19ABC	Park Ward	Drophead coupé	12-62	USA		H. Dahlberg	
BC40XA	20ABC	H. J. Mulliner	2-door saloon	1-63	UK	871 EYX	R. Valls	
BC42XA	21ABC	Park Ward	Drophead coupé	1-63	UK	JM 122	J. Mills	
BC44LXA	22ABC	H. J. Mulliner	Flying Spur saloon	10-62	USA		Mrs S. Busch	
BC46XA	23ABC	Park Ward	2-door saloon	5-63	UK		B. Myers	
BC48LXA	24ABC	Park Ward	Drophead coupé	12-62	Belgium		A. Denis	
BC50LXA	25ABC	Park Ward	Drophead coupé	1-63	USA		W. Findlay	
BC52LXA	26ABC	H. J. Mulliner	2-door saloon	2-63	Switzerland		E. Chamay	
BC54XA	27ABC	H. J. Mulliner	Flying Spur saloon	1-63	UK		J. Boyden	
BC56LXA	28ABC	Park Ward	Drophead coupé	5-63	France		P. Bernard	
BC58XA	29ABC	H. J. Mulliner	2-door saloon	1-63	UK	EWR 1	Edmundo Ros Orchestras Ltd	
BC60XA	30ABC	Park Ward	Drophead coupé	1-63	UK	996 EYV	Francis Sumner (Holdings) Ltd	
BC62XA	31ABC	H. J. Mulliner	Flying Spur saloon	1-63	UK	GM 7	G. Martineau	
BC64XA	32ABC	James Young	Saloon	2-63	UK	3 FGX	Sir L. Bagrit	
BC66XA	33ABC	Park Ward	Drophead coupé	2-63	UK	519 EGK	G. Sinclair Noble	
BC68LXA	34ABC	Park Ward	Drophead coupé	3-63	USA		C. DuBois	
BC70LXA	35ABC	Park Ward	Drophead coupé	4-63	Monaco		Conte L. di Valgiurata	
BC72LXA	36ABC	H. J. Mulliner	Flying Spur saloon	3-63	USA		S. Swenson	
BC74XA	37ABC	H. J. Mulliner	Flying Spur saloon	7-63	UK	300 GLX	R. Brookes	
BC76XA	38ABC	James Young	2-door saloon	5-63	UK		Relgan Ltd	
BC78XA	39ABC	James Young	Saloon	4-63	UK	782 FLP	I. Sanderson	
BC80LXA	40ABC	Park Ward	Drophead coupé	3-63	USA		Peoples Express Co.	
BC82LXA	41ABC	Park Ward	2-door saloon	3-63	Switzerland		G. Filipinetti	
BC84XA	42ABC	H. J. Mulliner	Flying Spur saloon	3-63	UK		B. Jenks	
BC86LXA	43ABC	Park Ward	2-door saloon	3-63	UK	508 EGK	G. Cantor	
BC88XA	44ABC	H. J. Mulliner	2-door saloon	2-63	UK	NE 211	N. Easterman	
BC90XA	45ABC	H. J. Mulliner	Flying Spur saloon	4-63	UK	3553 PH	F. Would	
BC92XA	46ABC	H. J. Mulliner	2-door saloon	5-63	UK	VCL 8	J. Barbour	
BC94XA	47ABC	H. J. Mulliner	Flying Spur saloon	3-63	UK	990 EXP	A. Holmes	
BC96XA	48ABC	Park Ward	Drophead coupé	4-63	UK		Freeman, Hardy & Willis	
BC98LXA	49ABC	Park Ward	2-door saloon	5-63	UK	568 EGK	S. Le Fiell	
BC100XA	50ABC	H. J. Mulliner	2-door saloon	3-63	UK	400 FXB	S. Chaffey	

S3 CONTINENTAL

Chassis no.	Eng. no.	Coachbuilder	Body style	Del.	Country	UK reg. no.	Original owner	Remarks
BC102LXA	51ABC	Park Ward	Drophead coupé	3-63	UK	538 EGK	Mrs B. Wilkes	
BC104LXA	52ABC	H. J. Mulliner	2-door saloon	7-63	UK	530 EGK	W. Warren	
BC106LXA	53ABC	Park Ward	2-door saloon	10-63	UK	647 EGK	R. Sicre	
BC108XA	54ABC	H. J. Mulliner	Flying Spur saloon	5-63	UK		Cmdr D. Miller	
BC110XA	55ABC	Park Ward	Drophead coupé	4-63	UK	200 WKP	J. Cox	
BC112XA	56ABC	Park Ward	2-door saloon	5-63	UK		E. Miller	
BC114XA	57ABC	H. J. Mulliner	Flying Spur saloon	4-63	UK	1 FOO	H. Swift	
BC116LXA	58ABC	Park Ward	2-door saloon	6-63	USA		W. Rosenberg	
BC118LXA	59ABC	H. J. Mulliner	Flying Spur saloon	5-63	UK	547 EGK	T. Abbo	
BC120XA	60ABC	H. J. Mulliner	2-door saloon	4-63	UK	OLM 7	Countess of Suffolk & Berkshire	
BC122XA	61ABC	Park Ward	Drophead coupé	4-63	UK	500 FLL	Lt. Col. R. Bellamy	
BC124XA	62ABC	Park Ward	Drophead coupé	4-63	UK		D. Ward	
BC126XA	63ABC	Park Ward	2-door saloon	4-63	UK	AWB 22	A. Berner	
BC128XA	64ABC	H. J. Mulliner	Flying Spur saloon	4-63	UK		C. Miller	
BC130LXA	65ABC	Park Ward	2-door saloon	6-63	USA		H. Hoffman	
BC132XA	66ABC	Park Ward	2-door saloon	4-63	UK	500 LG	Rolls-Royce Ltd	Conduit St. Trials car
BC134XA	67ABC	James Young	Saloon	7-63	UK	472 FXD	Highams Ltd	
BC136XA	68ABC	Park Ward	Drophead coupé	5-63	UK	1 EBE	G. Trill	
BC138XA	69ABC	Park Ward	2-door saloon	5-63	UK	NM 44	N. Moore	
BC140XA	70ABC	H. J. Mulliner	Flying Spur saloon	5-63	UK	GH 82	G. Hochschild	
BC142XA	71ABC	Park Ward	2-door saloon	5-63	UK	HC 11	H. Gressman	
BC144LXA	72ABC	H. J. Mulliner	Flying Spur saloon	5-63	UK	584 EGK	H. Florman	
BC146LXA	73ABC	Park Ward	Drophead coupé	5-63	USA		J. Calvillo	
BC148XA	74ABC	Park Ward	2-door saloon	6-63	UK	771 FXT	J. Shellim	
BC150XA	75ABC	H. J. Mulliner	Flying Spur saloon	5-63	UK	J 143	J. Hood	
BC152XA	76ABC	Park Ward	2-door saloon	5-63	UK	RG 27	R. Gooda	
BC154LXA	77ABC	Park Ward	2-door saloon	7-63	France		B. Dierckx de Casterle	
BC156XA	78ABC	H. J. Mulliner	Flying Spur saloon	7-63	UK	CE 12	Lady Fox	
BC158XA	79ABC	James Young	2-door saloon	7-63	UK		Opus Plant Ltd	
BC160XA	80ABC	Park Ward	Drophead coupé	6-63	UK	FWE 2	F. Eske	
BC162XA	81ABC	Park Ward	2-door saloon	5-63	UK	RF 188	D. Facchino	
BC164XA	82ABC	H. J. Mulliner	Flying Spur saloon	6-63	UK		P. Cadbury	
BC166LXA	83ABC	Park Ward	2-door saloon	6-63	USA		Mrs S. Harrah	
BC168XA	84ABC	H. J. Mulliner	Flying Spur saloon	6-63	UK	950 FYO	L. Townson	
BC170XA	85ABC	Park Ward	2-door saloon	6-63	UK	H 22	Mrs E. Gilston	
BC172XA	86ABC	H. J. Mulliner	Flying Spur saloon	6-63	UK	YVH 140	C. Sumrie	
BC174XA	87ABC	Park Ward	2-door saloon	7-63	UK	MS 21	M. Summers	
BC2XB	1BBC	H. J. Mulliner	Flying Spur saloon	6-63	UK	964 FYN	W. Turriff	
BC4XB	2BBC	Park Ward	Drophead coupé	6-63	NL		Sir A. Noble	
BC6XB	3BBC	H. J. Mulliner	Flying Spur saloon	7-63	UK	260 DER	Sirdall Plant Ltd	
BC8LXB	4BBC	Park Ward	2-door saloon	6-63	UK	587 EGK	R. Parish	
BC10XB	5BBC	Park Ward	2-door saloon	7-63	UK	URN 5	W. Lawson	
BC12LXB	6BBC	Park Ward	2-door saloon	5-63	UK	567 EGK	A. Nast	
BC14XB	7BBC	H. J. Mulliner	Flying Spur saloon	7-63	UK	SYM 877	Platt Metals Ltd	
BC16XB	8BBC	Park Ward	2-door saloon	8-63	UK	5 GXB	Major G. Blundell-Brown	
BC18LXB	9BBC	Park Ward	Drophead coupé	8-63	USA		E. Clark	
BC20LXB	10BBC	Park Ward	2-door saloon	8-63	USA		E. Foote	
BC22LXB	11BBC	H. J. Mulliner	Flying Spur saloon	5-63	UK	584 EGK	H. Rosenthal	
BC24LXB	12BBC	Park Ward	Drophead coupé	8-63	USA		Harry Belafonte	

S3 CONTINENTAL

Chassis no.	Eng. no.	Coachbuilder	Body style	Del.	Country	UK reg. no.	Original owner	Remarks
BC26XB	13BBC	Park Ward	2-door saloon	8-63	UK	66 HAX	Saunders Valve Co. Ltd	
BC28LXB	14BBC	Park Ward	2-door saloon	8-63	Lebanon		Mrs R. Hani-Salam	
BC30LXB	15BBC	H. J. Mulliner	Flying Spur saloon	8-63	NL		F. van der Meyden	
BC32XB	16BBC	James Young	Saloon	9-63	UK	300 YKT	W. Stromeyer	
BC34XB	17BBC	Park Ward	2-door saloon	8-63	UK	OWU 10	Mrs Y. Jacobson	
BC36XB	18BBC	H. J. Mulliner	Flying Spur saloon	8-63	UK		Hammer Film Productions Ltd	
BC38XB	19BBC	Park Ward	Drophead coupé	8-63	UK	WLR 1	M. Rayne	
BC40XB	20BBC	Park Ward	2-door saloon	8-63	UK	517 GLN	J. Trup	
BC42XB	21BBC	Park Ward	2-door saloon	8-63	UK	702 GLR	J. Durlacher	
BC44XB	22BBC	H. J. Mulliner	Flying Spur saloon	9-63	UK	SLL 1	G. Davis	
BC46XB	23BBC	Park Ward	Drophead coupé	9-63	UK	600 KOF	Wetenhall Cooper Ltd	
BC48XB	24BBC	Park Ward	2-door saloon	9-63	UK	SNH 567	E. Travis	
BC50XB	25BBC	Park Ward	2-door saloon	8-63	UK	622 EGK	Sir Duncan Orr-Lewis	
BC52XB	26BBC	H. J. Mulliner	Flying Spur saloon	8-63	UK	650 GLY	Aladdin Industries Ltd	
BC54LXB	27BBC	H. J. Mulliner	Flying Spur saloon	9-63	NL		J. van der Meyden	
BC56LXB	28BBC	Park Ward	2-door saloon	8-63	UK	624 EGK	L. Gilmour	
BC58XB	29BBC	Park Ward	2-door saloon	9-63	UK	456 GUW	P. Cussins	
BC60LXB	30BBC	Park Ward	Drophead coupé	10-63	USA		Jayne Mansfield	
BC62LXB	31BBC	Park Ward	Drophead coupé	9-63	Switzerland		K. Gentsch-Schubert	
BC64XB	32BBC	Park Ward	2-door saloon	10-63	UK	100 FMO	E. Cole	
BC66LXB	33BBC	H. J. Mulliner	Flying Spur saloon	12-63	UK	677 EGK	R. Bialetti	1963 Paris Salon
BC68XB	34BBC	James Young	Saloon	1-64	UK		J. Hartley	
BC70XB	35BBC	James Young	Saloon	2-64	UK	HD 7000	H. Dare & Son Ltd	
BC72XB	36BBC	Park Ward	Drophead coupé	10-63	UK	TOP 555	R. Freimuth	
BC74XB	37BBC	H. J. Mulliner	Flying Spur saloon	9-63	UK		B. Lyner	
BC76XB	38BBC	Park Ward	2-door saloon	10-63	UK		J. Jelly	
BC78XB	39BBC	Park Ward	Drophead coupé	10-63	UK	545 GXP	J. McEnnery	
BC80LXB	40BBC	Park Ward	2-door saloon	10-63	France		R. Kahn-Sriber	
BC82XB	41BBC	H. J. Mulliner	Flying Spur saloon	10-63	UK	GS 666	G. Sanderson	
BC84XB	42BBC	Park Ward	2-door saloon	10-63	UK	HS 1	Sir W. Lithgow	
BC86XB	43BBC	H. J. Mulliner	Flying Spur saloon	2-64	UK		D. Mackinnon	
BC88LXB	44BBC	Park Ward	Drophead coupé	2-64	UK		Stauss Turnbull & Co.	
BC90XB	45BBC	Park Ward	2-door saloon	10-63	UK		W. Whitton	
BC92LXB	46BBC	H. J. Mulliner	Flying Spur saloon	12-63	Lebanon		Sheikh Moubarak Abdallah	
BC94XB	47BBC	Park Ward	2-door saloon	11-63	UK		A. Bryant	
BC96XB	48BBC	Park Ward	2-door saloon	1-64	UK	783 GXX	R. Stephens	
BC98LXB	49BBC	Park Ward	2-door saloon	3-64	Belgium		J. Zuylen	
BC100LXB	50BBC	Park Ward	Drophead coupé	10-63	USA		J. Lilly	
BC2XC	1CBC	Park Ward	2-door saloon	11-63	UK	4004 TU	P. Brocklehurst	
BC4XC	2CBC	H. J. Mulliner	Flying Spur saloon	11-63	UK	430 EXP	T. Phillips	
BC6XC	3CBC	Park Ward	2-door saloon	11-63	UK	LJK 10	Castrol Ltd	
BC8XC	4CBC	Park Ward	Drophead coupé	12-63	UK		H. Silley	
BC10XC	5CBC	Park Ward	Drophead coupé	12-63	UK		J. Reynolds	
BC12LXC	6CBC	Park Ward	2-door saloon	12-63	USA		R. Sinclaire	
BC14XC	7CBC	Park Ward	2-door saloon	11-63	UK		A. Wilkinson	
BC16XC	8CBC	H. J. Mulliner	Flying Spur saloon	9-63	UK		F. Craddock	
BC18LXC	9CBC	Park Ward	2-door saloon	11-63	UK	637 EGK	L. Wasserman	
BC20XC	10CBC	Park Ward	2-door saloon	11-63	UK	777 HVA	T. Coughtrie	
BC22LXC	11CBC	H. J. Mulliner	Flying Spur saloon	11-63	UK	645 EGK	B. Bement	

S3 CONTINENTAL

Chassis no.	Eng. no.	Coachbuilder	Body style	Del.	Country	UK reg. no.	Original owner	Remarks
BC24LXC	12CBC	H. J. Mulliner	Flying Spur saloon	12-63	UK	608 EGK	B. Martin	
BC26XC	13CBC	Park Ward	2-door saloon	12-63	UK	UXY 95	R. Burr	
BC28LXC	14CBC	Park Ward	2-door saloon	12-63	UK	668 EGK	SPA Gruppo Zanon	
BC30XC	15CBC	Park Ward	Drophead coupé	12-63	UK	JLC 123	J. Cohen	
BC32LXC	16CBC	Park Ward	2-door saloon	12-63	USA		J. Merrick	
BC34XC	17CBC	H. J. Mulliner	Flying Spur saloon	2-64	UK	GEF 853	A. Holmes	
BC36XC	18CBC	Park Ward	2-door saloon	12-63	UK		A. Perry	
BC38XC	19CBC	Park Ward	2-door saloon	2-64	UK	H 1	R. McLeod	Specially shortened
BC40XC	20CBC	Park Ward	2-door saloon	12-63	UK	WB 3253	Sir W. Beale OBE	
BC42XC	21CBC	H. J. Mulliner	Flying Spur saloon	1-64	UK		Newmans (Midlands) Ltd	
BC44XC	22CBC	Park Ward	Drophead coupé	1-64	UK	777 WYA	R. Sharman-Crawford	
BC46LXC	23CBC	Park Ward	2-door saloon	1-64	USA		C. Huthsing	
BC48LXC	24CBC	Park Ward	2-door saloon	1-64	UK	682 EGK	P. Zage	
BC50XC	25CBC	Park Ward	2-door saloon	1-64	UK	906 GYV	Extertise Ltd	
BC52XC	26CBC	Park Ward	Drophead coupé	1-64	UK	999 GWT	H. Crossley	
BC54XC	27CBC	James Young	Saloon	1-64	UK		W. Airey & Son Ltd	
BC56XC	28CBC	Park Ward	2-door saloon	1-64	UK	MB 50	Lady M. Barlow	
BC58XC	29CBC	H. J. Mulliner	Flying Spur saloon	2-64	UK		R. Moore	
BC60XC	30CBC	Park Ward	Drophead coupé	1-64	UK	905 GYV	Earl of Inchcape	
BC62XC	31CBC	Park Ward	2-door saloon	2-64	UK		Sir A. Wheeler	
BC64XC	32CBC	Park Ward	Drophead coupé	2-64	UK	3864 VU	James Barnes Ltd	
BC66XC	33CBC	Park Ward	2-door saloon	1-64	UK	DON 700	G. Brittain	
BC68XC	34CBC	Park Ward	2-door saloon	2-64	UK	5050 DF	D. Fry	
BC70XC	35CBC	Park Ward	Drophead coupé	2-64	UK	HLB 239	G. Worthington	
BC72XC	36CBC	Park Ward	2-door saloon	3-64	UK	866 GGK	W. Lawson	
BC74XC	37CBC	H. J. Mulliner	Flying Spur saloon	3-64	SA		R. Heinrich	
BC76XC	38CBC	James Young	2-door saloon	3-64	Switzerland		H. Appenzeller	
BC78XC	39CBC	Park Ward	Drophead coupé	2-64	UK	147 HJJ	J. Abrahams	
BC80XC	40CBC	Park Ward	2-door saloon	2-64	UK	MCA 4	Sir Robert McAlpine & Sons Ltd	
BC82XC	41CBC	H. J. Mulliner	Flying Spur saloon	2-64	UK		J. Edwards	
BC84XC	42CBC	Park Ward	Drophead coupé	3-64	UK	HSE 666	Lt. Col. G. Kynoch	
BC86XC	43CBC	H. J. Mulliner	Flying Spur saloon	2-64	UK		H. Laing	
BC88LXC	44CBC	Park Ward	2-door saloon	3-64	UK		E. Taubman	
BC90LXC	45CBC	Park Ward	2-door saloon	10-64	UK	AGN 517 B	L. Reed	
BC92XC	46CBC	H. J. Mulliner	Flying Spur saloon	3-64	UK	KRN 7	J. Dewhurst	
BC94XC	47CBC	Park Ward	2-door saloon	3-64	UK	MWB 1	Col. M. Batchelor CBE	
BC96XC	48CBC	Park Ward	Drophead coupé	3-64	UK	7 HYH	Dr F. Campbell Golding	
BC98LXC	49CBC	Park Ward	2-door saloon	3-64	Switzerland		G. Embiricos	
BC100XC	50CBC	H. J. Mulliner	Flying Spur saloon	3-64	UK	854 GGK	A. O'Neil	
BC102XC	51CBC	Park Ward	Drophead coupé	4-64	UK		R.S. Mead Ltd	
BC104XC	52CBC	Park Ward	2-door saloon	4-64	UK	323 EUF	C. Shrubsall	
BC106XC	53CBC	H. J. Mulliner	Flying Spur saloon	3-64	UK	340 HLR	H. Lipman	
BC108XC	54CBC	H. J. Mulliner	Flying Spur saloon	4-64	UK	JW 8	J. Walton	
BC110XC	55CBC	Park Ward	Drophead coupé	3-64	UK		Emu Wine Co. Ltd	
BC112XC	56CBC	Park Ward	2-door saloon	4-64	UK		I. Spencer	
BC114XC	57CBC	Park Ward	2-door saloon	4-64	UK		R. Hughes	
BC116XC	58CBC	Park Ward	2-door saloon	4-64	UK	SCB 1	R. Baco	
BC118XC	59CBC	H. J. Mulliner	Flying Spur saloon	4-64	USA		L. Edwards	
BC120XC	60CBC	Park Ward	2-door saloon	5-64	UK	ADG 368 B	Mrs D. Daly	
BC122XC	61CBC	H. J. Mulliner	Flying Spur saloon	5-64	UK	JXS 2	R. Forrest	

S3 CONTINENTAL

Chassis no.	Eng. no.	Coachbuilder	Body style	Del.	Country	UK reg. no.	Original owner	Remarks
BC124XC	62CBC	Park Ward	2-door saloon	6-64	UK	RFC 36	K. Craggs	
BC126LXC	63CBC	Park Ward	Drophead coupé	5-64	Italy		Mrs R. Del Monaco	
BC128LXC	64CBC	H. J. Mulliner	Flying Spur saloon	5-64	UK	AGN 534 B	A. Knowles	
BC130XC	65CBC	Park Ward	Drophead coupé	6-64	UK	GRK 8	G. Kennerley	
BC132XC	66CBC	Park Ward	2-door saloon	6-64	UK		Major J. Trusted	
BC134XC	67CBC	H. J. Mulliner	Flying Spur saloon	6-64	UK	BGU 68 B	C. Dugan-Chapman	
BC136LXC	68CBC	Park Ward	Drophead coupé	2-64	USA		S. Long	
BC138XC	69CBC	Park Ward	2-door saloon	6-64	UK	CPL 600 B	F. Gree	
BC140XC	70CBC	H. J. Mulliner	Flying Spur saloon	6-64	UK	VSN 202	The Misses MacFarlane	
BC142XC	71CBC	Park Ward	Drophead coupé	6-64	UK		K. Showering	
BC144XC	72CBC	Park Ward	Drophead coupé	7-64	UK	TJ 21	A. Jones	
BC146XC	73CBC	Park Ward	Drophead coupé	8-64	UK	888 D	Malcolm Sanderson Developments	
BC148XC	74CBC	Park Ward	2-door saloon	7-64	UK	AGT 38 B	W. Knight	
BC150XC	75CBC	H. J. Mulliner	Flying Spur saloon	9-64	UK		Hon. D. Wills	
BC152XC	76CBC	Park Ward	Drophead coupé	7-64	UK	BLX 520 B	A. Weinstock	
BC154XC	77CBC	Park Ward	2-door saloon	8-64	UK		Woodfall Film Productions Ltd	
BC156XC	78CBC	Park Ward	2-door saloon	9-64	UK	DSG 1	D. Grant	
BC158XC	79CBC	Park Ward	Drophead coupé	11-64	UK		Major J. Wilkinson-Latham	
BC160LXC	80CBC	Park Ward	2-door saloon	9-64	France		P. Bernard	
BC162XC	81CBC	H. J. Mulliner	Flying Spur saloon	8-64	Australia		Screenings Pty Ltd	
BC164XC	82CBC	H. J. Mulliner	Flying Spur saloon	11-64	UK		Sir Henry Lunn Ltd	
BC166XC	83CBC	Park Ward	2-door saloon	11-64	UK		W.J. Turpin (Greenwich) Ltd	
BC168XC	84CBC	Park Ward	2-door saloon	11-64	UK		Bluemel Bros. (Shopfitters) Ltd	
BC170XC	85CBC	Park Ward	2-door saloon	11-64	UK		P. Cadbury	
BC172XC	86CBC	Park Ward	Drophead coupé	12-64	UK	CLK 1 B	Mrs N. Bell	
BC174XC	87CBC	Park Ward	2-door saloon	12-64	UK	CUV 800 C	G. Biggs	
BC176XC	88CBC	Park Ward	Drophead coupé	12-64	UK		G. Smith	
BC178LXC	89CBC	H. J. Mulliner	Flying Spur saloon	12-64	UK	DGC 557 B	D. Tuttle	
BC180XC	90CBC	Park Ward	2-door saloon	12-64	UK	DSC 44	Dart Spring Co. Ltd	
BC182XC	91CBC	Park Ward	Drophead coupé	1-65	UK	DJB 900 C	Nems Enterprises Ltd	
BC184XC	92CBC	Park Ward	2-door saloon	12-64	UK	GR 24	G. Ronson	
BC186XC	93CBC	H. J. Mulliner	Flying Spur saloon	12-64	UK		A. Bolton	
BC188XC	94CBC	Park Ward	2-door saloon	1-65	UK	1 FGP	H. Oppenheim	
BC190XC	95CBC	Park Ward	2-door saloon	2-65	UK		T. Westbrook	
BC192LXC	96CBC	H. J. Mulliner	Flying Spur saloon	3-65	Switzerland		G. Burrus	
BC194XC	97CBC	Park Ward	2-door saloon	2-65	UK	EBP 736 C	Major M. Smithers	
BC196LXC	98CBC	Park Ward	2-door saloon	1-65	UK	DGY 6 C	T. Owen	
BC198XC	99CBC	H. J. Mulliner	Flying Spur saloon	1-65	UK		N. Jackson (Farmers) Ltd	
BC200XC	100CBC	James Young	Saloon	2-65	UK	ABH 50 C	Reckitt & Colman Holdings Ltd	
BC202LXC	101CBC	Graber	Drophead coupé	5-67	Switzerland			
BC2XD	1DBC	Park Ward	Drophead coupé	2-65	UK		A. Sanderson	
BC4XD	2DBC	James Young	Saloon	3-65	UK	DUC 220 C	J. Edwards	
BC6XD	3DBC	H. J. Mulliner	Flying Spur saloon	4-65	UK	EGB 850 C	J. Lawrence	
BC8XD	4DBC	Park Ward	Drophead coupé	3-65	UK	DLR 643 C	Plessey Ltd	
BC10XD	5DBC	Park Ward	Drophead coupé	3-65	UK	SSM 11	S. Myers	
BC12XD	6DBC	James Young	2-door saloon	3-65	UK	EDC 348 C	Freeman (London) Ltd	1965 Geneva Show
BC14XD	7DBC	Park Ward	2-door saloon	3-65	UK		M. Felton	
BC16XD	8DBC	Park Ward	Drophead coupé	3-65	Denmark		King of Denmark	
BC18XD	9DBC	H. J. Mulliner	Flying Spur saloon	4-65	Belgium		Mme S. Jacquette	

S3 CONTINENTAL

Chassis no.	Eng. no.	Coachbuilder	Body style	Del.	Country	UK reg. no.	Original owner	Remarks
BC20LXD	10DBC	Park Ward	Drophead coupé	3-65	Switzerland		P. Weiller	
BC22XD	11DBC	Park Ward	2-door saloon	3-65	UK	AJB 1	Boyce Hatton & Co.	
BC24XD	12DBC	H. J. Mulliner	Flying Spur saloon	4-65	UK	LP 4000	J.E. Cohen & Co. Ltd	
BC26XD	13DBC	Park Ward	2-door saloon	3-65	UK	HGF 32	H. Freye	
BC28XD	14DBC	Park Ward	Drophead coupé	4-65	UK		Sir Robert McAlpine & Sons Ltd	
BC2XE	1EBC	H. J. Mulliner	Flying Spur saloon	3-65	Australia		Sir Tom Barr-Smith	
BC4XE	2EBC	Park Ward	2-door saloon	4-65	UK	WW 15	William Whittingham Ltd	
BC6LXE	3EBC	H. J. Mulliner	Flying Spur saloon	5-65	Belgium		R. Janssen	
BC8XE	4EBC	James Young	Saloon	5-65	UK		B. Jenks	
BC10XE	5EBC	Park Ward	2-door saloon	4-65	UK	DCO 52 C	S. Thomas	
BC12XE	6EBC	Park Ward	2-door saloon	4-65	UK	JR 9	B.I. Transports Ltd	
BC14XE	7EBC	Park Ward	2-door saloon	5-65	UK	EUK 100 C	H. Wilkins	
BC16XE	8EBC	H. J. Mulliner	Flying Spur saloon	5-65	UK		R. Baker	
BC18XE	9EBC	James Young	Saloon	5-65	UK	ELL 486 C	A. Holmes	
BC20XE	10EBC	Park Ward	Drophead coupé	5-65	UK	EUU 735 C	Capt. J. Simpson	
BC22XE	11EBC	Park Ward	2-door saloon	5-65	UK	HUP 1 C	H. Stephenson	
BC24XE	12EBC	Park Ward	Drophead coupé	6-65	UK	DUJ 888 C	Virient Greenhouse (Shrewsbury) Ltd	Ranelagh, UK
BC26XE	13EBC	Park Ward	2-door saloon	6-65	UK	GCX 882 C	Thomas Preston Ltd	
BC28XE	14EBC	H. J. Mulliner	Flying Spur saloon	6-65	UK	EDD 934 C	Sir K. Peacock	
BC30XE	15EBC	Park Ward	2-door saloon	5-65	UK		W.C. French & Co. Ltd	
BC32LXE	16EBC	Park Ward	Drophead coupé	6-65	UK	DGY 97 C	N. Greene	
BC34XE	17EBC	Park Ward	2-door saloon	6-65	UK		Glanmore Investments Ltd	
BC36XE	18EBC	H. J. Mulliner	Flying Spur saloon	6-65	UK	NTE 999 C	Windy Arbour Colliery Co.	
BC38XE	19EBC	James Young	Saloon	7-65	UK	DGY 75 C	A. Graham	
BC40XE	20EBC	Park Ward	Drophead coupé	8-65	UK		W. Myers	
BC42XE	21EBC	Park Ward	2-door saloon	7-65	UK	DGY 245 C	R. Billam	
BC44LXE	22EBC	James Young	Saloon	11-65	Kuwait		Sheikh Jaber Al-Ali As-Salem Al-Sabah	
BC46XE	23EBC	James Young	Saloon	8-65	UK		E. Rex Makin & Co.	
BC48LXE	24EBC	H. J. Mulliner	Flying Spur saloon	7-65	Monaco		Baron M. Fassini	
BC50XE	25EBC	Park Ward	2-door saloon	9-65	UK		A. Slater	
BC52XE	26EBC	Park Ward	2-door saloon	3-66	UK	FOL 547	A. Gadsby	
BC54XE	27EBC	H. J. Mulliner	Flying Spur saloon	9-65	Rhodesia		R. Turner	
BC56XE								Completed as R-R Silver Cloud III LCSC83C
BC58XE	29EBC	Park Ward	2-door saloon	9-65	UK	DGY 271 C	C. Hough	
BC60XE	30EBC	H. J. Mulliner	Flying Spur saloon	9-65	UK		J. Hudson & Co.	
BC62XE	31EBC	Park Ward	Drophead coupé	11-65	UK	JM 88	J. Morgan	
BC64LXE	32EBC	Park Ward	Drophead coupé	8-65	USA		F. Dickey	
BC66XE	33EBC	Park Ward	2-door saloon	11-65	UK		E. Barr	
BC68XE	34EBC	H. J. Mulliner	Flying Spur saloon	10-65	UK	JLP 400 D	Rolling Stones Ltd	
BC70XE	35EBC	Park Ward	Drophead coupé	10-65	UK	GLM 25 C	Mallett & Sons Ltd	
BC72XE	36EBC	Park Ward	2-door saloon	11-65	UK	MC 98	John Peters Ltd	
BC74LXE	37EBC	H. J. Mulliner	Flying Spur saloon	10-65	UK	DGY 293 C	Kenney Construction Co. Ltd	
BC76XE	38EBC	H. J. Mulliner	Flying Spur saloon	10-65	UK	FLW 751 C	Macready's Metal Co. Ltd	
BC78XE	39EBC	H. J. Mulliner	Flying Spur saloon	12-65	UK	JLP 383 D	G. Coke	
BC80LXE	40EBC	Park Ward	Drophead coupé	11-65	USA		E. Wallach	
BC82XE	41EBC	Park Ward	Drophead coupé	11-65	UK		H. Lever	
BC84XE	42EBC	Park Ward	2-door saloon	11-65	UK	KPG 975 C	F. Cook	

S3 CONTINENTAL

Chassis no.	Eng. no.	Coachbuilder	Body style	Del.	Country	UK reg. no.	Original owner	Remarks
BC86XE	43EBC	Park Ward	Drophead coupé	11-65	UK	BOB 1	J. Charlesworth	
BC88XE	44EBC	H. J. Mulliner	Flying Spur saloon	11-65	UK	GYX 763 C	J. Brazil	
BC90XE	45EBC	Park Ward	Drophead coupé	11-65	UK	MCA 300	Sir Alfred McAlpine & Sons Ltd	
BC92XE	46EBC	Park Ward	Drophead coupé	11-65	UK	DKU 456 C	Parkland Mfg. Co. Ltd	
BC94XE	47EBC	H. J. Mulliner	Flying Spur saloon	12-65	UK		Col. H. Marsh	
BC96XE	48EBC	H. J. Mulliner	Flying Spur saloon	12-65	UK	NW 44	Astoria Holdings Ltd	
BC98LXE	49EBC	Park Ward	Drophead coupé	12-65	NL		A. Heineken	
BC100XE	50EBC	Park Ward	Drophead coupé	12-65	UK	JLX 111 D	J. Osborne	
BC102XE	51EBC	H. J. Mulliner	Flying Spur saloon	12-65	UK		J. Elliott Brown	
BC104LXE	52EBC	Park Ward	Drophead coupé	12-65	UK	DGY 299 C	S. Beyer	
BC106XE	53EBC	H. J. Mulliner	Flying Spur saloon	12-65	UK		Modern Engineering (Bristol) Ltd	
BC108XE	54EBC	Park Ward	Drophead coupé	12-65	SA		B. Skok	
BC110XE	55EBC	Park Ward	Drophead coupé	1-66	UK	555 B	J. Ainsworth	
BC112XE	56EBC	Park Ward	Drophead coupé	1-66	Channel Islands		N. Hamwee	
BC114XE	57EBC	H. J. Mulliner	Flying Spur saloon	1-66	UK		Sir Alfred McAlpine & Sons Ltd	
BC116XE	58EBC	H. J. Mulliner	Flying Spur saloon	1-66	UK	JLB 747 D	Brownhill Holdings Ltd	
BC118XE	59EBC	Park Ward	Drophead coupé	1-66	UK		Mrs B. Blundell	
BC120XE	60EBC	Park Ward	Drophead coupé	1-66	UK	JLD 4 D	L. Bart	

INDEX

Airbrush, use by coachwork designers 86-89
Airflow Streamlines 170
Albany Jig & Tool 170
Allen, Bill, coachwork designer 16, 129, 162, 165, 174
Anti-locking (ABS) brakes 183
Attlee, Clement 12
Automatic gearbox, introduction of 31
   standard equipment 69
Automatic Ride Control 183
Automobile Club de France 23
Automobile Club of Great Britain and Ireland (later RAC) 148

Barclay, Jack Ltd
   acquisition of James Young Ltd 155
   Jack Barclay Continental 197, 201
   Jack Barclay Platinum Azure 198, 202
Bentley cars
   4¼-litre 8, 9
   Azure 195, 197-200, 202, 205, 206
   Bentley VIII 15
   Camargue 174, 180
   Continental, development of 8-23
   Continental R Type 17, 18, 27-56, 126, 163
   Continental S1 27-93, 146, 174, 191
   Continental S2 94-121, 147-150, 154
   Continental S3 122-145, 151
   Continental (1984-95) 156, 157, 162, 178, 179, 181-189
   Continental R 190-199, 201, 203, 205, 207, 210-212
   Continental S 192
   Continental T 197, 203, 204, 208-212
   Continental Turbo 183-185
   Corniche (1939) 8-10, 17
   Corniche (1971-84) 157, 158, 161, 162, 167-177, 180, 186-189
   proposed replacement for, 177
   Mk V 8, 10-12, 170
   Mk VI 11, 13-18, 23, 27, 28, 30
   R Type 13, 17, 23, 56
   S Type (see Continental S1, S2, S3) 126, 127, 174
   T Series 159, 167-170, 173, 174
   T2 173-176
Blatchley, John ('JPB'), coachwork stylist 13, 14, 15, 28, 23, 42, 43, 46, 49, 72, 102, 103, 129, 154, 159, 160, 162-165, 170, 174
Bourne, Martin, coachwork designer 172
'Burma' project 164

Chapron, coachwork modified by 51

Citroën patents 169
Clan Foundry 13
Clay (or wax) modelling 146, 149, 150, 160, 162-165
Coachwork evolution by airbrush 86-89
'Comet' ('Scalded Cat') 10-12
Corniche (see Bentley cars)
'Corniche II' 11-13, 15-16, 18, 126, 150
Cosworth 164
'Cresta' 12, 15-16
Crewe, Car Division move to 10, 11
Cripps, Sir Stafford 11, 12

Dowty, Boulton & Paul 170

Earls Court Motor Show 14
Embiricos, André 8
'Embiricos' Bentley (B27LE) 8-9, 14, 15, 162
Evernden, Ivan ('Ev') 13-15, 22, 162
Experimental Department 12, 13, 22, 162
   move to Crewe 13

'F'-head valve layout 32
Facel Metallon 11, 13
Feller, Fritz 165
Flying Spur saloon 77, 78, 85, 103, 109-113, 129, 147. 149
Four-shoe front brakes 95, 144
   discontinued 129
Franay coachwork 52, 53
Franco-Britannic Autos 11, 13
Freestone & Webb 148

Gauntlett, Victor 23, 39
General Motors 38, 170, 187, 211
Girling 'Autostatic' brakes 58
Graber coachwork 28, 50, 90
Greenley, Ken 190, 191
Grylls, Shadwell Harry ('Gry') 60, 95, 110, 174
Gurney Nutting (coachbuilder) 13, 160, 162

Hay H.S.F. 8
Heffernan, John 190, 191
Hooper & Co. 148, 155, 156, 82-85, 123
   acquisition by Daimler and then BSA 156
   coachwork by 82-84, 119
Hucknall, Flight Test Establishment 15, 162
Hull, Graham (stylist) 164

251

Hydraulic tappets 97, 143, 186, 210
Hythe Road
   Mulliner Park Ward relocation to 159/162
   service & repair depot 38

International Automotive Design 190

James Young Ltd 72, 115-118, 129, 148, 154, 155
   acquisition by Jack Barclay Ltd 155
   coachwork by 80, 81, 115-118, 120, 121, 141, 142
Jenner, Cecily 14, 15
Johnson, Claude 148
Johnstone, Arthur Talbot 77, 84, 149

King of Denmark, car built for 138
Köng, coachwork modified by 50
Koren, Vilhelm (stylist) 102-105, 110, 129, 132-134, 149, 151, 174
'Korenental' 101, 110

Le Mans 24-hour Race 8, 9
'Lightweight' construction 14, 11, 20, 149
Lillie Hall 112, 134, 138
Llewellyn Smith, Dr F. 13, 14, 103, 149, 154, 174

McLeod, R. G., cars built for 41, 81, 120, 136, 137
McNeil, A. F. (coachwork designer) 72, 154, 155, 162
Manual gearbox (on S1) 62, 69, 82
Marchal lamps 19, 27
Medcalf, Bill 39
Montlhéry, France 22
Moseley, George 15, 84, 87, 149, 162
Motor Show, Earls Court 14
Motorways, British roads prior to advent of 8
Mulliner, Henry Jervis 148, 150
Mulliner, H. J. & Co. 11, 13-15, 20, 27, 28, 33, 69-72, 103, 129, 131, 146-150, 155, 126-27, 162
   acquisition by John Croall   148
   acquisition by Rolls-Royce Ltd (and merger with Park Ward)   28, 103, 129, 149, 150, 157-159
   Bedford Park Works 147, 148
   coachwork by 7, 14, 16-31, 33-41, 51, 58-63, 77-80, 85, 86, 87, 96-100, 109-112, 120, 122, 123, 139-141, 146-148
   formation of (see also Flying Spur)   148
Mulliner Park Ward (and H. J. Mulliner, Park Ward Ltd) 124, 129, 131, 133, 149, 151, 155, 168, 170, 174

'Nepal' project (Continental R) 190
Nye, Herbert 30, 60, 77, 149

'Olga' prototype Bentley Continental 18-26, 28, 38

Park Sheet Metal 160

Park, W. M. 150
Park Ward & Co. 14, 27, 28, 65, 68, 70-72, 103, 129, 150-156, 158, 159, 160
   coachwork by 12, 42-49, 64-76, 88, 89, 101-108, 124-139, 151-153
   experimental department 151, 156
   formation of 150
   merger with H.J. Mulliner 28, 103, 129, 149, 150, 157/159
Paulin, Georges 8-10, 14
Perry, Richard 179
Pininfarina 11, 13, 15, 28, 51, 149, 174, 180, 195, 197, 200
Porlock Hill 10, 12
Pourtout coachwork 8-10
Power-assisted steering, introduction of 57, 60/63
Pressed Steel Co. (and Pressed Steel Fisher) 162, 170
'Project 90' concept car 163, 190, 191

Radford, Harold Ltd 15
Rationalised Range 8-10, 17, 32
'Reynolds Metal' 14, 20, 149
Read, Milford 15
Rivers, Osmond 156
Robotham, William Arthur 8
Rolls, C. S. & Co. 148

Saginaw steering 170
'Scalded Cat' 10-12
Scott, Jack ('JS') 13, 154
Sedgwick, Stanley 23, 38
Self-levelling suspension, introduction of 167, 169, 170
'Siam' project (S Type) 163, 164
Sleator, Walter ('Sr') 11, 13, 15, 20
Synchromesh gearbox (on S1) 62, 69, 82

Talamo, Carlo, special Continental R built for 207
'Teleflex' window mechanism 37
'Tibet' project 164

V8 engine, development and introduction of 94-97, 100
Vanvooren coachwork 8, 10

Waller, Ivan ('IMW') 8
Ward, C. W. (Charlie) 150, 153, 154
Ward, Peter 179, 190
Watts, Stanley (Park Ward Technical Director) 14, 15, 149, 162
Wax ('Clay') modelling 146, 149, 150, 160, 162-165
West, Ronald 95
Wharton, Peter ('PJW') 28, 43, 47, 89, 101, 105, 122, 124, 154, 159
Wind tunnel testing of coachwork shapes 15
Wood, P. & A. 23, 39
Woodwark, Chris 195

Young, James (see James Young Ltd)

HANWELLS of LONDON W7 3ST

Bentley & Rolls-Royce

Quality Sales and Car Hire for the discerning driver.
Largest independent Used Bentley and Used Rolls-Royce specialist in the world.
Established for over 35 years. 60 vehicles usually in stock.

FULL WORKSHOP FACILITIES • 2 YEAR WARRANTY ON EVERY MODEL • FULLY TRAINED STAFF • EASILY ACCESSIBLE

Always Bentley Azures and Continental Rs in stock

HANWELLS BENTLEY & ROLLS-ROYCE, The Broadway, 86-91 Uxbridge Road, London W7 3ST, UK
Phone: 44 (0) 207 436 2070 Fax: 44 (0) 207 436 3110 www.hanwells.com

Whether your requirements are for Used Bentley or Used Rolls Royce purchase, Servicing or Car Hire (Self Drive or Chauffeur Driven) we can meet your needs!

P & A Wood

Rolls-Royce and Bentley Heritage Dealers

Sales, Service, Repairs, Spare Parts
and Complete Restorations

"Attention to Detail"

P & A Wood, Great Easton, Dunmow, Essex CM6 2HD, England
Telephone: 01371 870848   Fax: 01371 870810   E-mail: enquiries@pa-wood.co.uk   www.pa-wood.co.uk

BENTLEY MKVI – ROLLS-ROYCE SILVER WRAITH, DAWN & CLOUD, BENTLEY R & S-SERIES

Hardback • 25x20.7cm • £35.00*
• 176 pages • 160+ colour & b&w photos
• ISBN: 978-1-845840-68-6

The development and production history of the elegant and luxurious mainstream Rolls-Royce and Bentley models built between 1947 and 1965. Arguably, these cars – all built on chassis and echoing pre-war practices – were the last of the 'traditional' Rolls-Royce and Bentley models. Many, many of these cars have survived to the present day: all are eminently collectible. Covering concept, design and development, production, promotion, publicity and the coachbuilt cars. There is also helpful practical advice on buying and running these cars today, together with appendices of chassis number sequences and dates, build numbers and modifications and development by chassis number. Illustrated with over 160 black and white and colour photos, this book is a must have for anyone interested in automotive history.

*p&p extra. Call 01305 260068 for details. Prices subject to change.

ROLLS-ROYCE SILVER SHADOW & BENTLEY T-SERIES – THE ESSENTIAL BUYER'S GUIDE

Paperback • 19.5x13.9cm • £9.99*
• 64 pages • 100 colour photos
• ISBN: 978-1-845841-46-1

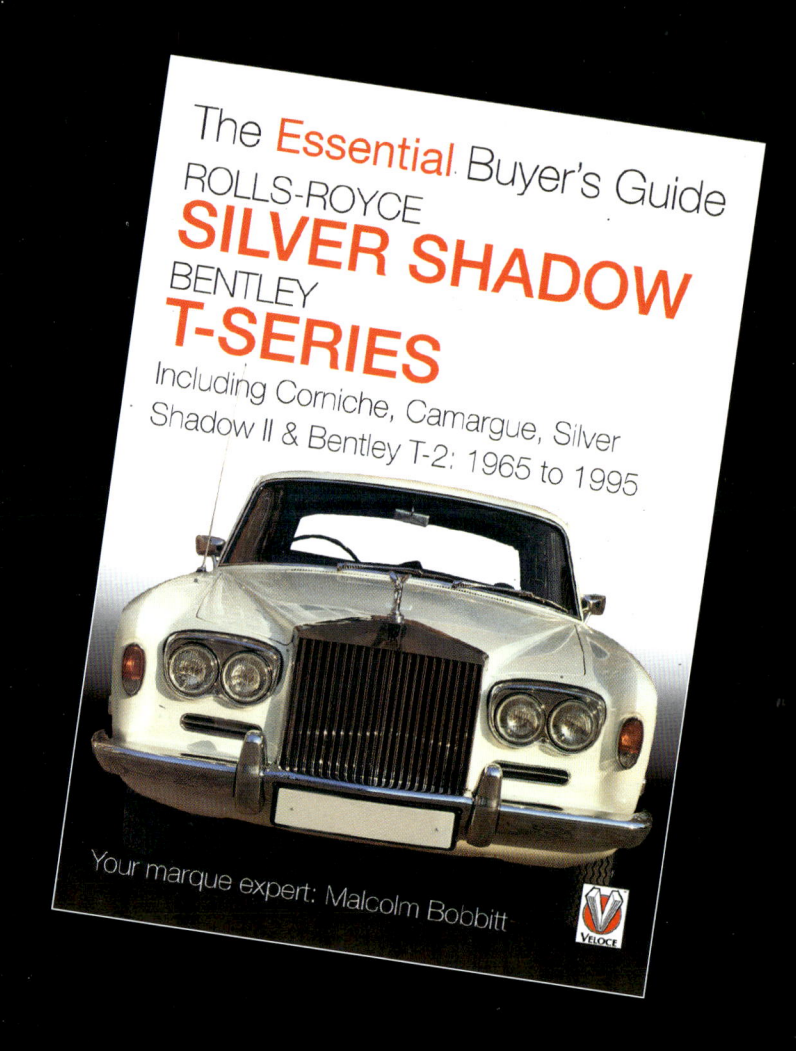

The essential guide to purchasing a Silver Shadow or Bentley T, which allows both novice and accustomed Rolls-Royce and Bentley enthusiasts to appraise a potential purchase with professional confidence, identifying what to look for in order to acquire the right car at the right price. With Malcolm Bobbitt's concise and easy-to-follow guide, packed with sound advice, and backed up by specially selected illustrations, the route through checking a car's provenance and true condition is made all the easier. Packed with the right information, this is your passport to the Rolls-Royce and Bentley community.

*p&p extra. Call 01305 260068 for details. Prices subject to change.

WELCOME TO...

ULTIMATE PORSCHE 911
GT3
COLLECTION

Cast your mind back to 1999. The Porsche 911 had just ditched its air-cooled engine in favour of a flat six cooled by water, the 996 completely revised over its predecessor in both appearance, proportion and engineering. Without a Turbo model to raise the pulses of enthusiasts, who had to make do with only C2s or C4s in either Coupe or Cabriolet form, general reception to this new era of 911 was lukewarm. But Porsche had an ace up its sleeve, duly unveiling a fresh model to add new fire to the water-cooled 911's primitive line-up. Designed as a track-capable road car, Porsche's GT3 was to bridge a sizeable gap between the opulent Carrera and hardcore RS of old.

If the public at the time needed any convincing as to this new GT3's credentials, sales material which included 'GT1-derived engine' and 'Nürburgring lap record' certainly helped. This though was to be a car adorned with licence plates, applying the 911's mantra of 'complete everyday usability' and taking things up a notch. As Porsche itself said in its first release to the media on this new model: "In its driving behaviour the 911 GT3 is designed and built for extremely sporting and agile handling, offering an excellent feeling for the road at all times."

As it was the GT3 began a rich legacy of intensive, precision engineering, which continues to this day. That it is considered so iconic at just 25 years old is remarkable – for context, the 911 itself by the age of 25 was very nearly dead, never mind decorated. Nothing in its class is so young yet so revered, the GT3 being one of Porsche's greatest ever success stories.

FUTURE

ULTIMATE PORSCHE 911
GT3
COLLECTION

Future PLC Quay House, The Ambury, Bath, BA1 1UA

Bookazine Editorial
Editor **Lee Sibley**
Senior Art Editor **Stephen Williams**
Head of Art & Design **Greg Whitaker**
Editorial Director **Jon White**
Managing Director **Grainne McKenna**

Total 911 Editorial
Editor **Lee Sibley**
Art Editor **Jamie Schildhauer**
Operations Editor **Cliff Hope**

Photography
All copyrights and trademarks are recognised and respected

Advertising
Media packs are available on request
Commercial Director **Clare Dove**

International
Head of Print Licensing **Rachel Shaw**
licensing@futurenet.com
www.futurecontenthub.com

Circulation
Head of Newstrade **Tim Mathers**

Production
Head of Production **Mark Constance**
Production Project Manager **Matthew Eglinton**
Advertising Production Manager **Joanne Crosby**
Digital Editions Controller **Jason Hudson**
Production Managers **Keely Miller, Nola Cokely, Vivienne Calvert, Fran Twentyman**

Printed in the UK

Distributed by Marketforce – www.marketforce.co.uk
For enquiries, please email: mfcommunications@futurenet.com

Ultimate Porsche 911 GT3 Collection First Edition (TNB6416)
© 2024 Future Publishing Limited

We are committed to only using magazine paper which is derived from responsibly managed, certified forestry and chlorine-free manufacture. The paper in this bookazine was sourced and produced from sustainable managed forests, conforming to strict environmental and socioeconomic standards.

All contents © 2024 Future Publishing Limited or published under licence. All rights reserved. No part of this magazine may be used, stored, transmitted or reproduced in any way without the prior written permission of the publisher. Future Publishing Limited (company number 2008885) is registered in England and Wales. Registered office: Quay House, The Ambury, Bath BA1 1UA. All information contained in this publication is for information only and is, as far as we are aware, correct at the time of going to press. Future cannot accept any responsibility for errors or inaccuracies in such information. You are advised to contact manufacturers and retailers directly with regard to the price of products/services referred to in this publication. Apps and websites mentioned in this publication are not under our control. We are not responsible for their contents or any other changes or updates to them. This magazine is fully independent and not affiliated in any way with the companies mentioned herein.

FUTURE Connectors. Creators. Experience Makers.

Future plc is a public company quoted on the London Stock Exchange (symbol: FUTR)
www.futureplc.com

Chief Executive Officer **Jon Steinberg**
Non-Executive Chairman **Richard Huntingford**
Chief Financial Officer **Sharjeel Suleman**

Tel +44 (0)1225 442 244

Part of the **Total 911** THE PORSCHE MAGAZINE bookazine series

CONTENTS

08
ROAD TESTS
Presenting an exciting mix of features showcasing every generation of Porsche 911 GT3 and its RS equivalent, from group tests to single drives

74
GT3 PORSCHE INDEX
Has our thrilling Porsche content got your wallet twitching? If so, you'll need our handy buying guides for the most popular examples, with input from trusted industry specialists

108
MODIFIED & MOTORSPORT
The home of the GT3 is the race track, after all, so we take a look at race cars past and present, as well as a special modified example from the pioneers at Sharkwerks

Contents | 7

ROAD TESTS

10
25 YEARS OF GT3
We kick off our quarter-century celebrations by looking at the evolution of the GT3 since 1999

22
996.1 V 992.1 GT3
We pit the very first GT3 against the latest… is newer really better?

32
997.1 V 997.2 GT3 RS
These thrilling Rennsports sit right in the sweet spot for the 997 genre. Which is the better modern classic GT3 RS?

44
996 GT3 RS
The once unloved GT3 RS is now highly desirable. We take one for a test drive to find out why

52
GT3 TOURINGS
The Touring offers a thrilling GT3 experience for those who wish to fly under the radar. We try the 991 and 992 generations

60
GT3 RS GENERATIONS
We take a look at the first ten years of GT3 RS with a group test on road and track

68
MANUAL GT3S
These days Porsche offers GT3s with PDK transmission… but how do the manual equivalents stack up?